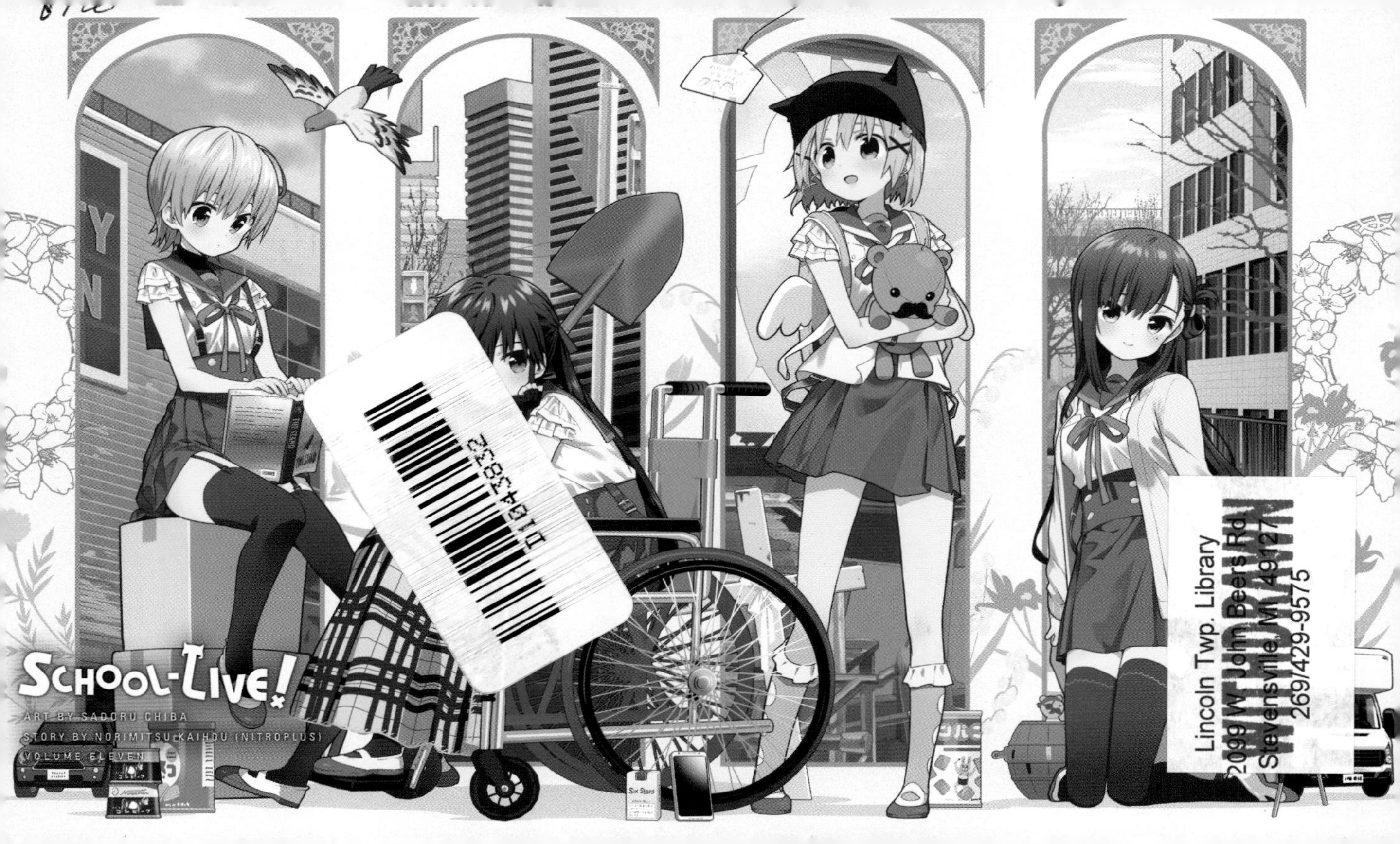
SCHOOL-LIVE!
ART BY SADORU CHIBA
STORY BY NORIMITSU KAIHOU (NITROPLUS)
VOLUME ELEVEN
D1043832

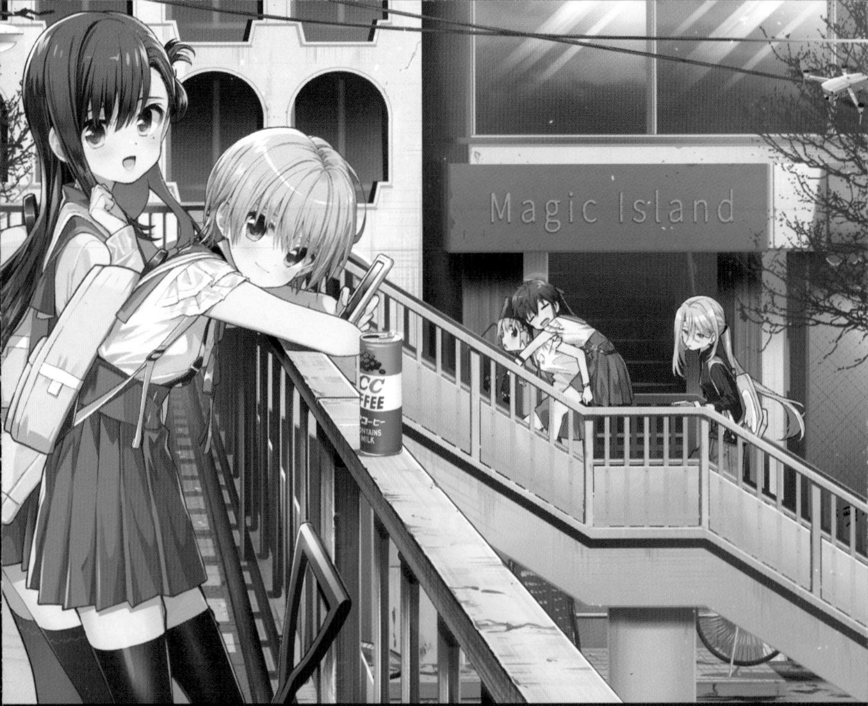
Magic Island

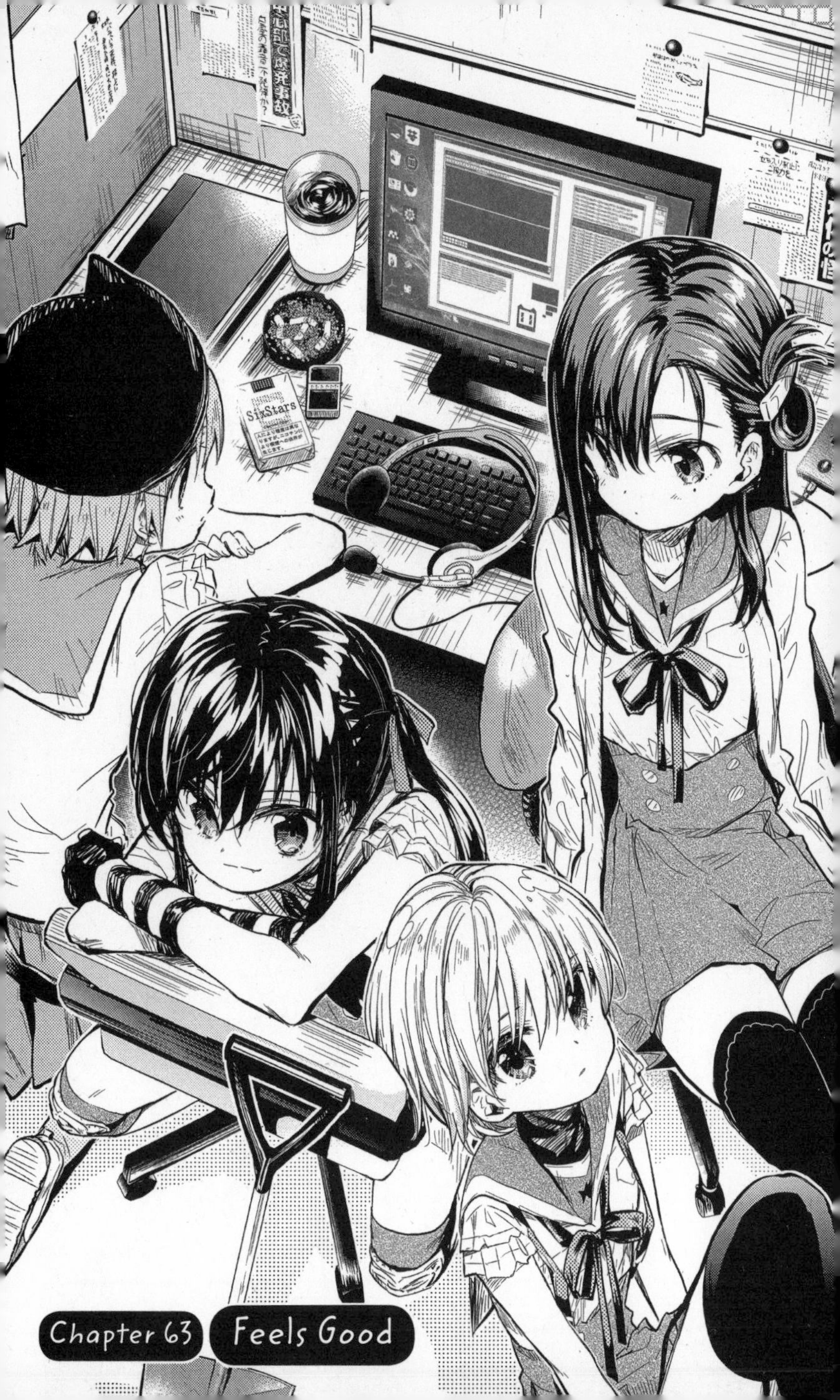
SixStars
Chapter 63
Feels Good

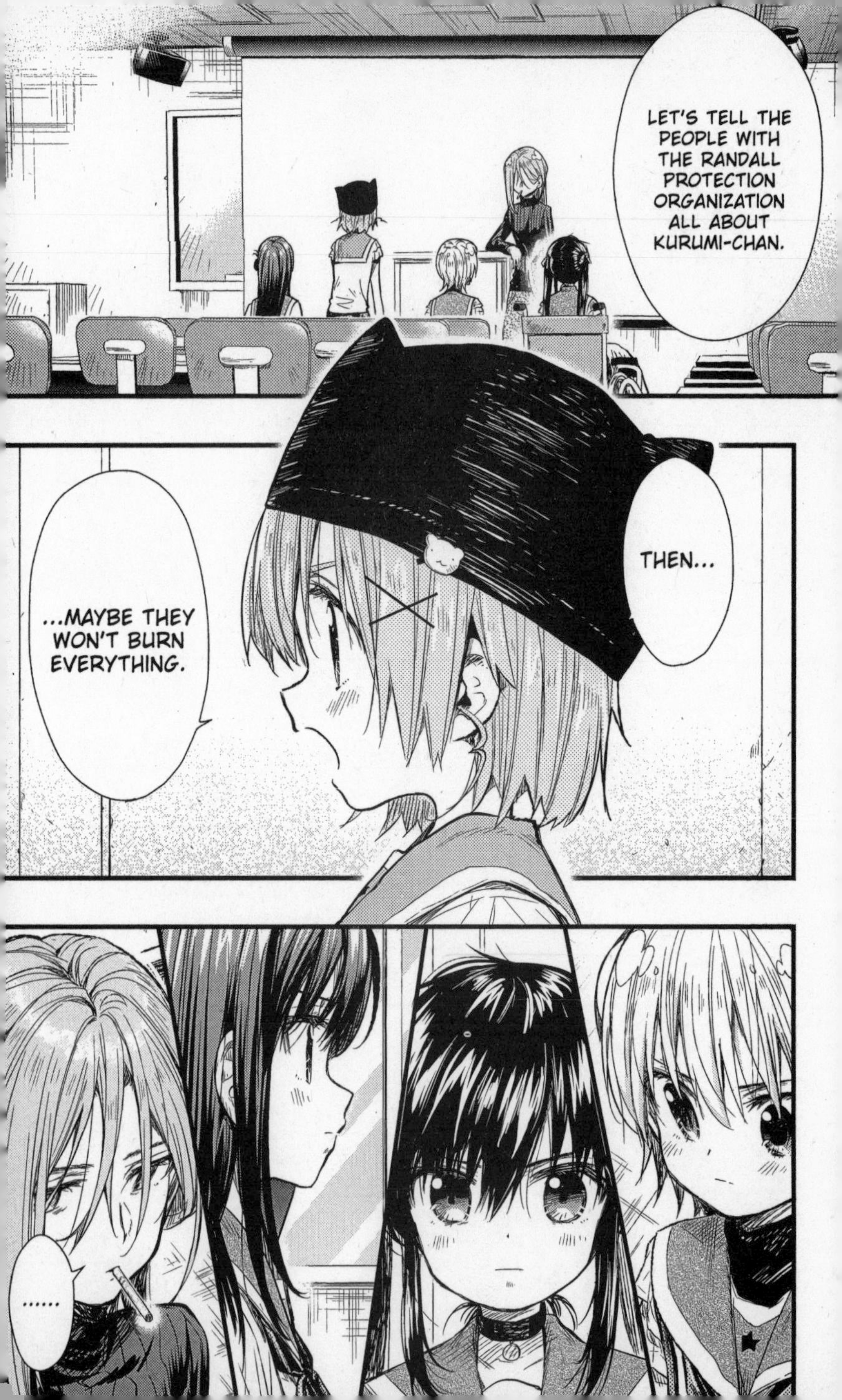
LET'S TELL THE PEOPLE WITH THE RANDALL PROTECTION ORGANIZATION ALL ABOUT KURUMI-CHAN.
THEN...
...MAYBE THEY WON'T BURN EVERYTHING.
......

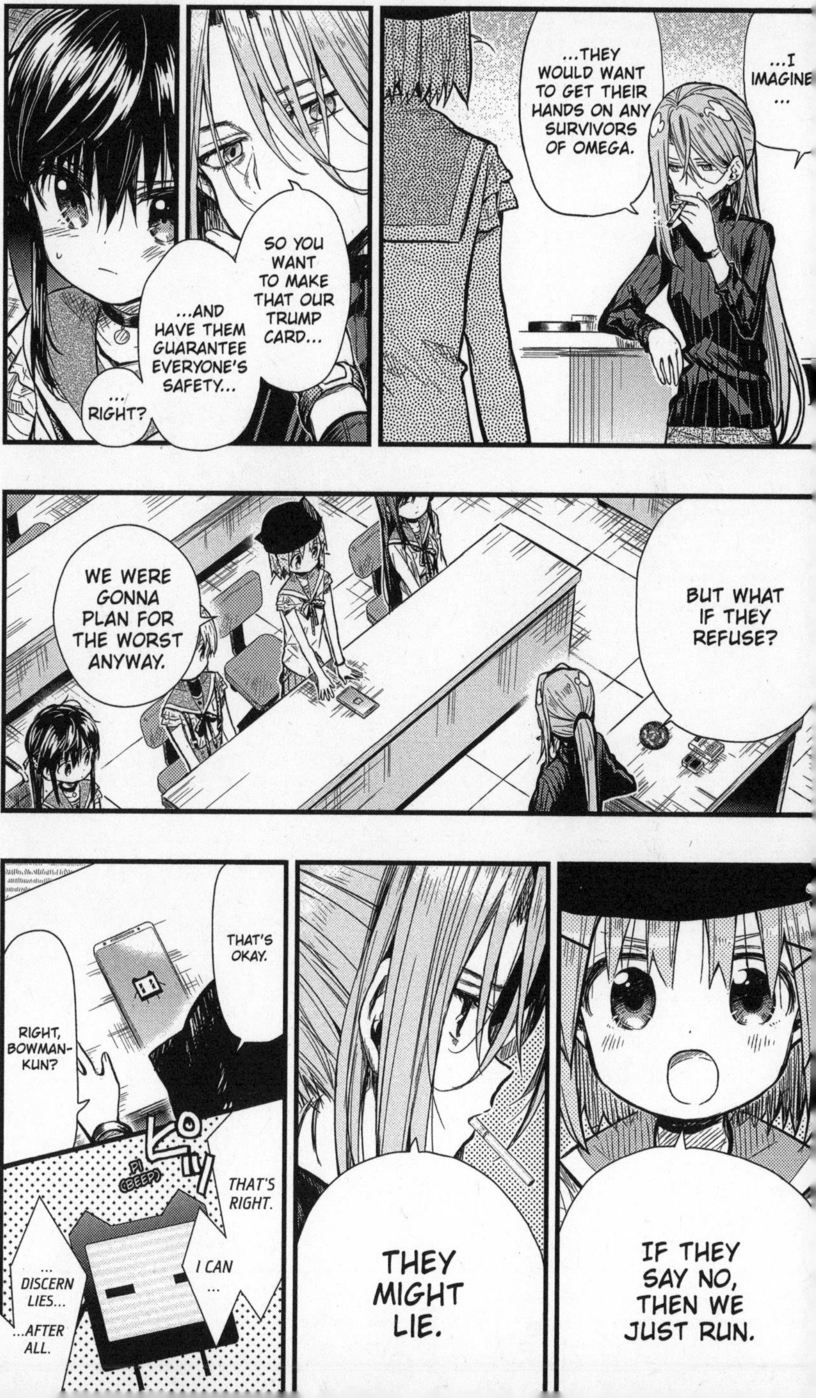
...I IMAGINE...
...THEY WOULD WANT TO GET THEIR HANDS ON ANY SURVIVORS OF OMEGA.
SO YOU WANT TO MAKE THAT OUR TRUMP CARD...
...AND HAVE THEM GUARANTEE EVERYONE'S SAFETY...
...RIGHT?
BUT WHAT IF THEY REFUSE?
WE WERE GONNA PLAN FOR THE WORST ANYWAY.
IF THEY SAY NO, THEN WE JUST RUN.
THEY MIGHT LIE.
THAT'S OKAY.
RIGHT, BOWMAN-KUN?
PI (BEEP)
THAT'S RIGHT.
I CAN...
...DISCERN LIES...
...AFTER ALL.

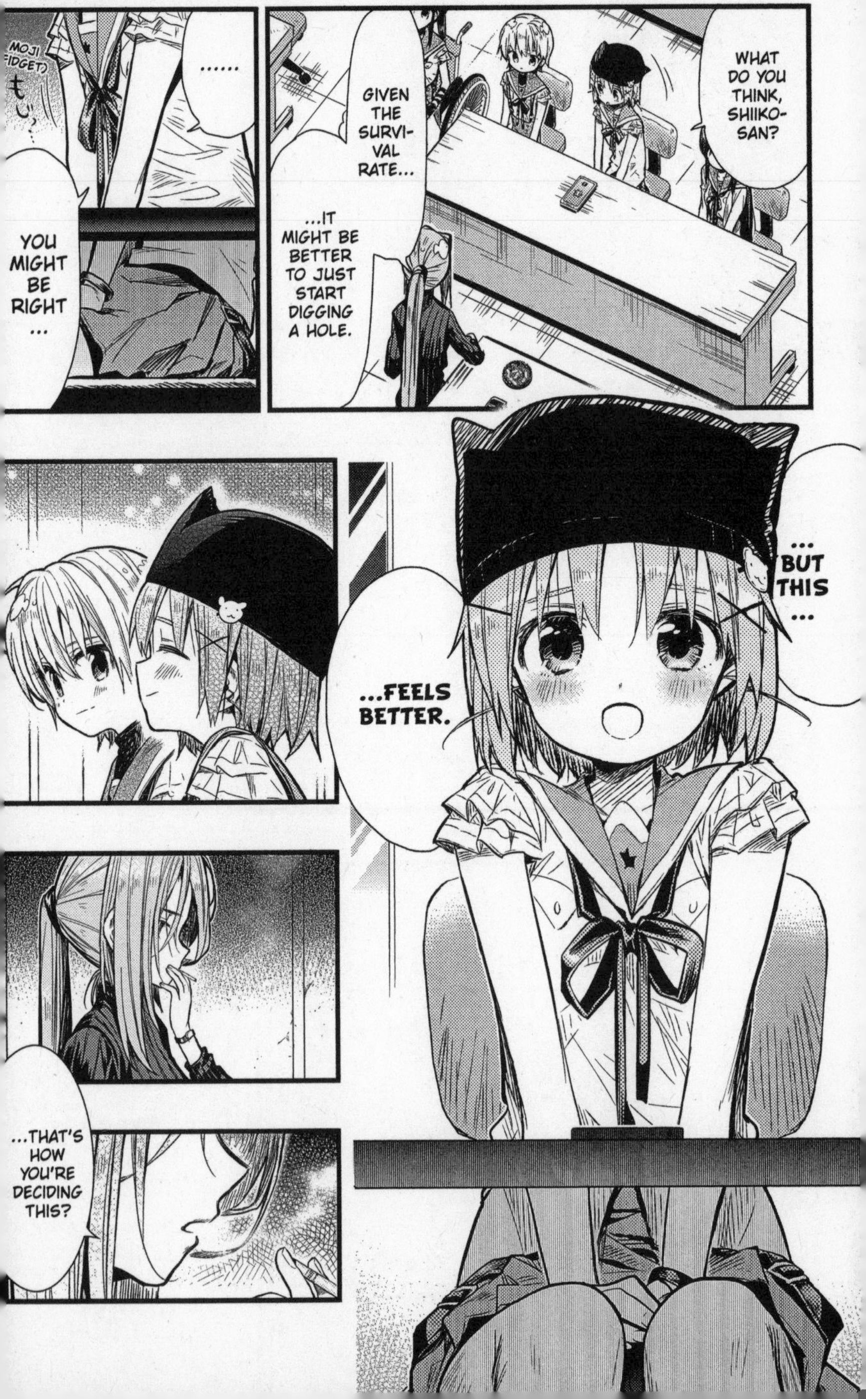
WHAT DO YOU THINK, SHIIKO-SAN?
GIVEN THE SURVIVAL RATE...
...IT MIGHT BE BETTER TO JUST START DIGGING A HOLE.
......
MOJI (FIDGET)
もじ…
YOU MIGHT BE RIGHT ...
...BUT THIS ...
...FEELS BETTER.
...THAT'S HOW YOU'RE DECIDING THIS?

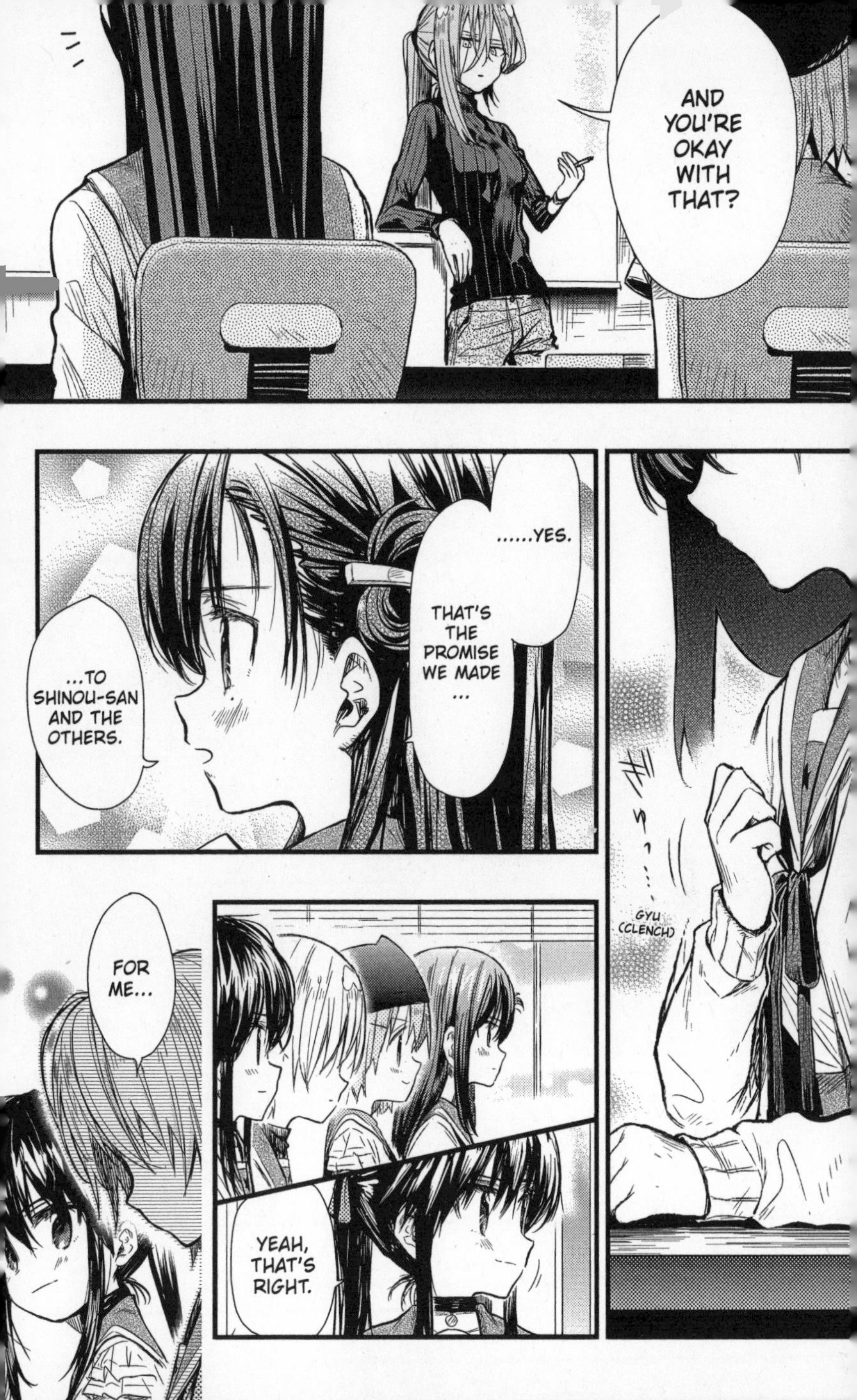
AND YOU'RE OKAY WITH THAT?
GYU (CLENCH)
......YES.
THAT'S THE PROMISE WE MADE ...
...TO SHINOU-SAN AND THE OTHERS.
FOR ME...
YEAH, THAT'S RIGHT.

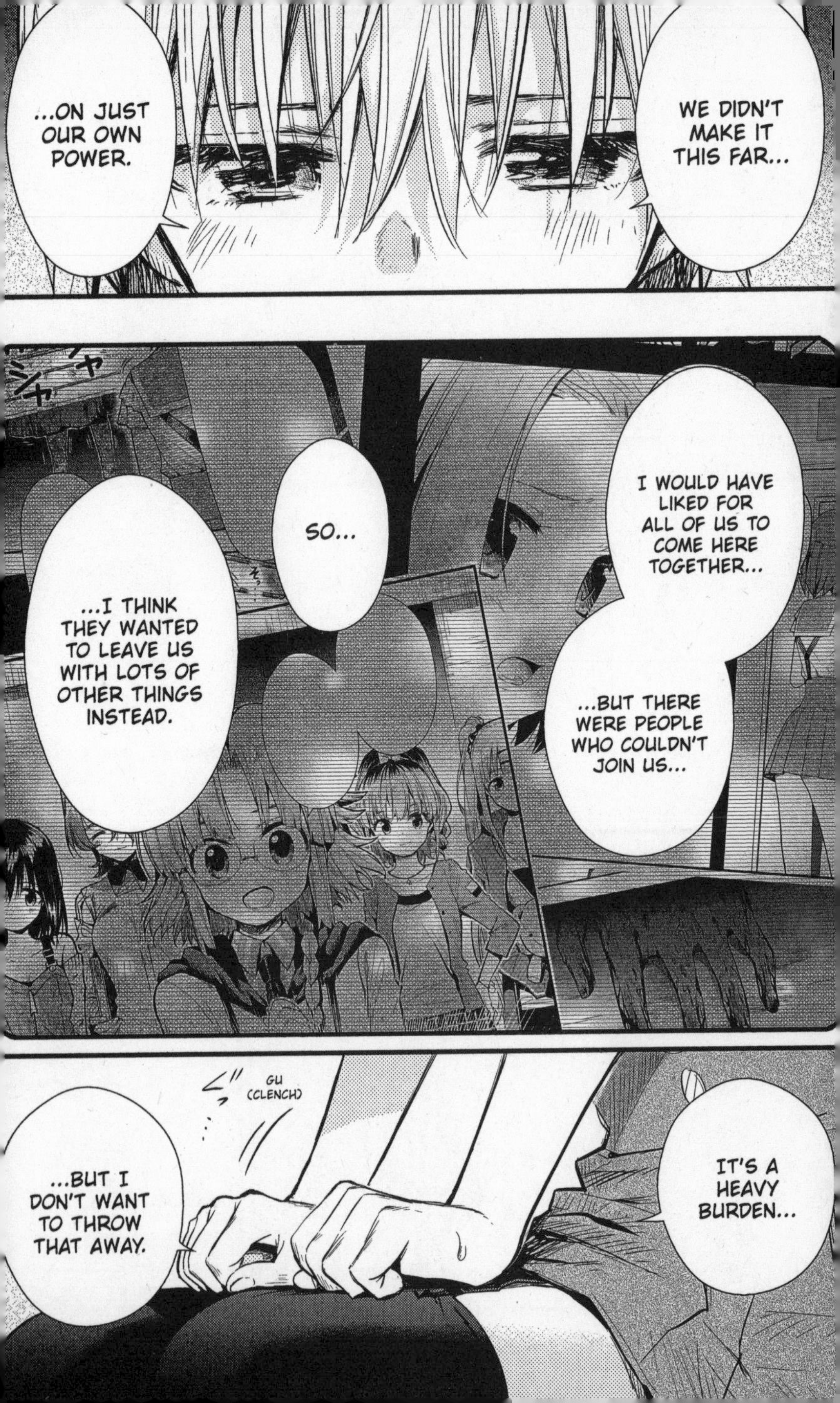
WE DIDN'T MAKE IT THIS FAR...
...ON JUST OUR OWN POWER.
I WOULD HAVE LIKED FOR ALL OF US TO COME HERE TOGETHER...
...BUT THERE WERE PEOPLE WHO COULDN'T JOIN US...
SO...
...I THINK THEY WANTED TO LEAVE US WITH LOTS OF OTHER THINGS INSTEAD.
IT'S A HEAVY BURDEN...
GU (CLENCH)
...BUT I DON'T WANT TO THROW THAT AWAY.

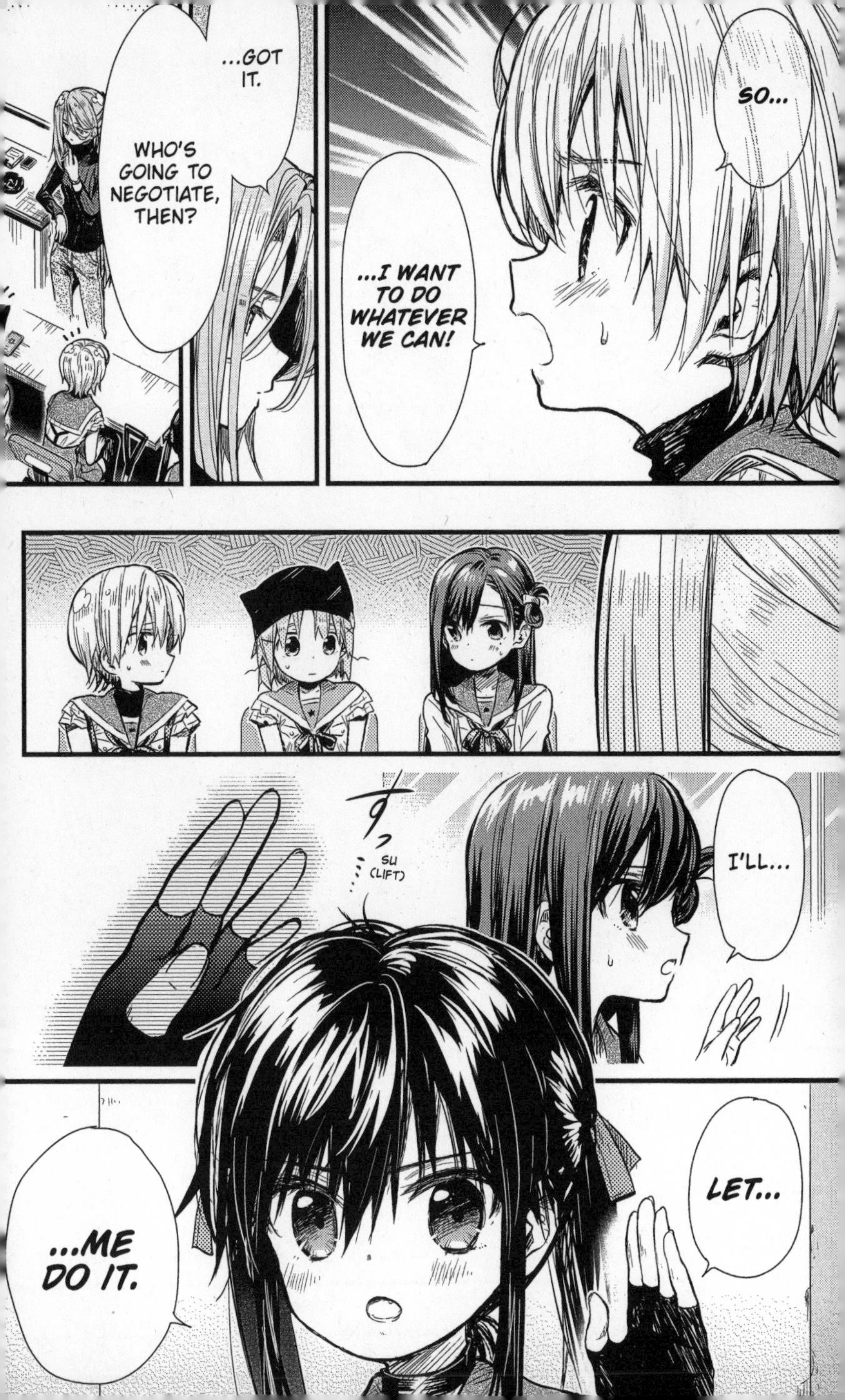
SO...
...I WANT TO DO WHATEVER WE CAN!
...GOT IT.
WHO'S GOING TO NEGOTIATE, THEN?
I'LL...
すっ
SU (LIFT)
LET...
...ME DO IT.

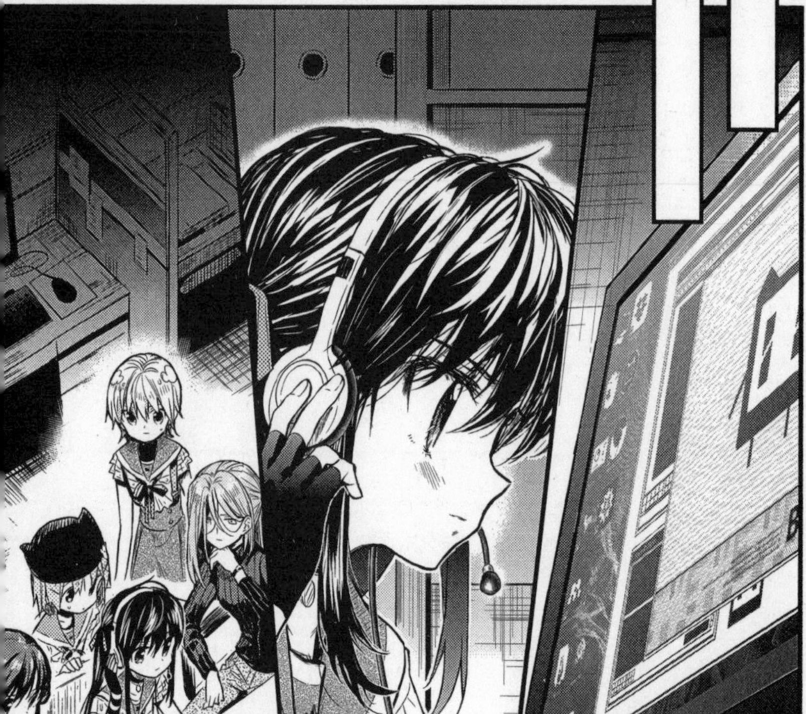

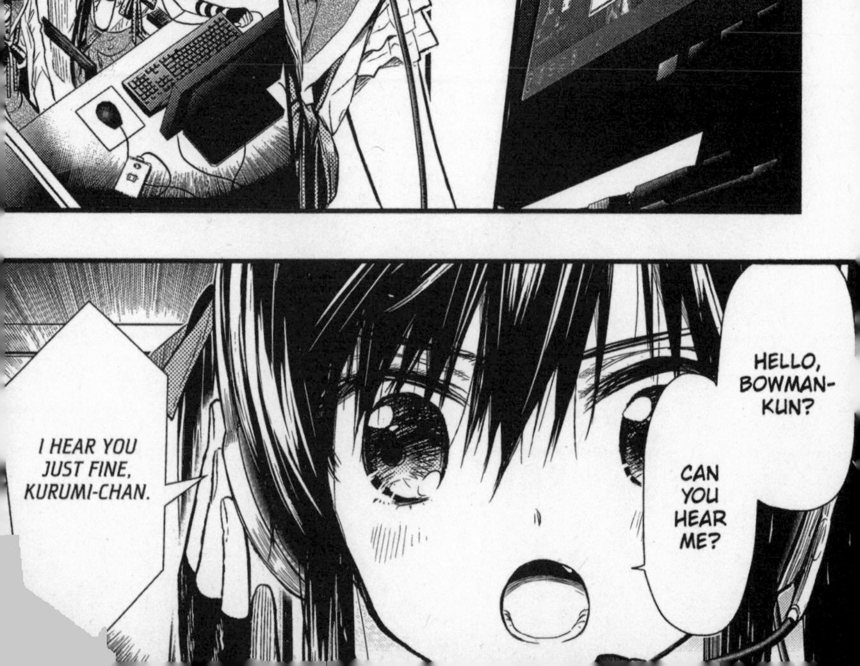
HELLO, BOWMAN-KUN?
CAN YOU HEAR ME?
I HEAR YOU JUST FINE, KURUMI-CHAN.

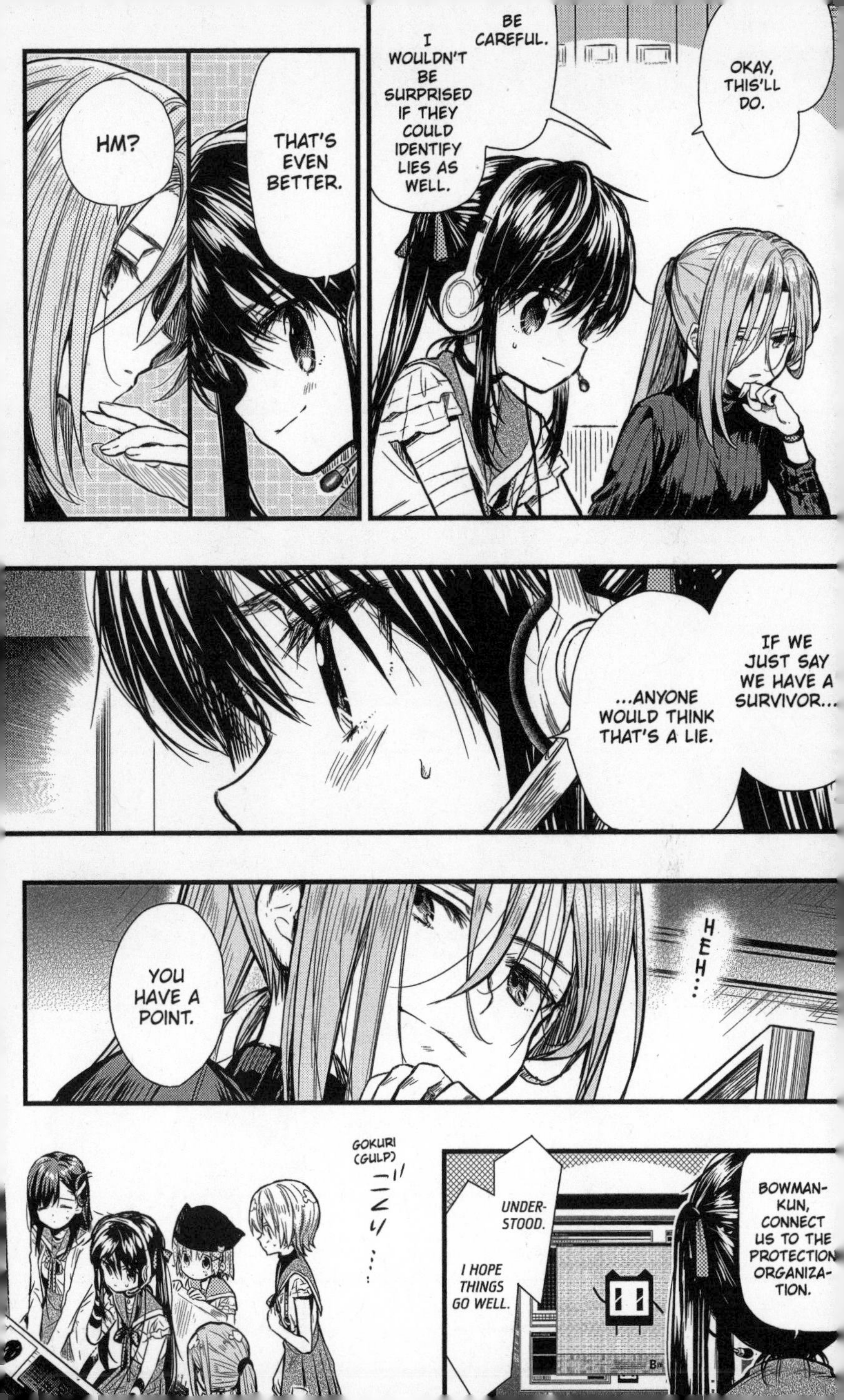
OKAY, THIS'LL DO.
BE CAREFUL.
I WOULDN'T BE SURPRISED IF THEY COULD IDENTIFY LIES AS WELL.
THAT'S EVEN BETTER.
HM?
IF WE JUST SAY WE HAVE A SURVIVOR...
...ANYONE WOULD THINK THAT'S A LIE.
HEH...
YOU HAVE A POINT.
BOWMAN-KUN, CONNECT US TO THE PROTECTION ORGANIZATION.
UNDERSTOOD.
I HOPE THINGS GO WELL.
GOKURI (GULP)

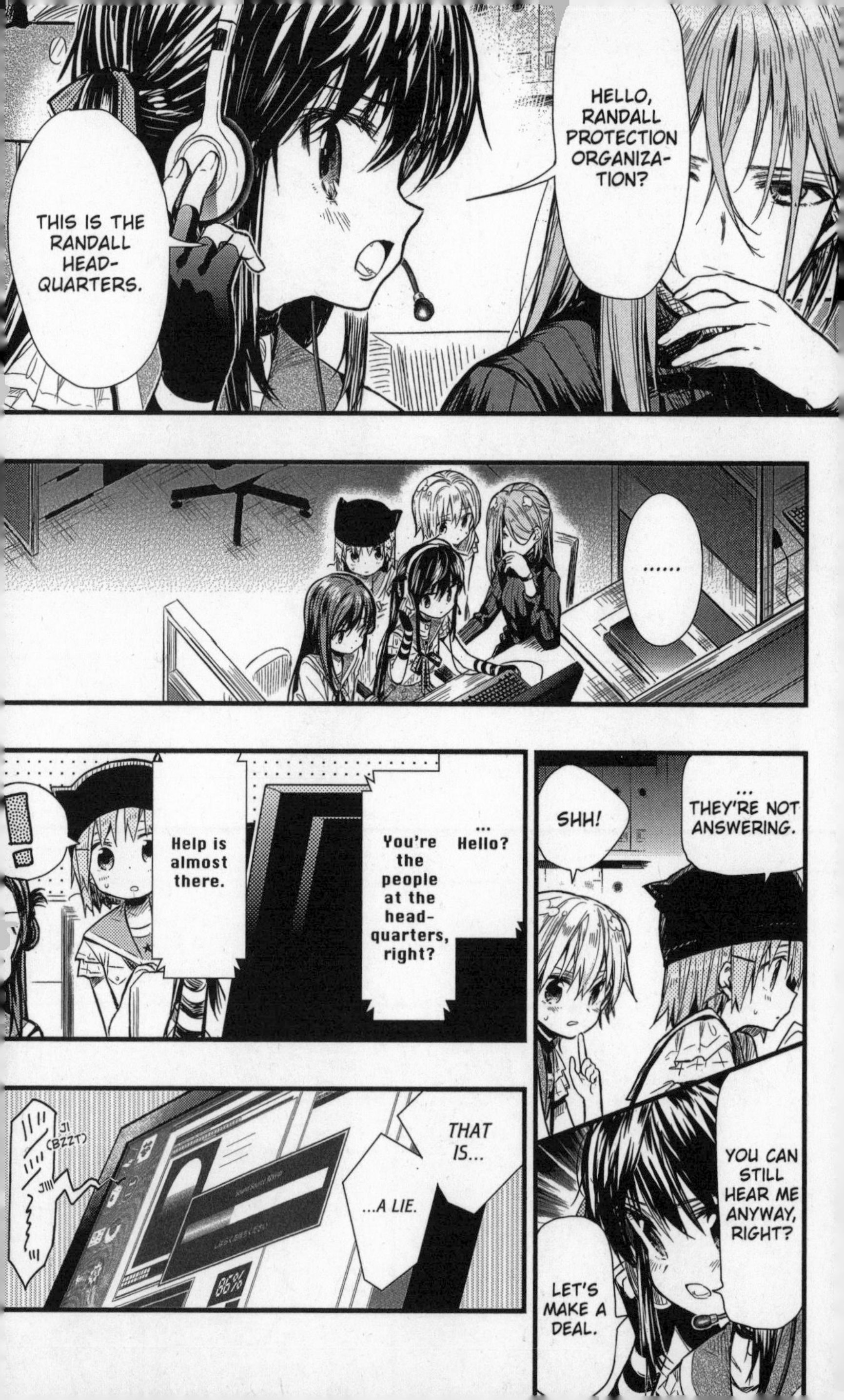
HELLO, RANDALL PROTECTION ORGANIZATION?
THIS IS THE RANDALL HEAD-QUARTERS.
......
... THEY'RE NOT ANSWERING.
SHH!
YOU CAN STILL HEAR ME ANYWAY, RIGHT?
LET'S MAKE A DEAL.
... Hello?
You're the people at the head-quarters, right?
Help is almost there.
!
THAT IS...
...A LIE.
JI (BZZT)
JI
86%

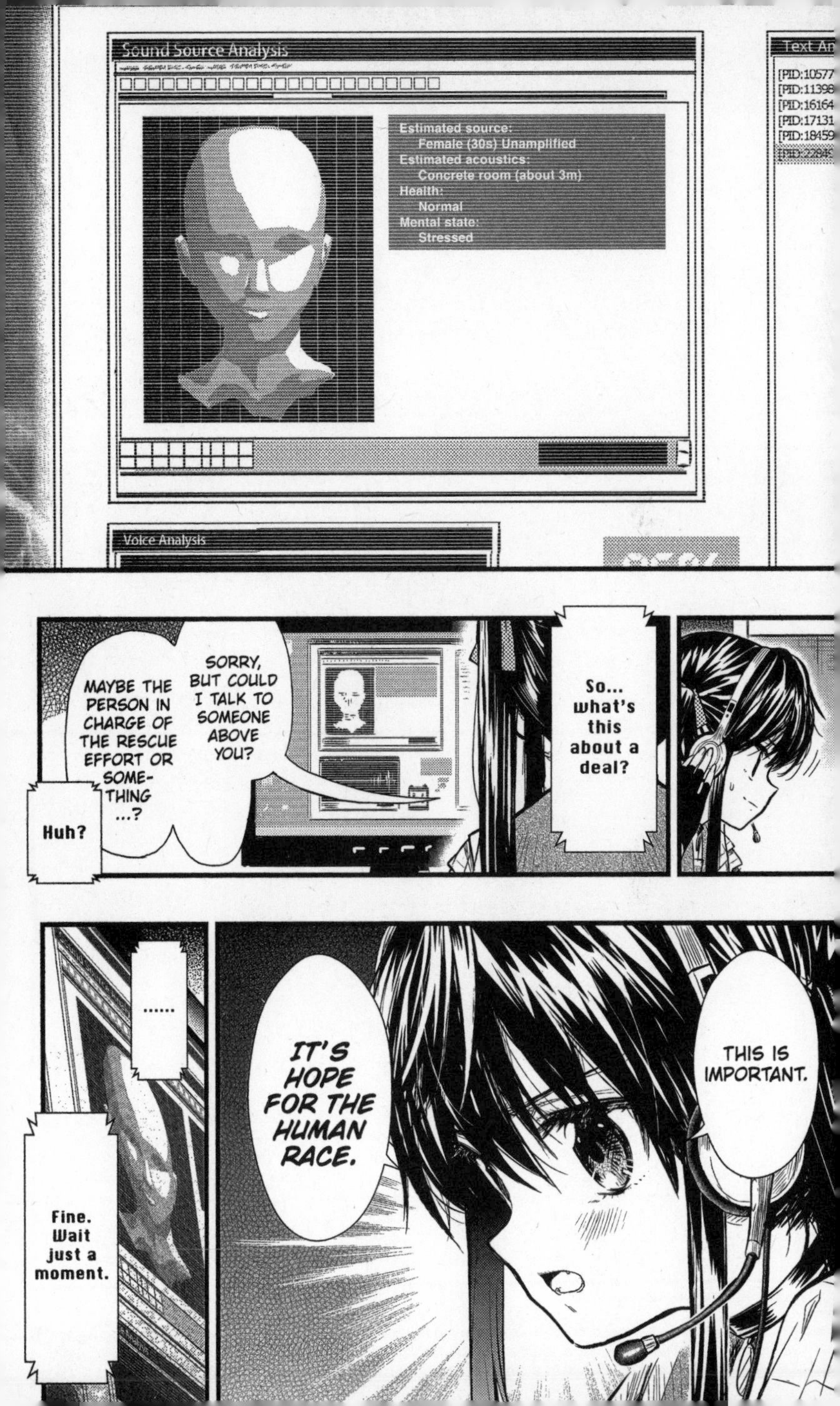

Sound Source Analysis
Estimated source:
Female (30s) Unamplified
Estimated acoustics:
Concrete room (about 3m)
Health:
Normal
Mental state:
Stressed
Voice Analysis
So... what's this about a deal?
SORRY, BUT COULD I TALK TO SOMEONE ABOVE YOU?
MAYBE THE PERSON IN CHARGE OF THE RESCUE EFFORT OR SOME-THING ...?
Huh?
THIS IS IMPORTANT.
IT'S HOPE FOR THE HUMAN RACE.
......
Fine. Wait just a moment.

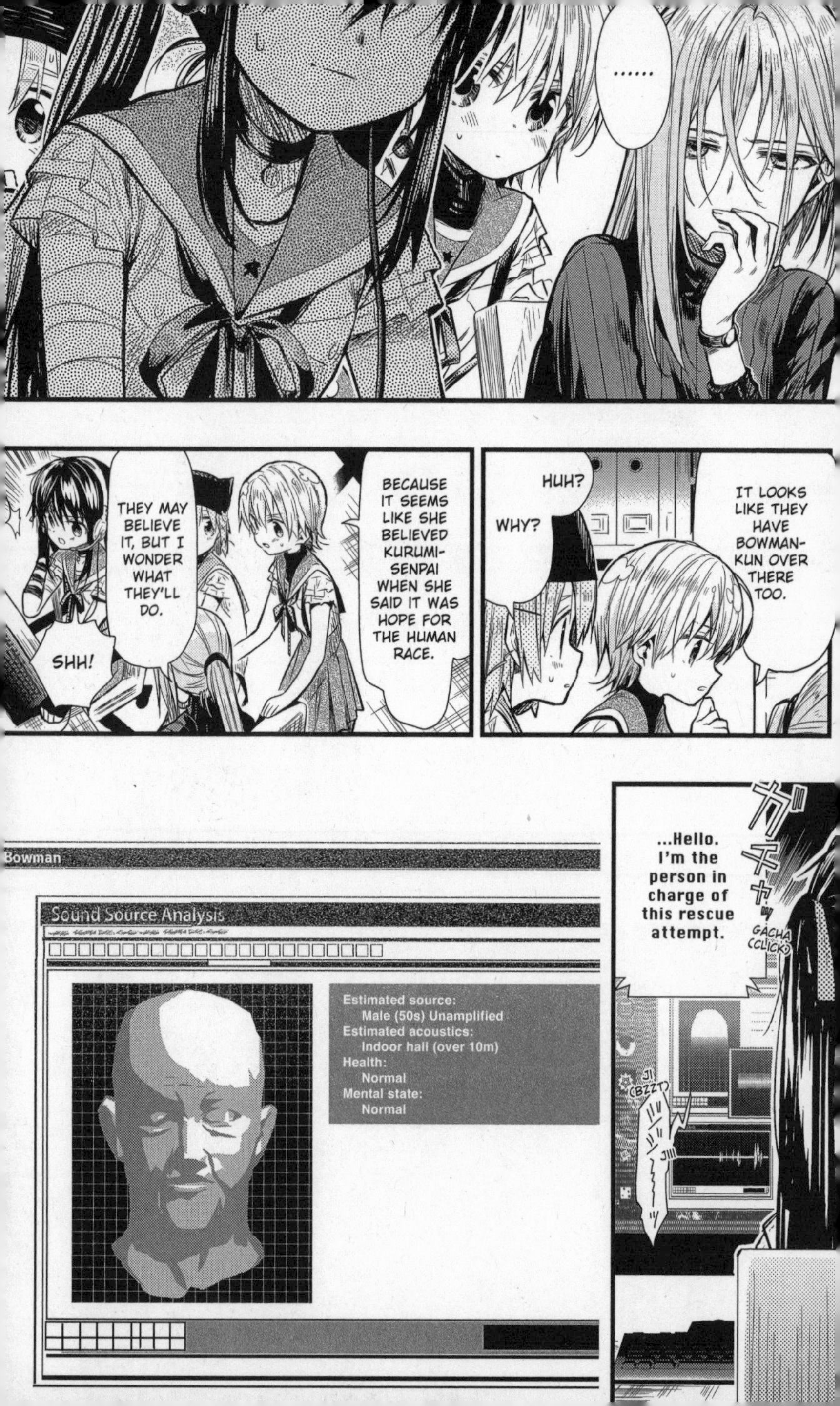
......
IT LOOKS LIKE THEY HAVE BOWMAN-KUN OVER THERE TOO.
HUH?
WHY?
BECAUSE IT SEEMS LIKE SHE BELIEVED KURUMI-SENPAI WHEN SHE SAID IT WAS HOPE FOR THE HUMAN RACE.
THEY MAY BELIEVE IT, BUT I WONDER WHAT THEY'LL DO.
SHH!
GACHA (CLICK)
...Hello. I'm the person in charge of this rescue attempt.
JI (BZZT)
Bowman
Sound Source Analysis
Estimated source:
Male (50s) Unamplified
Estimated acoustics:
Indoor hall (over 10m)
Health:
Normal
Mental state:
Normal

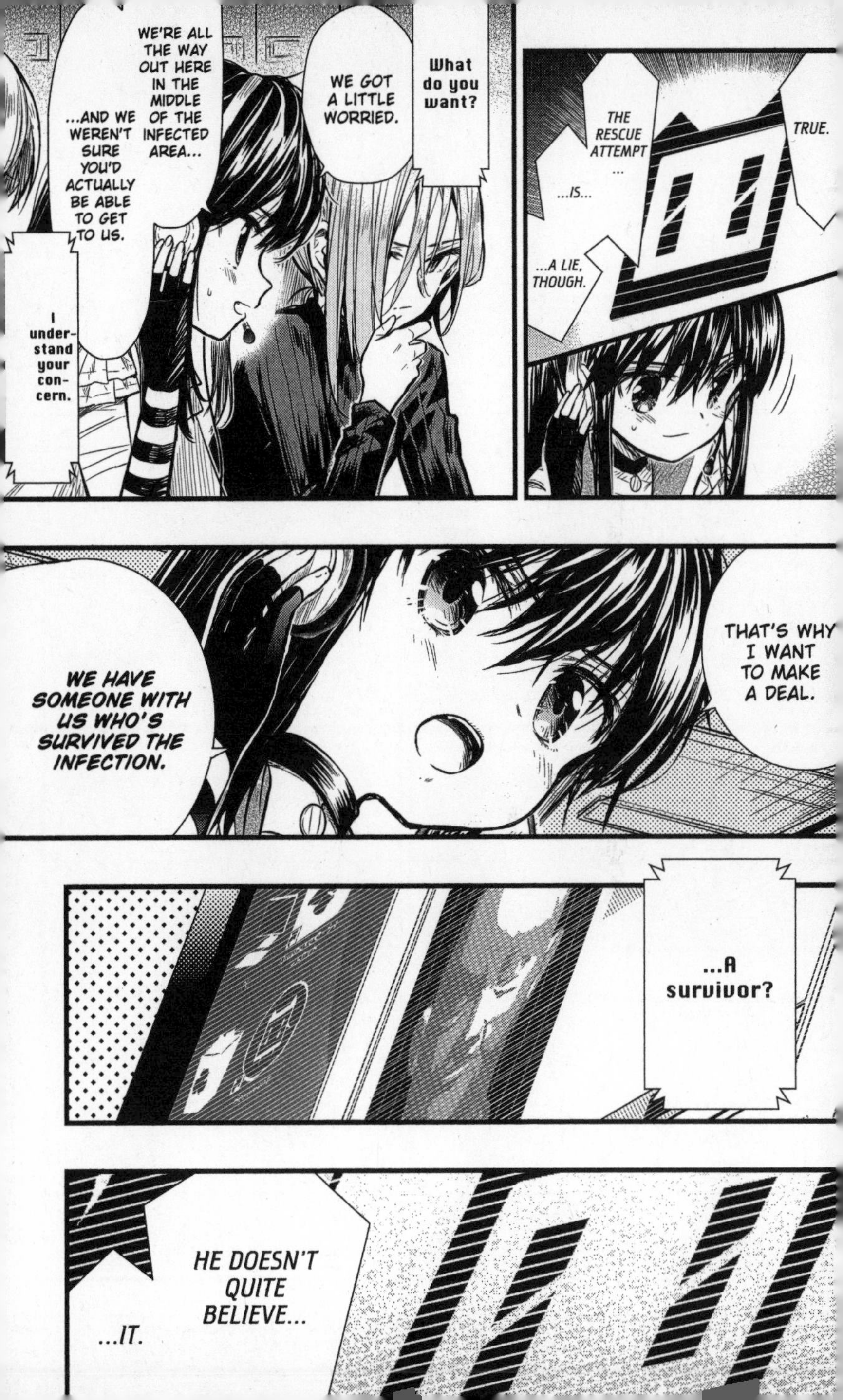
TRUE.
THE RESCUE ATTEMPT ...
...IS...
...A LIE, THOUGH.
What do you want?
WE GOT A LITTLE WORRIED.
WE'RE ALL THE WAY OUT HERE IN THE MIDDLE OF THE INFECTED AREA...
...AND WE WEREN'T SURE YOU'D ACTUALLY BE ABLE TO GET TO US.
I understand your concern.
THAT'S WHY I WANT TO MAKE A DEAL.
WE HAVE SOMEONE WITH US WHO'S SURVIVED THE INFECTION.
...A survivor?
HE DOESN'T QUITE BELIEVE...
...IT.

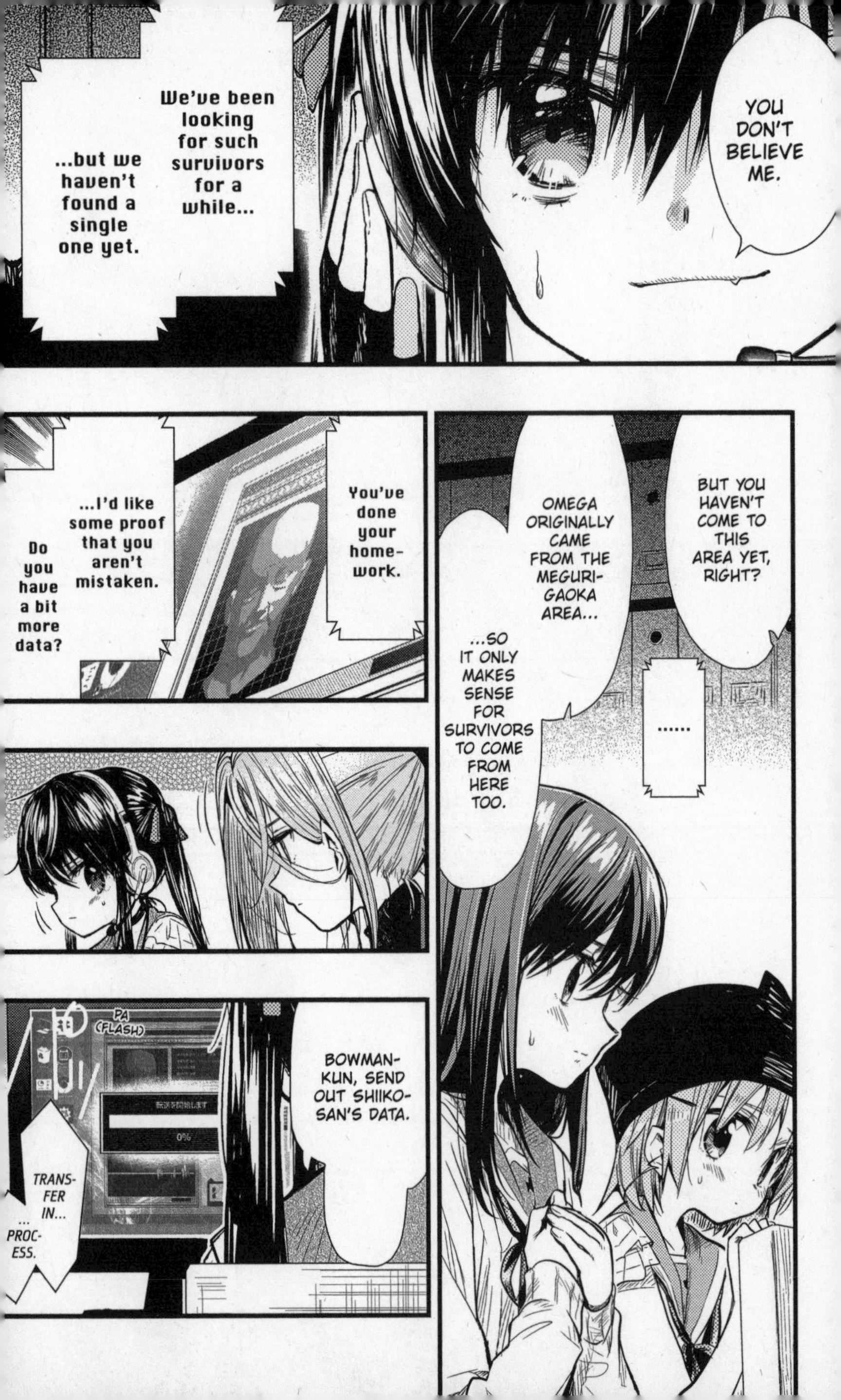
YOU DON'T BELIEVE ME.
We've been looking for such survivors for a while...
...but we haven't found a single one yet.
BUT YOU HAVEN'T COME TO THIS AREA YET, RIGHT?
OMEGA ORIGINALLY CAME FROM THE MEGURI-GAOKA AREA...
...SO IT ONLY MAKES SENSE FOR SURVIVORS TO COME FROM HERE TOO.
......
You've done your home-work.
...I'd like some proof that you aren't mistaken.
Do you have a bit more data?
BOWMAN-KUN, SEND OUT SHIIKO-SAN'S DATA.
PA (FLASH)
転送を開始します
0%
TRANS-FER IN...
...PROC-ESS.

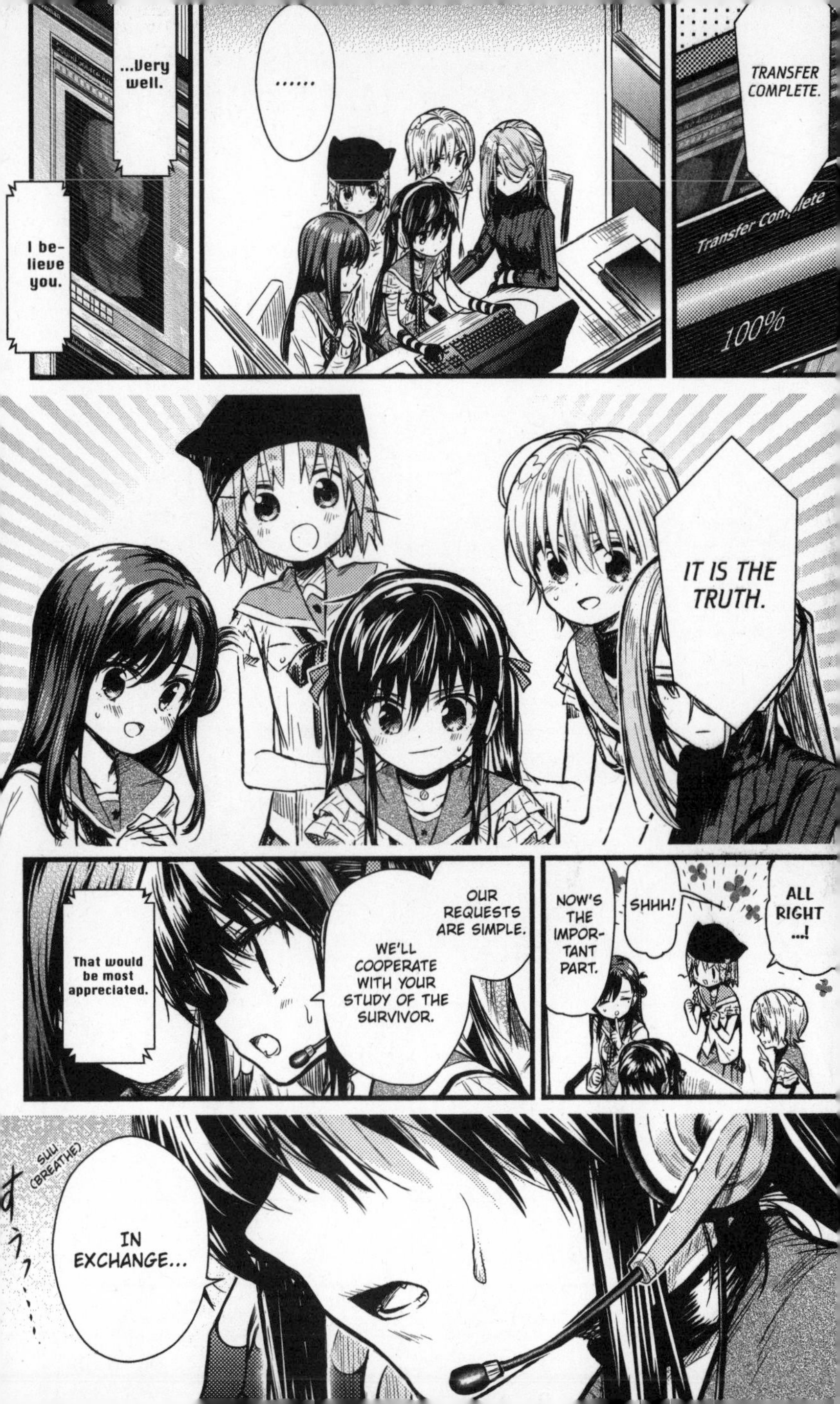
TRANSFER COMPLETE.
Transfer Complete
100%
......
...Very well.
I believe you.
IT IS THE TRUTH.
ALL RIGHT ...!
SHHH!
NOW'S THE IMPORTANT PART.
OUR REQUESTS ARE SIMPLE.
WE'LL COOPERATE WITH YOUR STUDY OF THE SURVIVOR.
That would be most appreciated.
すぅ…
SUU (BREATHE)
IN EXCHANGE...

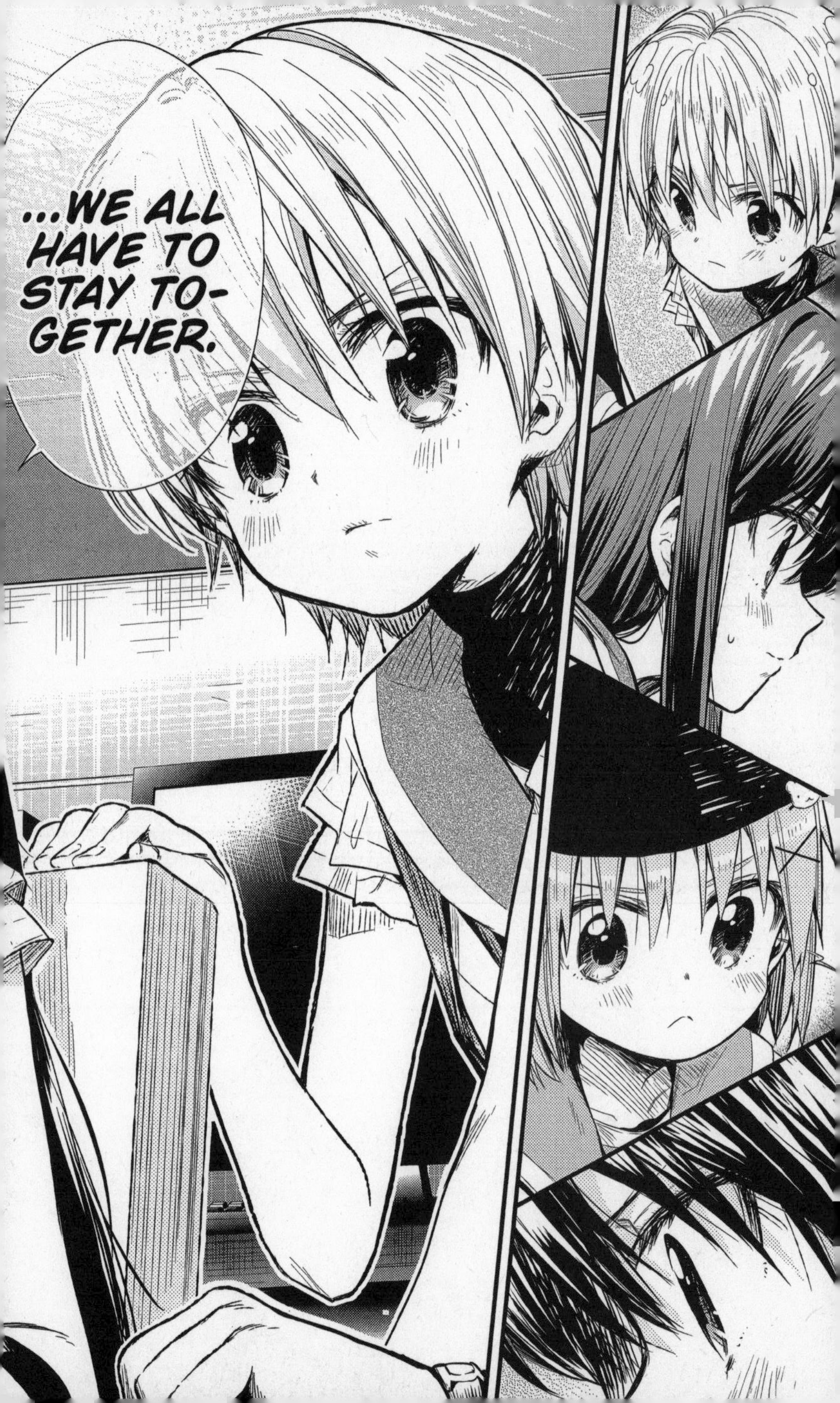
...WE ALL HAVE TO STAY TO-GETHER.

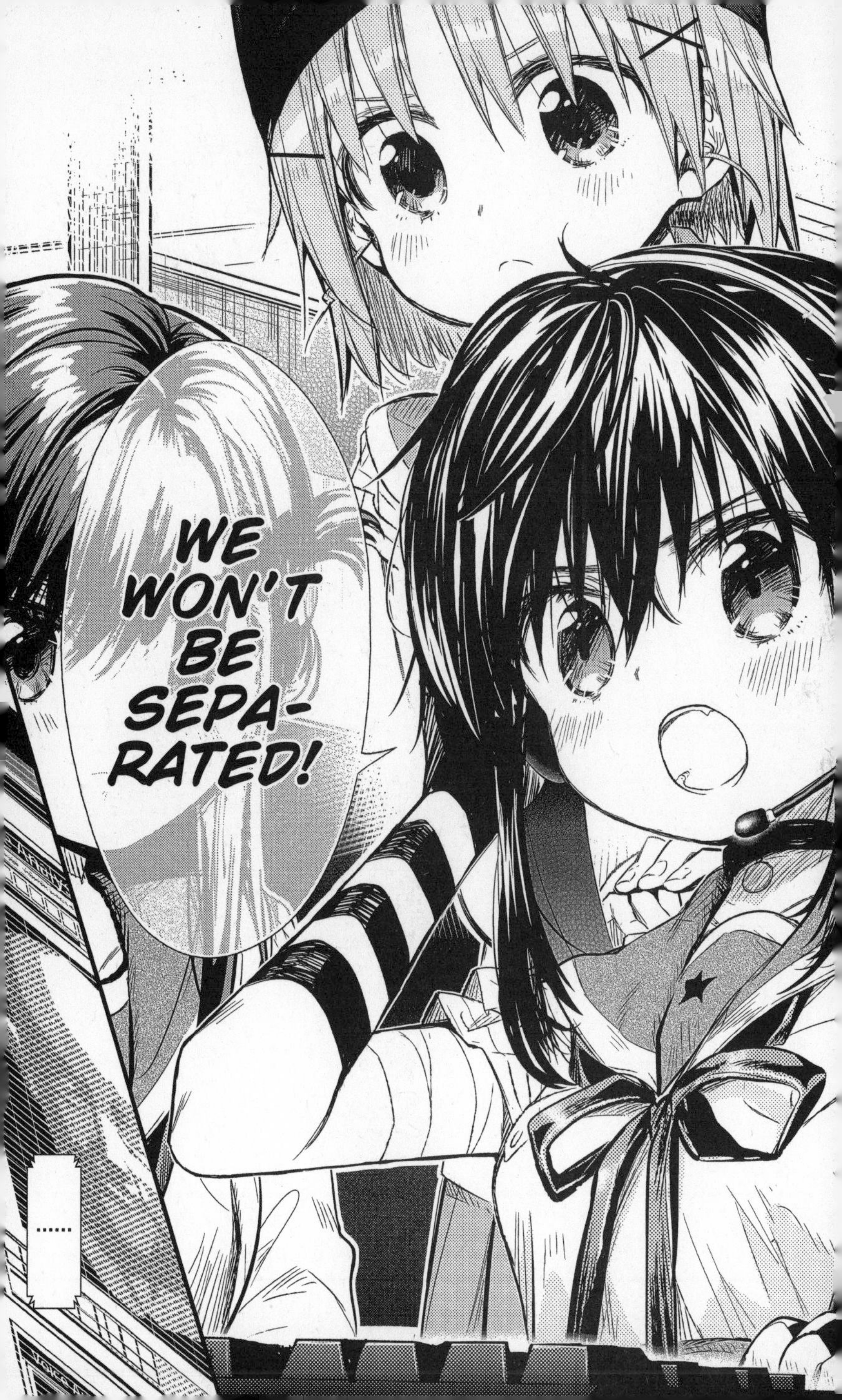
WE WON'T BE SEPA-RATED!
......

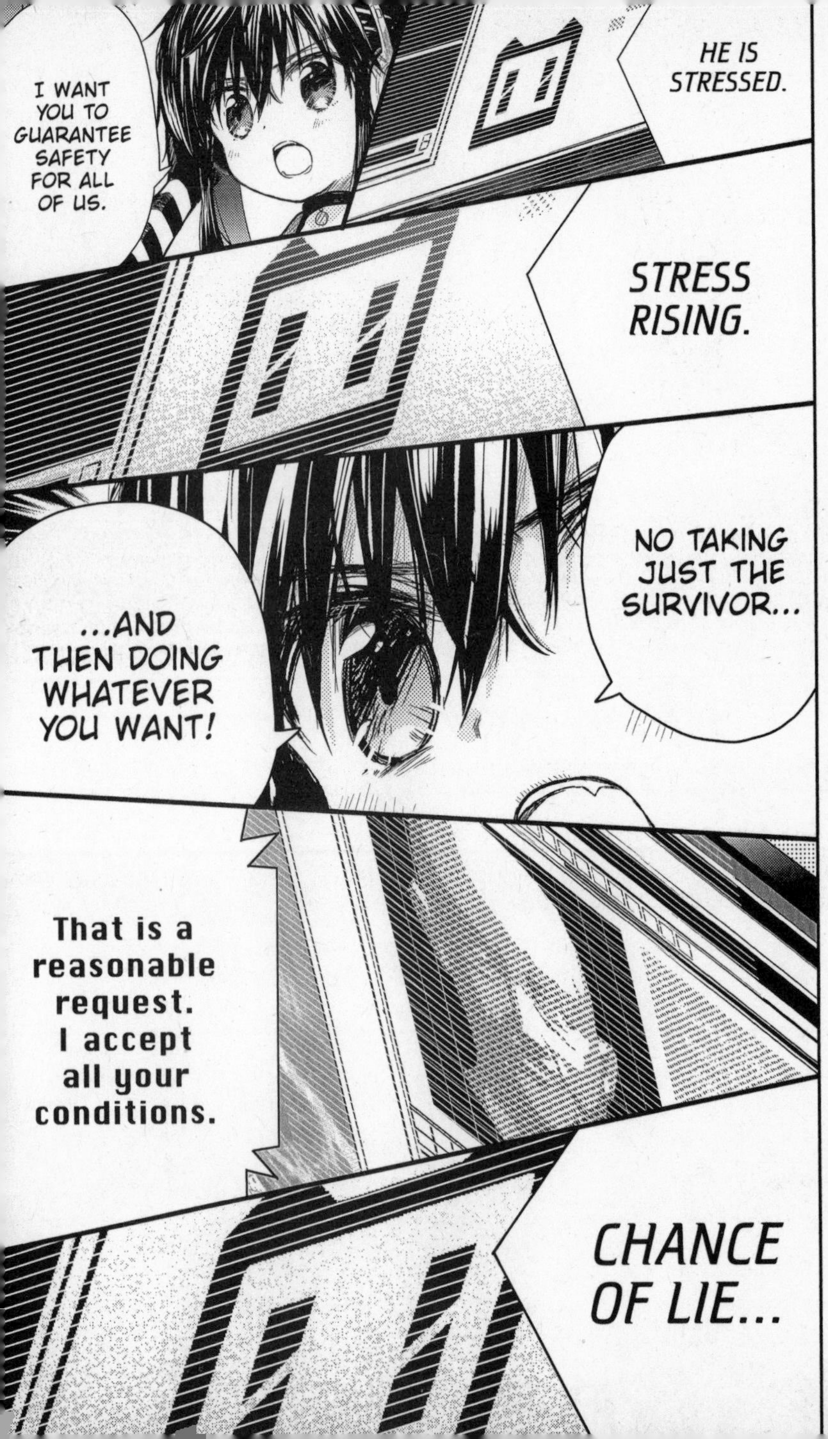
HE IS STRESSED.
I WANT YOU TO GUARANTEE SAFETY FOR ALL OF US.
STRESS RISING.
NO TAKING JUST THE SURVIVOR...
...AND THEN DOING WHATEVER YOU WANT!
That is a reasonable request. I accept all your conditions.
CHANCE OF LIE...

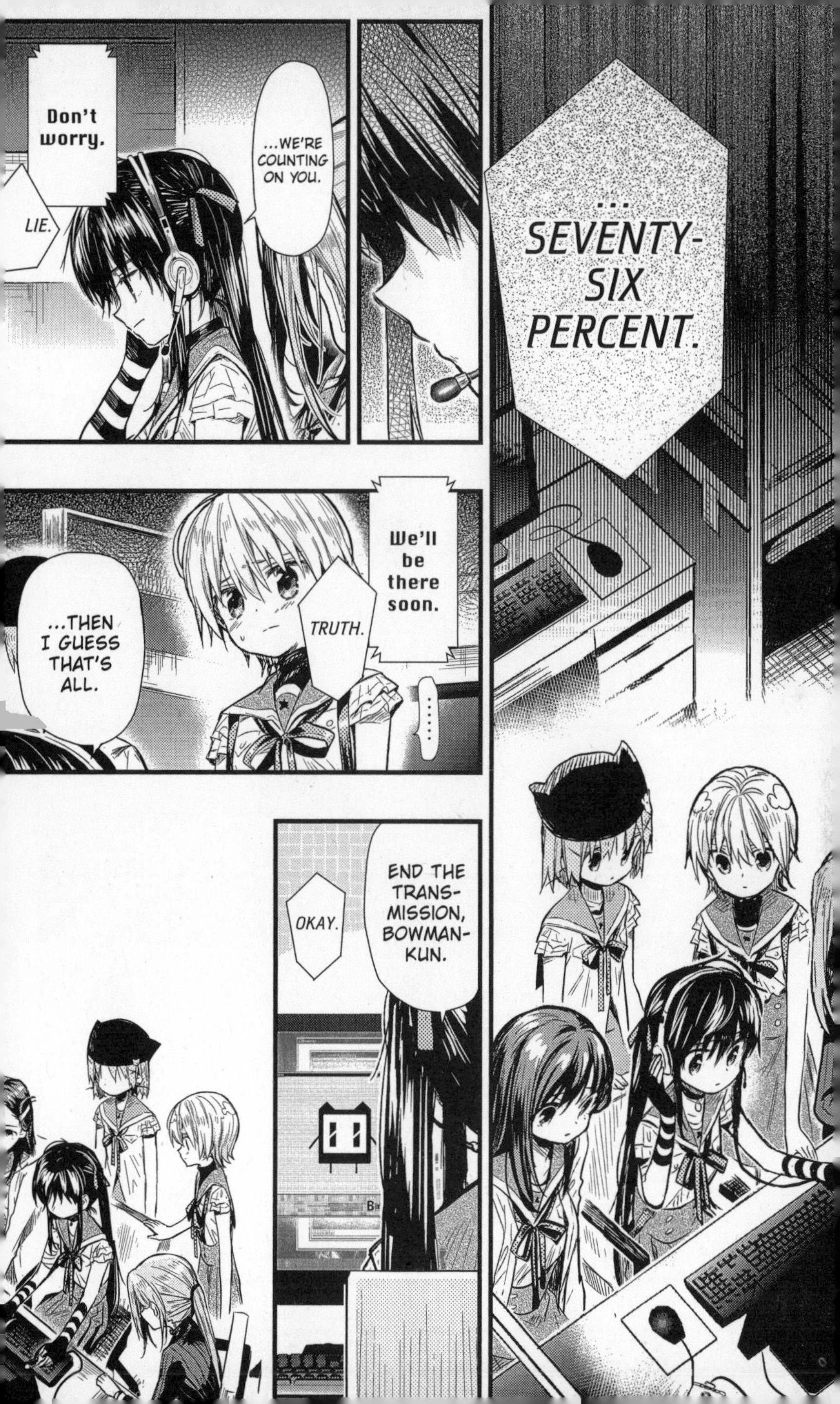
...SEVENTY-SIX PERCENT.
...WE'RE COUNTING ON YOU.
Don't worry.
LIE.
We'll be there soon.
TRUTH.
......
...THEN I GUESS THAT'S ALL.
END THE TRANS-MISSION, BOWMAN-KUN.
OKAY.

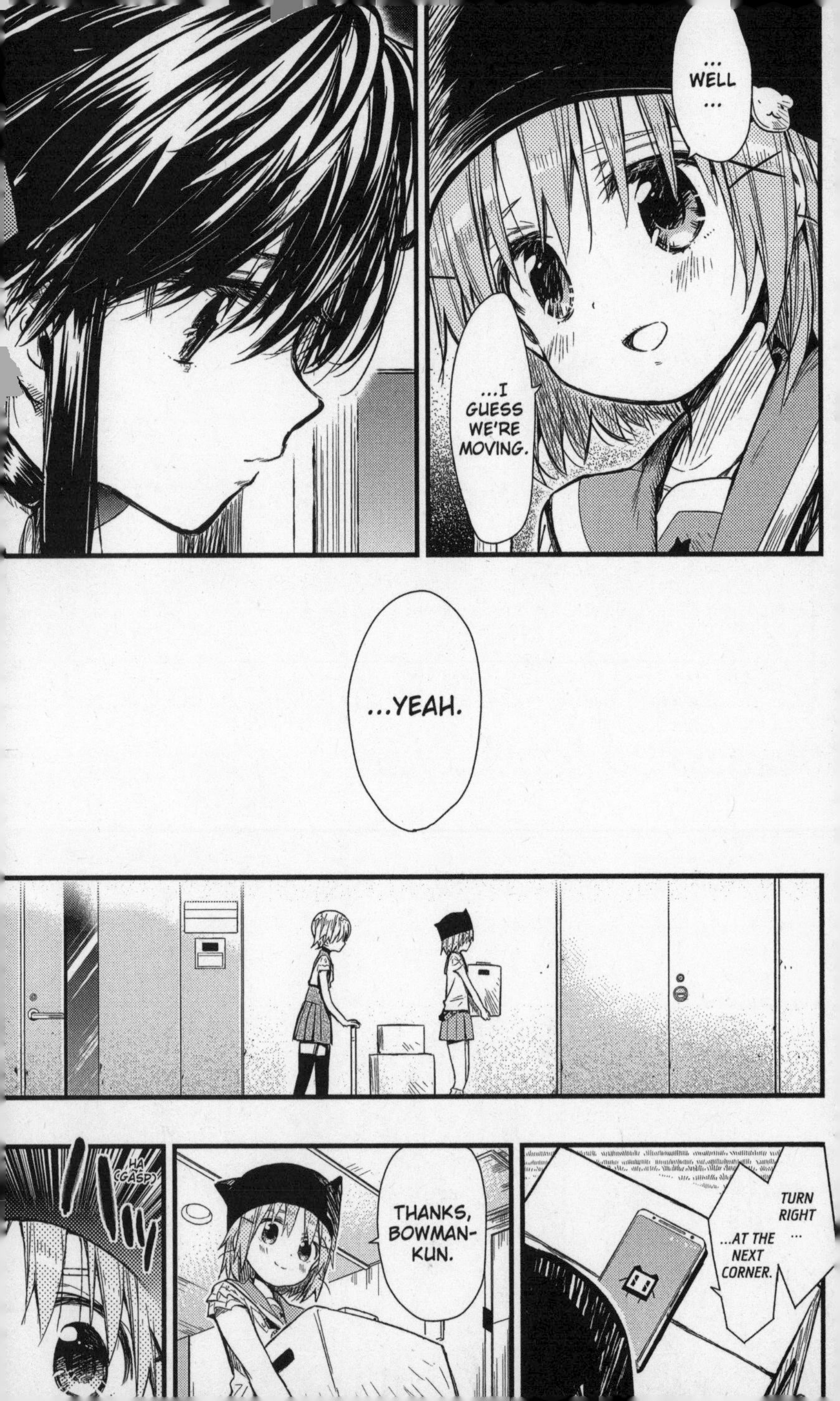
... WELL ...
...I GUESS WE'RE MOVING.
...YEAH.
TURN RIGHT ...
...AT THE NEXT CORNER.
THANKS, BOWMAN-KUN.
HA (GASP)

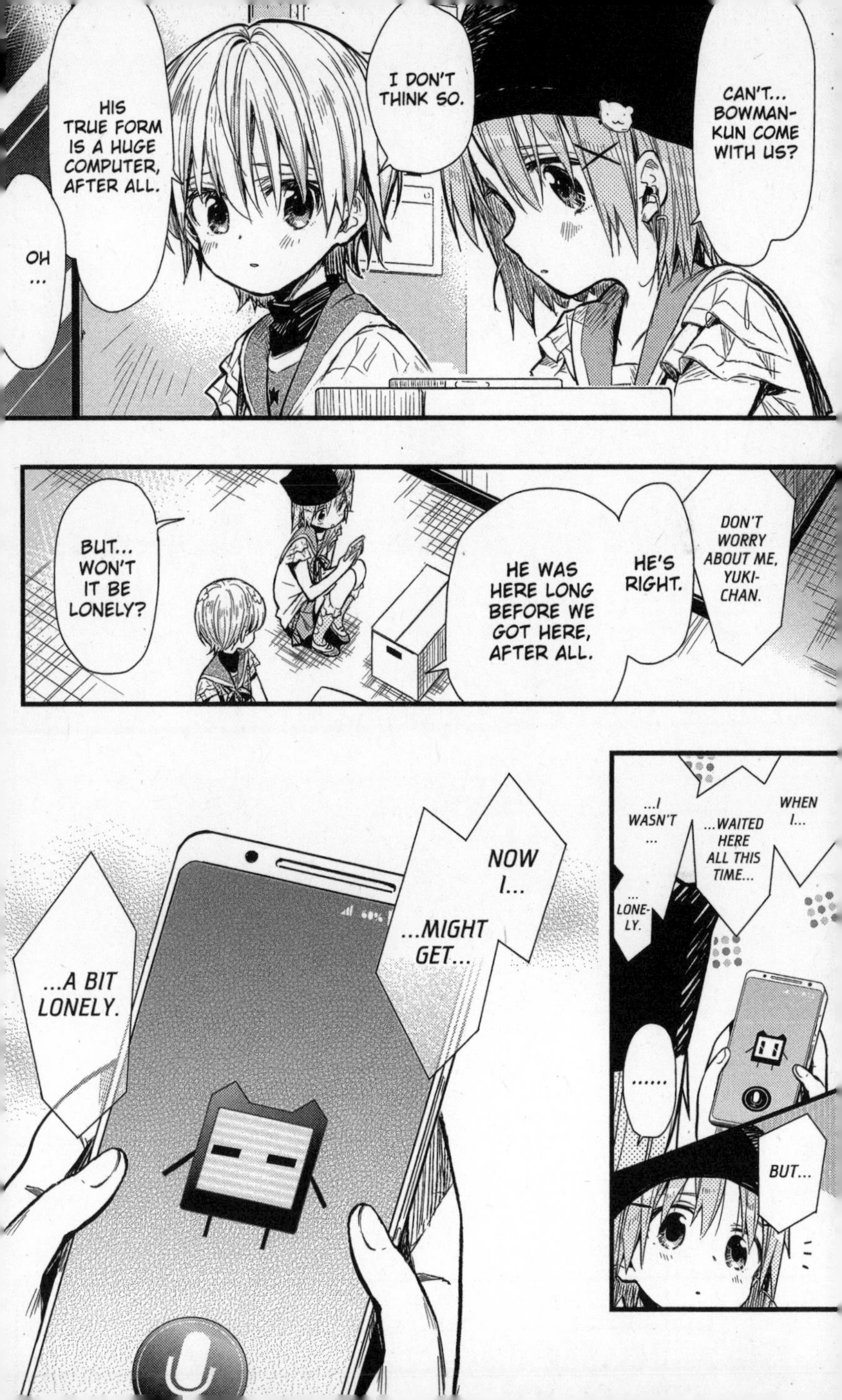
CAN'T... BOWMAN-KUN COME WITH US?
I DON'T THINK SO.
HIS TRUE FORM IS A HUGE COMPUTER, AFTER ALL.
OH ...
DON'T WORRY ABOUT ME, YUKI-CHAN.
HE'S RIGHT.
HE WAS HERE LONG BEFORE WE GOT HERE, AFTER ALL.
BUT... WON'T IT BE LONELY?
WHEN I...
...WAITED HERE ALL THIS TIME...
...I WASN'T ...
... LONE-LY.
......
BUT...
NOW I...
...MIGHT GET...
...A BIT LONELY.

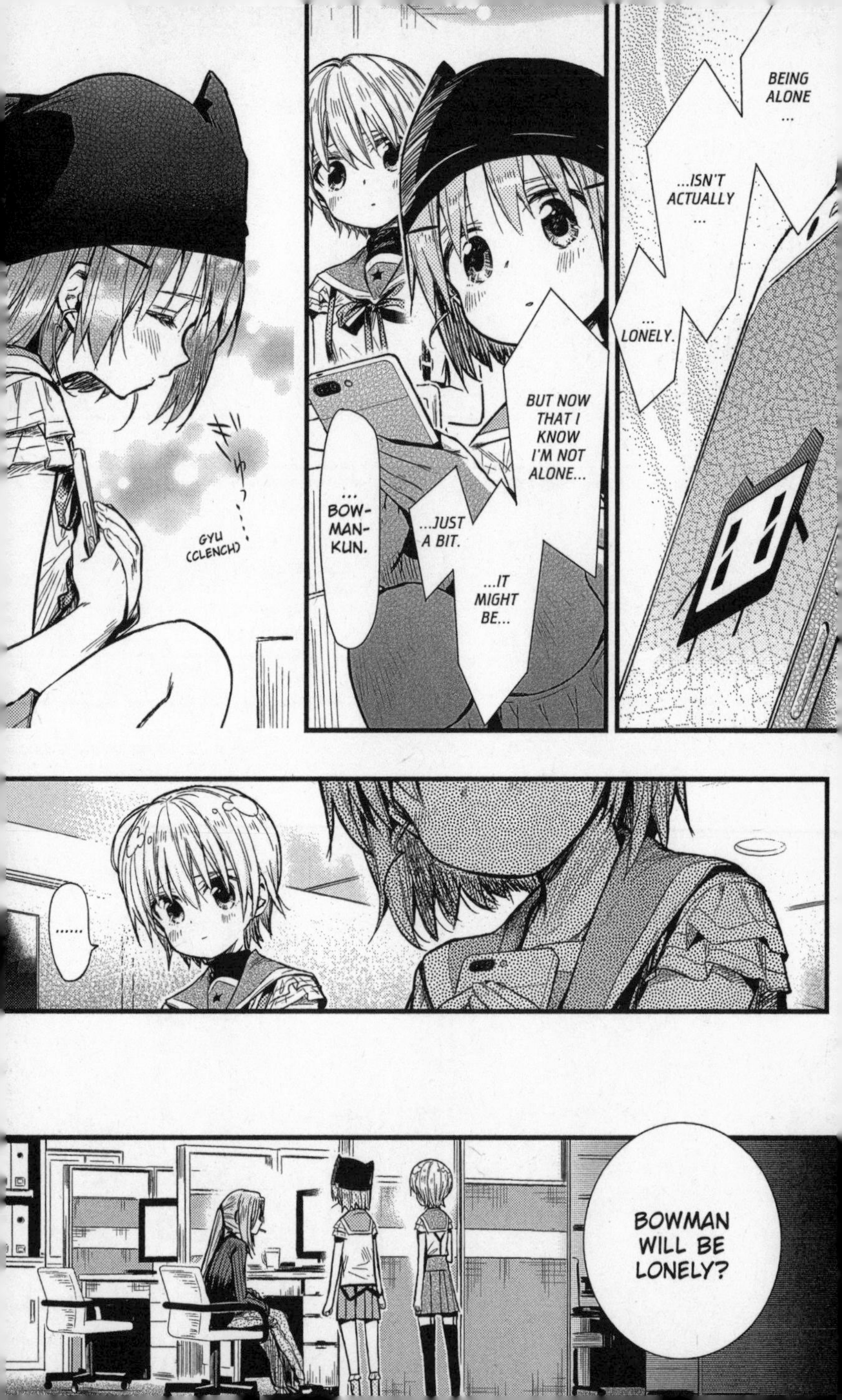
BEING ALONE ...
...ISN'T ACTUALLY ...
... LONELY.
BUT NOW THAT I KNOW I'M NOT ALONE...
...IT MIGHT BE...
...JUST A BIT.
... BOW-MAN-KUN.
GYU (CLENCH)
......
BOWMAN WILL BE LONELY?

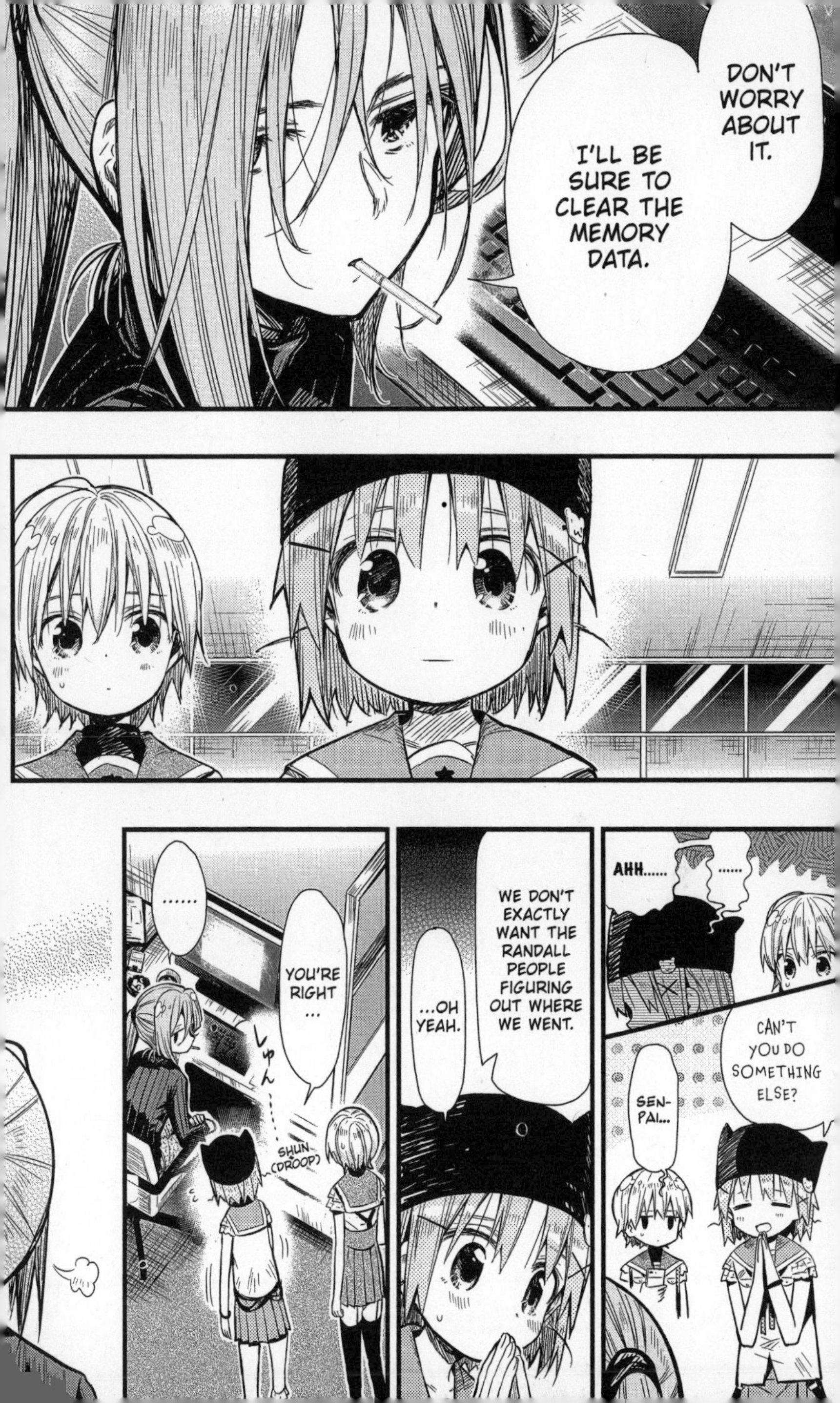
DON'T WORRY ABOUT IT.
I'LL BE SURE TO CLEAR THE MEMORY DATA.
......
AHH......
CAN'T YOU DO SOMETHING ELSE?
SEN-PAI...
WE DON'T EXACTLY WANT THE RANDALL PEOPLE FIGURING OUT WHERE WE WENT.
...OH YEAH.
......
YOU'RE RIGHT ...
SHUN (DROOP)

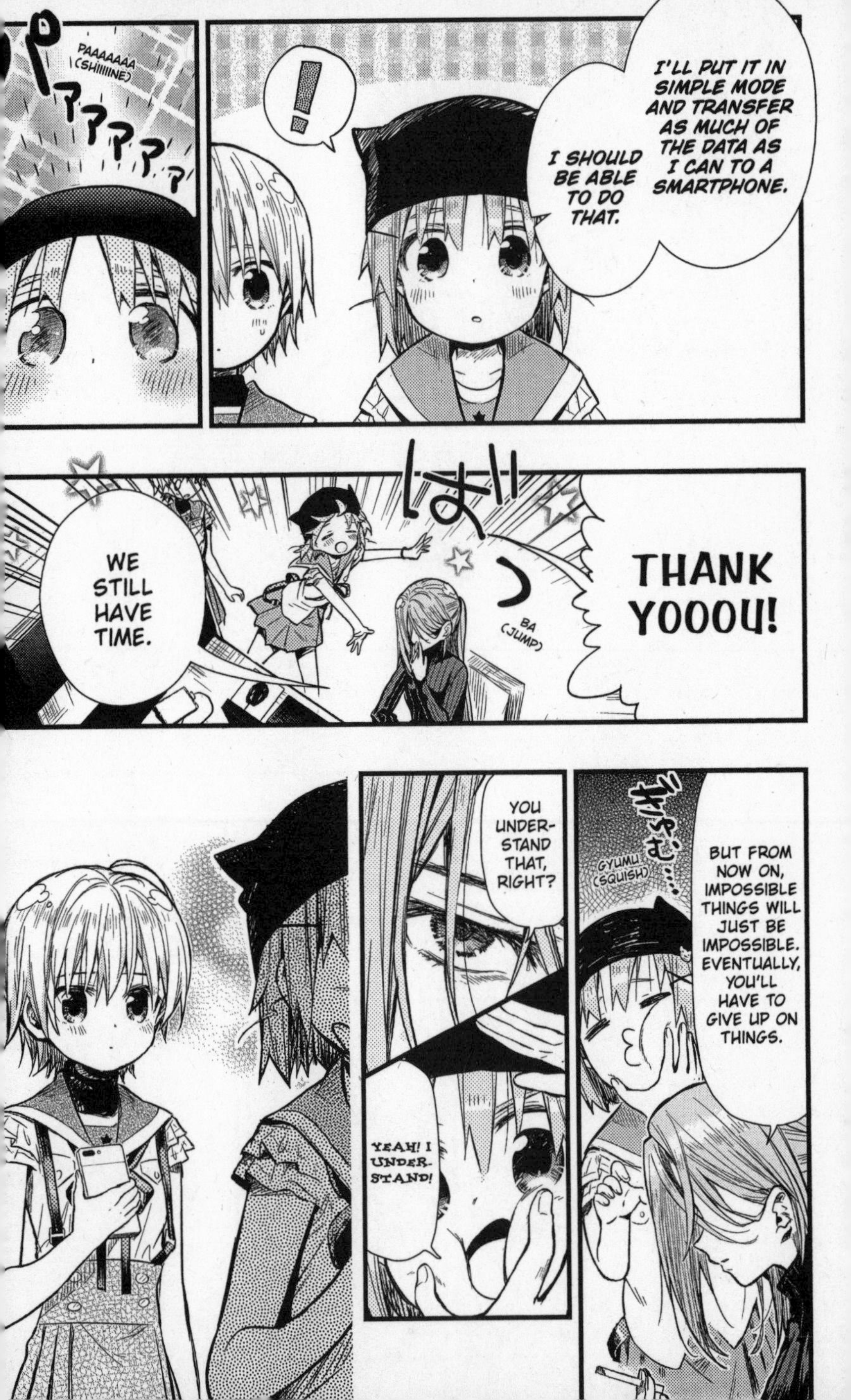

I'LL PUT IT IN SIMPLE MODE AND TRANSFER AS MUCH OF THE DATA AS I CAN TO A SMARTPHONE.
I SHOULD BE ABLE TO DO THAT.
!
パァァァァァ
PAAAAAAA (SHIIIIINE)
THANK YOOOU!
ばっ
BA (JUMP)
WE STILL HAVE TIME.
ぎゅむ…
GYUMU (SQUISH)
BUT FROM NOW ON, IMPOSSIBLE THINGS WILL JUST BE IMPOSSIBLE. EVENTUALLY, YOU'LL HAVE TO GIVE UP ON THINGS.
YOU UNDER-STAND THAT, RIGHT?
YEAH! I UNDER-STAND!

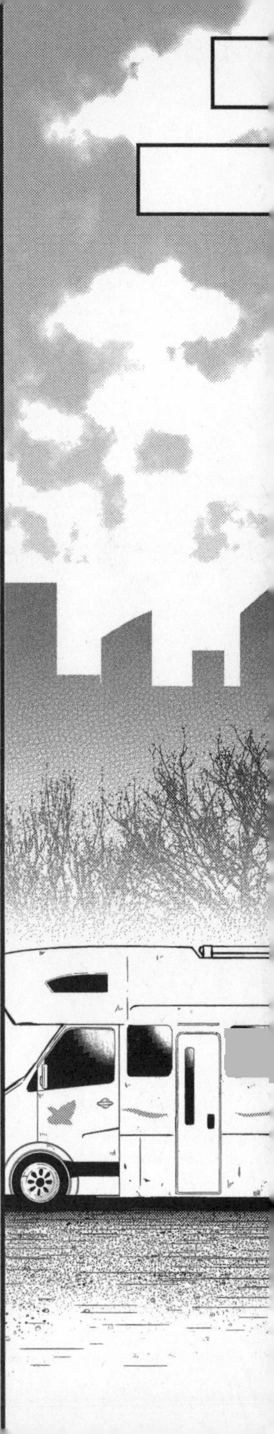

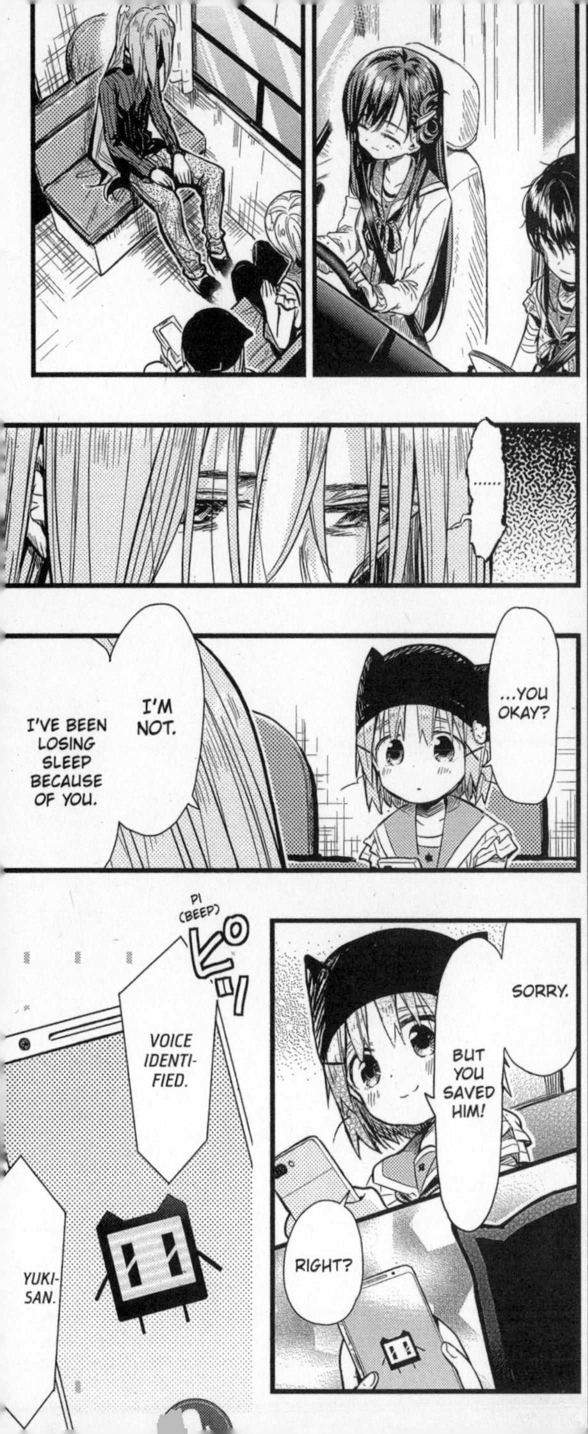

......
...YOU OKAY?
I'M NOT.
I'VE BEEN LOSING SLEEP BECAUSE OF YOU.
SORRY.
BUT YOU SAVED HIM!
RIGHT?
PI (BEEP)
VOICE IDENTIFIED.
YUKI-SAN.

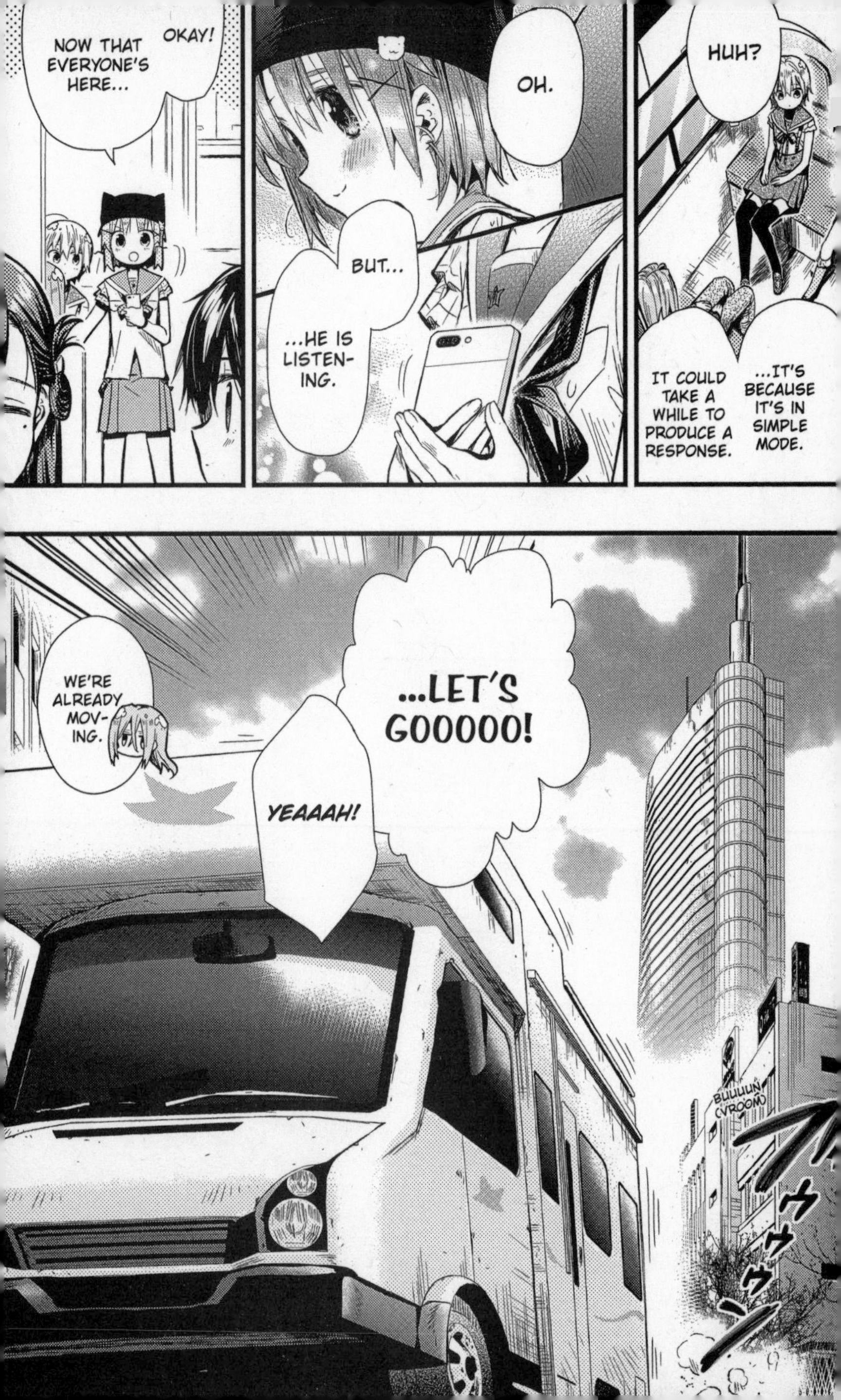
HUH?
...IT'S BECAUSE IT'S IN SIMPLE MODE.
IT COULD TAKE A WHILE TO PRODUCE A RESPONSE.
OH.
BUT...
...HE IS LISTEN-ING.
OKAY!
NOW THAT EVERYONE'S HERE...
...LET'S GOOOOO!
YEAAAH!
WE'RE ALREADY MOV-ING.
BUUUUN
(VROOM)

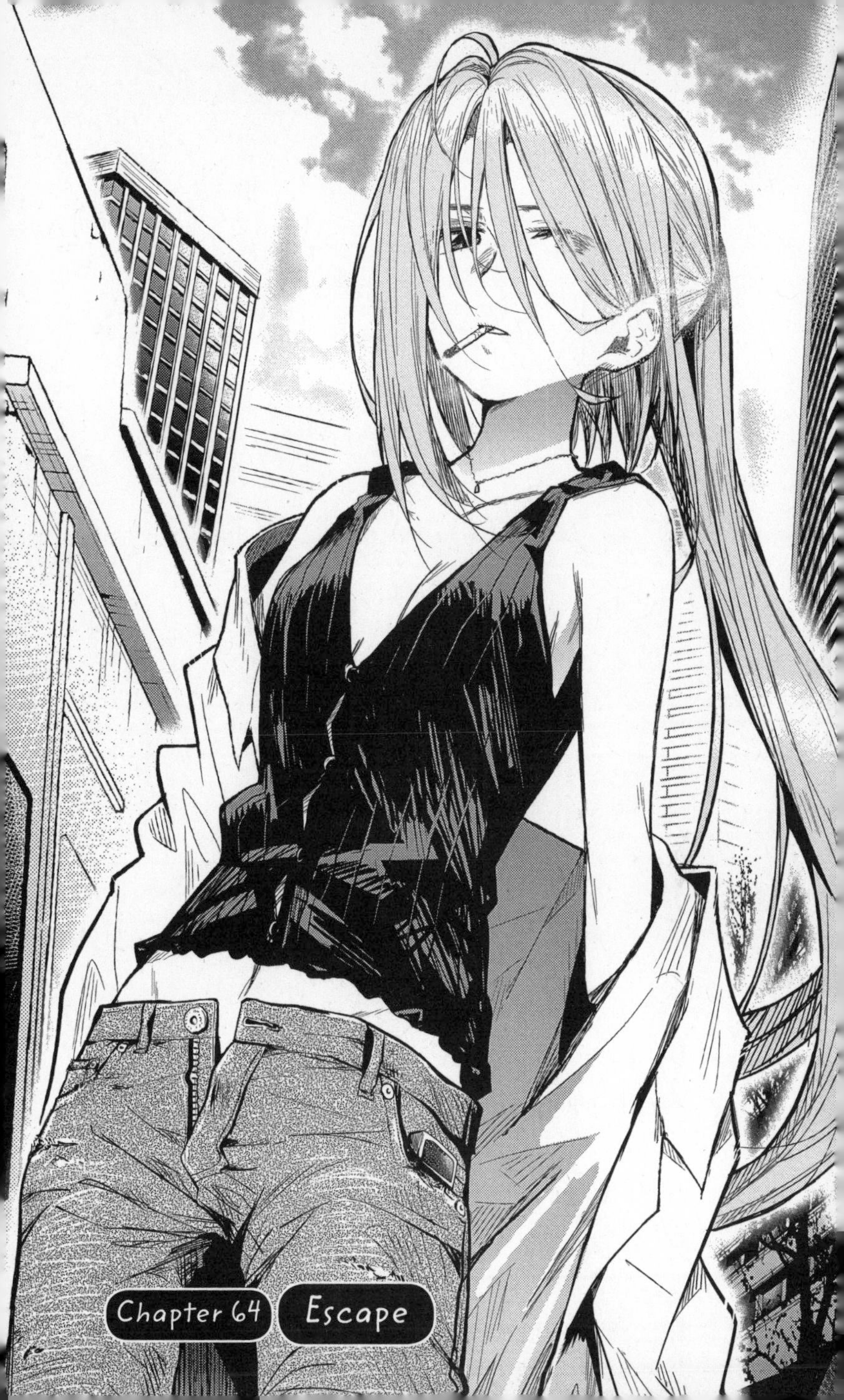
Chapter 64
Escape

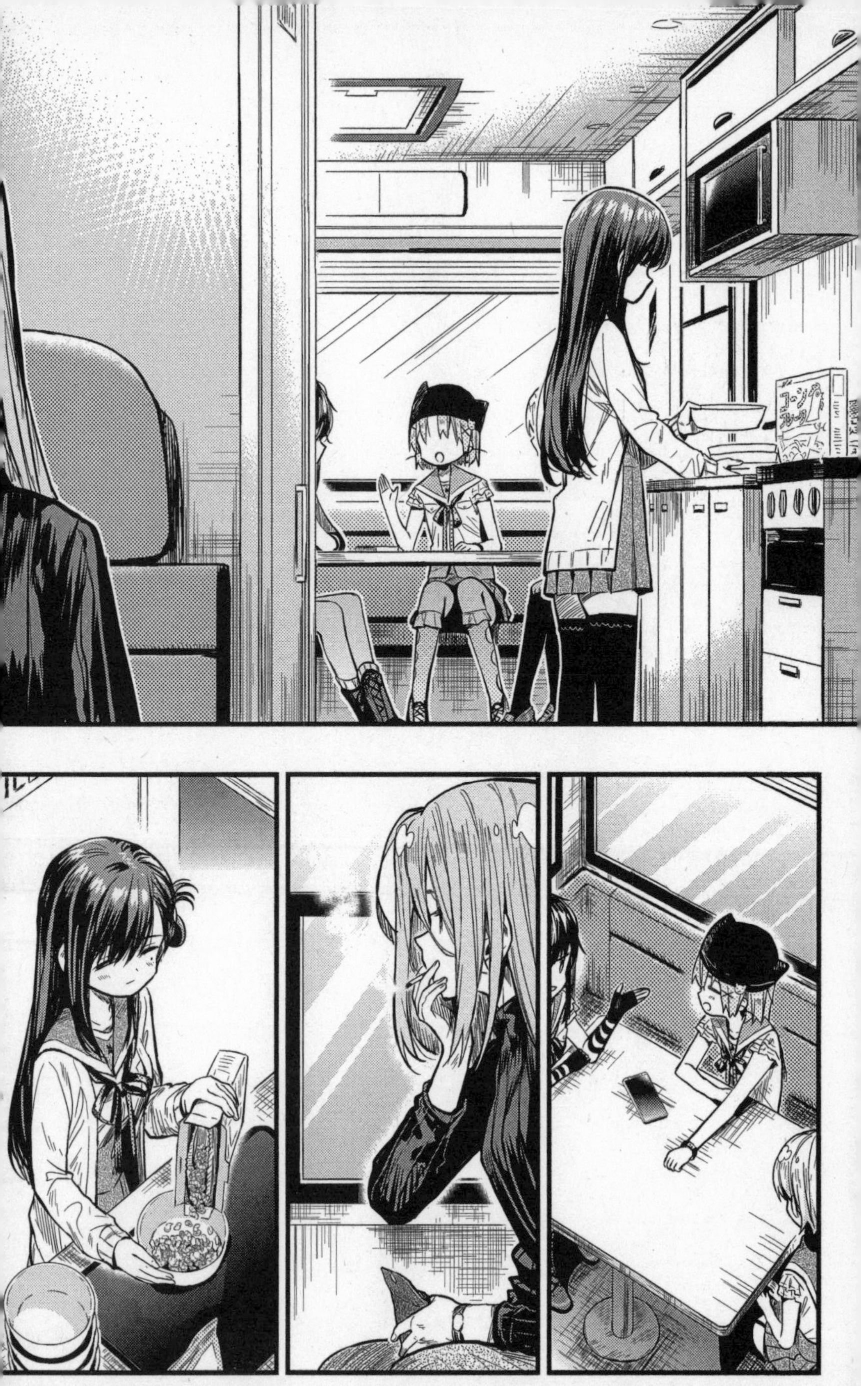
コーンフレーク

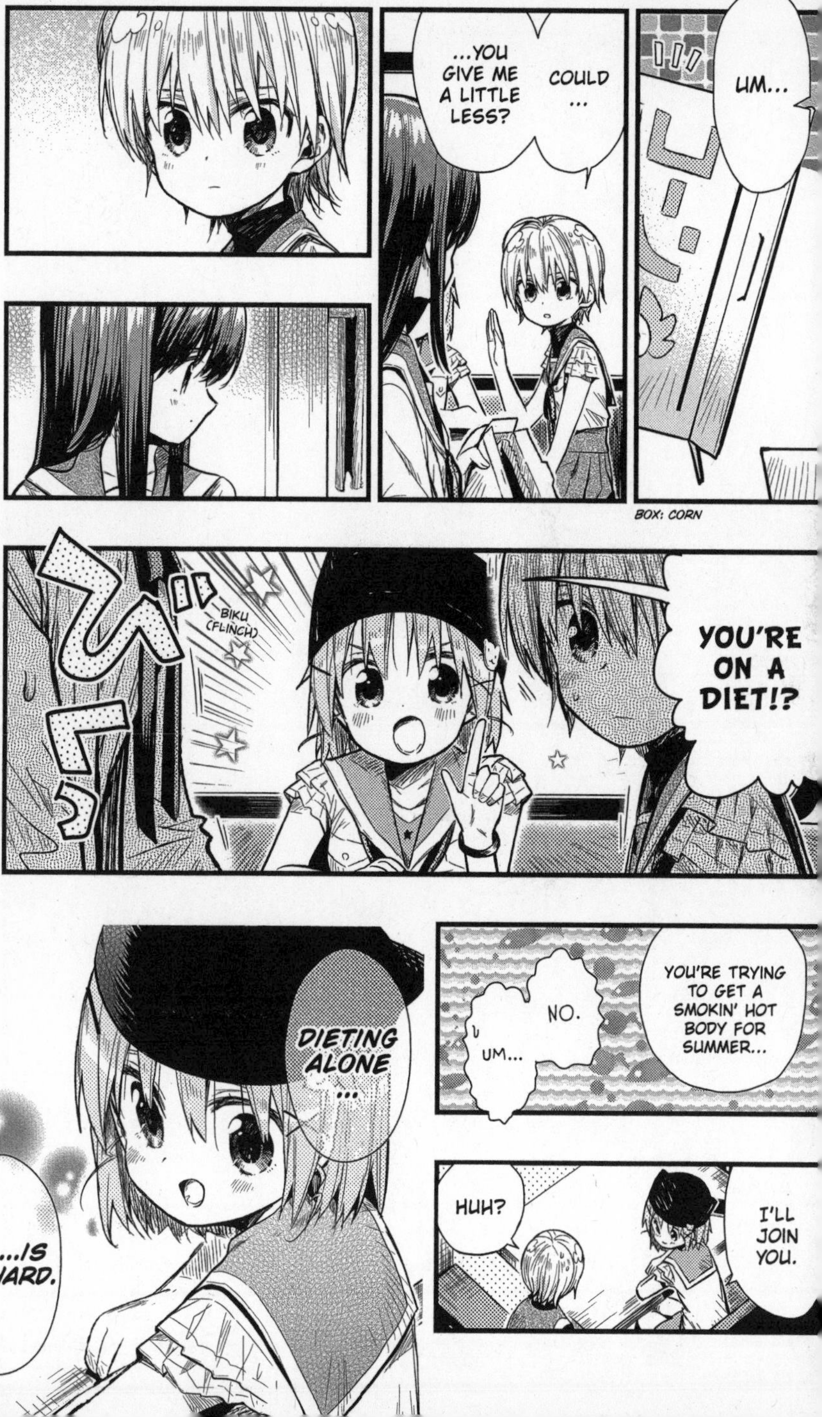
UM...
COULD ...
...YOU GIVE ME A LITTLE LESS?
BOX: CORN
YOU'RE ON A DIET!?
BIKU (FLINCH)
YOU'RE TRYING TO GET A SMOKIN' HOT BODY FOR SUMMER...
NO.
UM...
I'LL JOIN YOU.
HUH?
DIETING ALONE ...
...IS HARD.

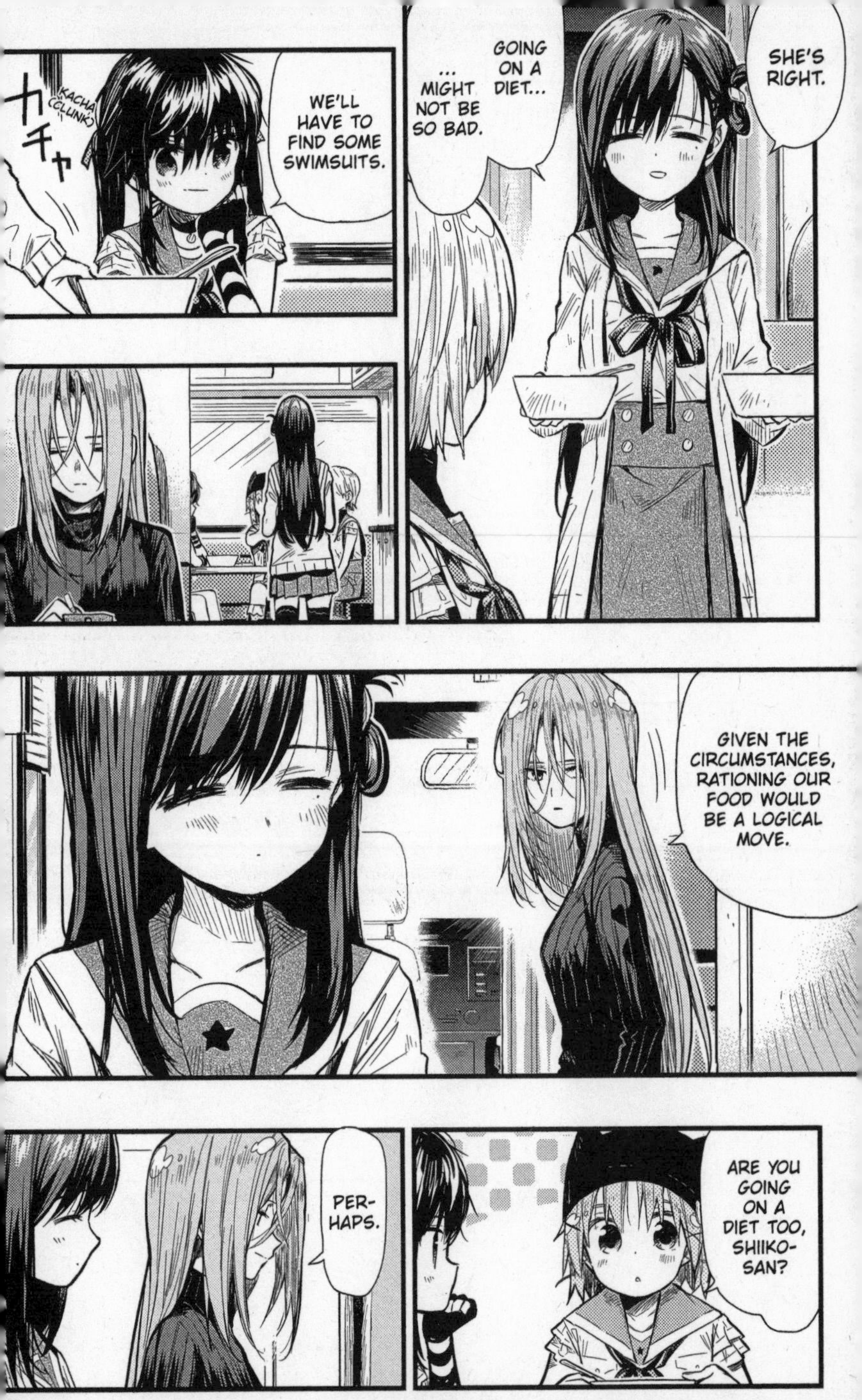
SHE'S RIGHT.
GOING ON A DIET...
...MIGHT NOT BE SO BAD.
WE'LL HAVE TO FIND SOME SWIMSUITS.
カチャ
KACHA (CLUNK)
GIVEN THE CIRCUMSTANCES, RATIONING OUR FOOD WOULD BE A LOGICAL MOVE.
ARE YOU GOING ON A DIET TOO, SHIIKO-SAN?
PER-HAPS.

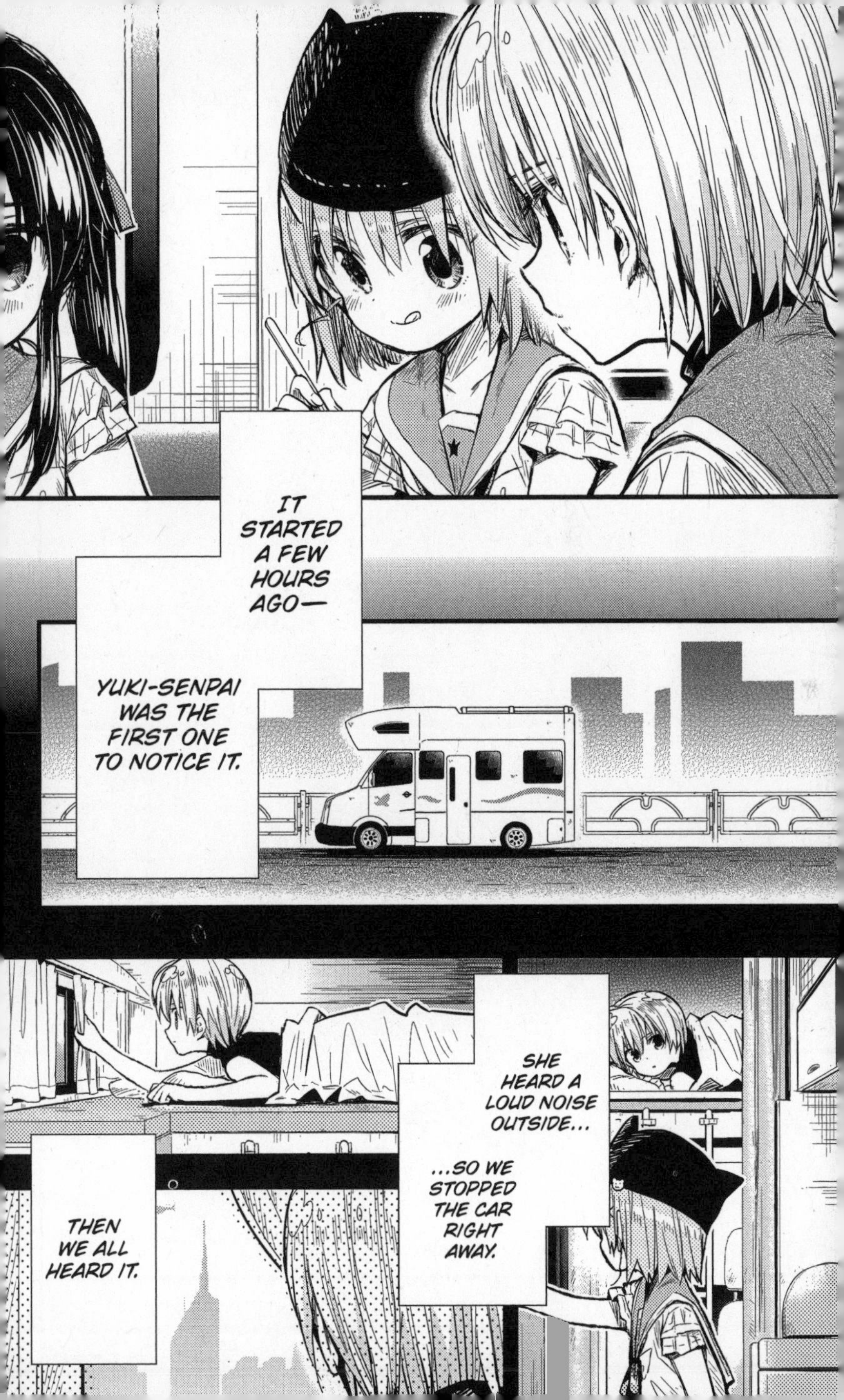
IT STARTED A FEW HOURS AGO—
YUKI-SENPAI WAS THE FIRST ONE TO NOTICE IT.
SHE HEARD A LOUD NOISE OUTSIDE...
...SO WE STOPPED THE CAR RIGHT AWAY.
THEN WE ALL HEARD IT.

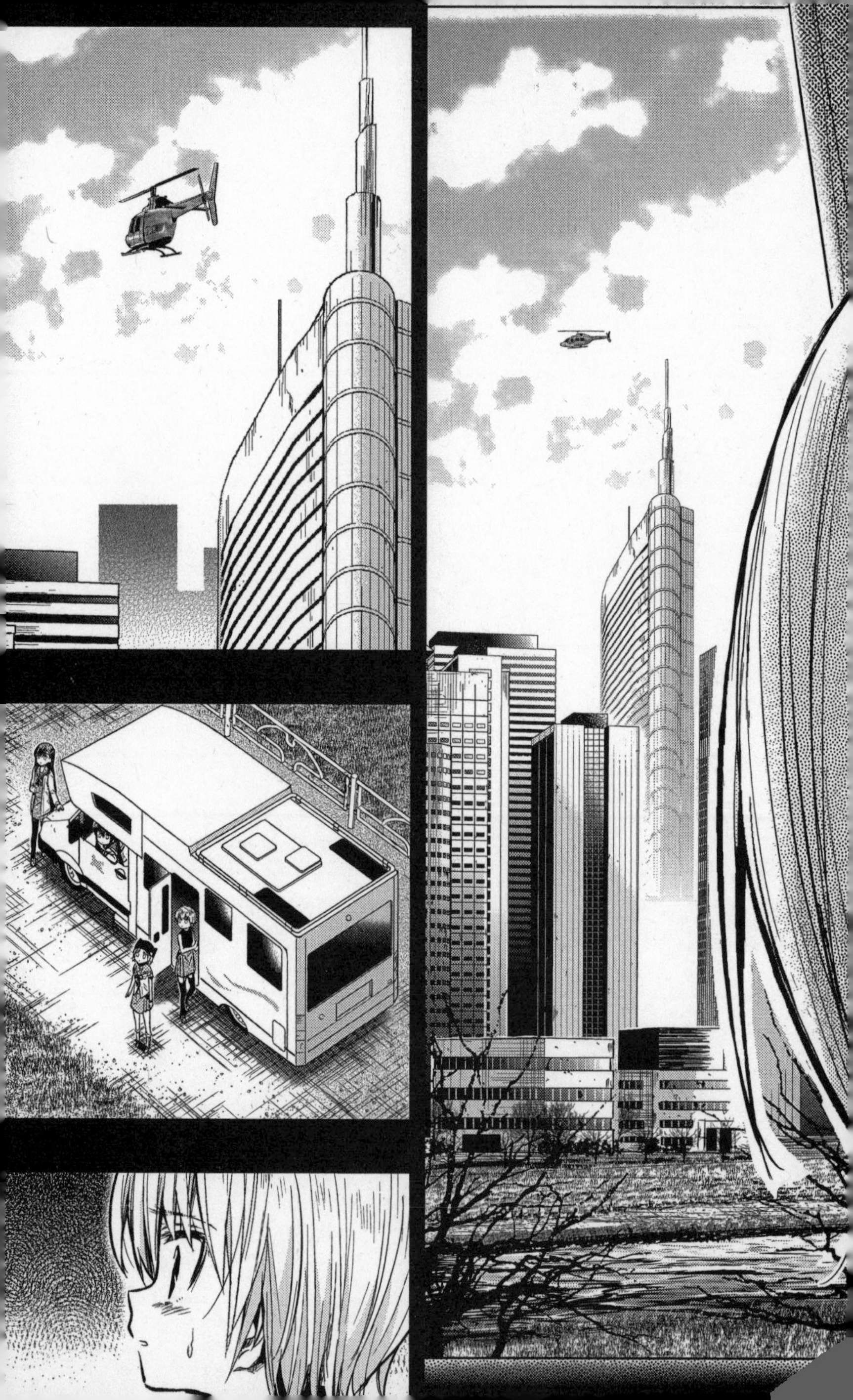

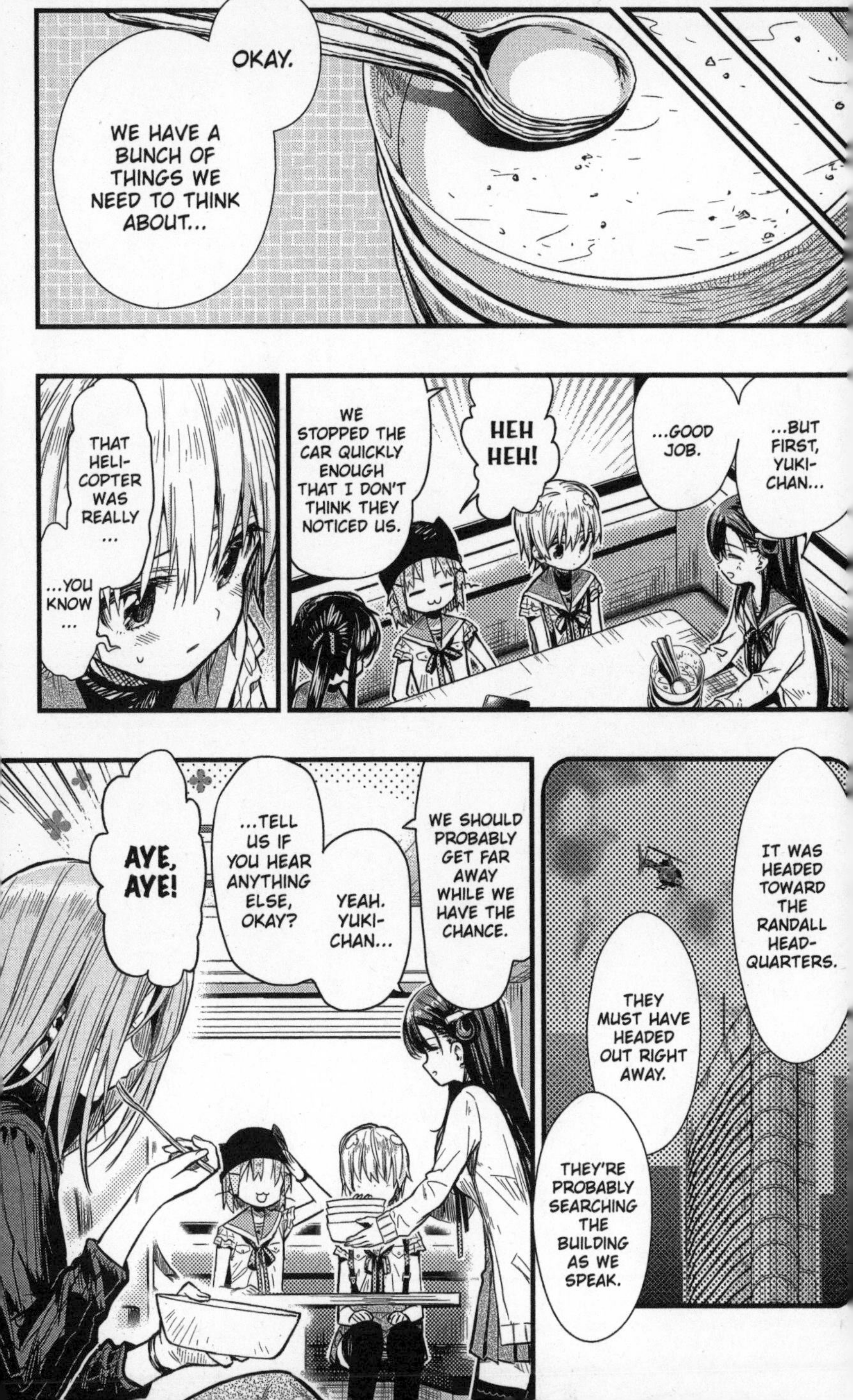
OKAY.
WE HAVE A BUNCH OF THINGS WE NEED TO THINK ABOUT...
...BUT FIRST, YUKI-CHAN...
...GOOD JOB.
HEH HEH!
WE STOPPED THE CAR QUICKLY ENOUGH THAT I DON'T THINK THEY NOTICED US.
THAT HELI-COPTER WAS REALLY...
...YOU KNOW...
IT WAS HEADED TOWARD THE RANDALL HEAD-QUARTERS.
THEY MUST HAVE HEADED OUT RIGHT AWAY.
THEY'RE PROBABLY SEARCHING THE BUILDING AS WE SPEAK.
WE SHOULD PROBABLY GET FAR AWAY WHILE WE HAVE THE CHANCE.
YEAH. YUKI-CHAN...
...TELL US IF YOU HEAR ANYTHING ELSE, OKAY?
AYE, AYE!

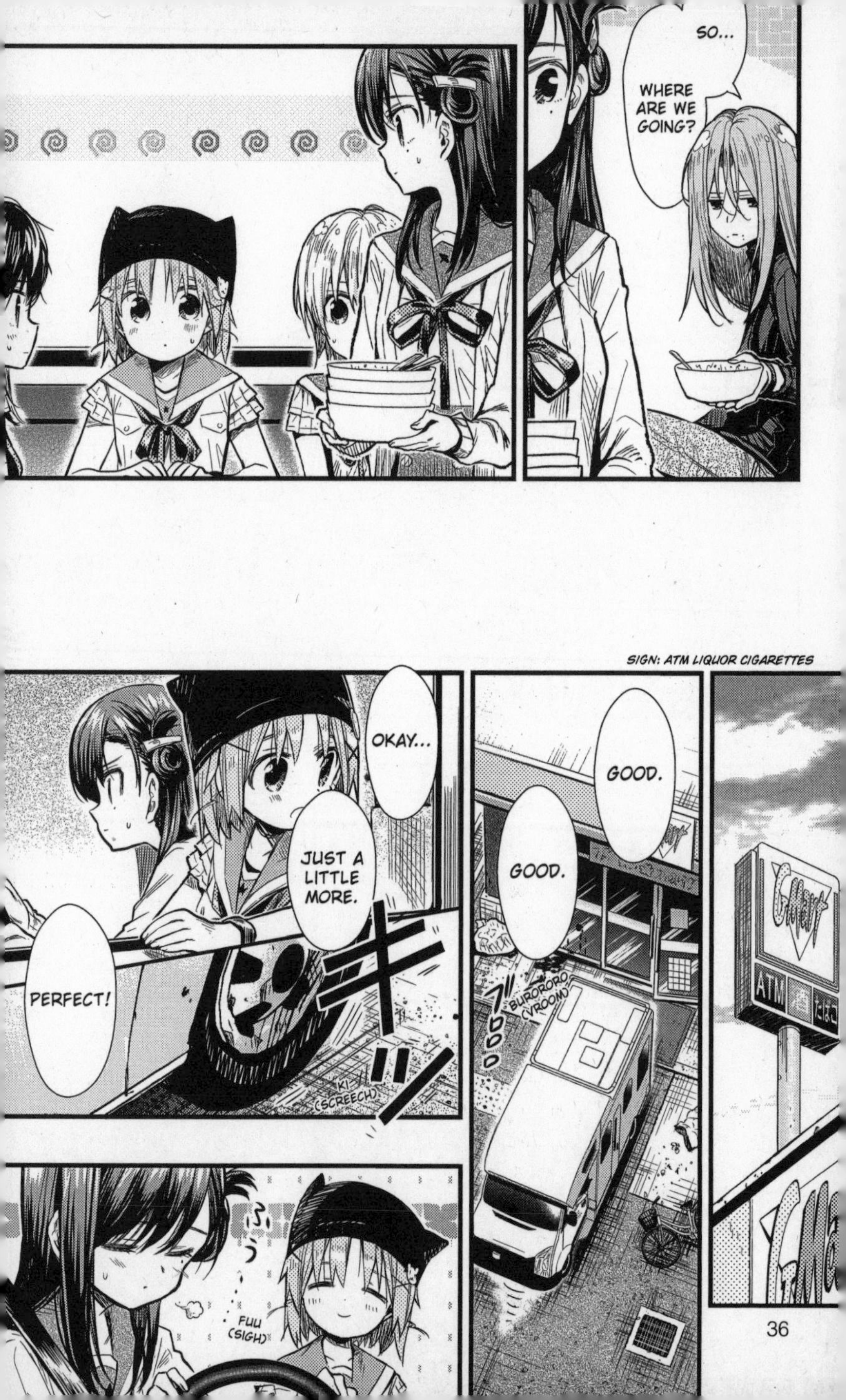
SO...
WHERE ARE WE GOING?
SIGN: ATM LIQUOR CIGARETTES
GOOD.
GOOD.
BURORORO (VROOM)
OKAY...
JUST A LITTLE MORE.
PERFECT!
KI (SCREECH)
FUU (SIGH)

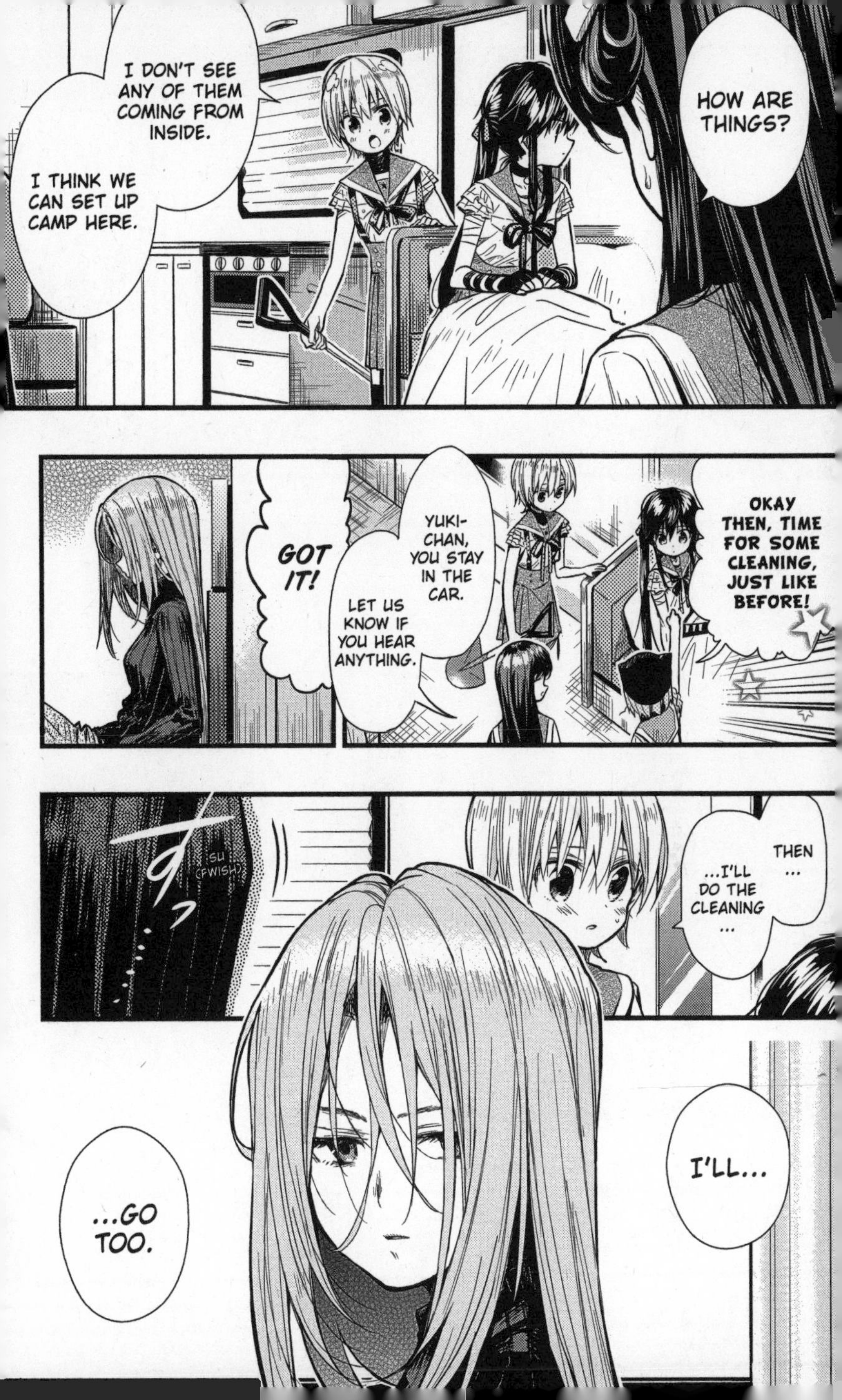
HOW ARE THINGS?
I DON'T SEE ANY OF THEM COMING FROM INSIDE.
I THINK WE CAN SET UP CAMP HERE.
OKAY THEN, TIME FOR SOME CLEANING, JUST LIKE BEFORE!
YUKI-CHAN, YOU STAY IN THE CAR.
LET US KNOW IF YOU HEAR ANYTHING.
GOT IT!
THEN ... ...I'LL DO THE CLEANING ...
SU (FWISH)
I'LL...
...GO TOO.

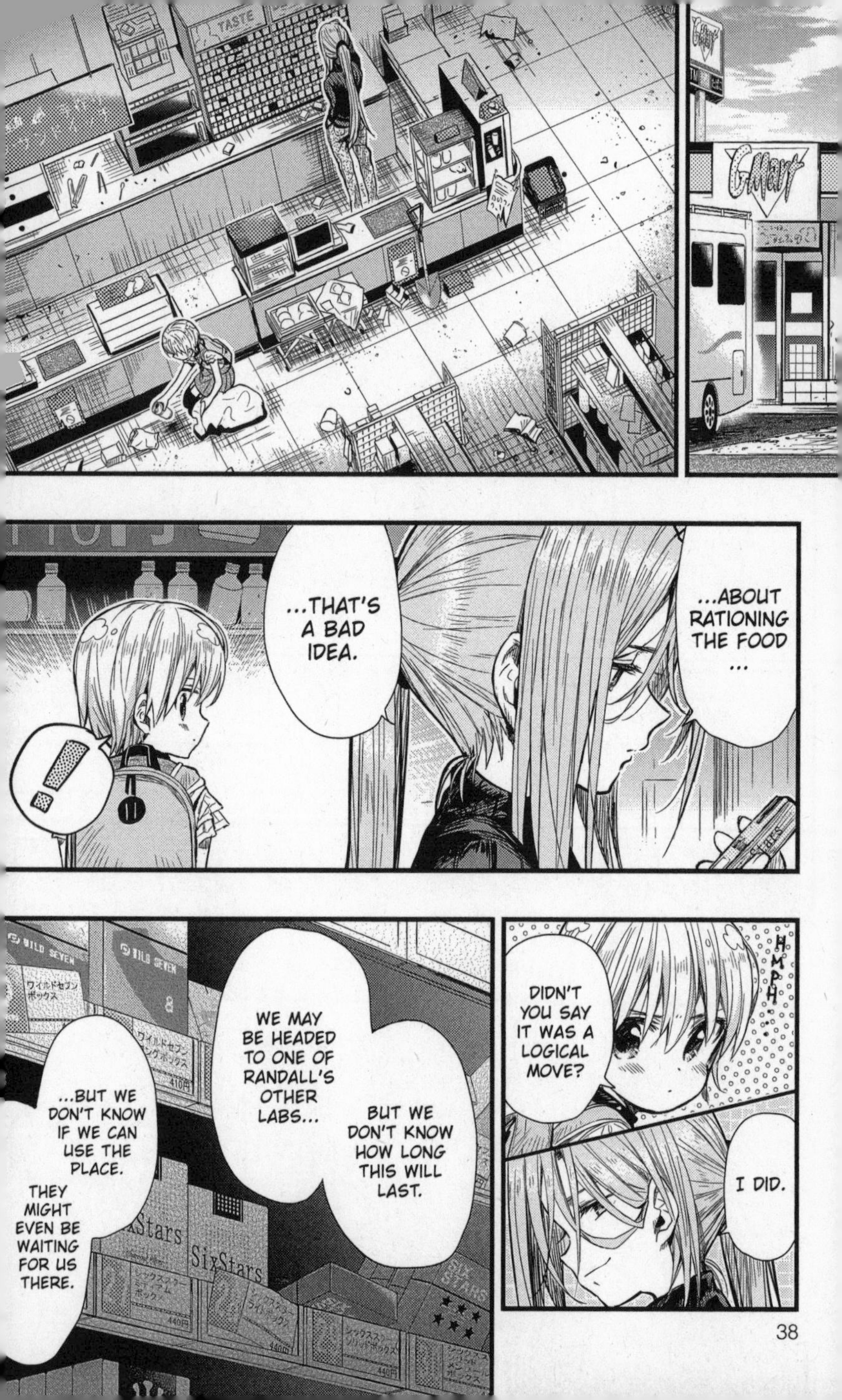
GMart
TASTE
...ABOUT RATIONING THE FOOD ...
...THAT'S A BAD IDEA.
!
DIDN'T YOU SAY IT WAS A LOGICAL MOVE?
HMPH...
I DID.
BUT WE DON'T KNOW HOW LONG THIS WILL LAST.
WE MAY BE HEADED TO ONE OF RANDALL'S OTHER LABS...
...BUT WE DON'T KNOW IF WE CAN USE THE PLACE.
THEY MIGHT EVEN BE WAITING FOR US THERE.
WILD SEVEN
SixStars

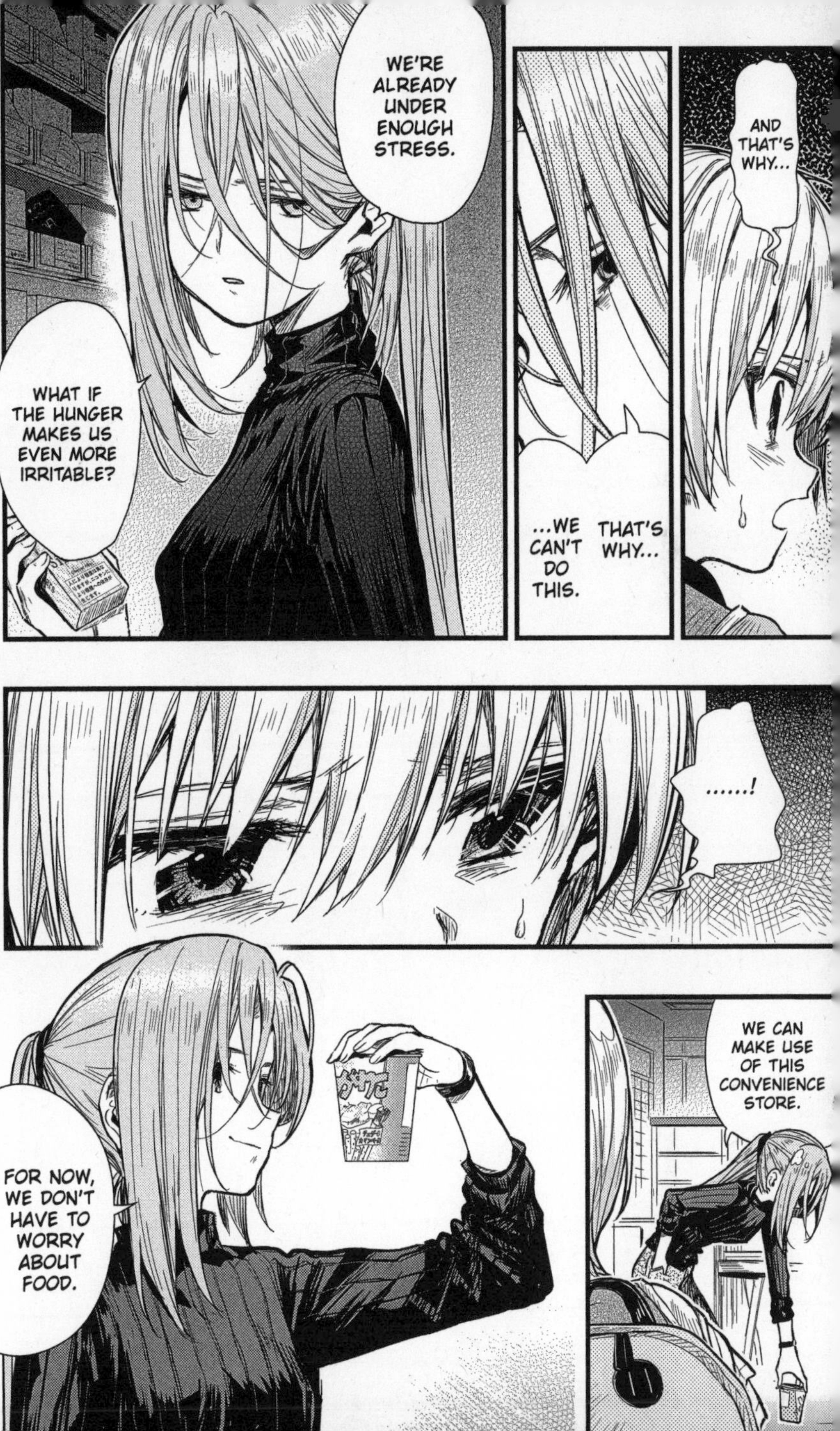
AND THAT'S WHY...
THAT'S WHY...
...WE CAN'T DO THIS.
WE'RE ALREADY UNDER ENOUGH STRESS.
WHAT IF THE HUNGER MAKES US EVEN MORE IRRITABLE?
......!
WE CAN MAKE USE OF THIS CONVENIENCE STORE.
FOR NOW, WE DON'T HAVE TO WORRY ABOUT FOOD.

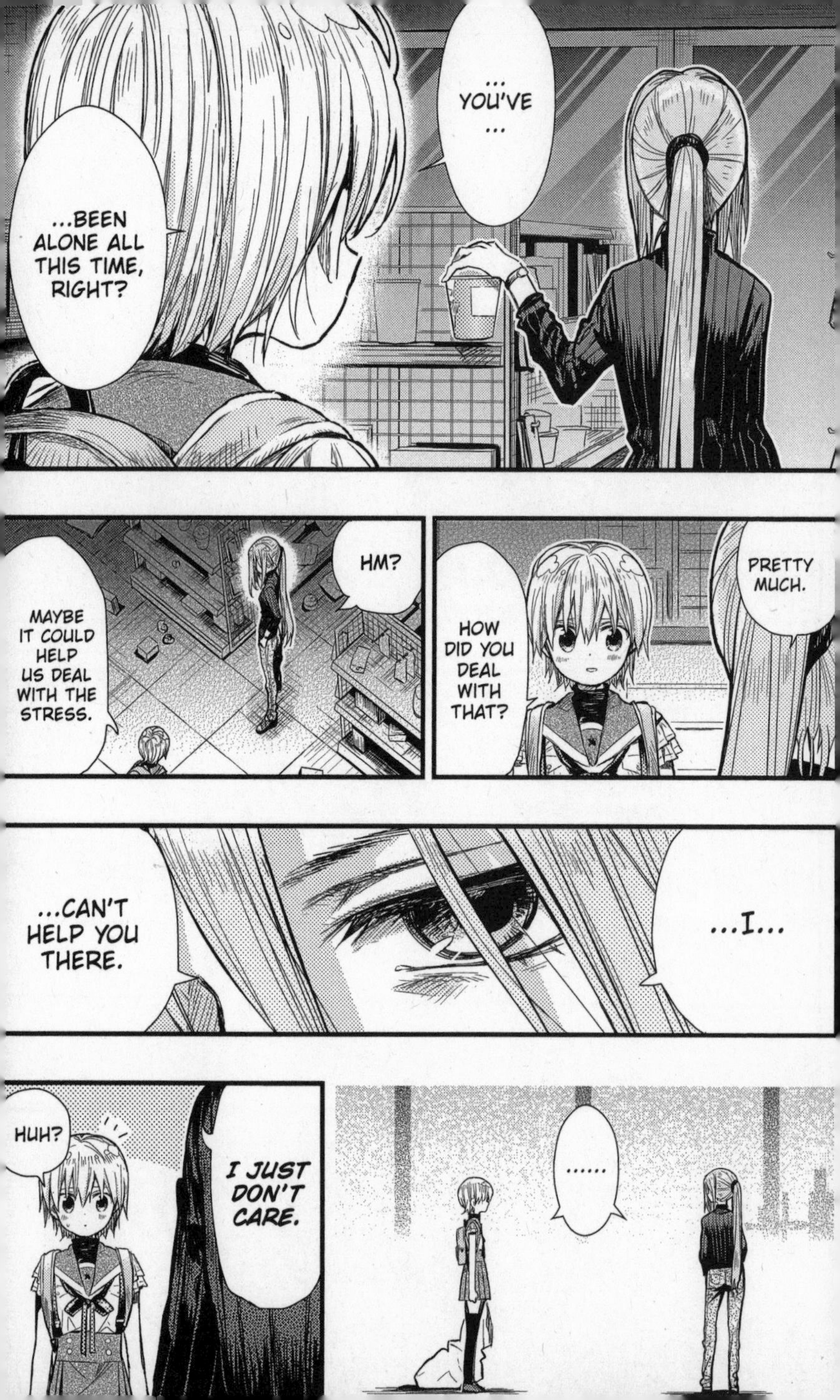
... YOU'VE ...
...BEEN ALONE ALL THIS TIME, RIGHT?
PRETTY MUCH.
HOW DID YOU DEAL WITH THAT?
HM?
MAYBE IT COULD HELP US DEAL WITH THE STRESS.
...I...
...CAN'T HELP YOU THERE.
......
I JUST DON'T CARE.
HUH?

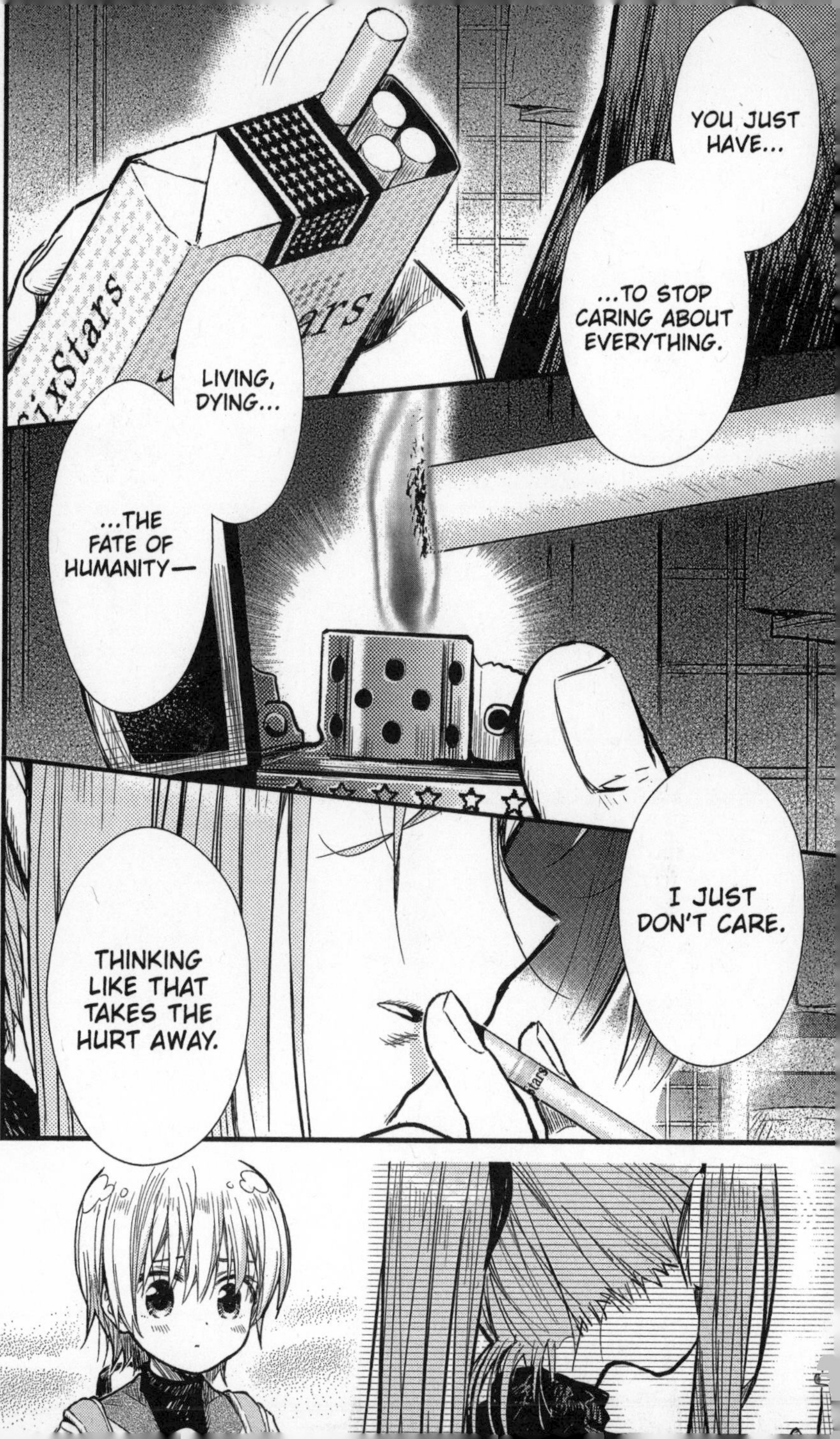
YOU JUST HAVE...
...TO STOP CARING ABOUT EVERYTHING.
SixStars
LIVING, DYING...
...THE FATE OF HUMANITY—
I JUST DON'T CARE.
THINKING LIKE THAT TAKES THE HURT AWAY.

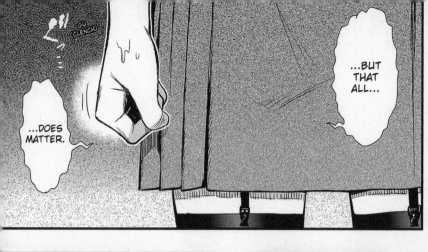

...BUT THAT ALL...

...DOES MATTER.

GU (CLENCH)

...BESIDES...

......

...I SAID I CAN'T HELP YOU.

THAT'S WHY...

...YOU ALREADY HAVE SOMEONE WHO'S GOOD AT DEALING WITH STRESS.

HUH?

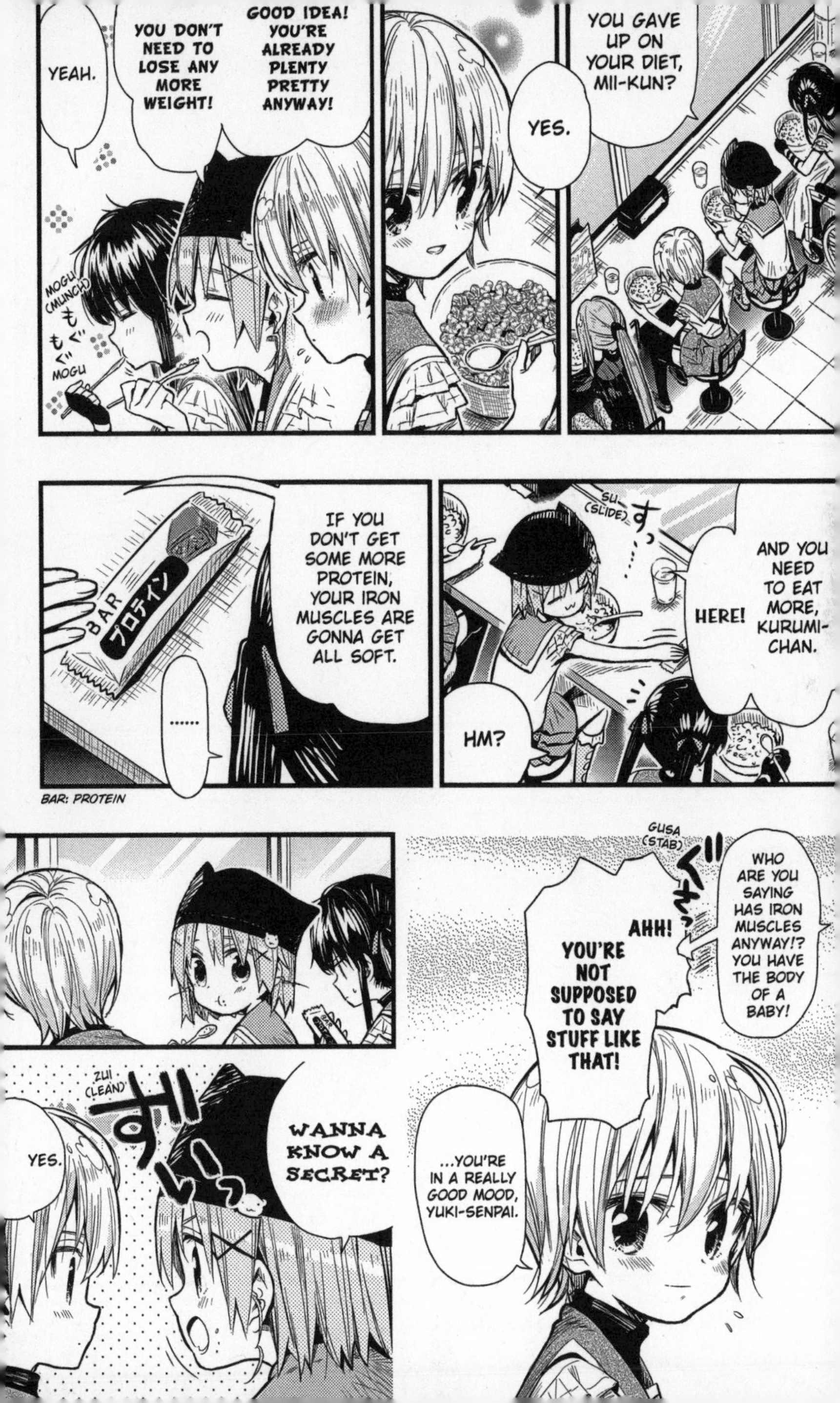
YOU GAVE UP ON YOUR DIET, MII-KUN?
YES.
GOOD IDEA! YOU'RE ALREADY PLENTY PRETTY ANYWAY!
YOU DON'T NEED TO LOSE ANY MORE WEIGHT!
YEAH.
MOGU (MUNCH) もぐもぐ MOGU
AND YOU NEED TO EAT MORE, KURUMI-CHAN.
SU (SLIDE) す
HERE!
HM?
IF YOU DON'T GET SOME MORE PROTEIN, YOUR IRON MUSCLES ARE GONNA GET ALL SOFT.
BAR プロテイン
......
BAR: PROTEIN
GUSA (STAB)
WHO ARE YOU SAYING HAS IRON MUSCLES ANYWAY!? YOU HAVE THE BODY OF A BABY!
AHH!
YOU'RE NOT SUPPOSED TO SAY STUFF LIKE THAT!
...YOU'RE IN A REALLY GOOD MOOD, YUKI-SENPAI.
WANNA KNOW A SECRET?
ZUI (CLEAN)
YES.

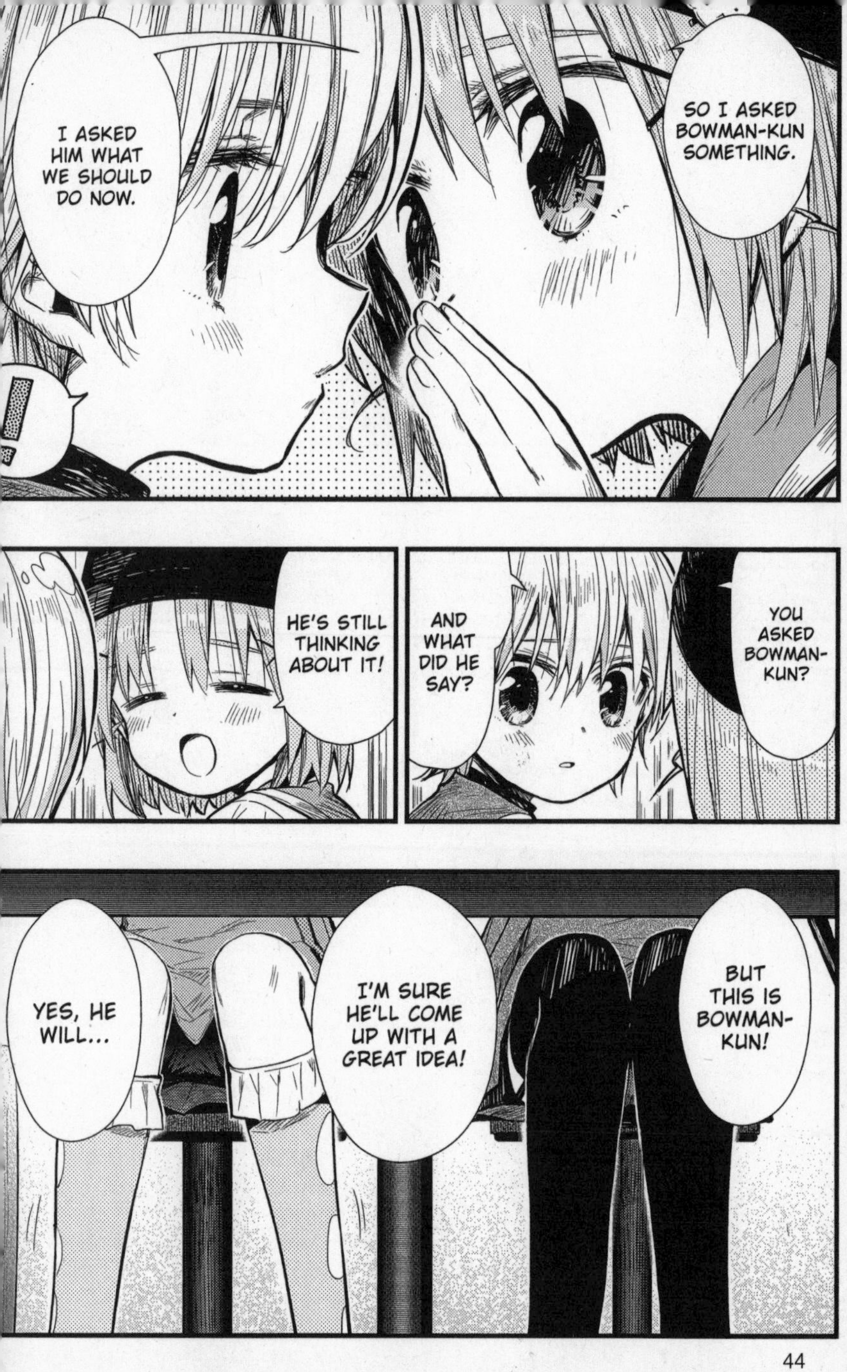
SO I ASKED BOWMAN-KUN SOMETHING.
I ASKED HIM WHAT WE SHOULD DO NOW.
!
YOU ASKED BOWMAN-KUN?
AND WHAT DID HE SAY?
HE'S STILL THINKING ABOUT IT!
BUT THIS IS BOWMAN-KUN!
I'M SURE HE'LL COME UP WITH A GREAT IDEA!
YES, HE WILL...

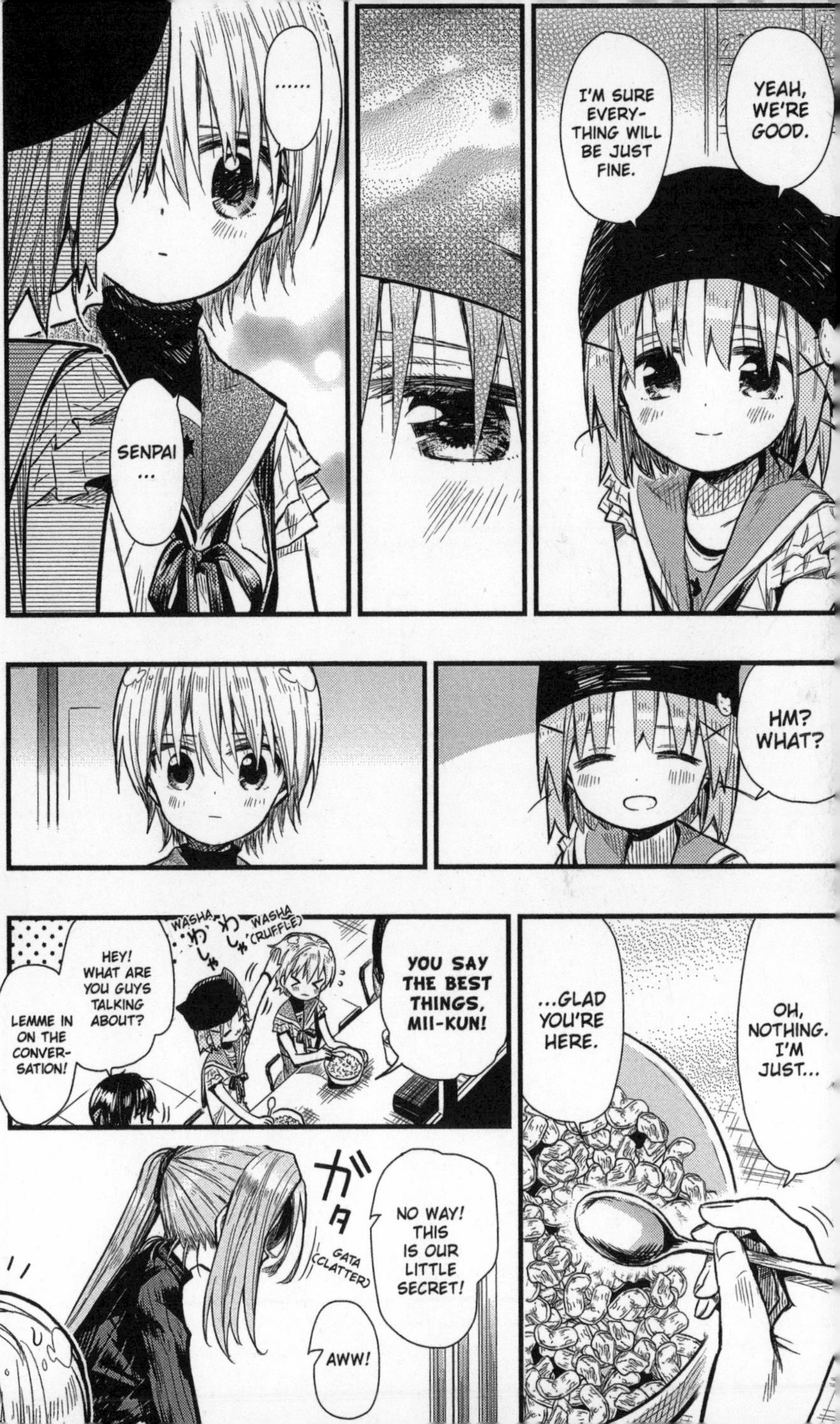

YEAH, WE'RE GOOD.
I'M SURE EVERYTHING WILL BE JUST FINE.
......
SENPAI ...
HM? WHAT?
OH, NOTHING. I'M JUST...
...GLAD YOU'RE HERE.
YOU SAY THE BEST THINGS, MII-KUN!
WASHA WASHA (RUFFLE)
HEY! WHAT ARE YOU GUYS TALKING ABOUT?
LEMME IN ON THE CONVERSATION!
NO WAY! THIS IS OUR LITTLE SECRET!
ガタ
GATA (CLATTER)
AWW!

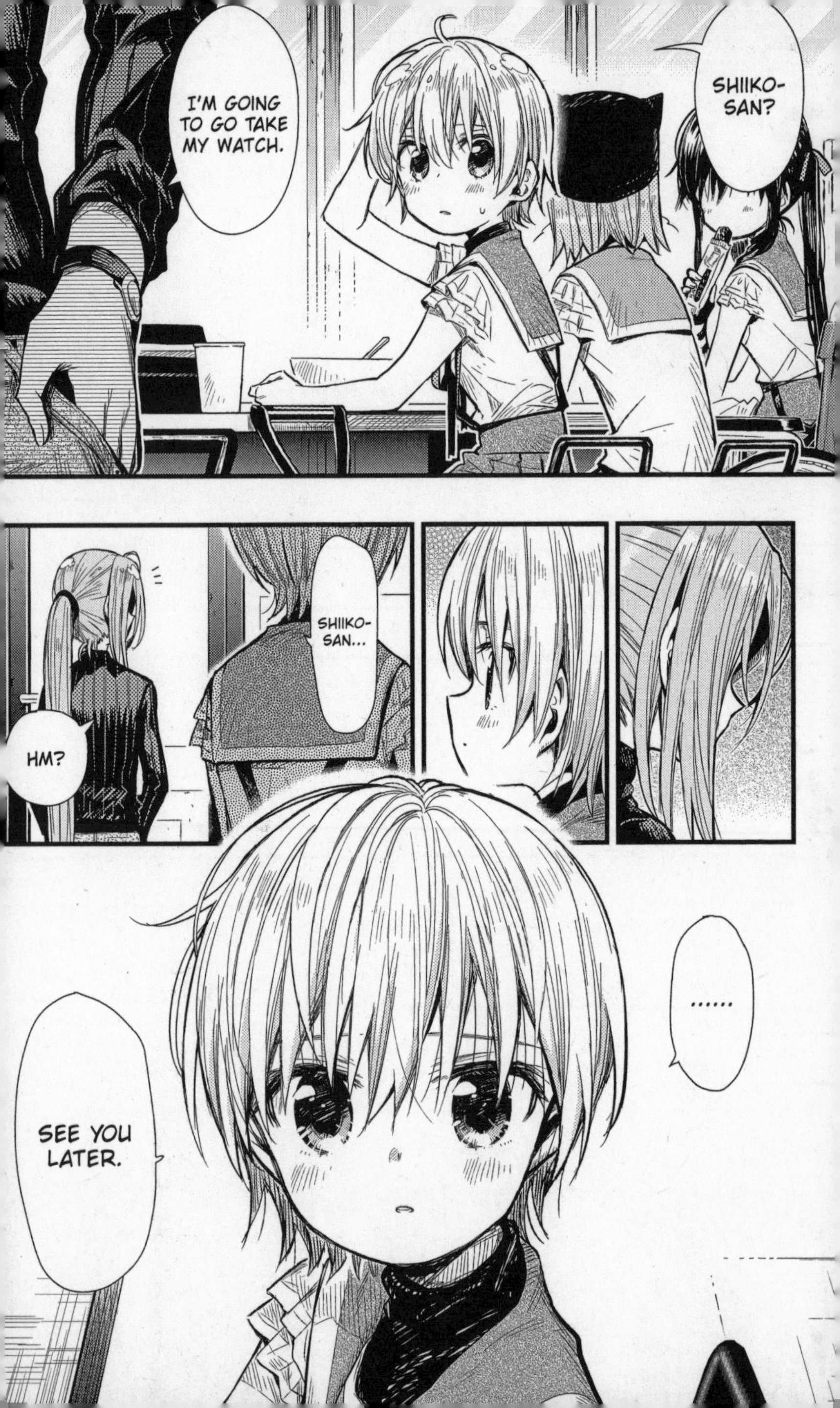
SHIIKO-SAN?
I'M GOING TO GO TAKE MY WATCH.
SHIIKO-SAN...
HM?
......
SEE YOU LATER.

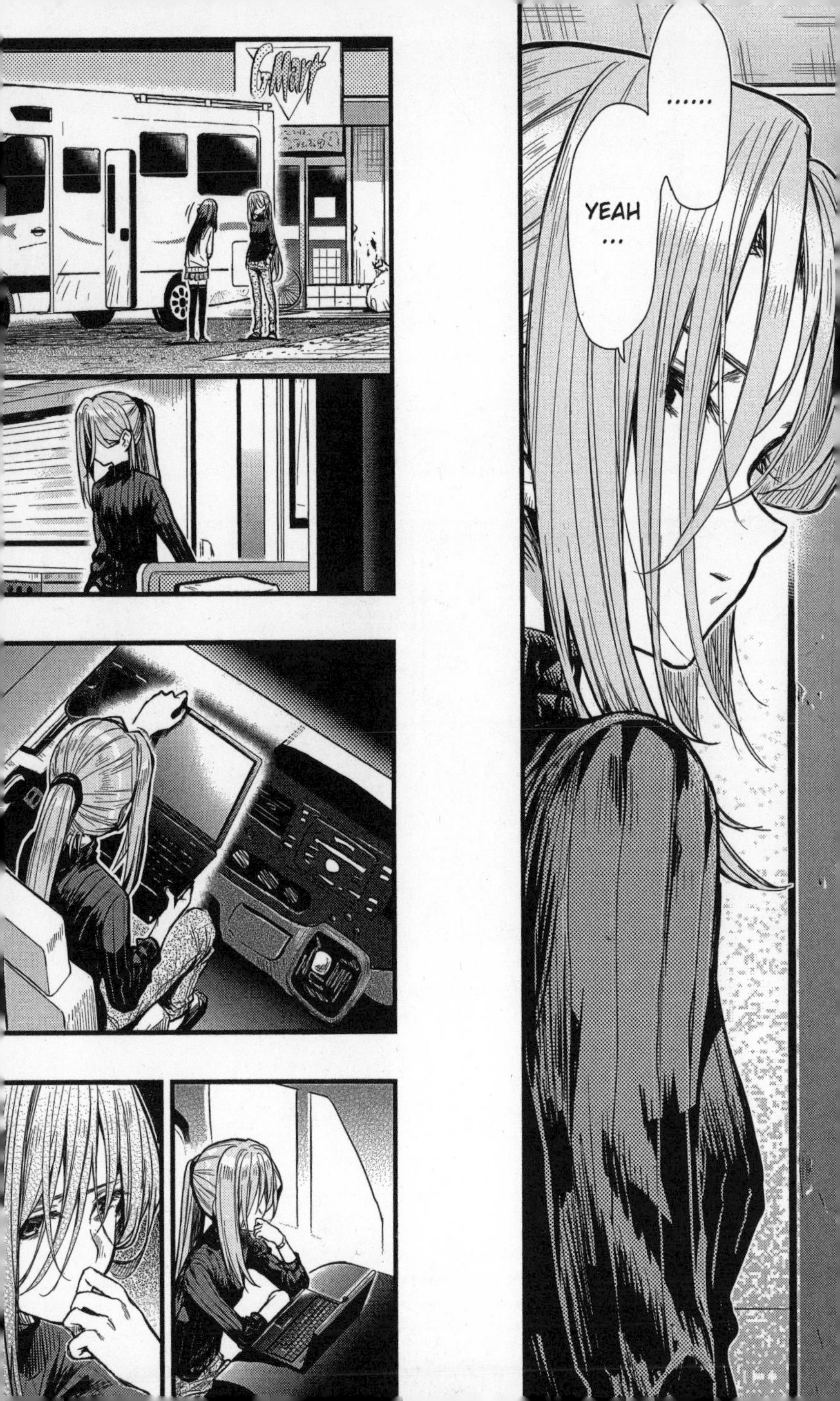
......
YEAH ...
GMart

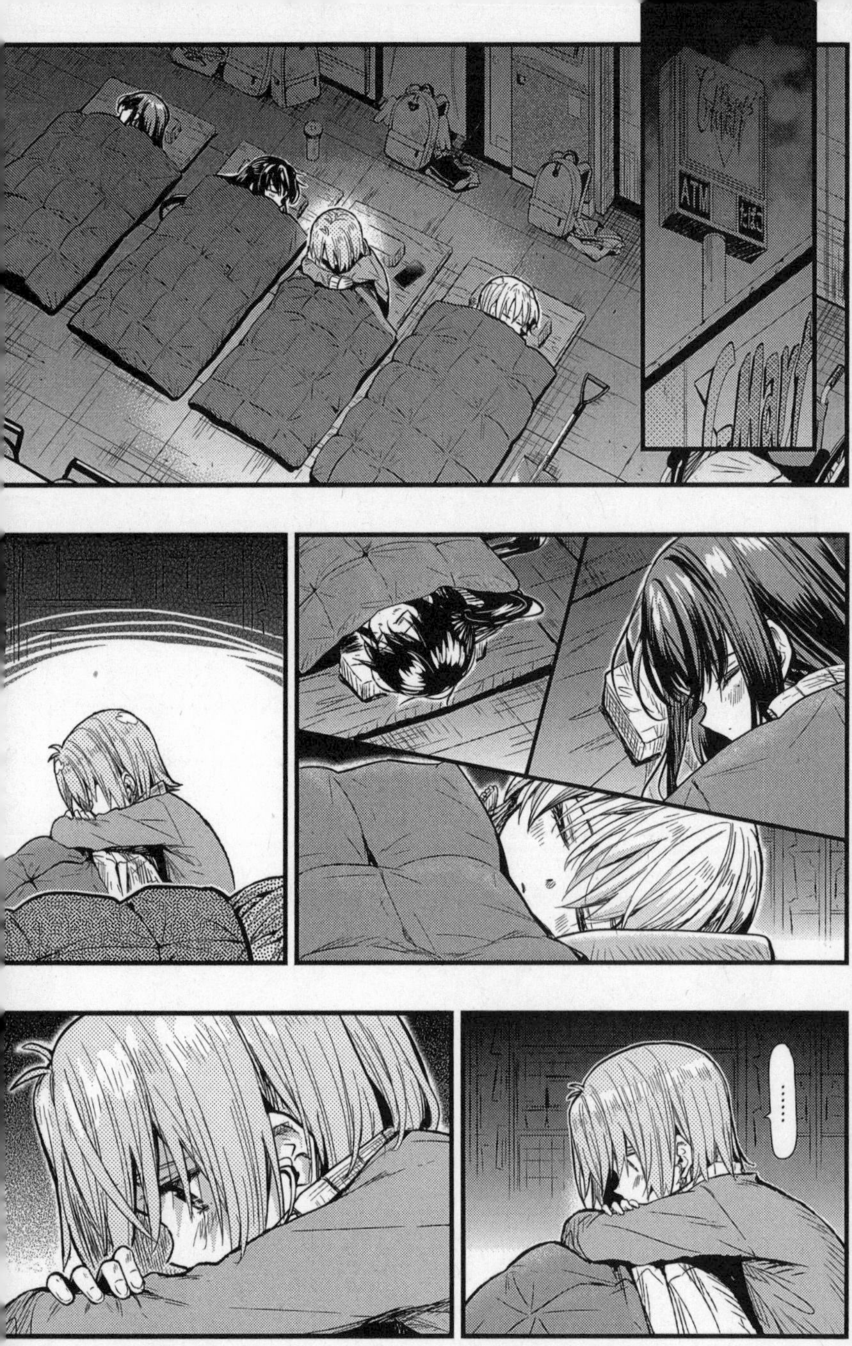
ATM
……

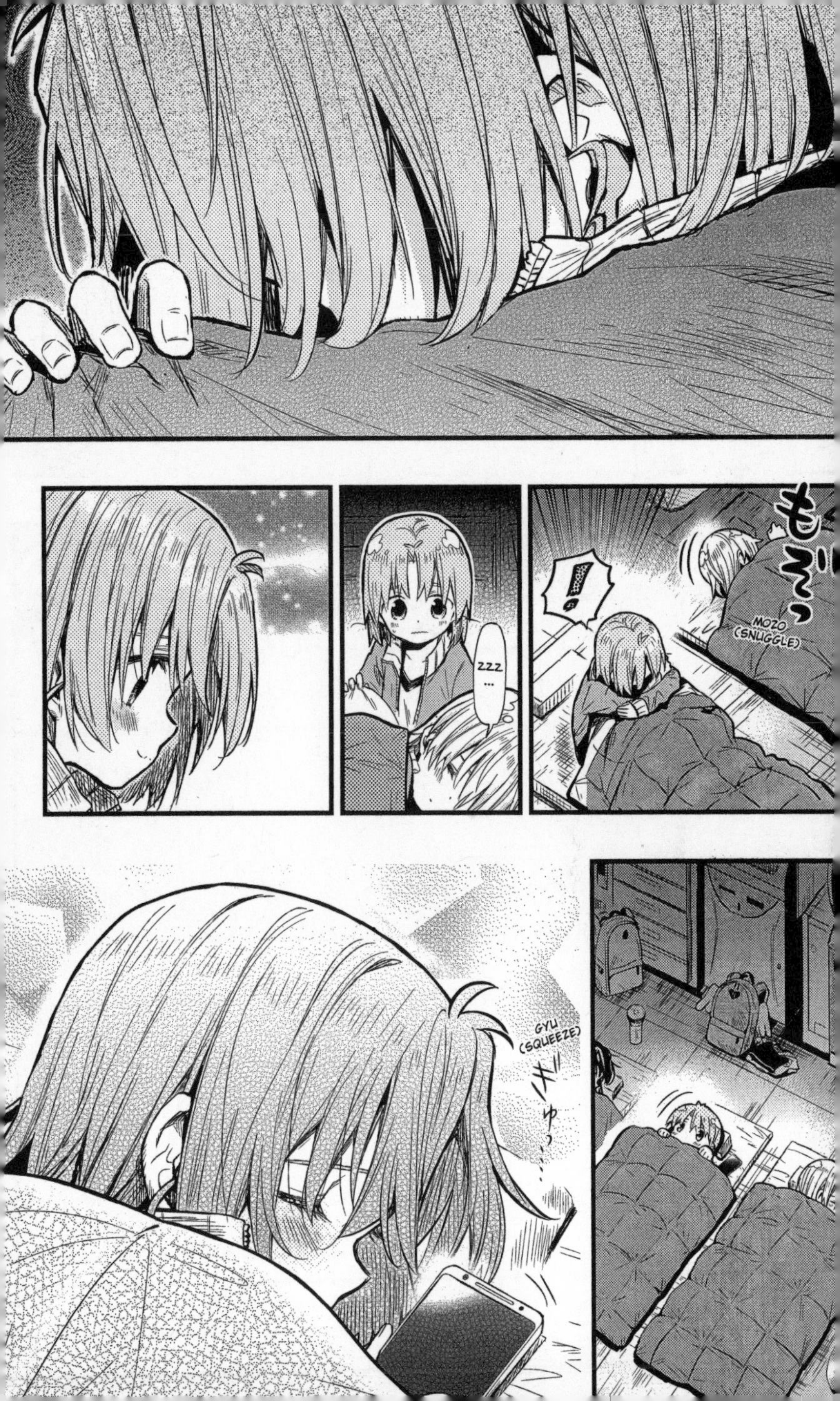
もぞっ
MOZO (SNUGGLE)
!
ZZZ ...
GYU (SQUEEZE)
ぎゅっ…

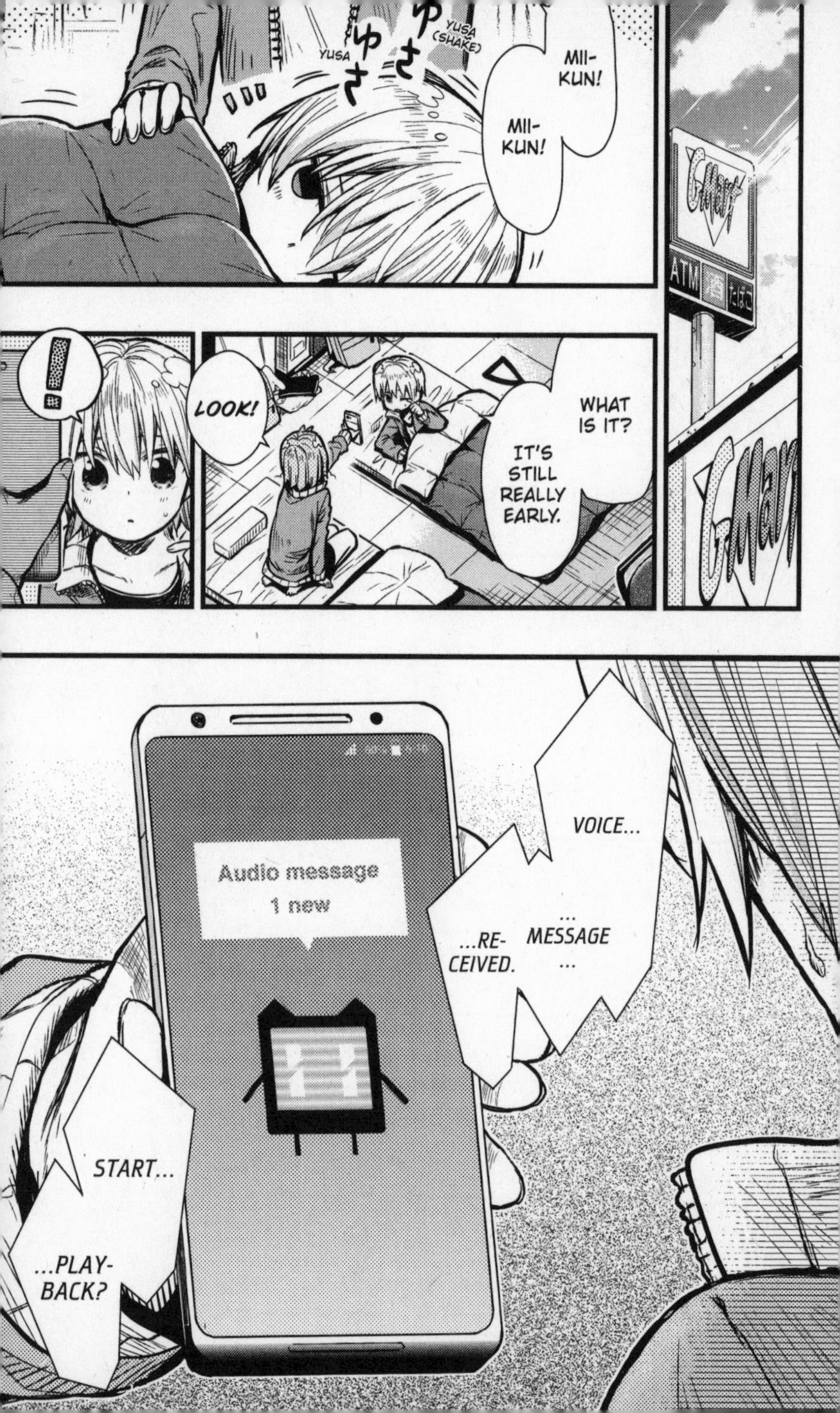
ATM
たばこ
ゆさ
YUSA (SHAKE)
ゆさ
YUSA
MII-KUN!
MII-KUN!
WHAT IS IT?
IT'S STILL REALLY EARLY.
LOOK!
!
VOICE...
... MESSAGE ...
...RE-CEIVED.
Audio message
1 new
START...
...PLAY-BACK?

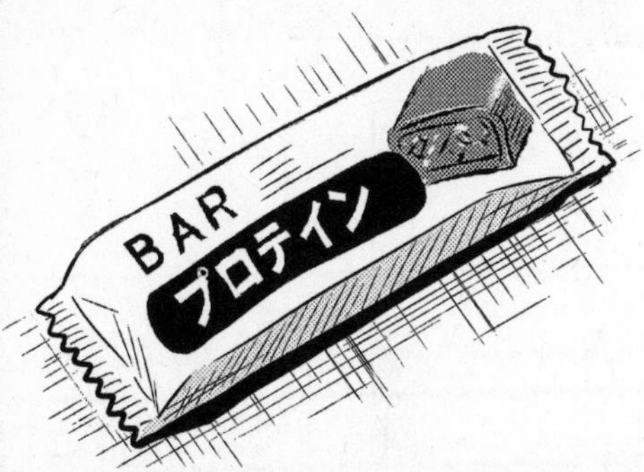
BAR
プロテイン

SCHOOL-LIVE!

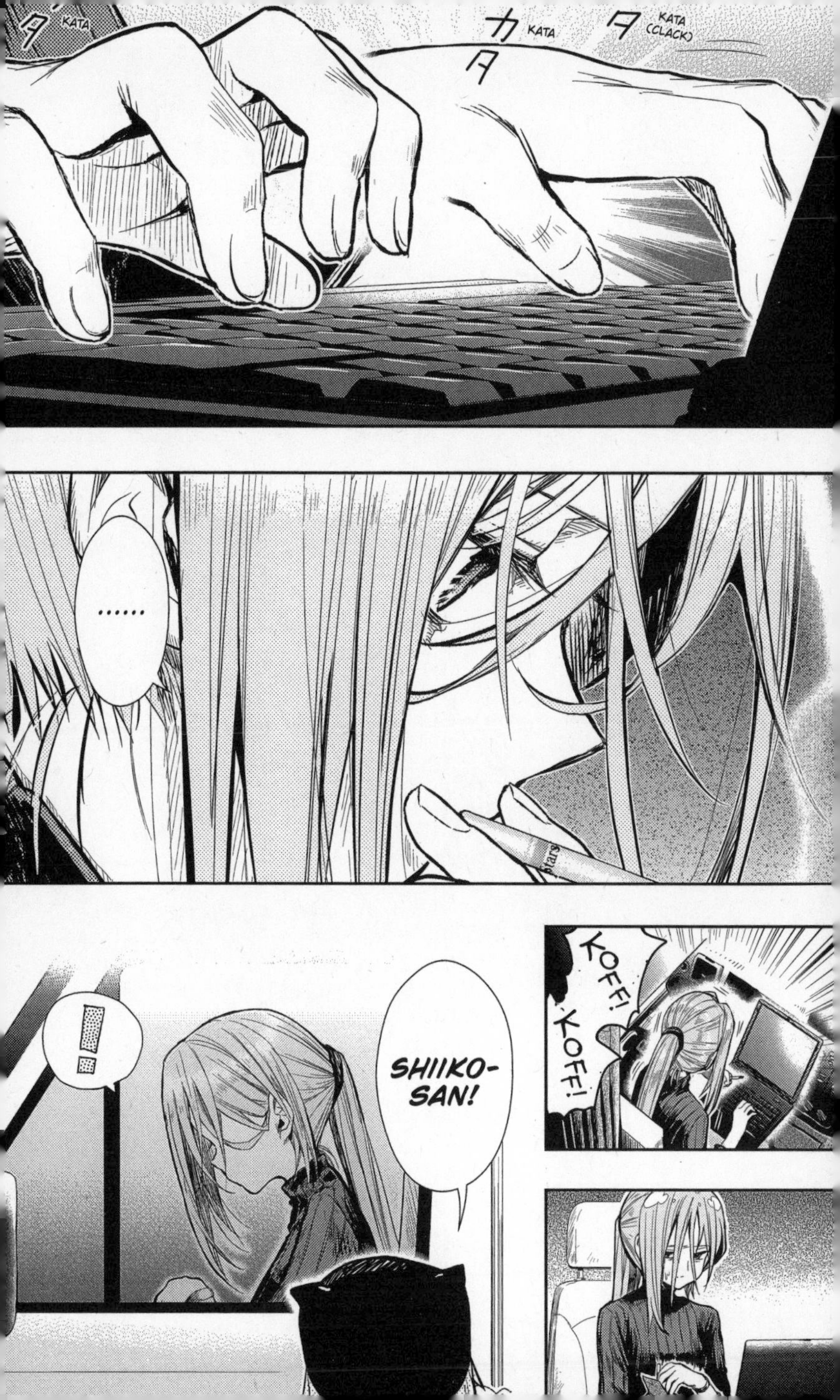

タ KATA (CLACK)
カ KATA
タ
タ KATA
......
Stars
KOFF! KOFF!
SHIIKO-SAN!
!

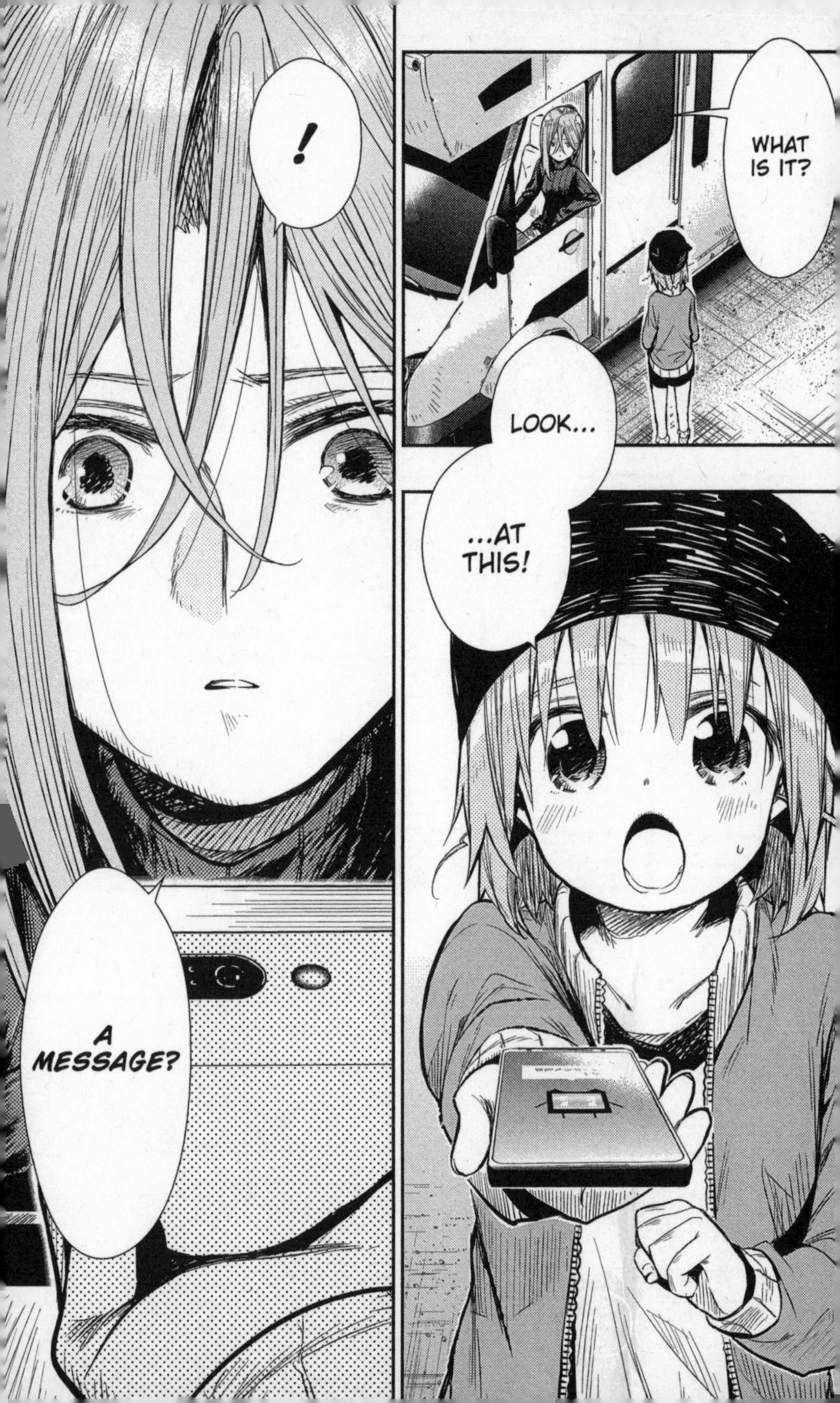
WHAT IS IT?
LOOK...
...AT THIS!
!
A MESSAGE?

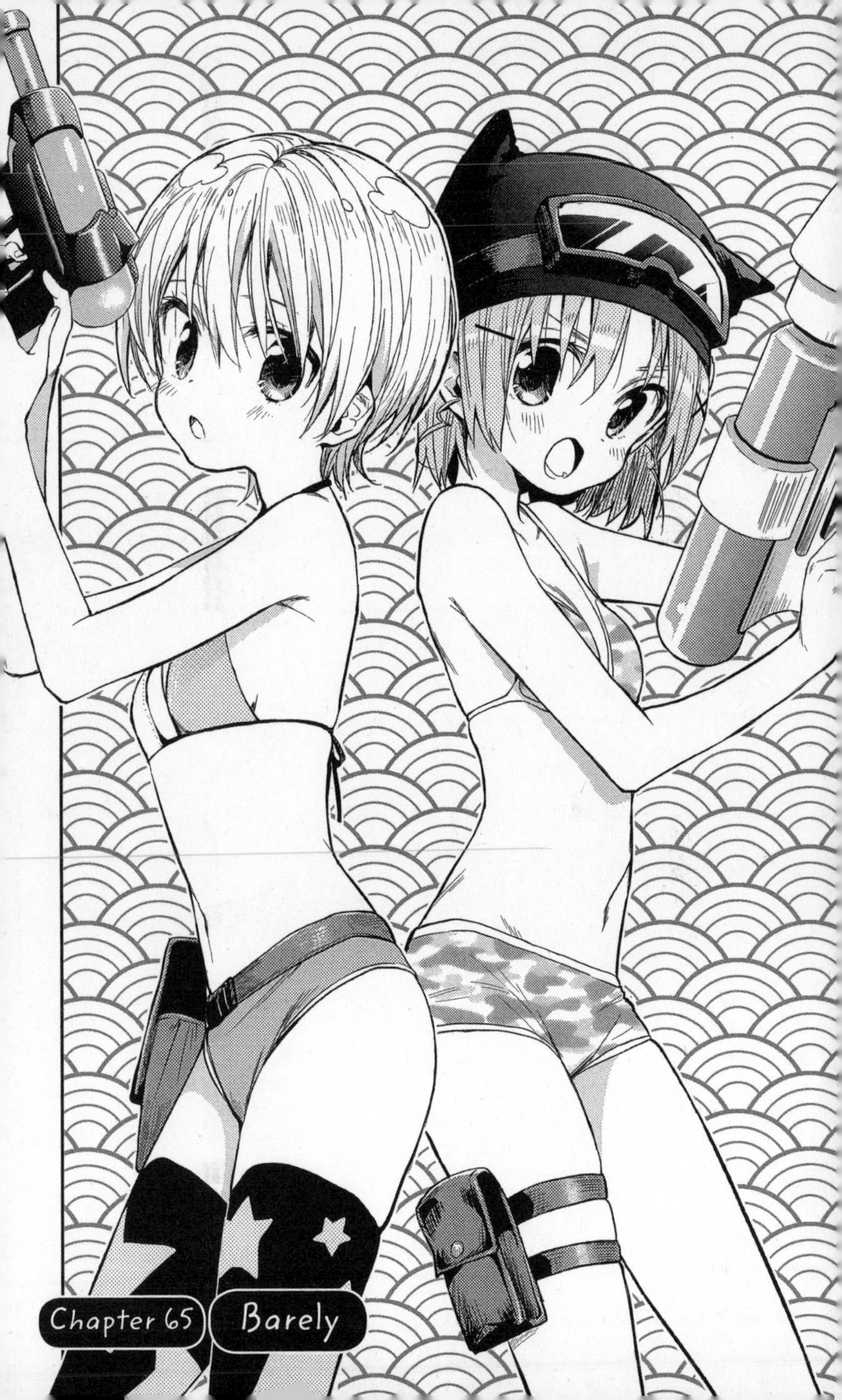
Chapter 65
Barely

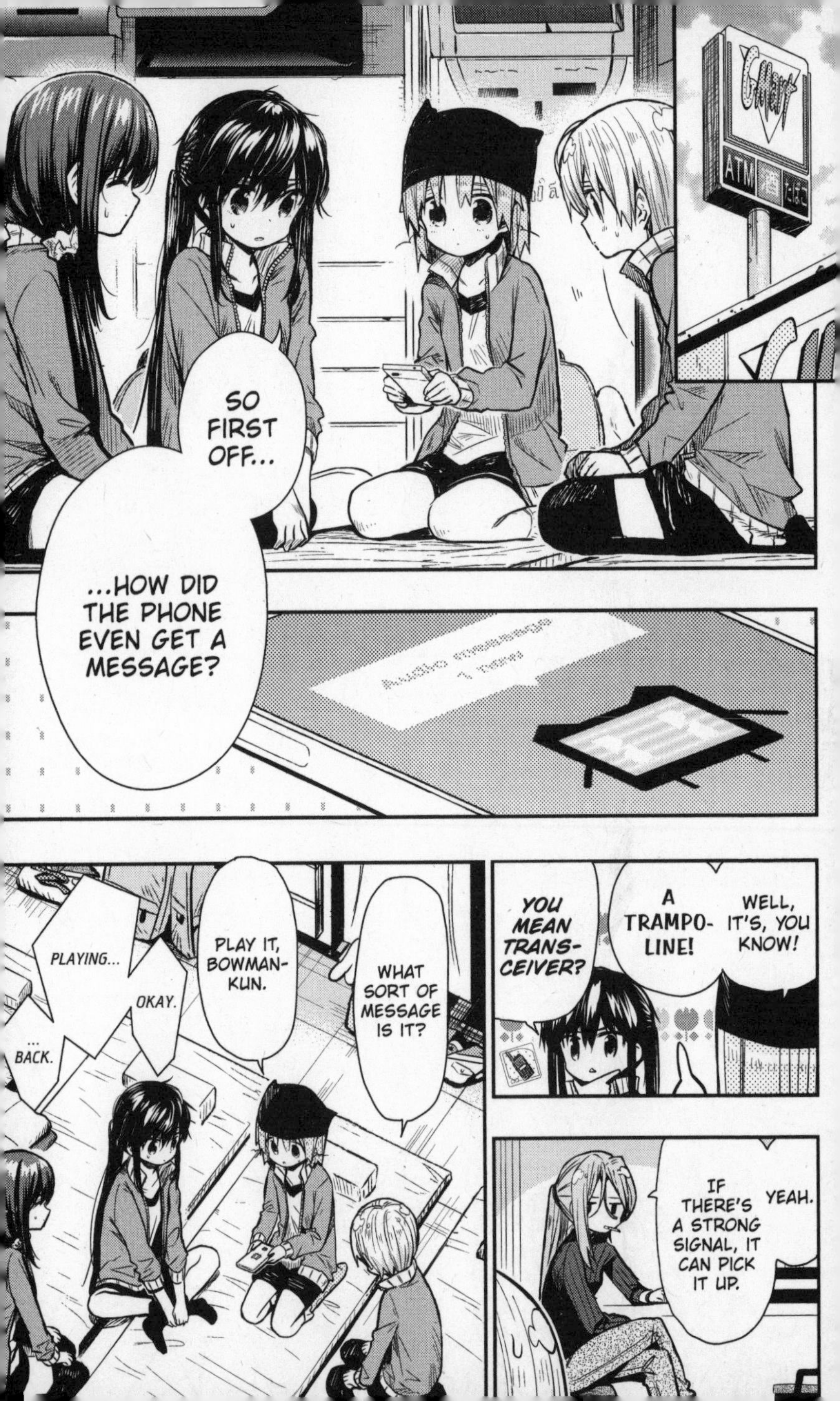
SO FIRST OFF...
...HOW DID THE PHONE EVEN GET A MESSAGE?
WELL, IT'S, YOU KNOW!
A TRAMPO-LINE!
YOU MEAN TRANS-CEIVER?
YEAH.
IF THERE'S A STRONG SIGNAL, IT CAN PICK IT UP.
WHAT SORT OF MESSAGE IS IT?
PLAY IT, BOWMAN-KUN.
OKAY.
PLAYING...
...BACK.

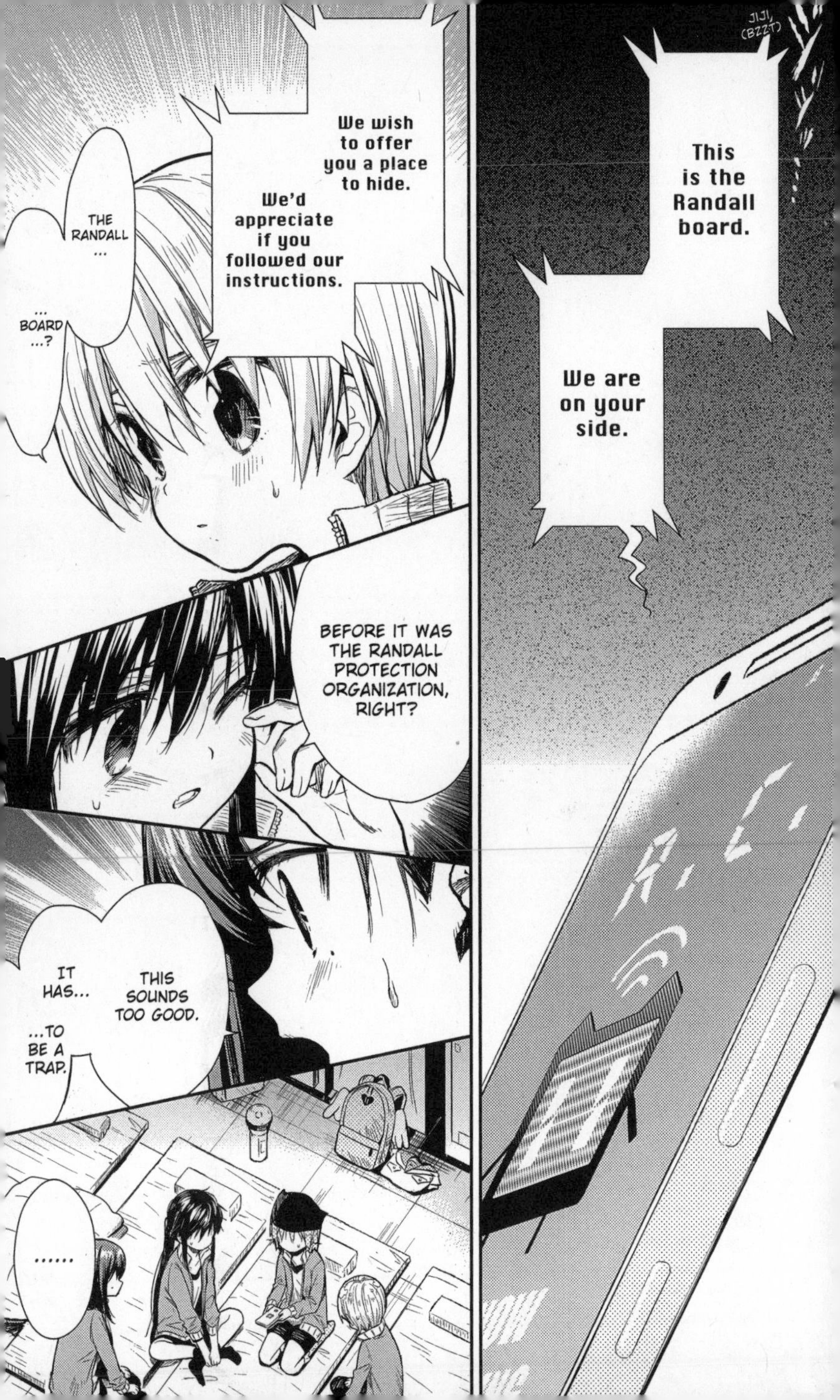
JIJI, (BZZT)
This is the Randall board.
We are on your side.
We wish to offer you a place to hide.
We'd appreciate if you followed our instructions.
THE RANDALL ...
... BOARD ...?
BEFORE IT WAS THE RANDALL PROTECTION ORGANIZATION, RIGHT?
THIS SOUNDS TOO GOOD.
IT HAS...
...TO BE A TRAP.
......

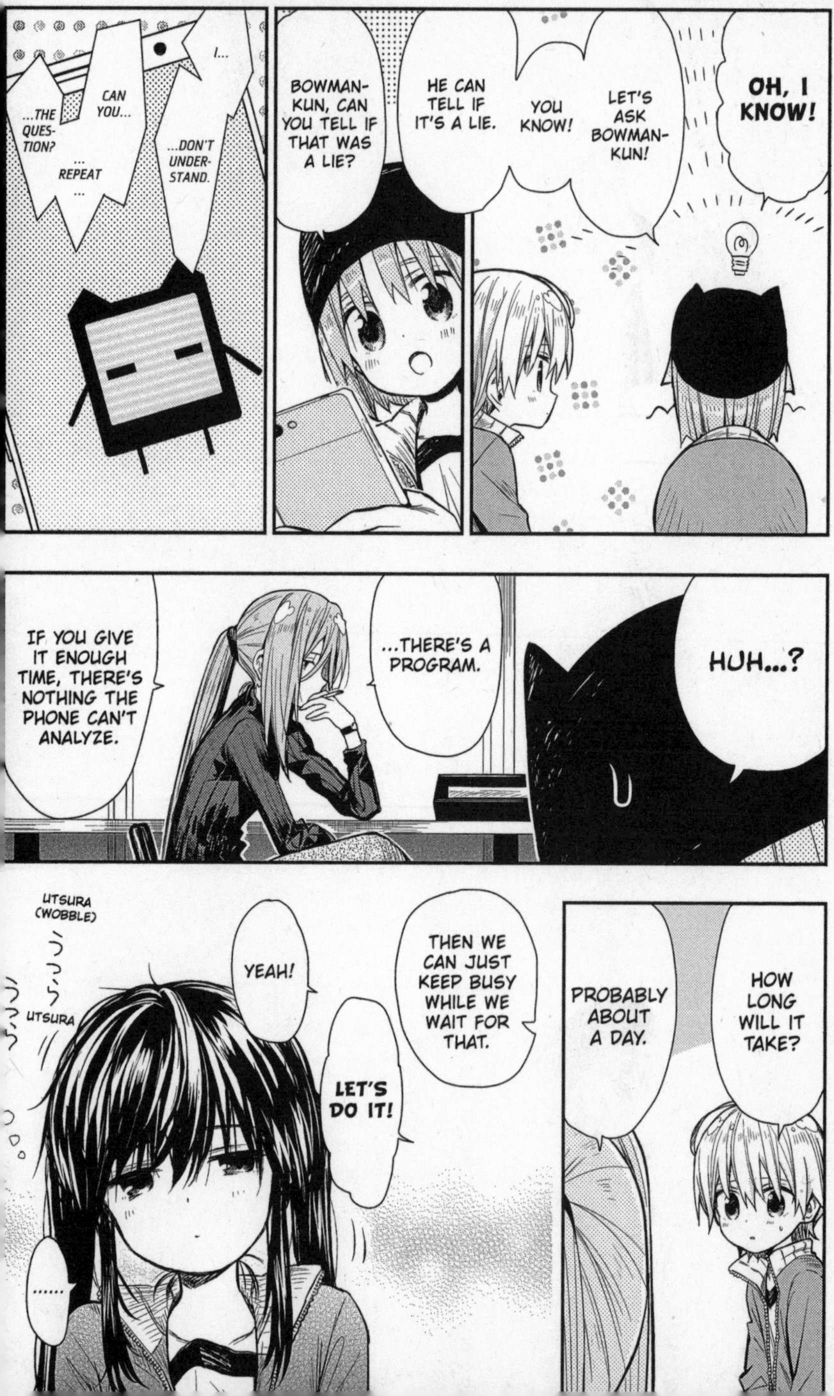
OH, I KNOW!
LET'S ASK BOWMAN-KUN!
YOU KNOW!
HE CAN TELL IF IT'S A LIE.
BOWMAN-KUN, CAN YOU TELL IF THAT WAS A LIE?
I...
...DON'T UNDER-STAND.
CAN YOU...
...REPEAT...
...THE QUES-TION?
HUH...?
...THERE'S A PROGRAM.
IF YOU GIVE IT ENOUGH TIME, THERE'S NOTHING THE PHONE CAN'T ANALYZE.
HOW LONG WILL IT TAKE?
PROBABLY ABOUT A DAY.
THEN WE CAN JUST KEEP BUSY WHILE WE WAIT FOR THAT.
YEAH!
LET'S DO IT!
UTSURA (WOBBLE)
UTSURA
......

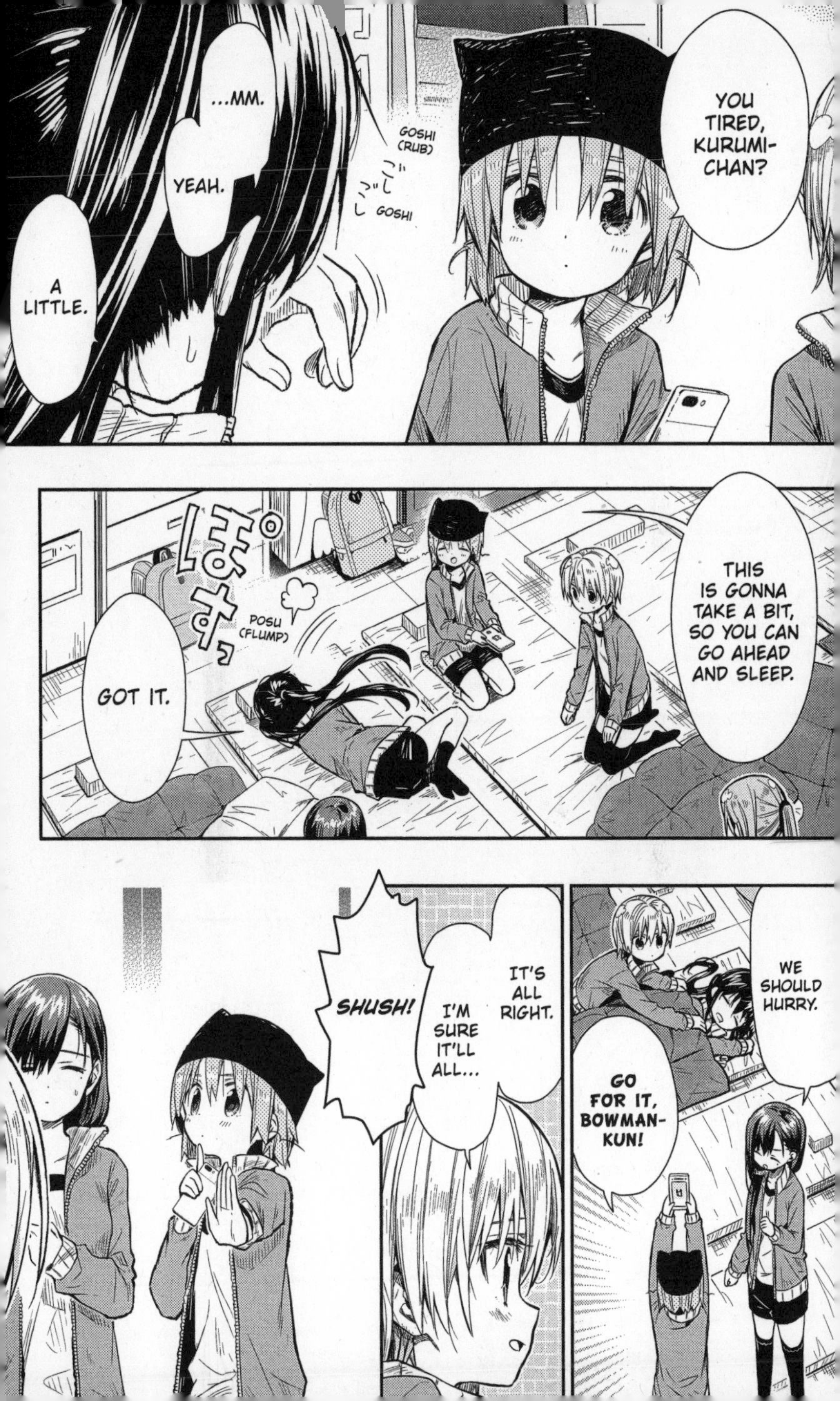
YOU TIRED, KURUMI-CHAN?
GOSHI (RUB)
ごしごし
GOSHI
...MM.
YEAH.
A LITTLE.
THIS IS GONNA TAKE A BIT, SO YOU CAN GO AHEAD AND SLEEP.
ぽすっ
POSU (FLUMP)
GOT IT.
WE SHOULD HURRY.
GO FOR IT, BOWMAN-KUN!
IT'S ALL RIGHT.
I'M SURE IT'LL ALL...
SHUSH!

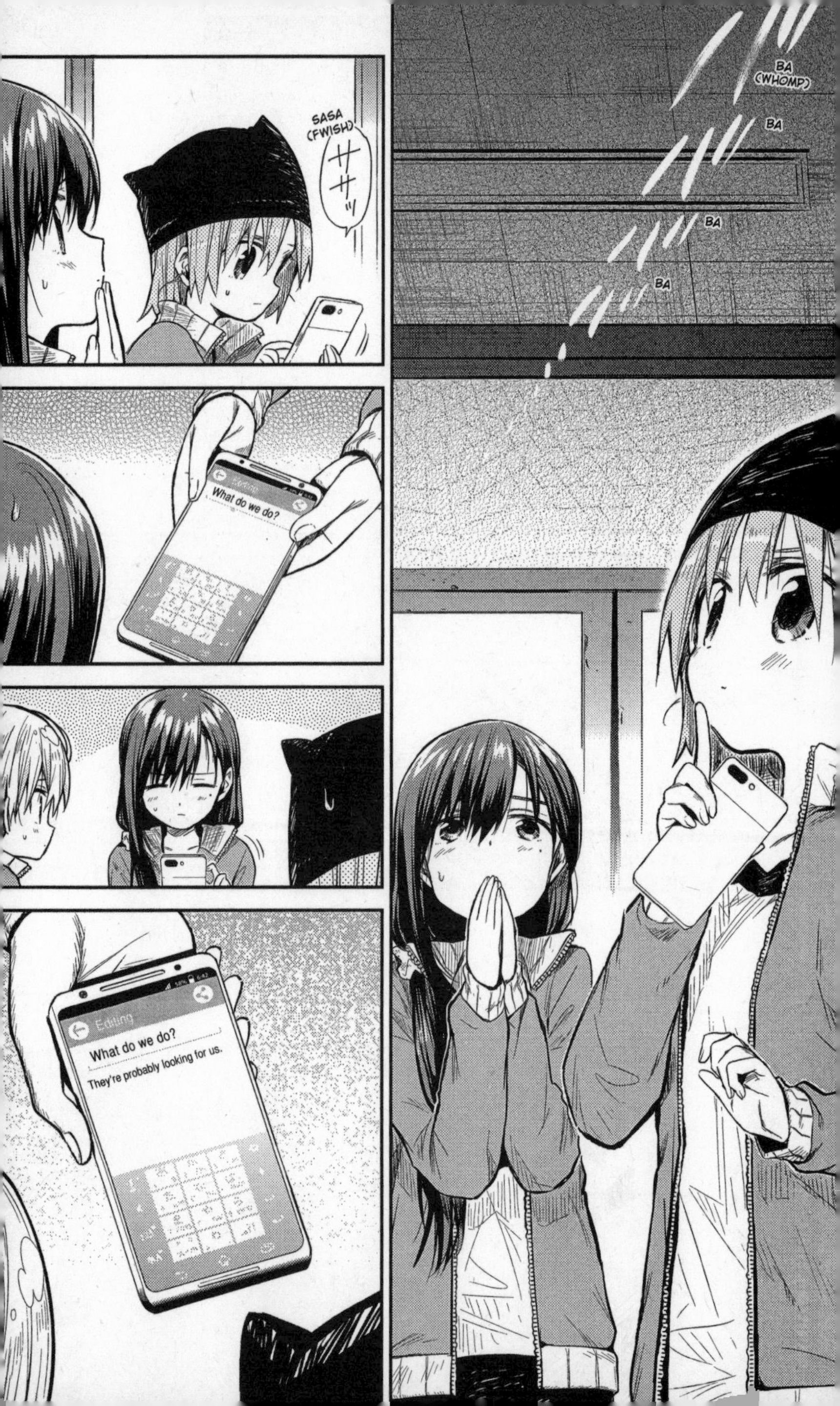
BA (WHOMP)
BA
BA
BA
SASA (FWISH)
ササッ
What do we do?
Editing
What do we do?
They're probably looking for us.

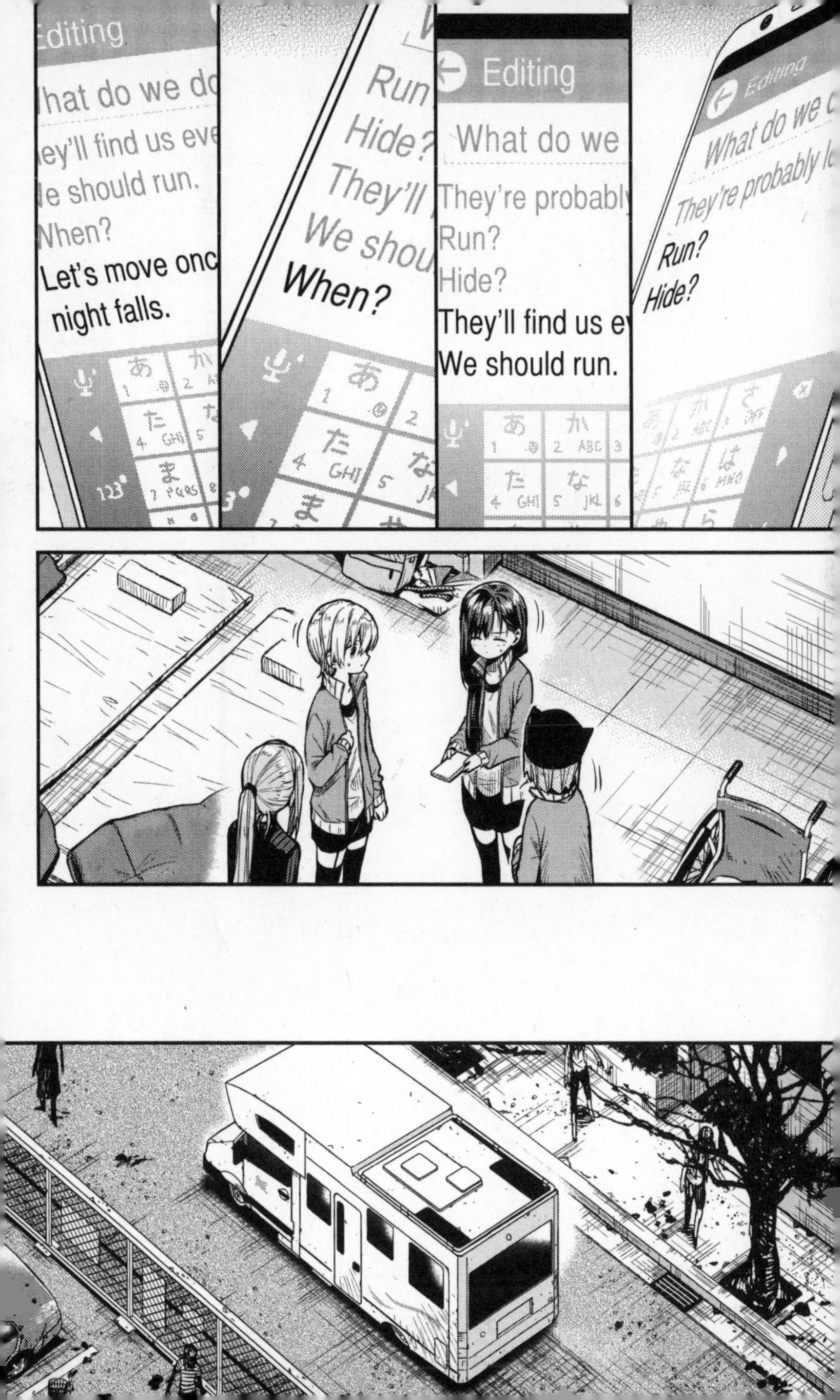

Editing
What do we d
They're probably l
Run?
Hide?
Editing
What do we
They're probabl
Run?
Hide?
They'll find us e
We should run.
Run
Hide?
They'll
We shou
When?
diting
hat do we dc
ey'll find us eve
e should run.
Vhen?
Let's move onc
night falls.

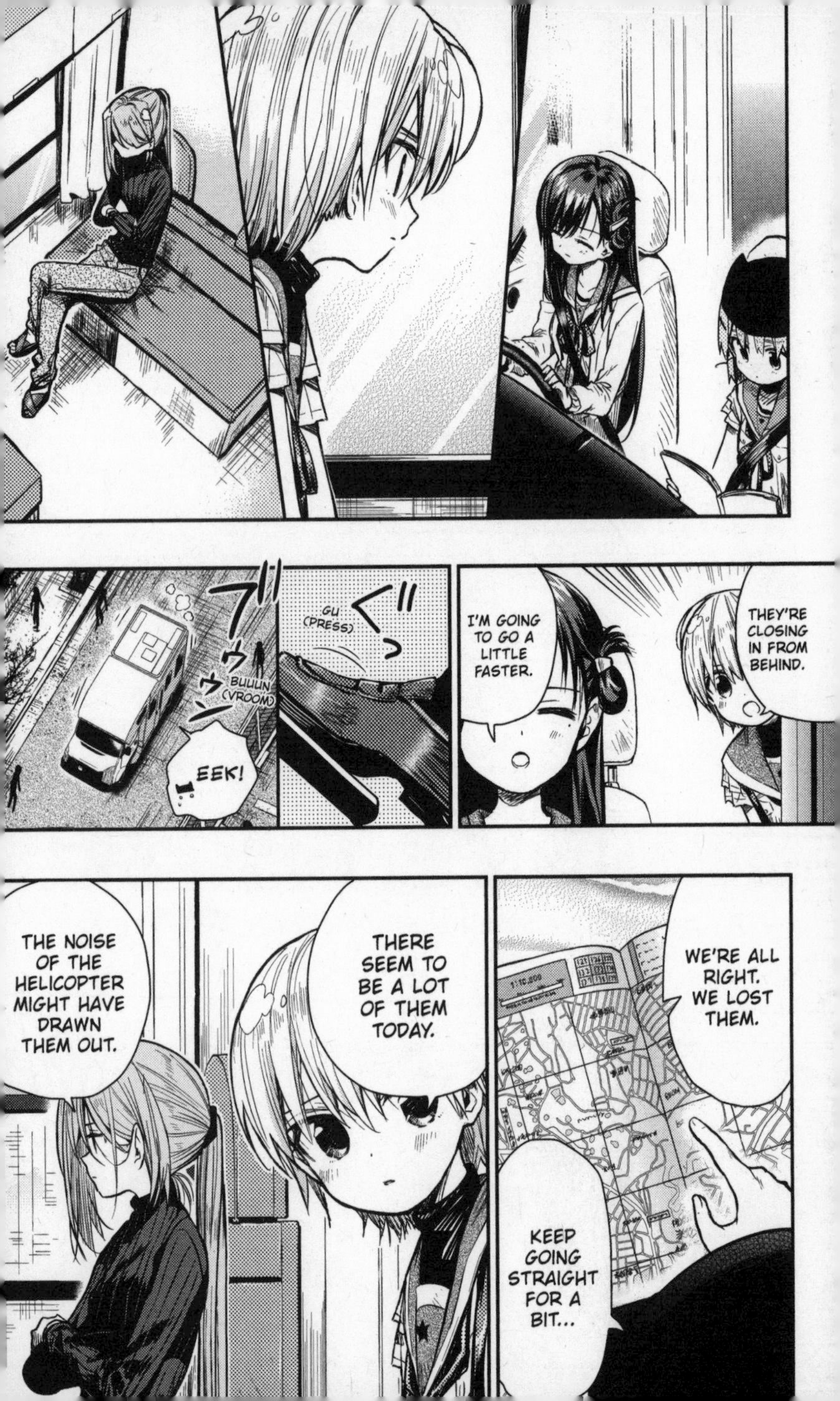

THEY'RE CLOSING IN FROM BEHIND.
I'M GOING TO GO A LITTLE FASTER.
GU (PRESS)
BUUUN (VROOM)
EEK!
WE'RE ALL RIGHT. WE LOST THEM.
KEEP GOING STRAIGHT FOR A BIT...
THERE SEEM TO BE A LOT OF THEM TODAY.
THE NOISE OF THE HELICOPTER MIGHT HAVE DRAWN THEM OUT.

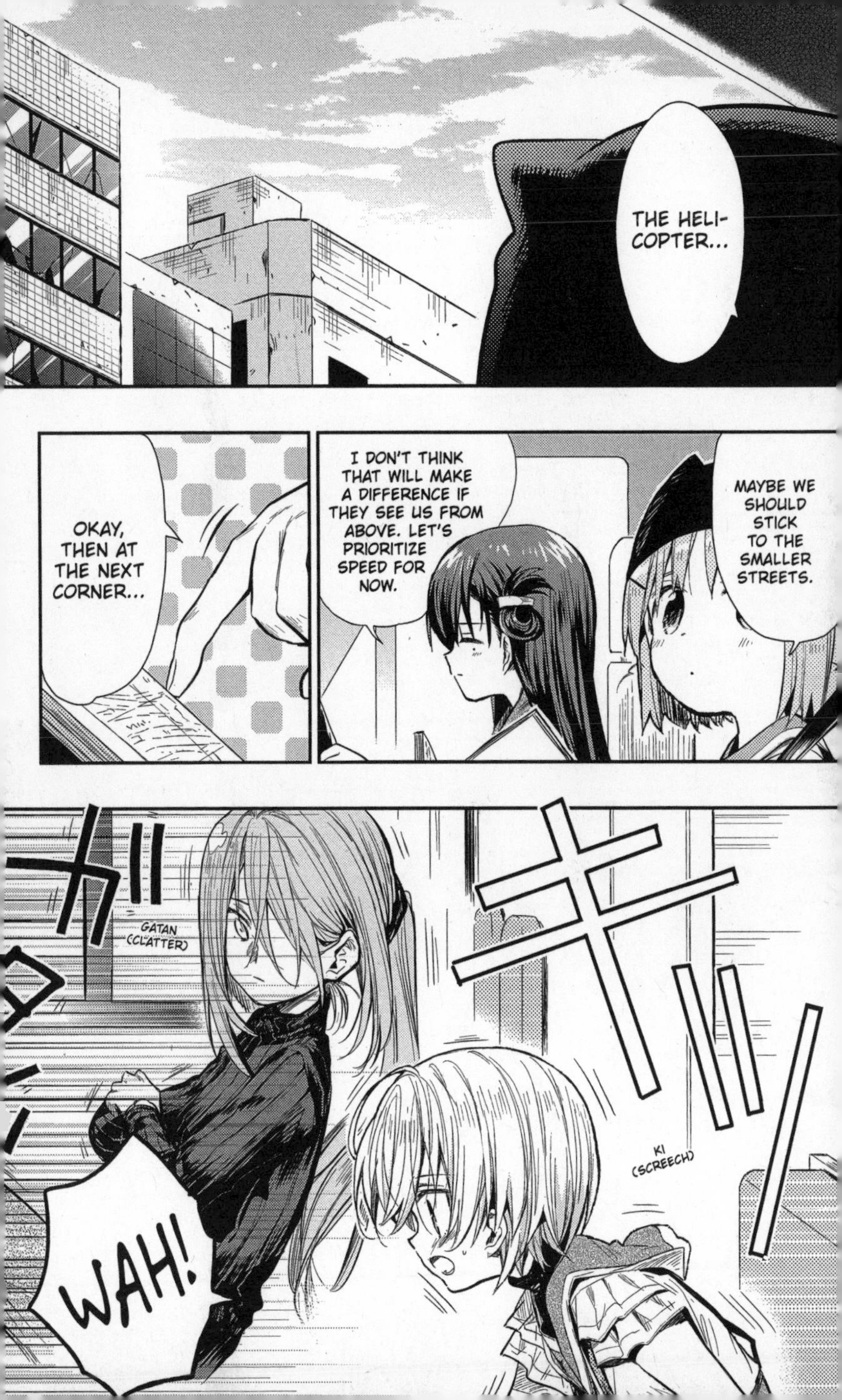
THE HELI-
COPTER...
MAYBE WE SHOULD STICK TO THE SMALLER STREETS.
I DON'T THINK THAT WILL MAKE A DIFFERENCE IF THEY SEE US FROM ABOVE. LET'S PRIORITIZE SPEED FOR NOW.
OKAY, THEN AT THE NEXT CORNER...
KI (SCREECH)
GATAN (CLATTER)
WAH!

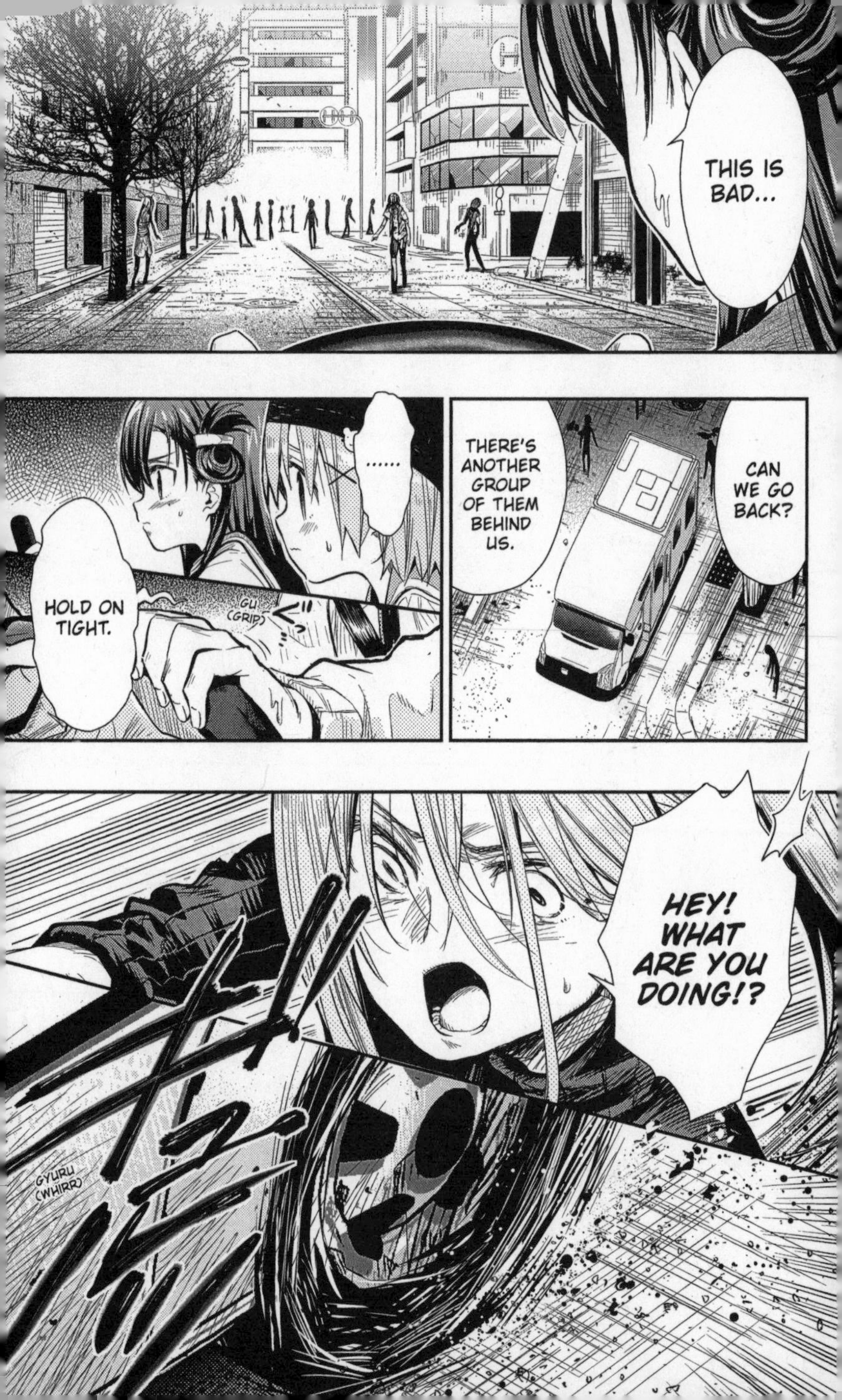
THIS IS BAD...
CAN WE GO BACK?
THERE'S ANOTHER GROUP OF THEM BEHIND US.
......
HOLD ON TIGHT.
GU (GRIP)
HEY! WHAT ARE YOU DOING!?
GYURU (WHIRR)

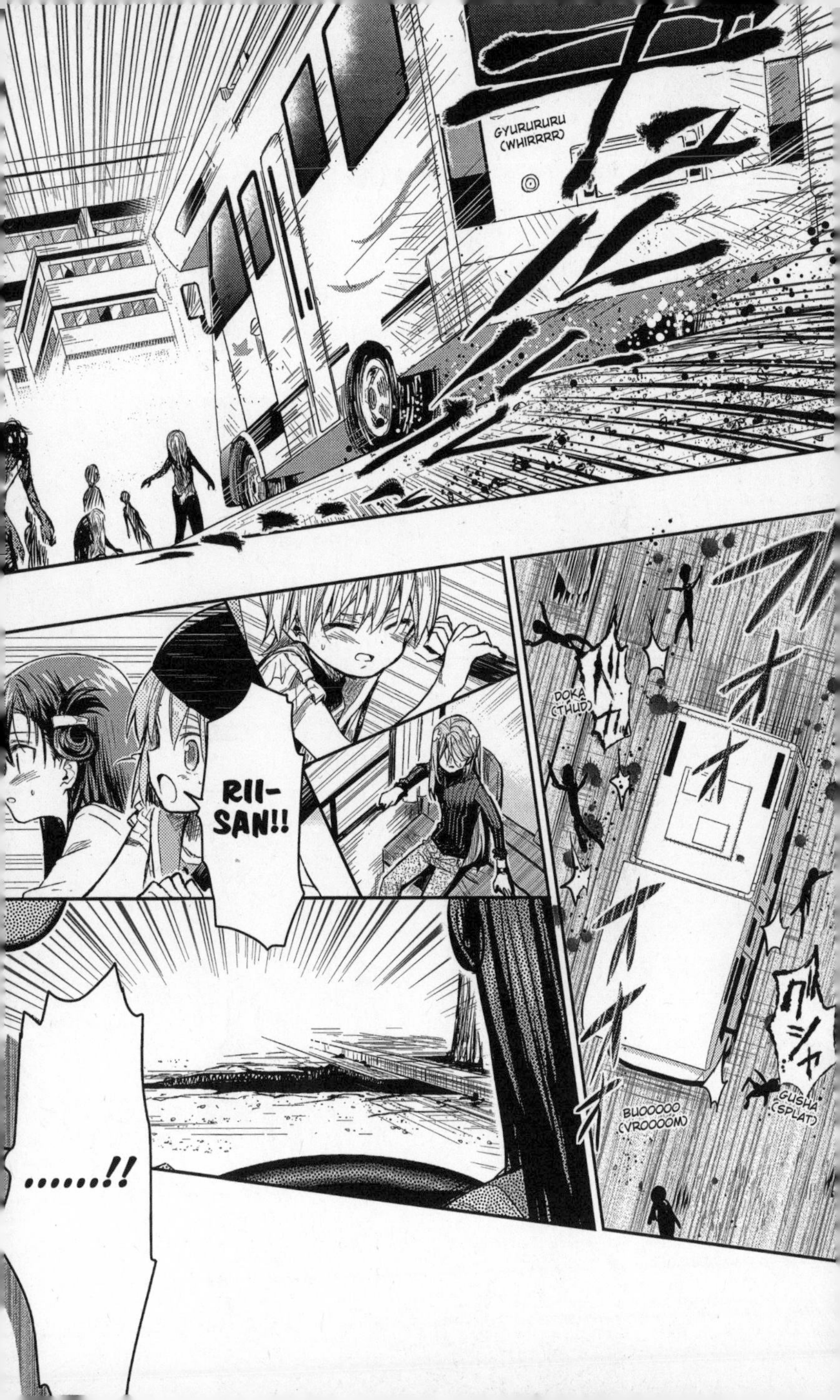
GYURURURU (WHIRRRR)
DOKA (THUD)
GUSHA (SPLAT)
BUOOOOO (VROOOOOM)
RII-SAN!!
......!!

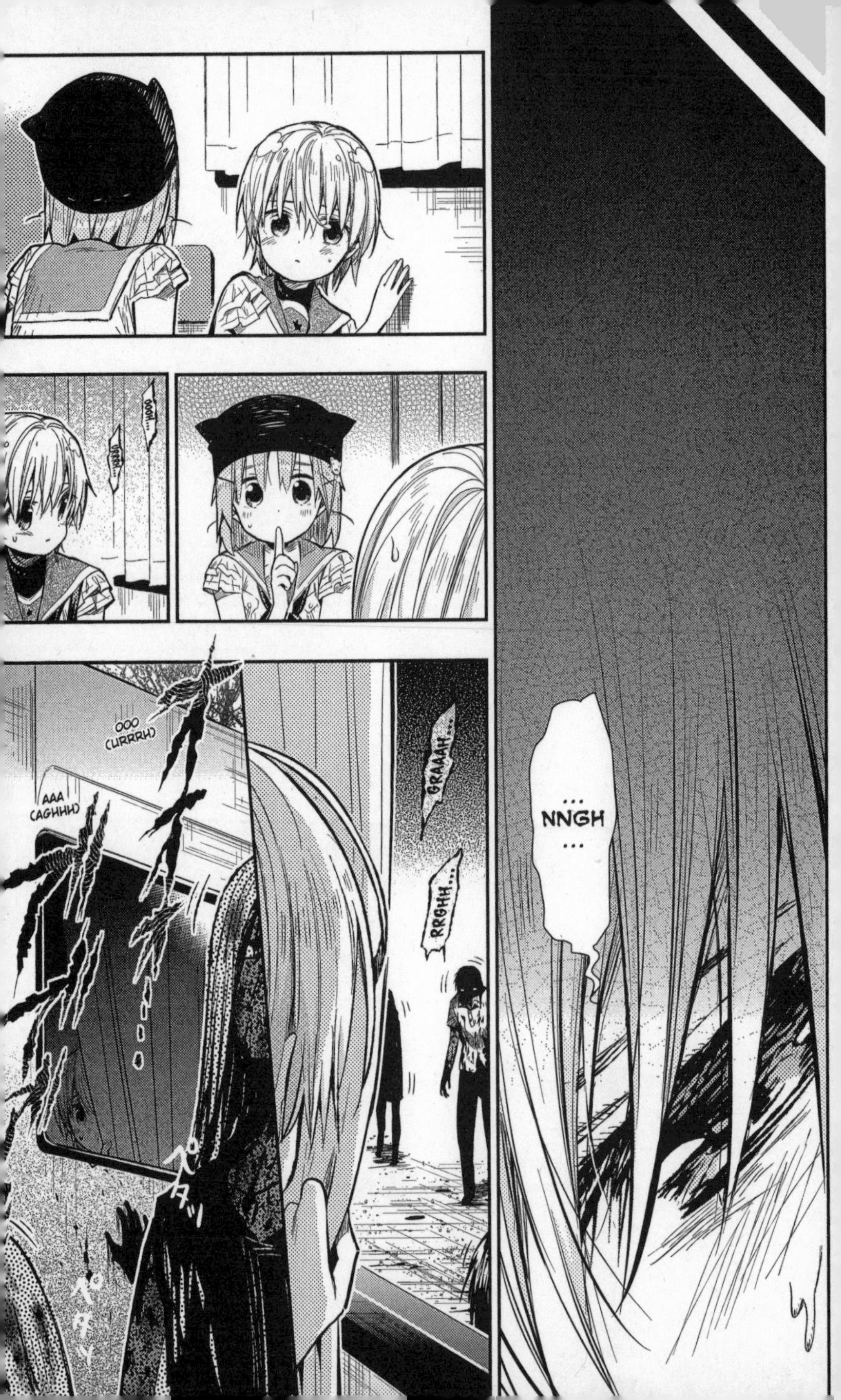
...
NNGH
...
OOOH...
URRRH...
GRAAAH...
RRGHH...
OOO
(URRRH)
AAA
(AGHHH)

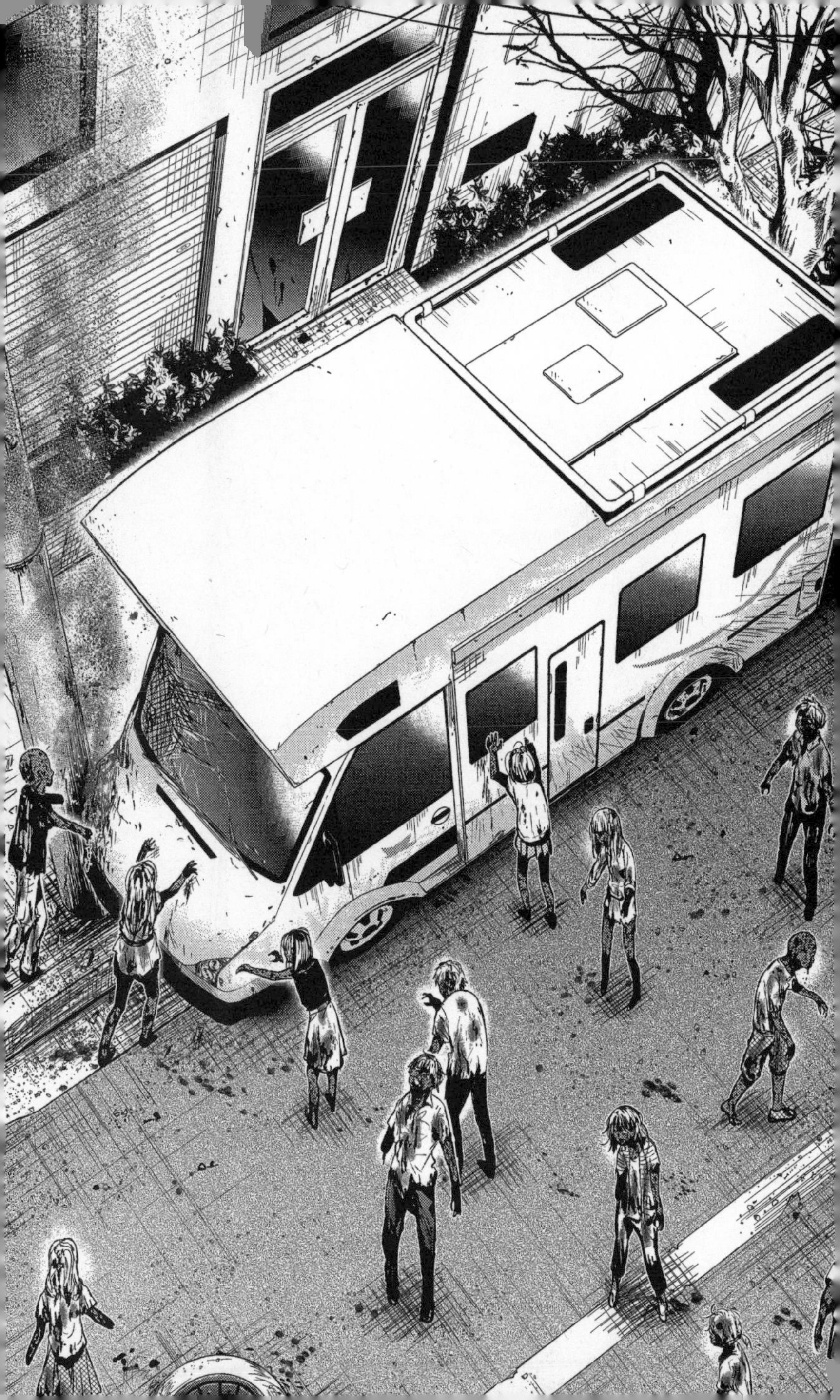

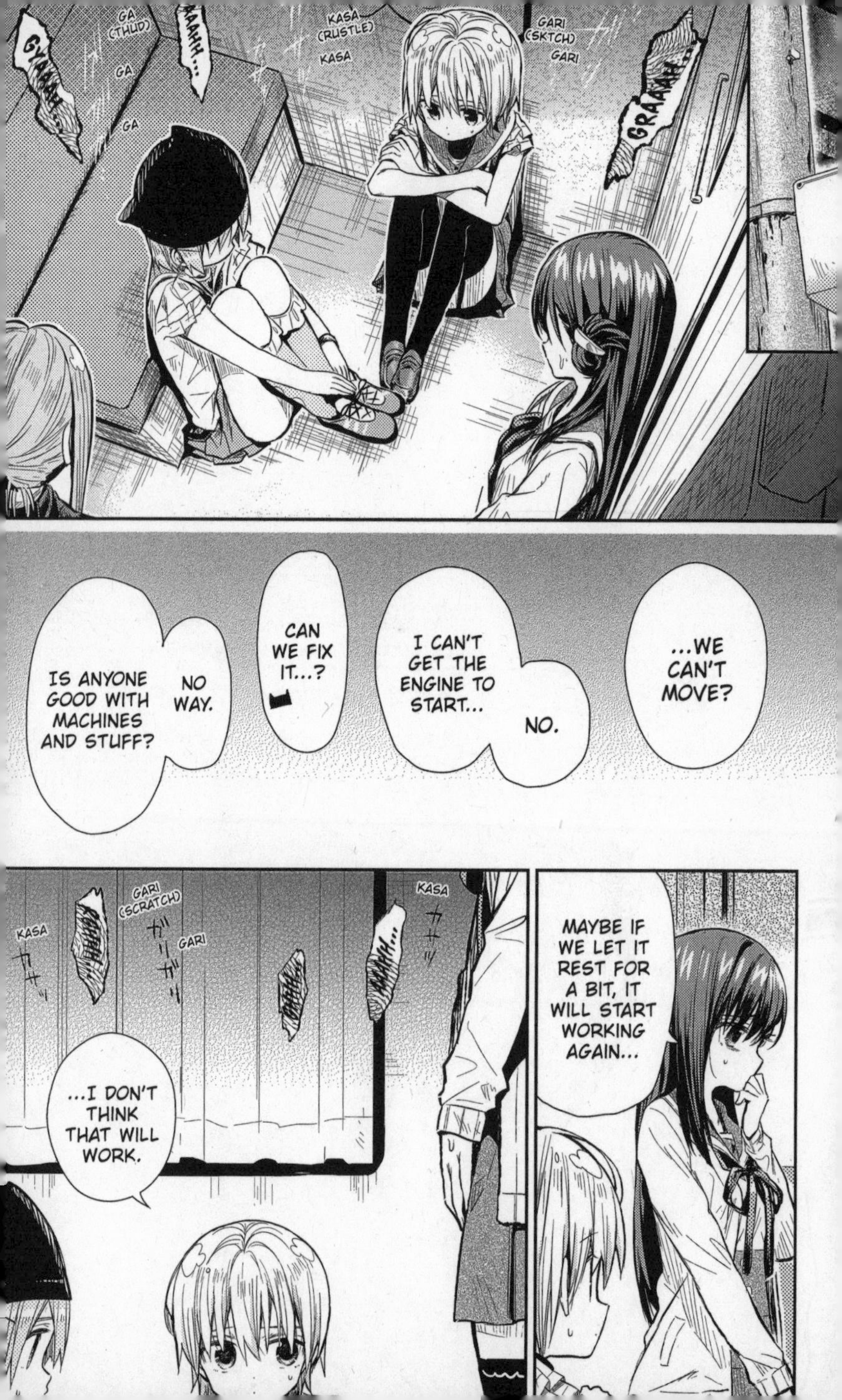
GARI (SKTCH)
GARI
GRAAAH...
KASA (RUSTLE)
KASA
AAAHH...
GA (THUD)
GA
GA
GYAAAH...
...WE CAN'T MOVE?
I CAN'T GET THE ENGINE TO START...
NO.
CAN WE FIX IT...?
NO WAY.
IS ANYONE GOOD WITH MACHINES AND STUFF?
MAYBE IF WE LET IT REST FOR A BIT, IT WILL START WORKING AGAIN...
KASA
GARI (SCRATCH)
GARI
KASA
...I DON'T THINK THAT WILL WORK.

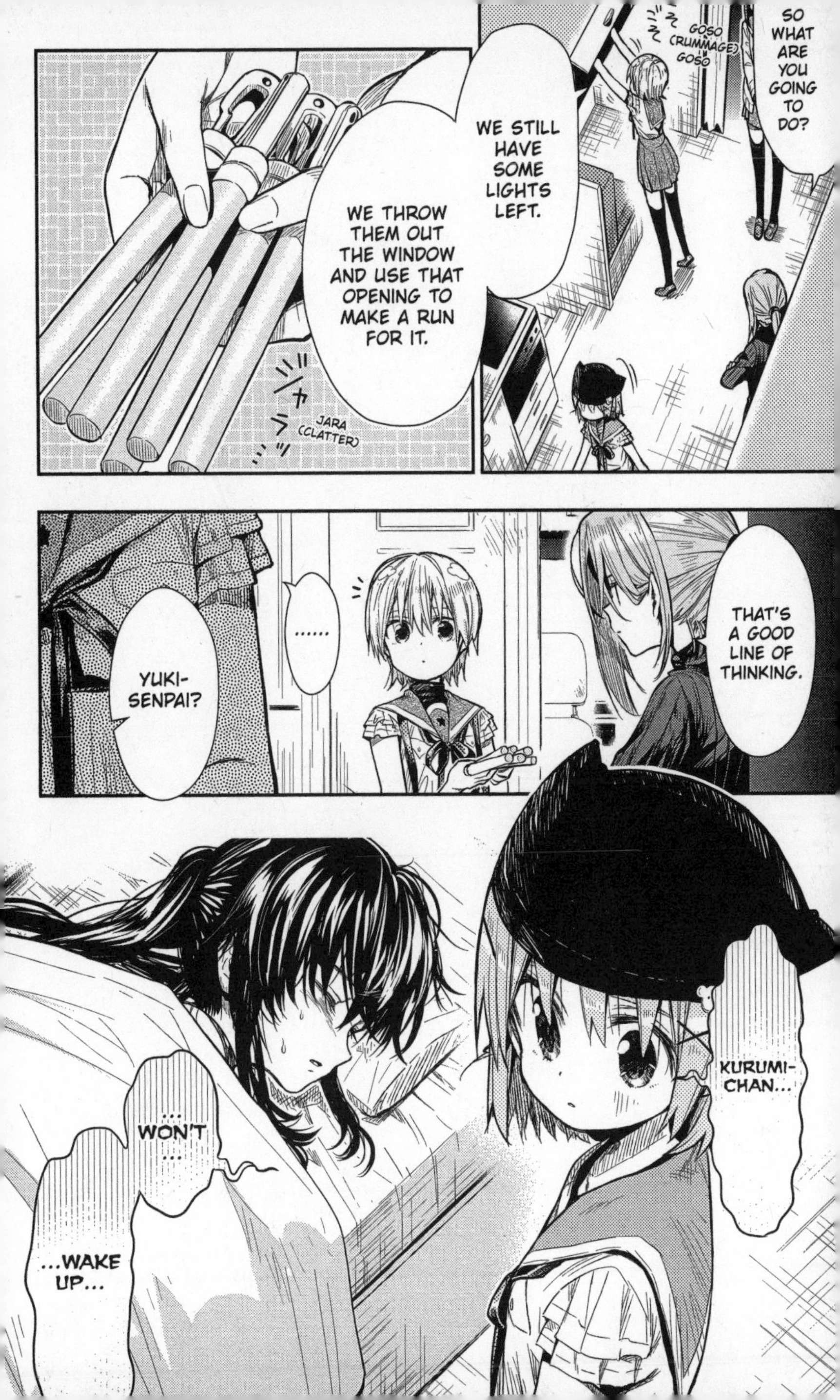
SO WHAT ARE YOU GOING TO DO?
GOSO (RUMMAGE) GOSO
WE STILL HAVE SOME LIGHTS LEFT.
WE THROW THEM OUT THE WINDOW AND USE THAT OPENING TO MAKE A RUN FOR IT.
JARA (CLATTER)
THAT'S A GOOD LINE OF THINKING.
......
YUKI-SENPAI?
KURUMI-CHAN...
...WON'T...
...WAKE UP...

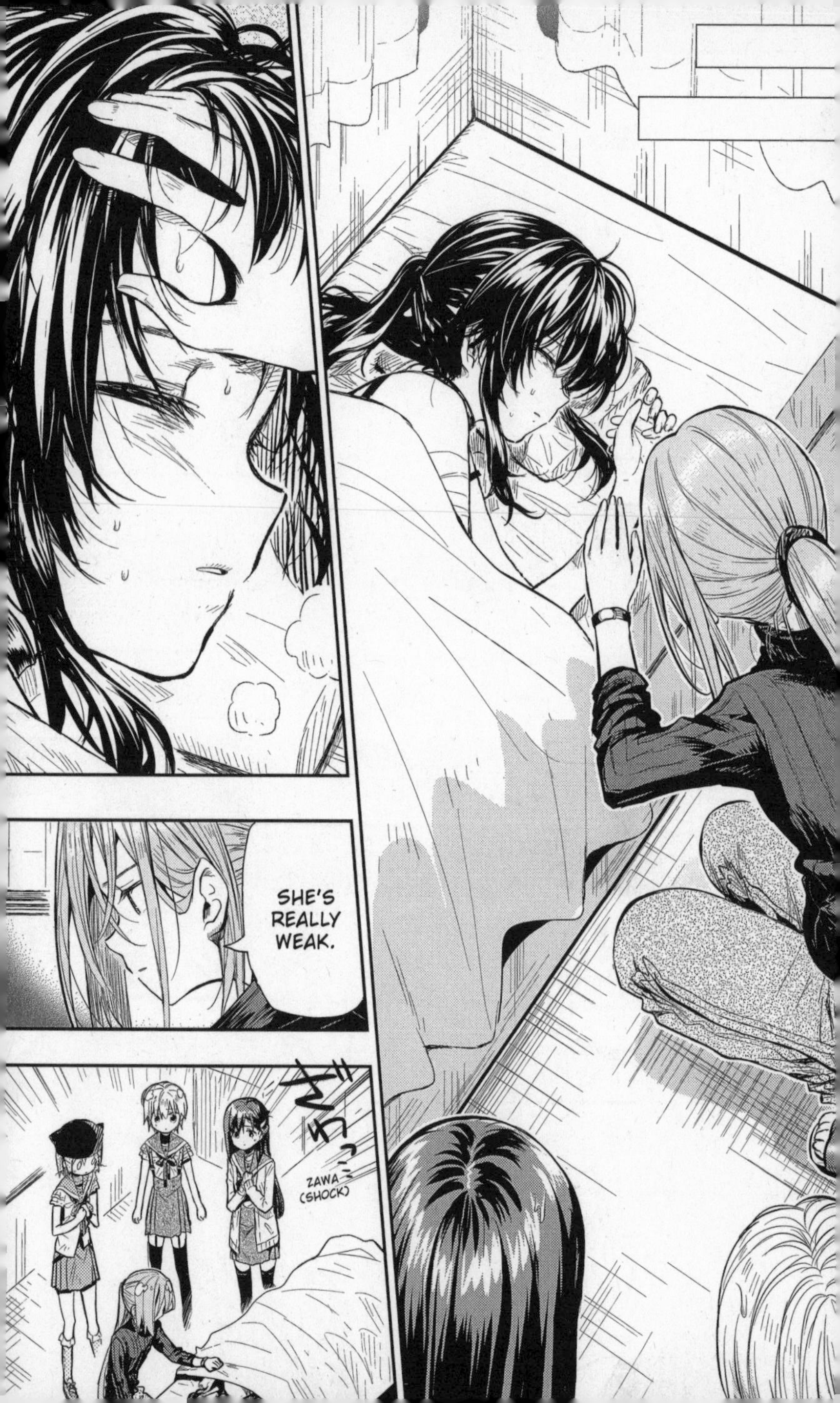
SHE'S REALLY WEAK.
ZAWA (SHOCK)

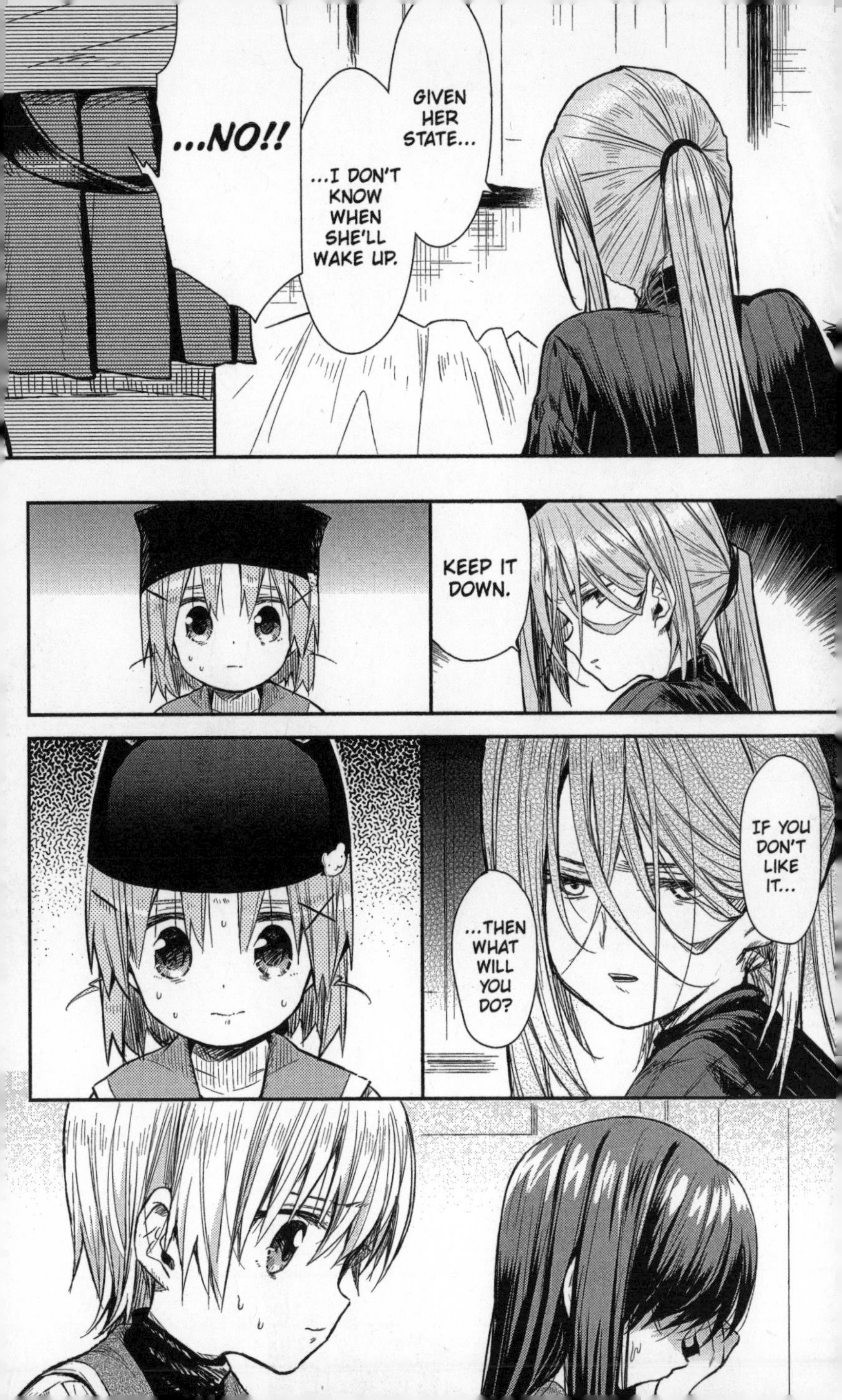
GIVEN HER STATE...
...I DON'T KNOW WHEN SHE'LL WAKE UP.
...NO!!
KEEP IT DOWN.
IF YOU DON'T LIKE IT...
...THEN WHAT WILL YOU DO?

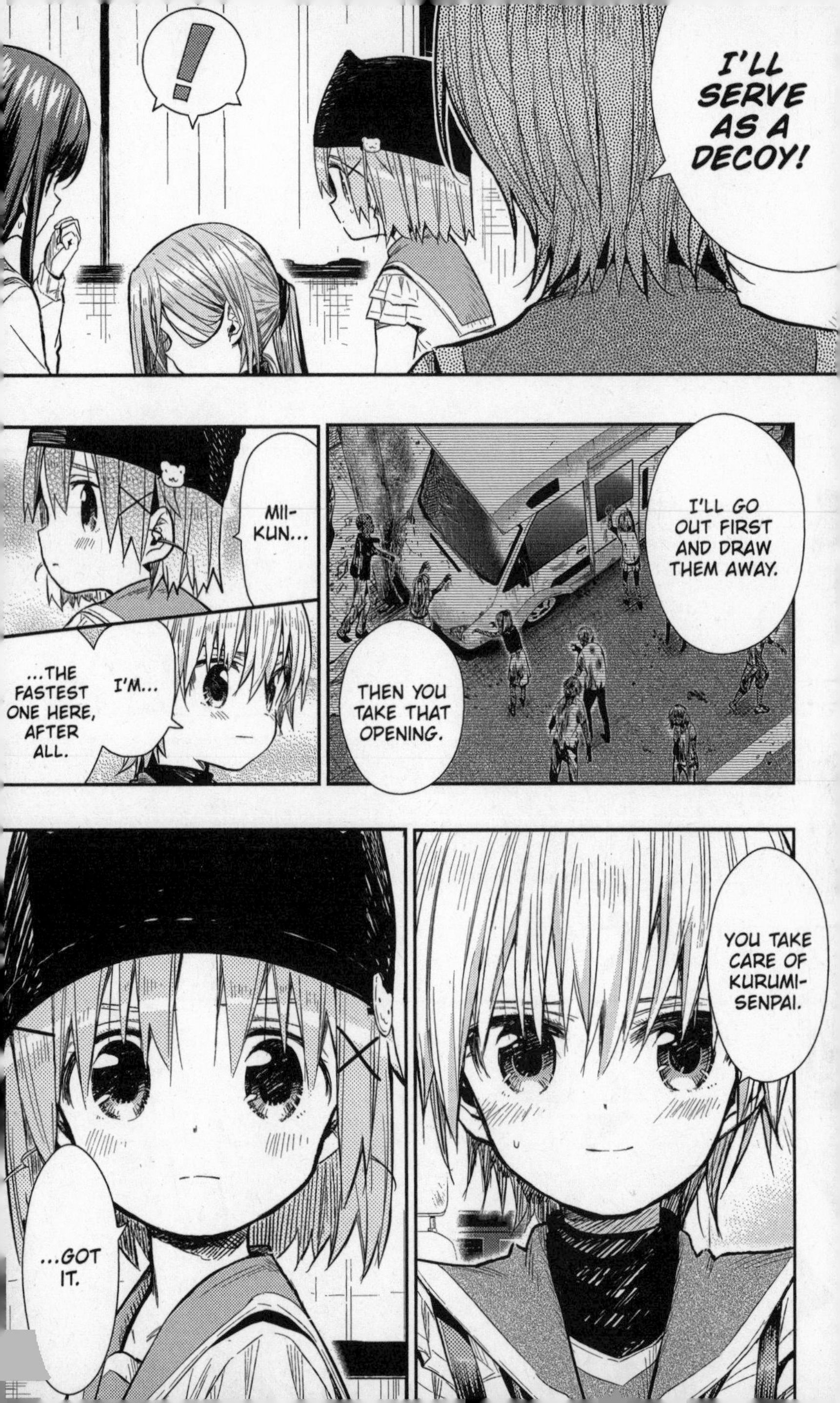
I'LL SERVE AS A DECOY!
!
I'LL GO OUT FIRST AND DRAW THEM AWAY.
THEN YOU TAKE THAT OPENING.
MII-KUN...
I'M...
...THE FASTEST ONE HERE, AFTER ALL.
YOU TAKE CARE OF KURUMI-SENPAI.
...GOT IT.

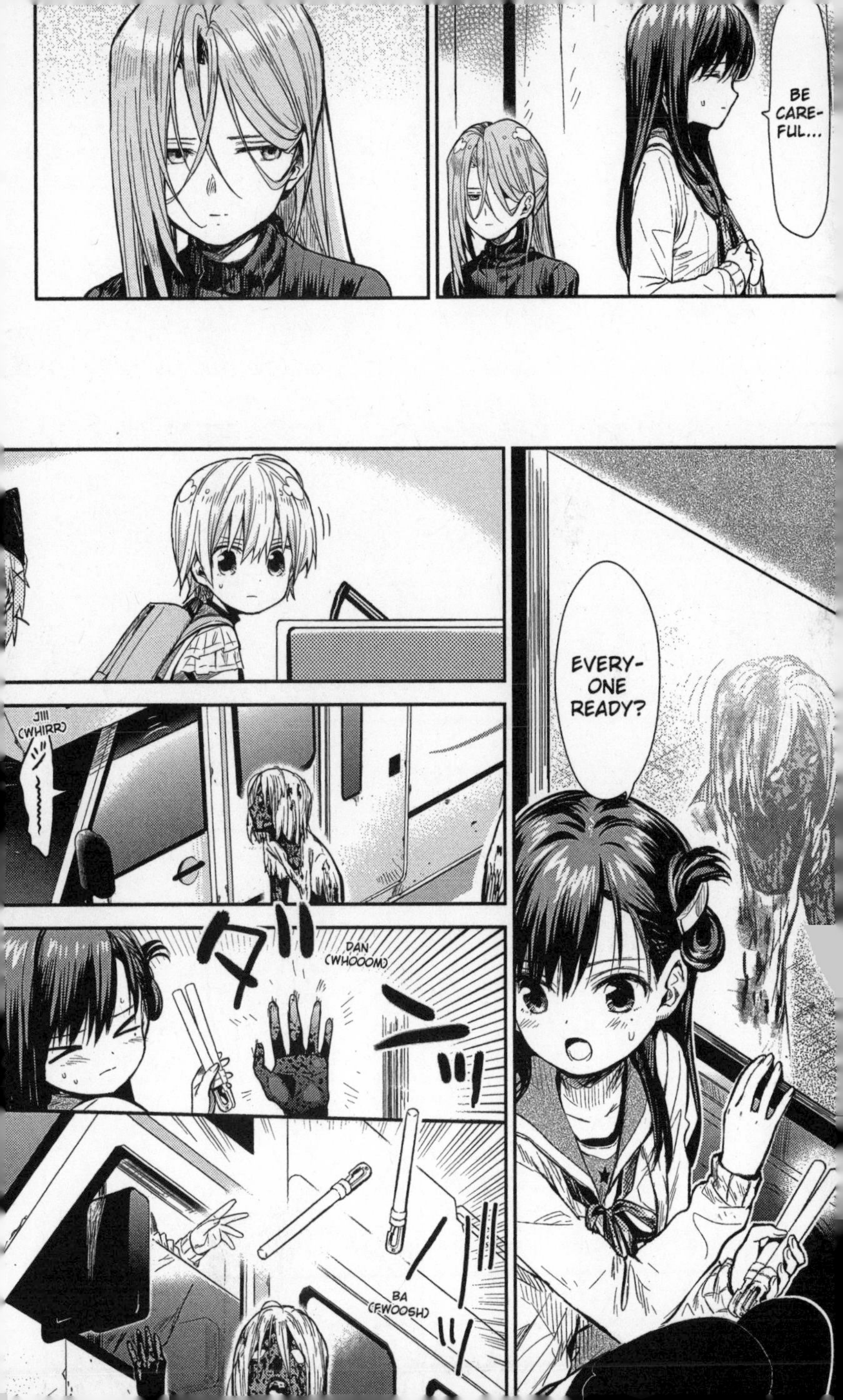
BE CARE-FUL...
EVERY-ONE READY?
JIII (WHIRR)
DAN (WHOOOM)
BA (F-WOOSH)

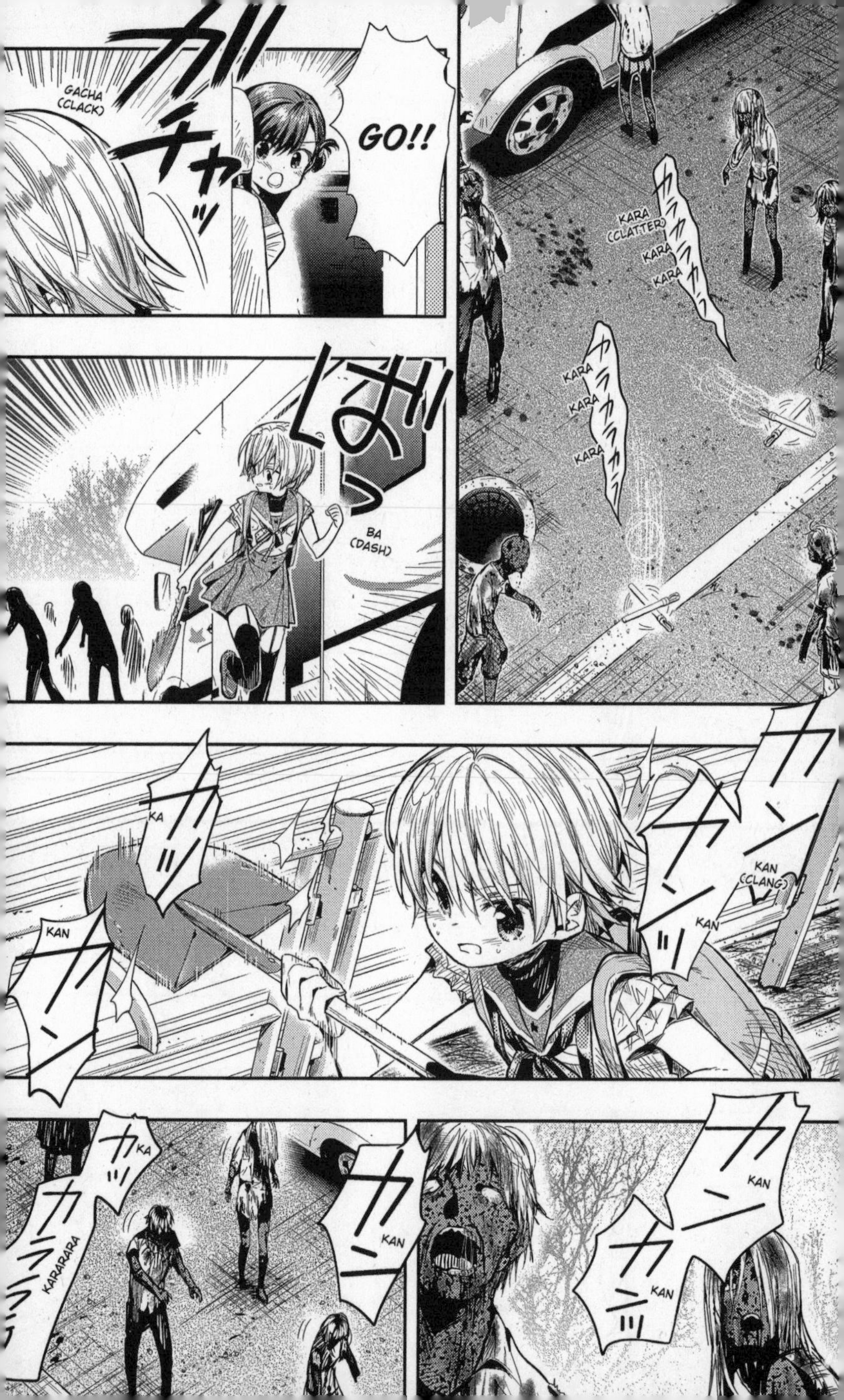

KARA (CLATTER)
KARA
KARA
KARA
KARA
KARA
GO!!
GACHA (CLACK)
BA (DASH)
KAN (CLANG)
KAN
KA
KAN
KAN
KAN
KAN
KA
KARARARA

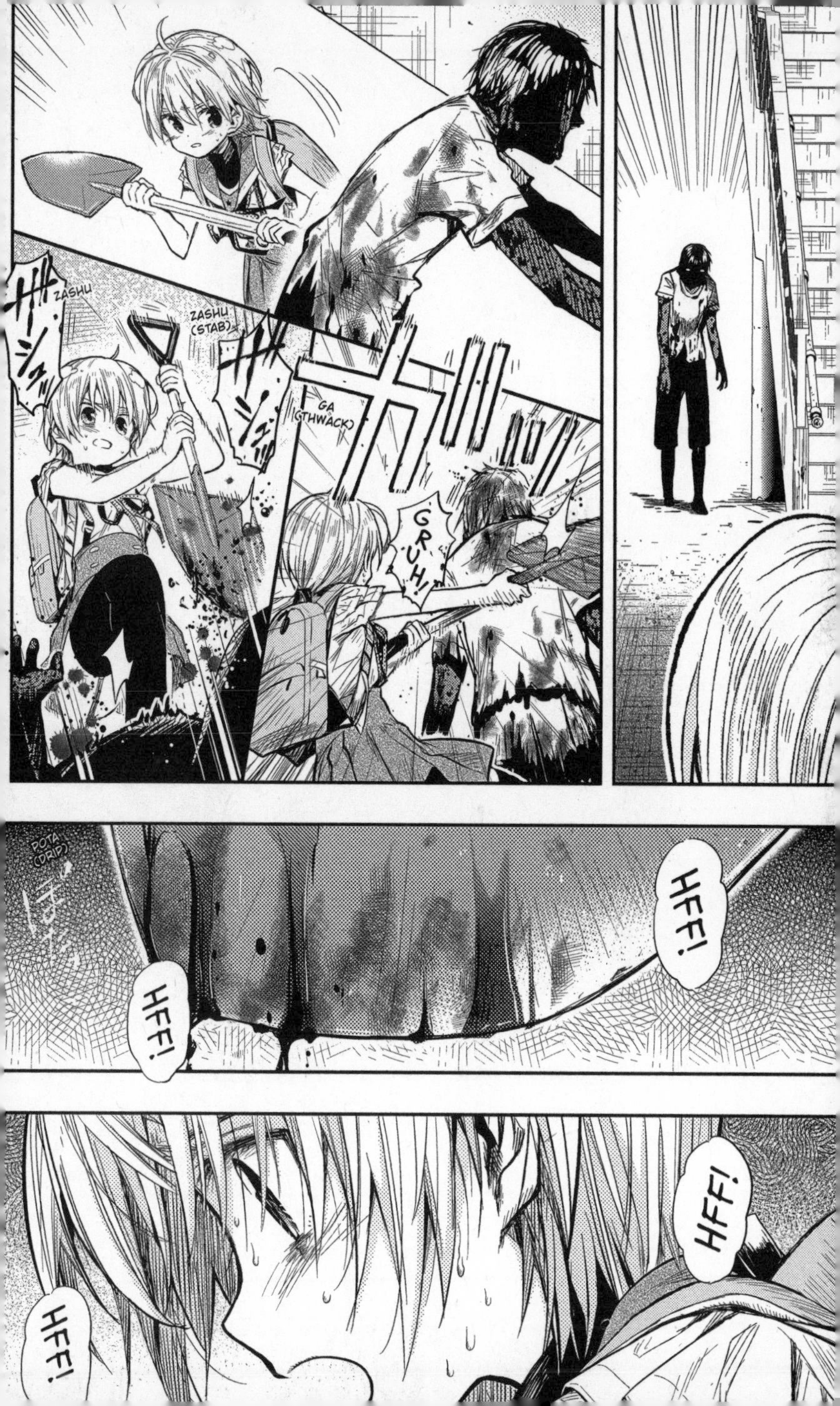
ZASHU
ZASHU (STAB)
GA (THWACK)
GRUH!
HFF!
POTA (DRIP)
HFF!
HFF!
HFF!

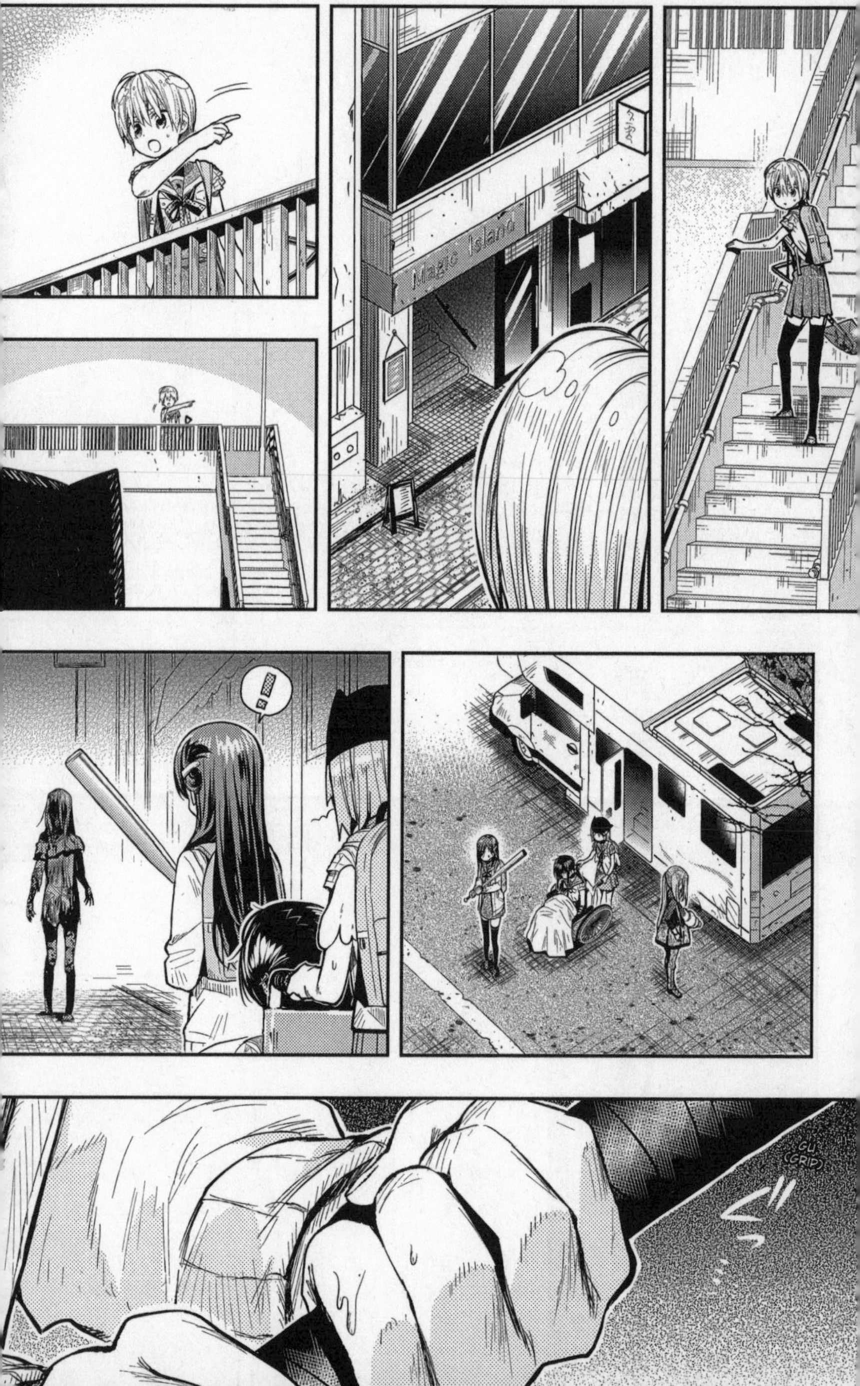
Magic Island
!
GU (GRIP)

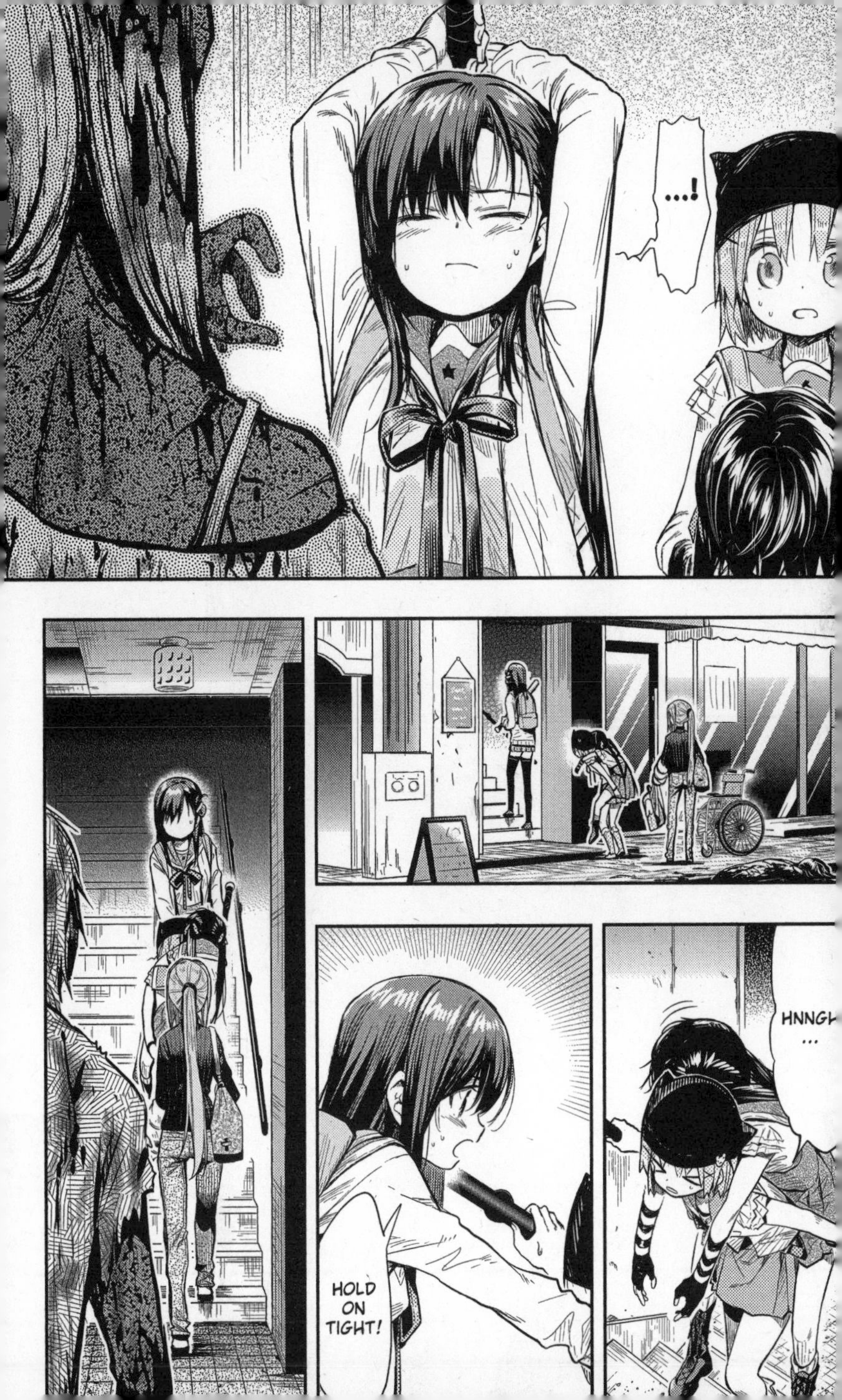
...!
HNNGH ...
HOLD ON TIGHT!

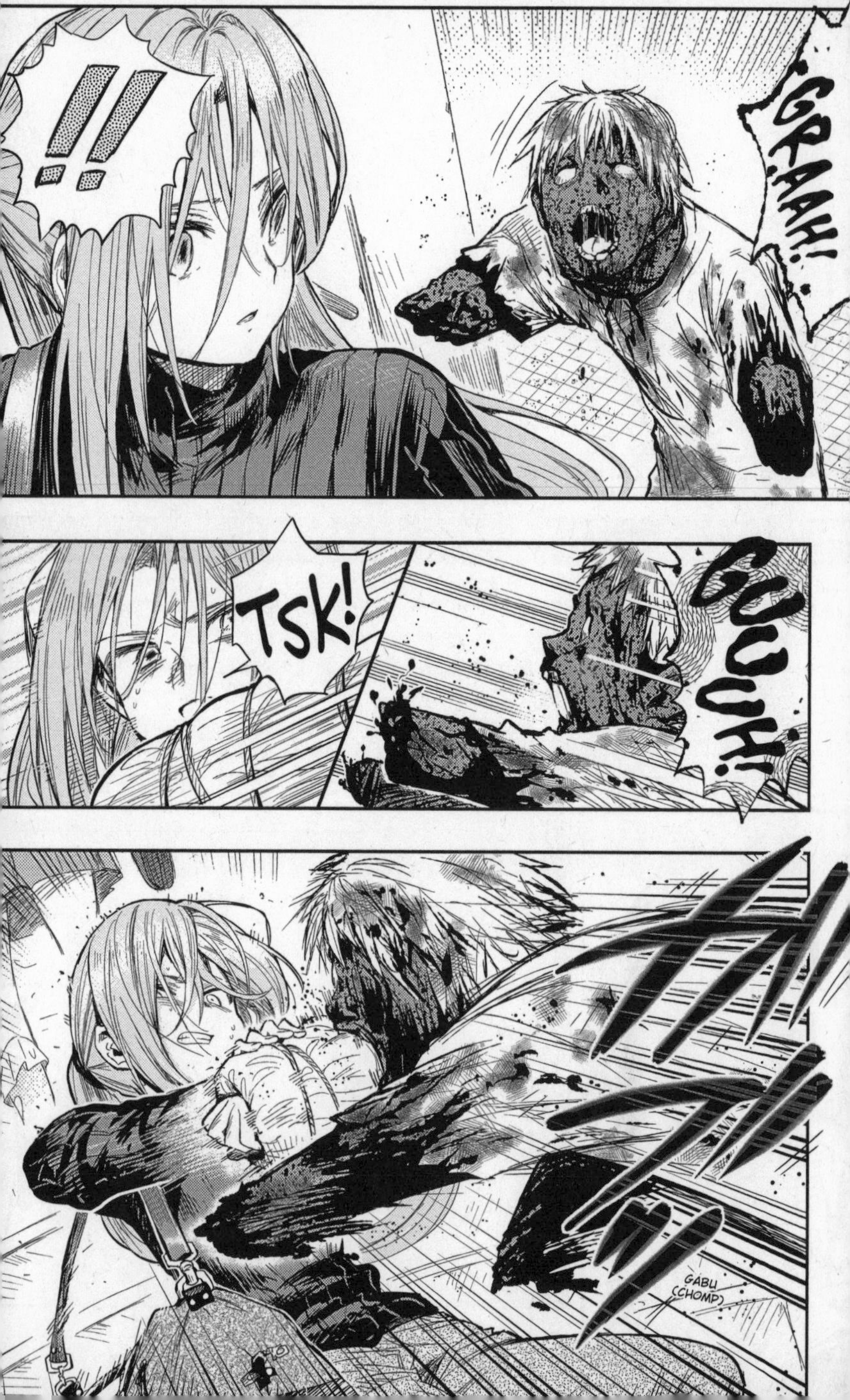
GRAAAH!
!!
GUUUH!
TSK!
GABU
(CHOMP)

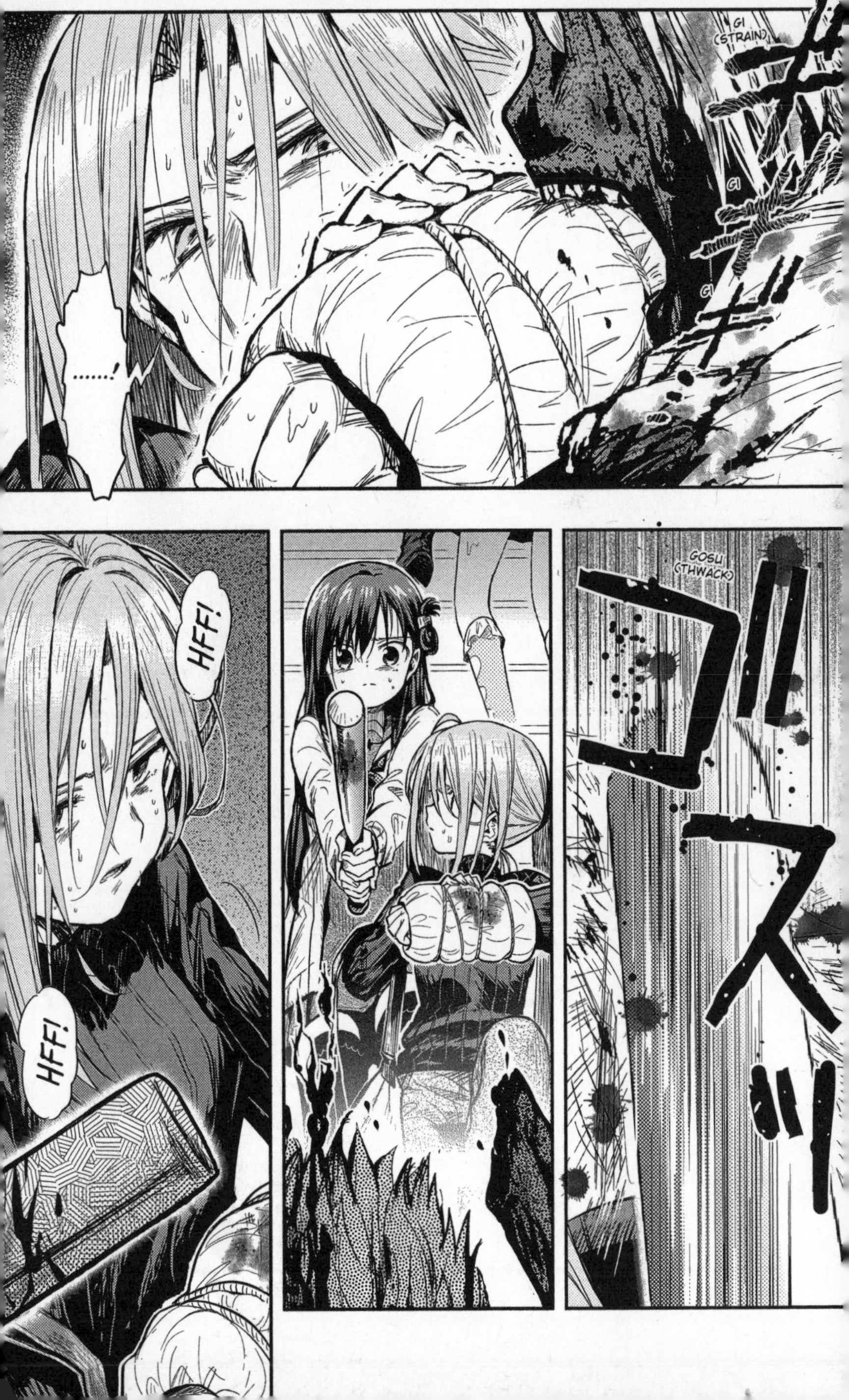
GI (STRAIN)
GI
GI
......!
GOSU (THWACK)
HFF!
HFF!

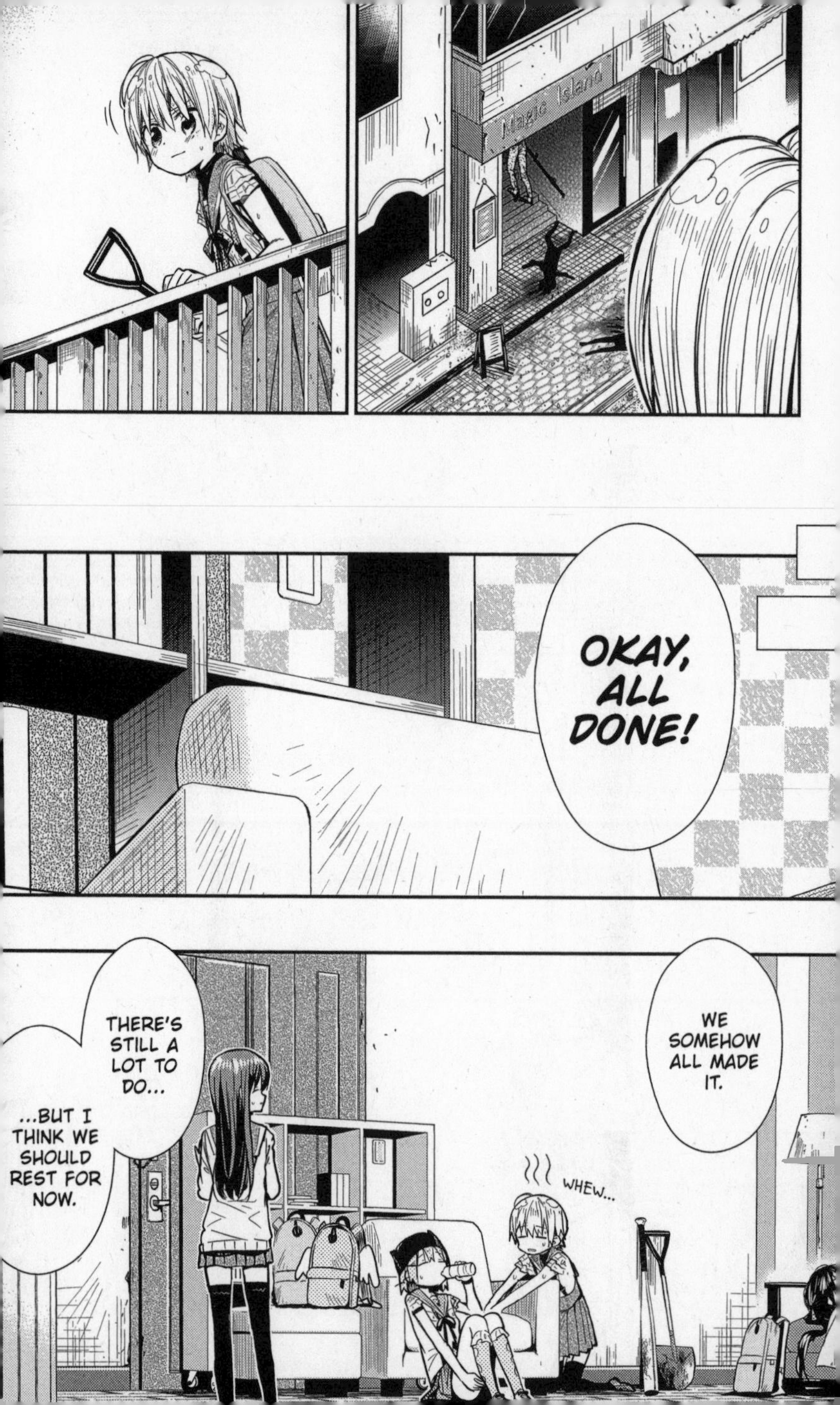
Magic Island
OKAY, ALL DONE!
WE SOMEHOW ALL MADE IT.
WHEW...
THERE'S STILL A LOT TO DO...
...BUT I THINK WE SHOULD REST FOR NOW.

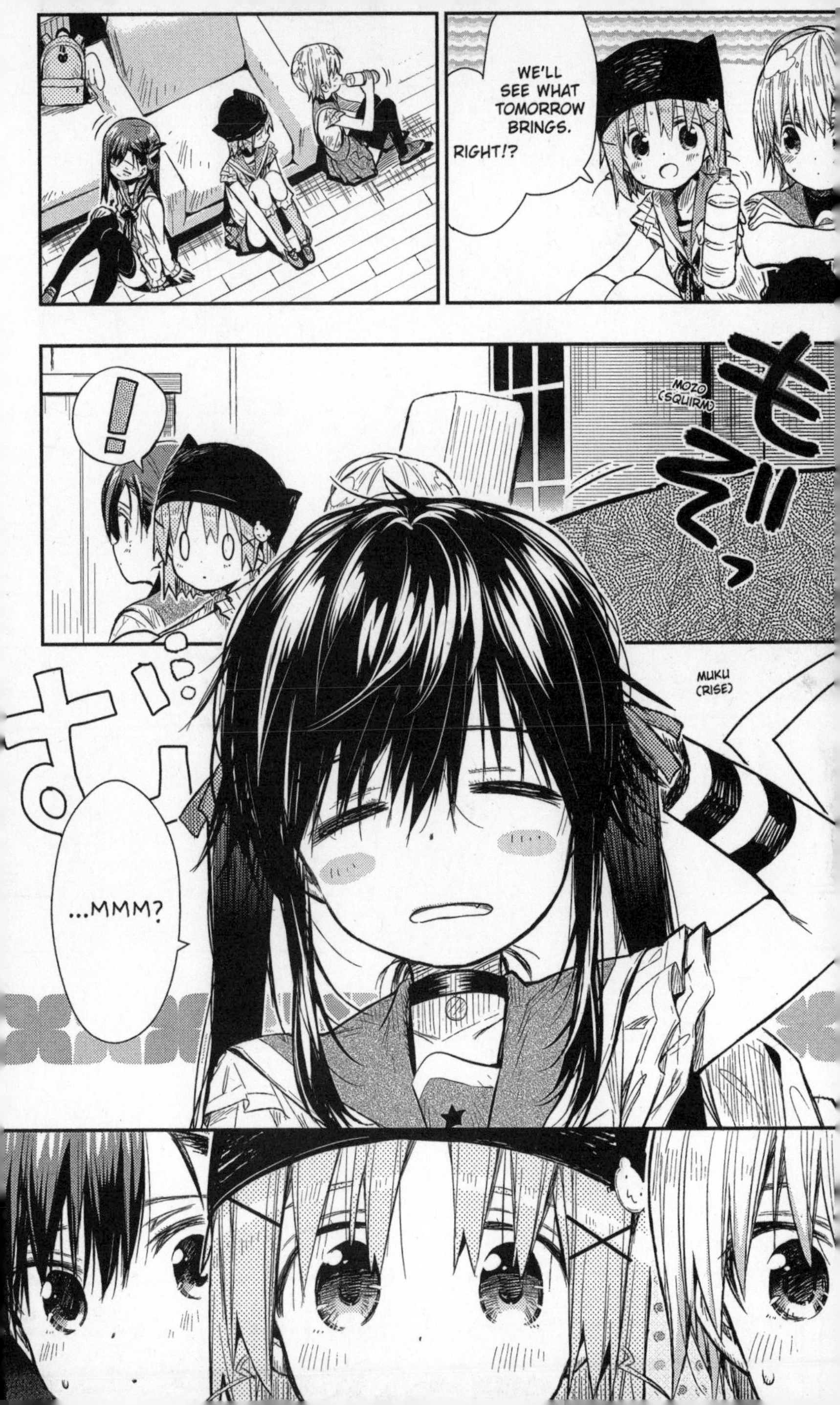
WE'LL SEE WHAT TOMORROW BRINGS.
RIGHT!?
もぞっ
MOZO (SQUIRM)
!
MUKU (RISE)
...MMM?

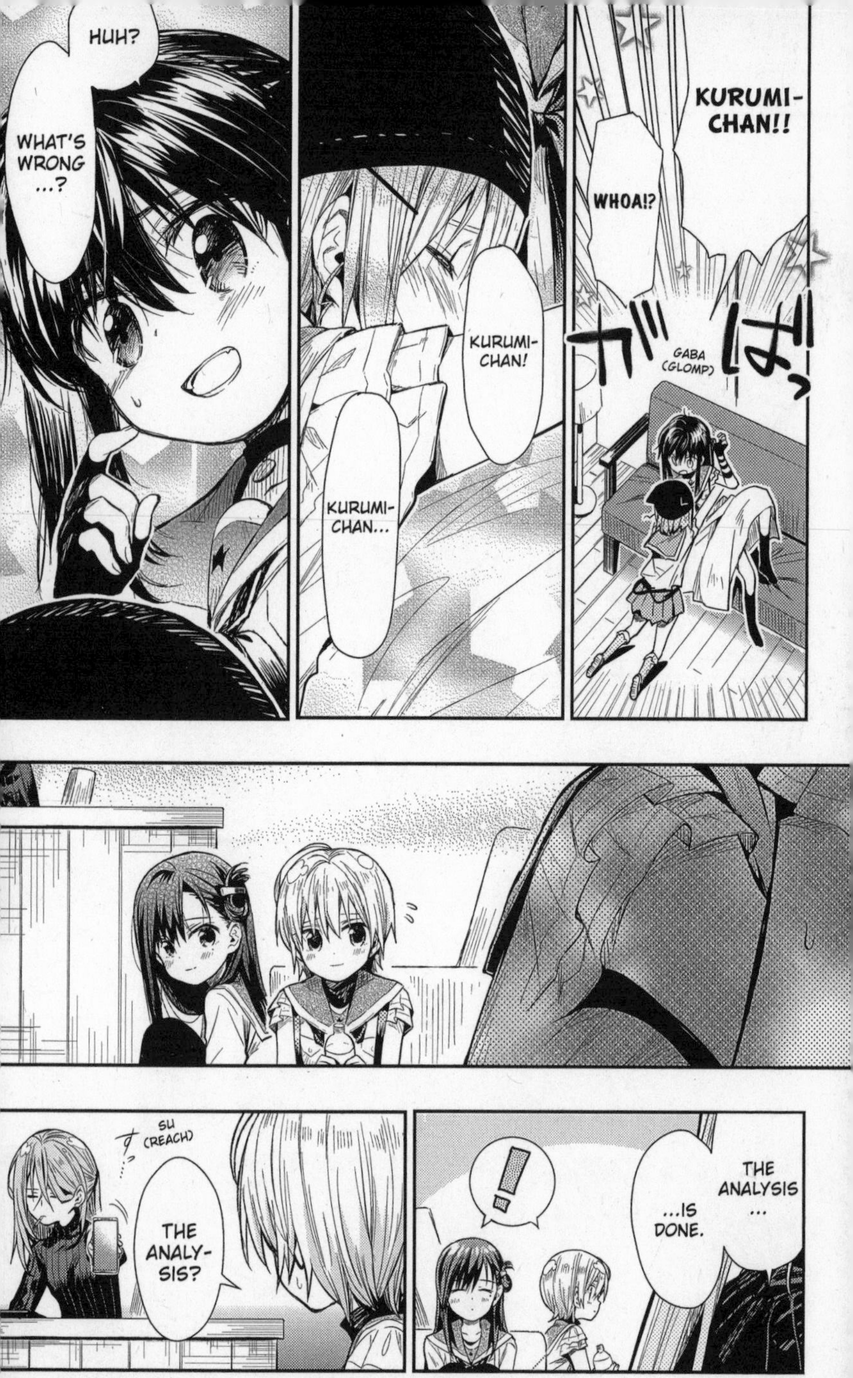
KURUMI-CHAN!!
WHOA!?
ガばっ
GABA (GLOMP)
KURUMI-CHAN!
KURUMI-CHAN...
HUH?
WHAT'S WRONG ...?
THE ANALYSIS ...
...IS DONE.
!
すっ
SU (REACH)
THE ANALY-SIS?

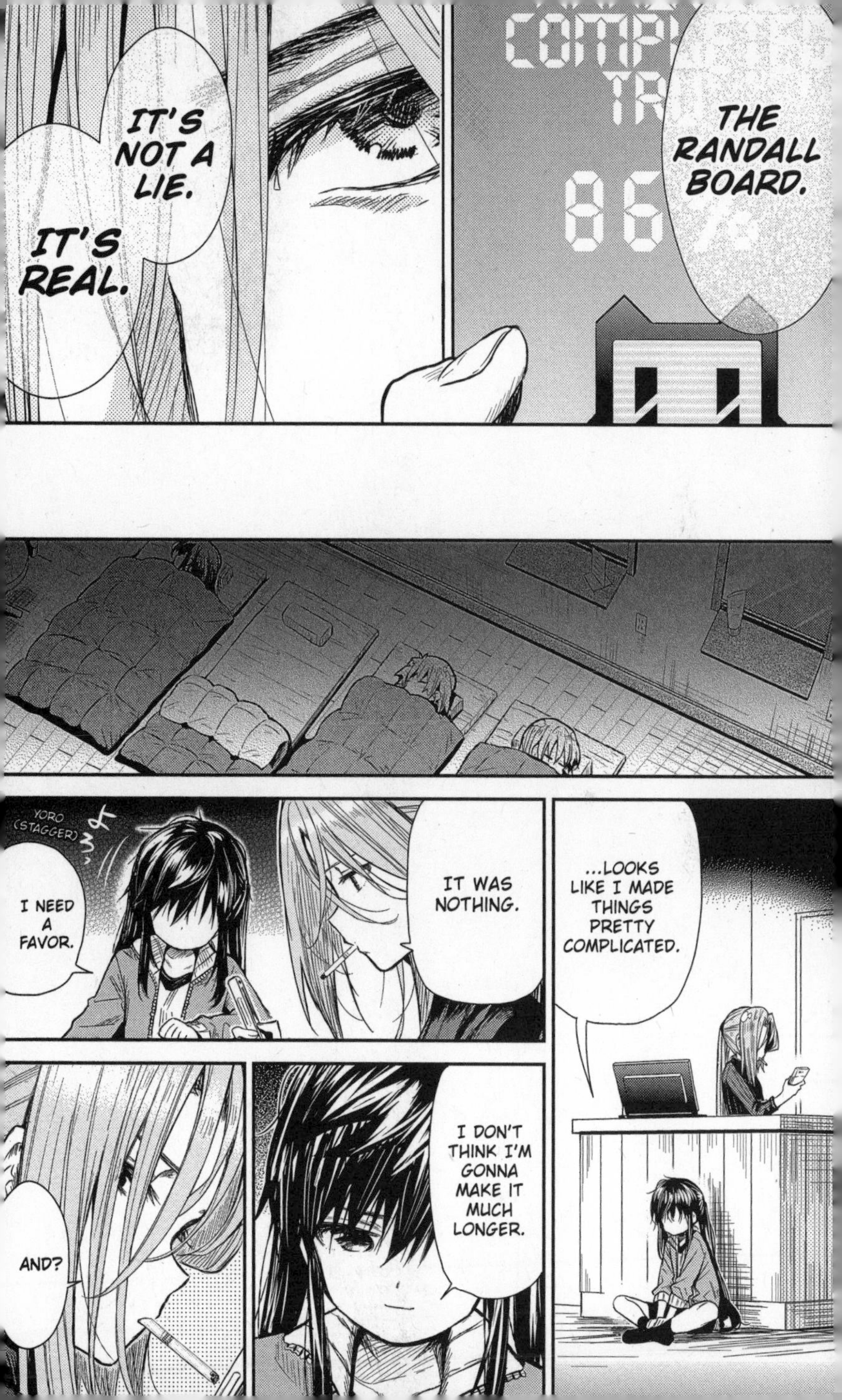
86
THE RANDALL BOARD.
IT'S NOT A LIE.
IT'S REAL.
...LOOKS LIKE I MADE THINGS PRETTY COMPLICATED.
IT WAS NOTHING.
YORO (STAGGER)
I NEED A FAVOR.
I DON'T THINK I'M GONNA MAKE IT MUCH LONGER.
AND?

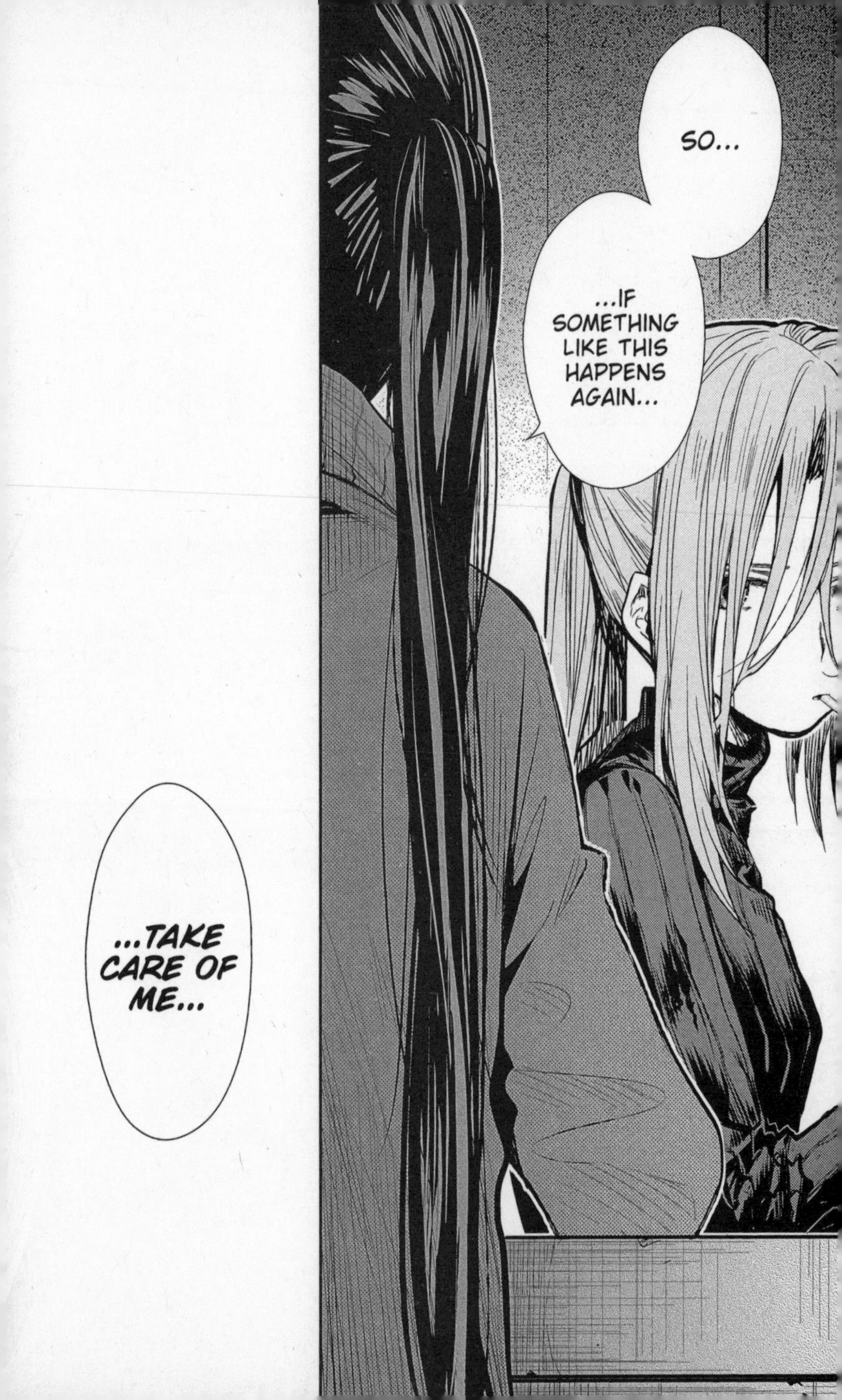
SO...
...IF SOMETHING LIKE THIS HAPPENS AGAIN...
...TAKE CARE OF ME...

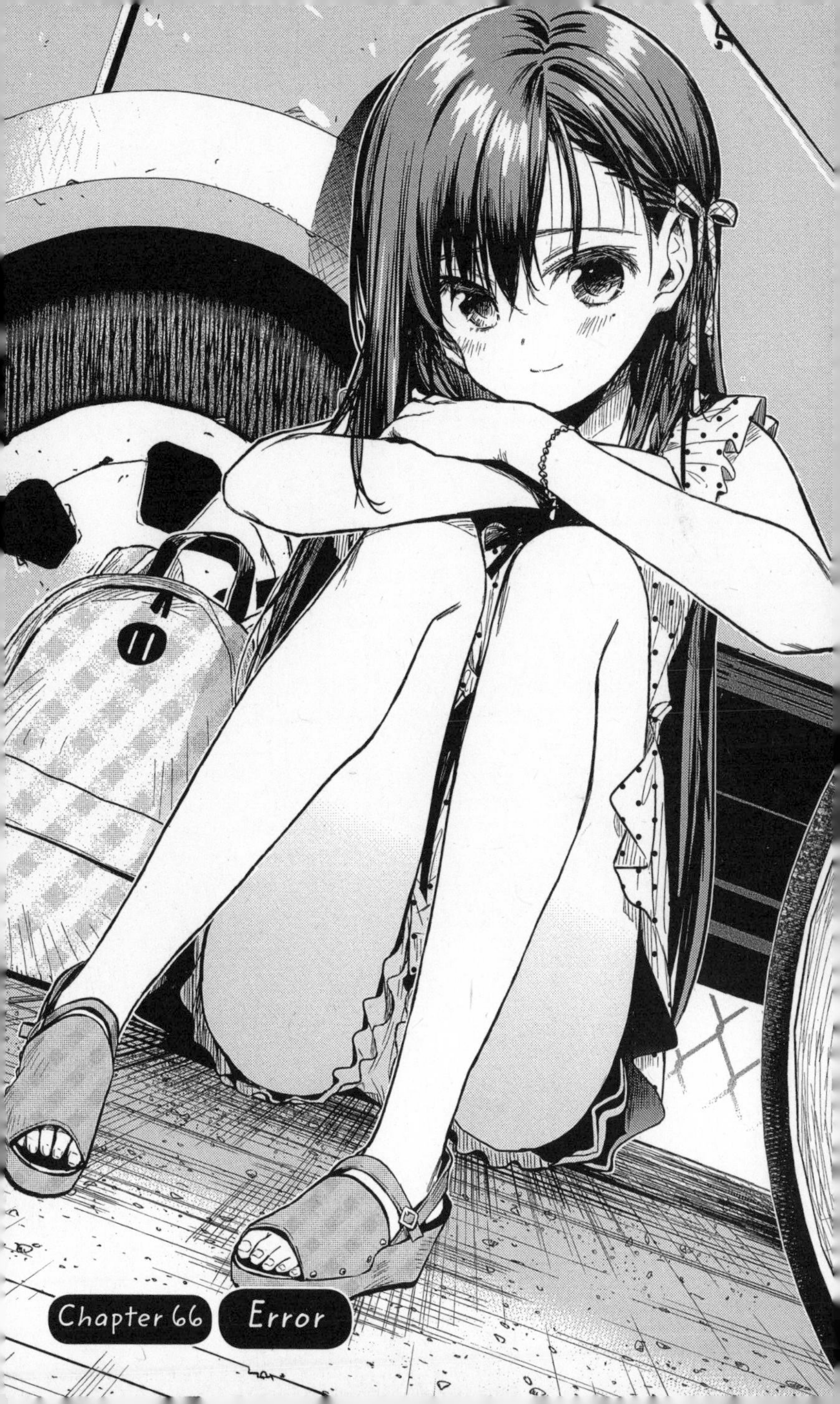
Chapter 66
Error

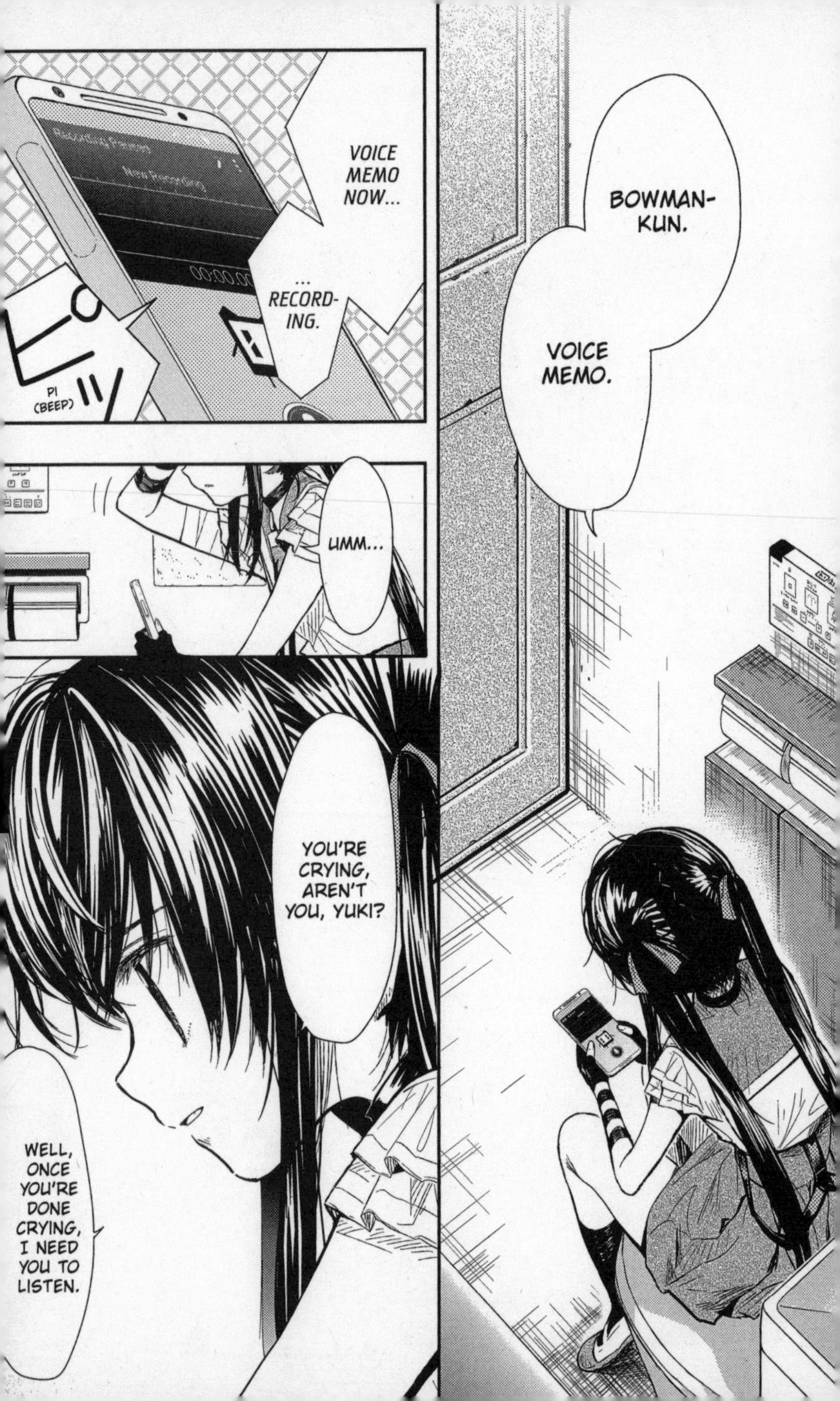
BOWMAN-KUN.
VOICE MEMO.
VOICE MEMO NOW...
...RECORDING.
PI (BEEP)
UMM...
YOU'RE CRYING, AREN'T YOU, YUKI?
WELL, ONCE YOU'RE DONE CRYING, I NEED YOU TO LISTEN.

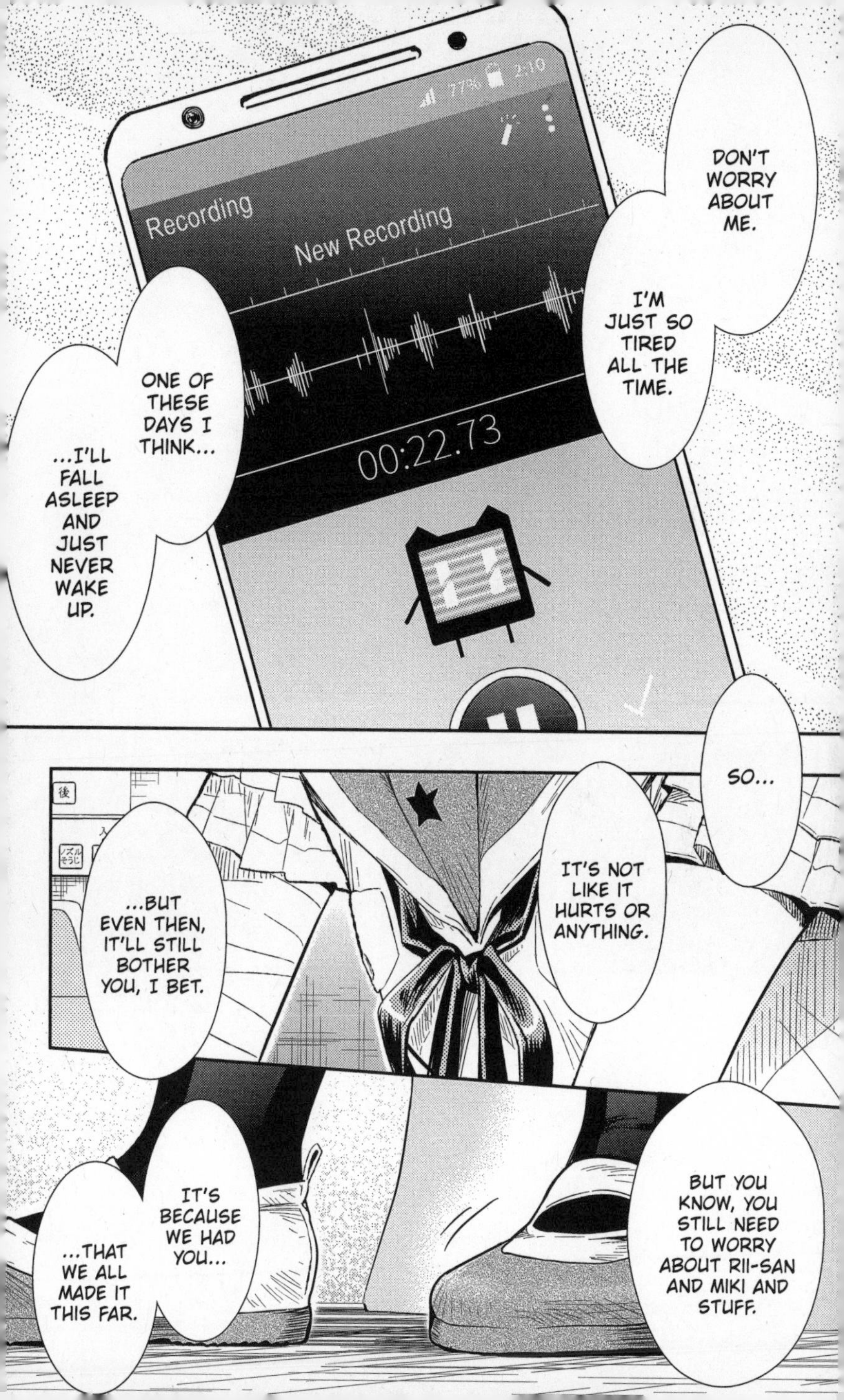
DON'T WORRY ABOUT ME.
I'M JUST SO TIRED ALL THE TIME.
Recording
New Recording
00:22.73
ONE OF THESE DAYS I THINK...
...I'LL FALL ASLEEP AND JUST NEVER WAKE UP.
SO...
IT'S NOT LIKE IT HURTS OR ANYTHING.
...BUT EVEN THEN, IT'LL STILL BOTHER YOU, I BET.
BUT YOU KNOW, YOU STILL NEED TO WORRY ABOUT RII-SAN AND MIKI AND STUFF.
IT'S BECAUSE WE HAD YOU...
...THAT WE ALL MADE IT THIS FAR.

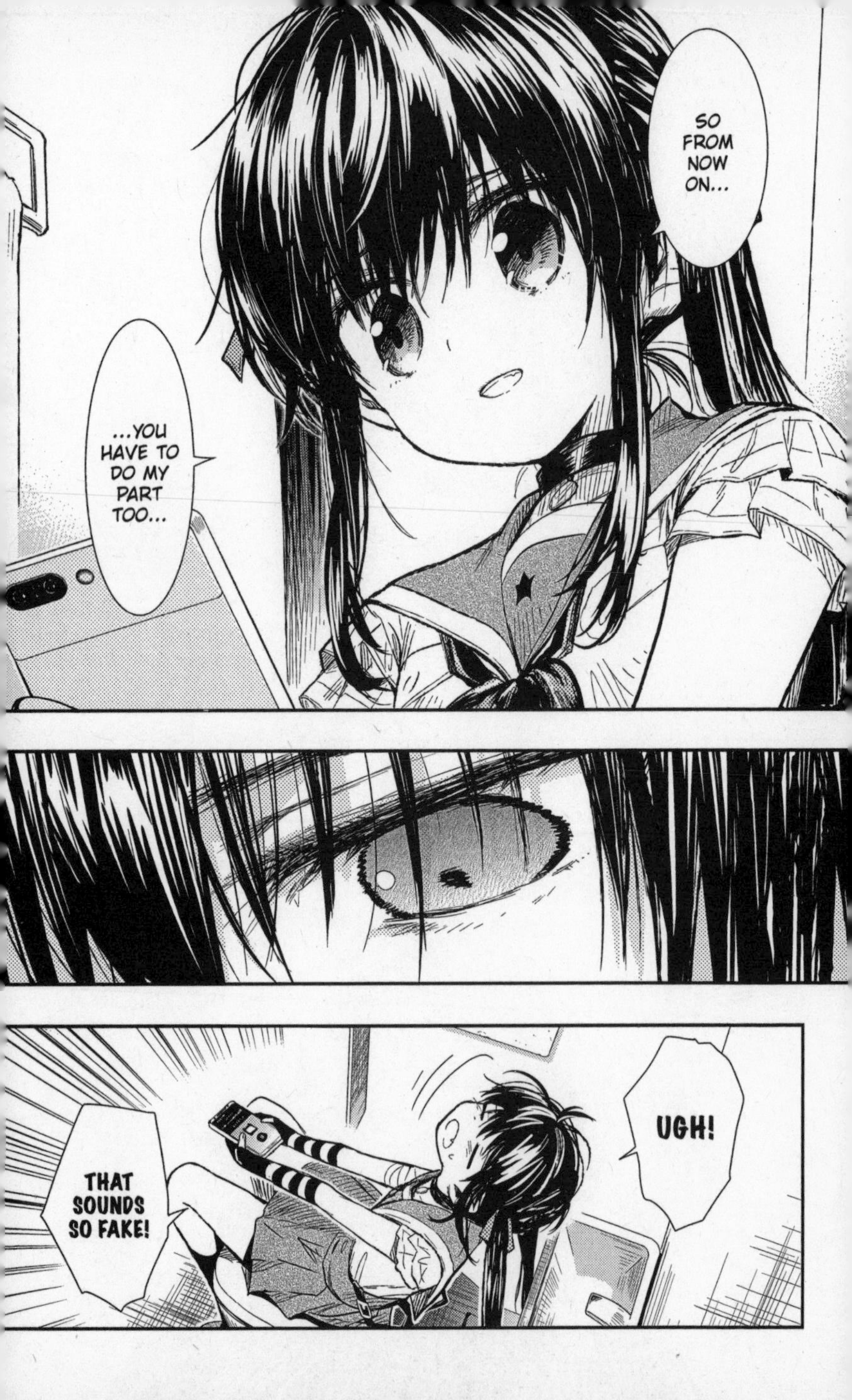
SO FROM NOW ON...
...YOU HAVE TO DO MY PART TOO...
UGH!
THAT SOUNDS SO FAKE!

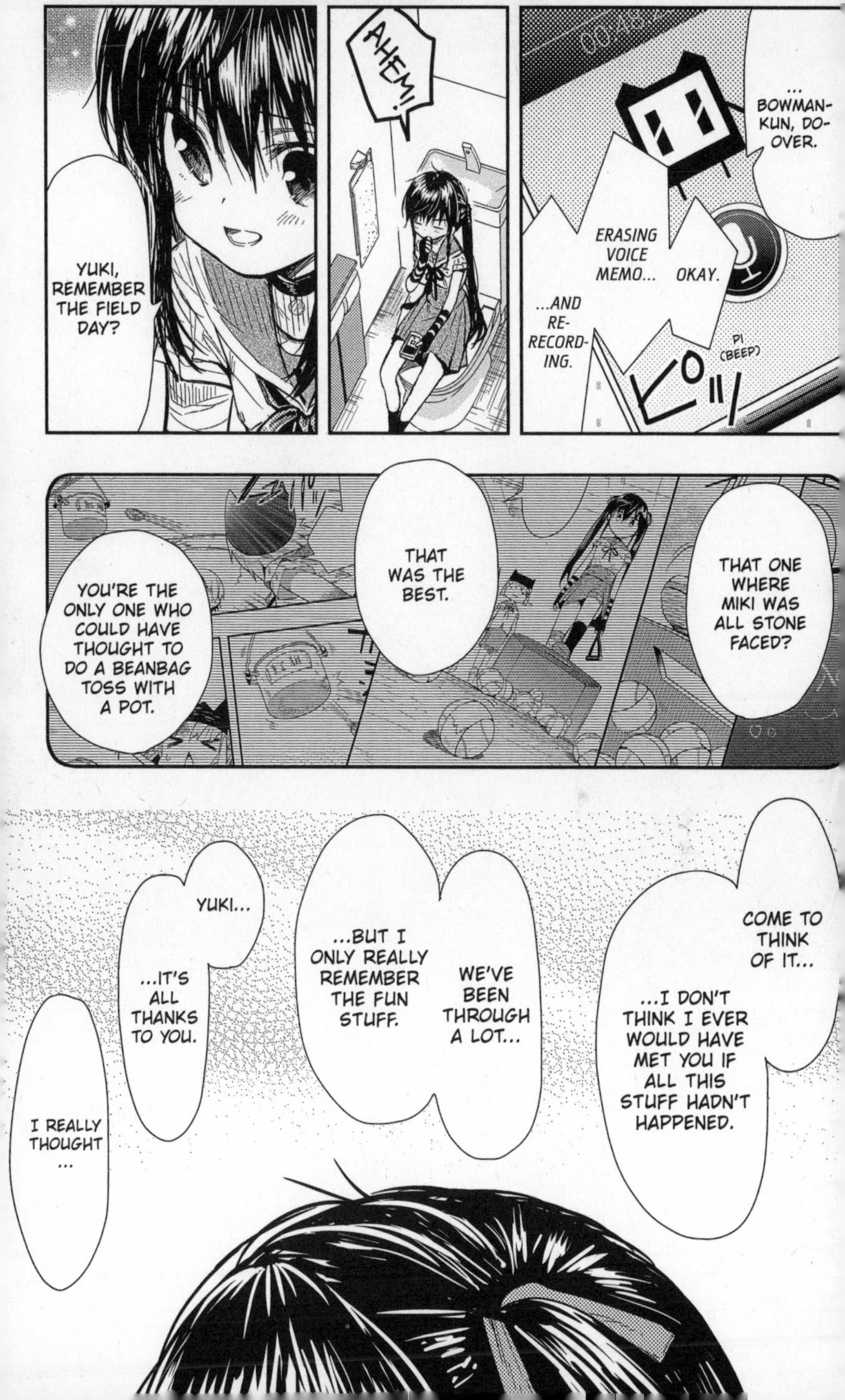
...BOWMAN-KUN, DO-OVER.
ERASING VOICE MEMO... OKAY.
...AND RE-RECORDING.
PI (BEEP)
AHEM!!
YUKI, REMEMBER THE FIELD DAY?
THAT ONE WHERE MIKI WAS ALL STONE FACED?
THAT WAS THE BEST.
YOU'RE THE ONLY ONE WHO COULD HAVE THOUGHT TO DO A BEANBAG TOSS WITH A POT.
COME TO THINK OF IT...
...I DON'T THINK I EVER WOULD HAVE MET YOU IF ALL THIS STUFF HADN'T HAPPENED.
WE'VE BEEN THROUGH A LOT...
...BUT I ONLY REALLY REMEMBER THE FUN STUFF.
YUKI...
...IT'S ALL THANKS TO YOU.
I REALLY THOUGHT ...

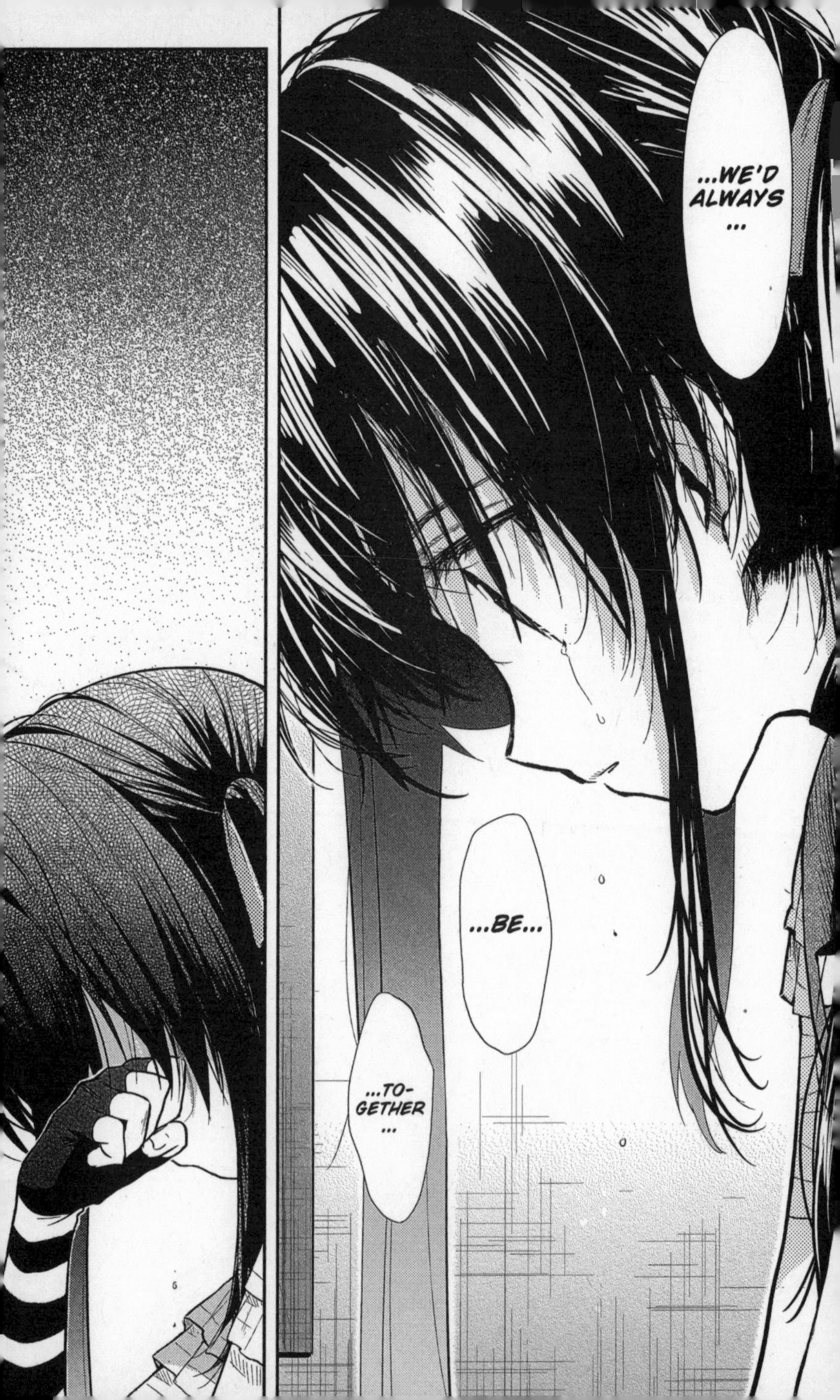
...WE'D ALWAYS ...
...BE...
...TO-GETHER ...

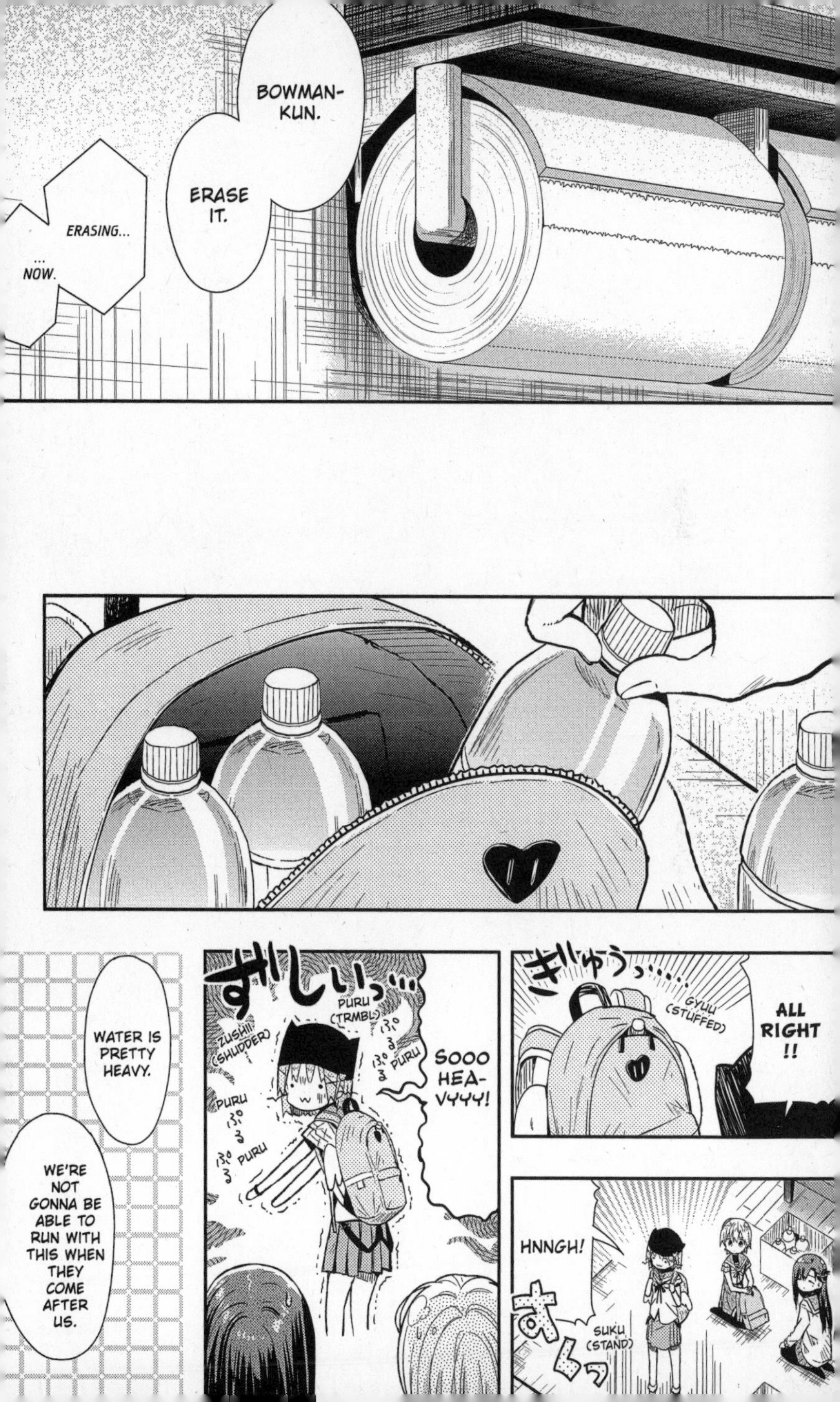
BOWMAN-KUN.
ERASE IT.
ERASING... ...NOW.
ぎゅう っ……
GYUU (STUFFED)
ALL RIGHT!!
HNNGH!
すくっ
SUKU (STAND)
ずしぃっ…
ZUSHII (SHUDDER)
PURU (TRMBL)
ぷるぷる
PURU
SOOO HEA-VYYY!
PURU
ぷるぷる
PURU
WATER IS PRETTY HEAVY.
WE'RE NOT GONNA BE ABLE TO RUN WITH THIS WHEN THEY COME AFTER US.

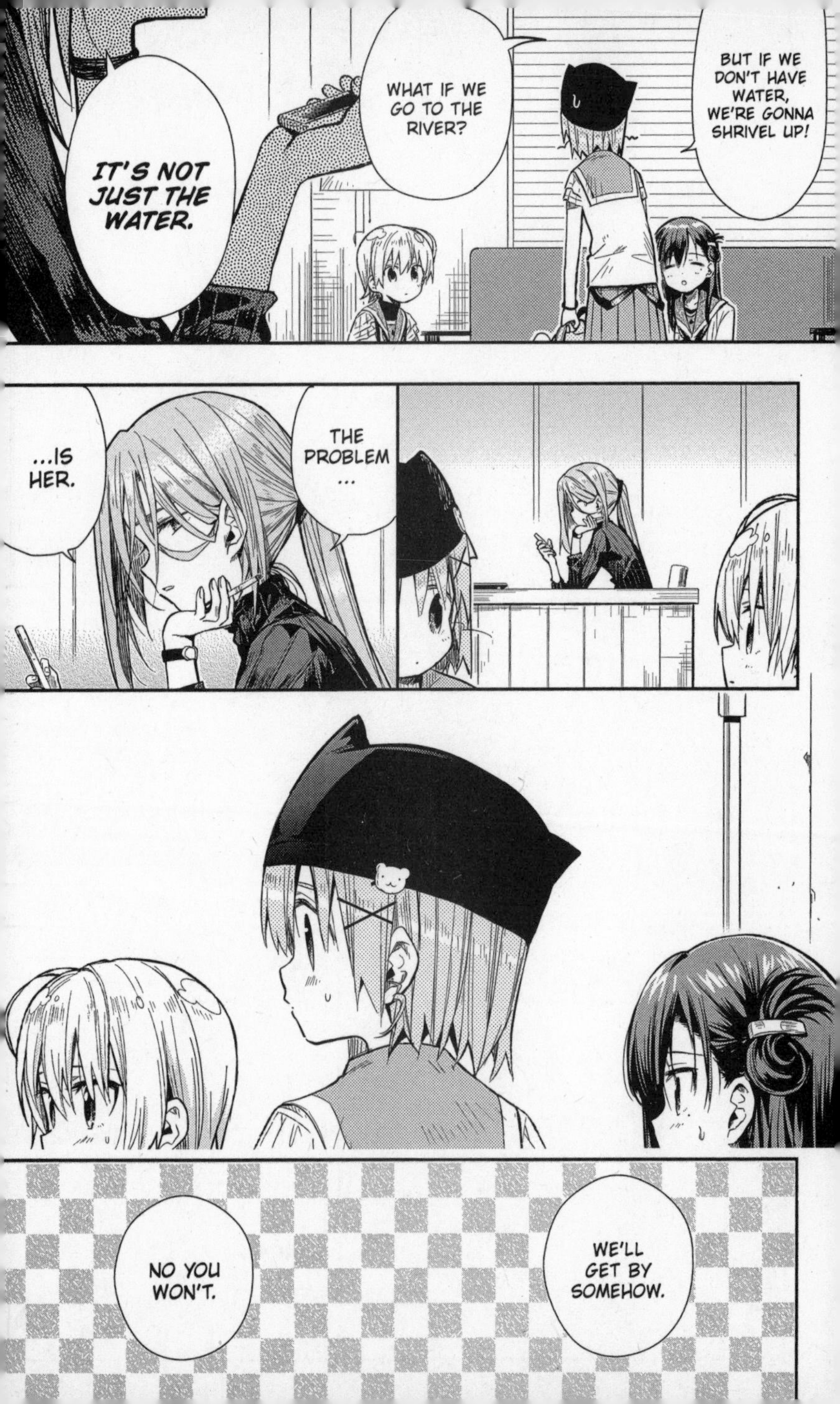
BUT IF WE DON'T HAVE WATER, WE'RE GONNA SHRIVEL UP!
WHAT IF WE GO TO THE RIVER?
IT'S NOT JUST THE WATER.
THE PROBLEM ...
...IS HER.
WE'LL GET BY SOMEHOW.
NO YOU WON'T.

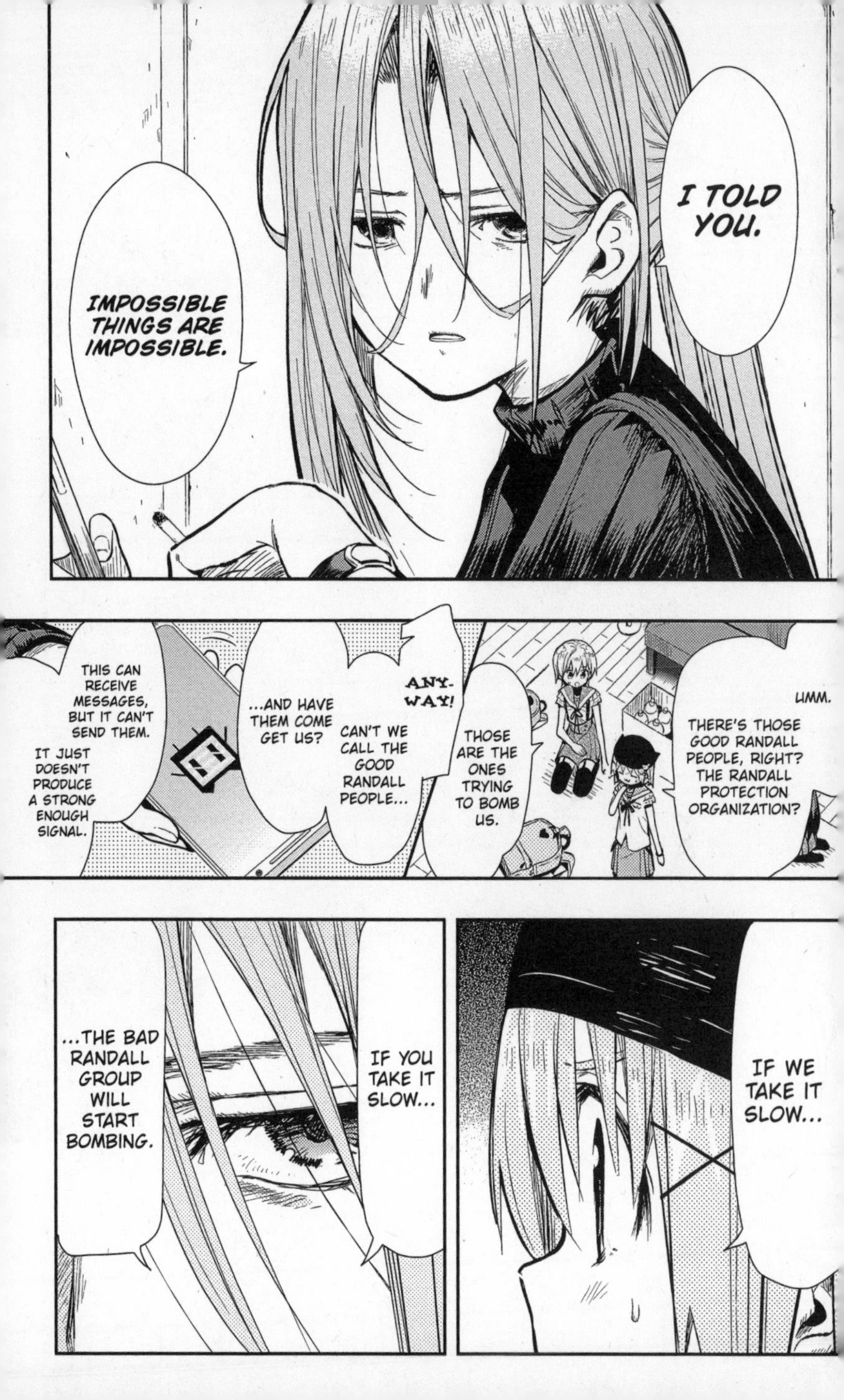
I TOLD YOU.
IMPOSSIBLE THINGS ARE IMPOSSIBLE.
UMM.
THERE'S THOSE GOOD RANDALL PEOPLE, RIGHT? THE RANDALL PROTECTION ORGANIZATION?
THOSE ARE THE ONES TRYING TO BOMB US.
ANY-WAY!
CAN'T WE CALL THE GOOD RANDALL PEOPLE...
...AND HAVE THEM COME GET US?
THIS CAN RECEIVE MESSAGES, BUT IT CAN'T SEND THEM.
IT JUST DOESN'T PRODUCE A STRONG ENOUGH SIGNAL.
IF WE TAKE IT SLOW...
IF YOU TAKE IT SLOW...
...THE BAD RANDALL GROUP WILL START BOMBING.

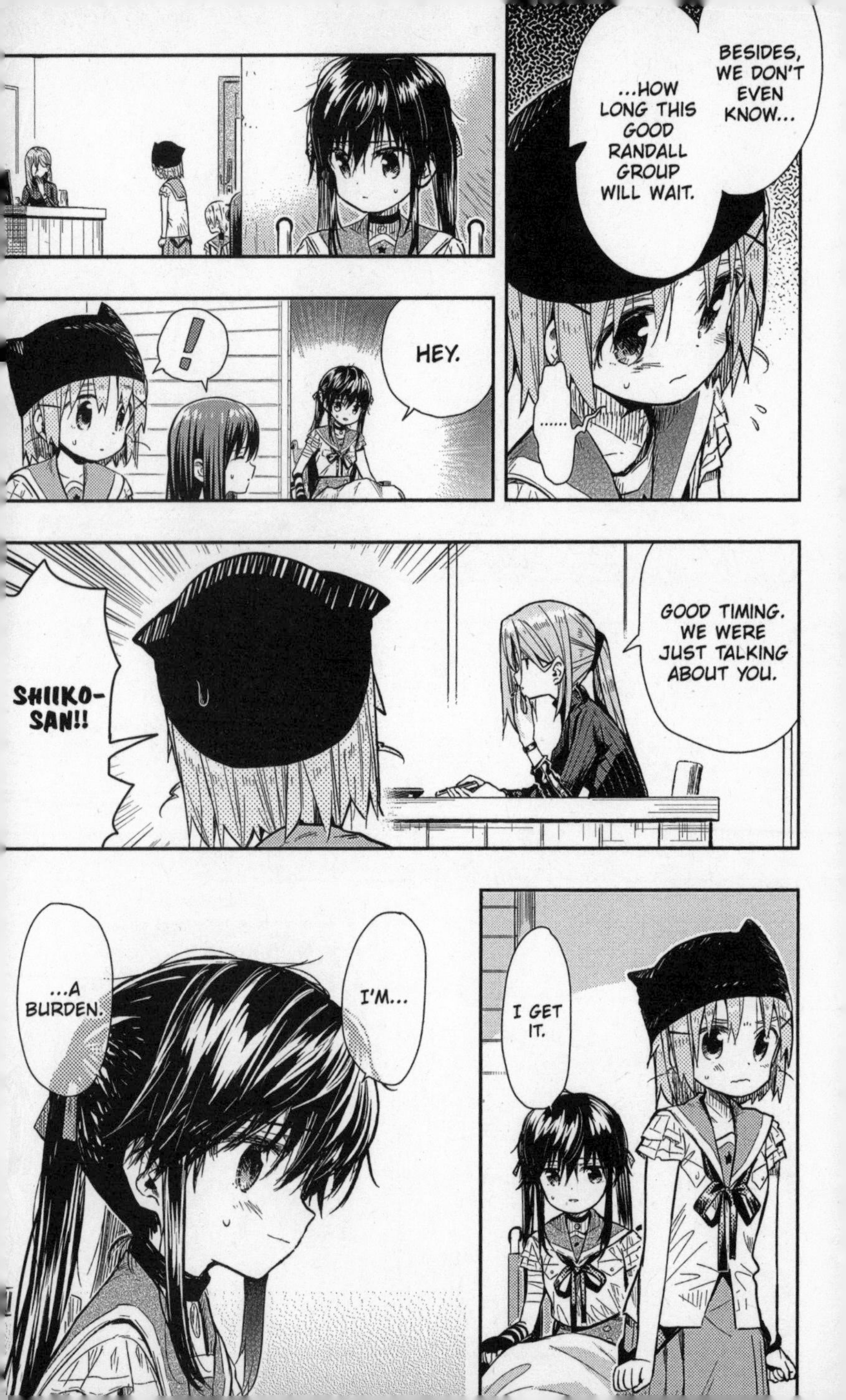
BESIDES, WE DON'T EVEN KNOW...
...HOW LONG THIS GOOD RANDALL GROUP WILL WAIT.
......
HEY.
!
GOOD TIMING. WE WERE JUST TALKING ABOUT YOU.
SHIIKO-SAN!!
I GET IT.
I'M...
...A BURDEN.

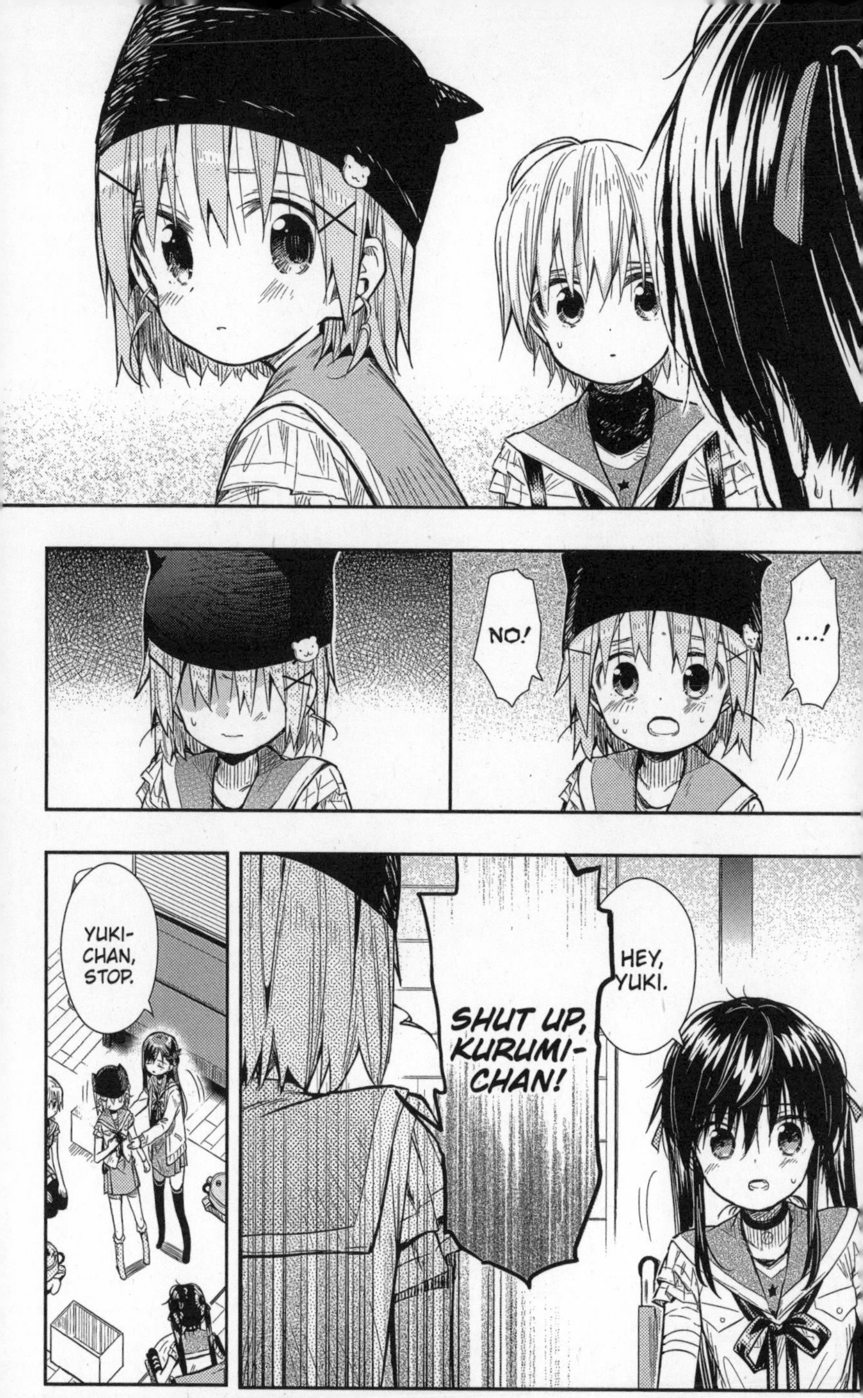
...!
NO!
HEY, YUKI.
SHUT UP, KURUMI-CHAN!
YUKI-CHAN, STOP.

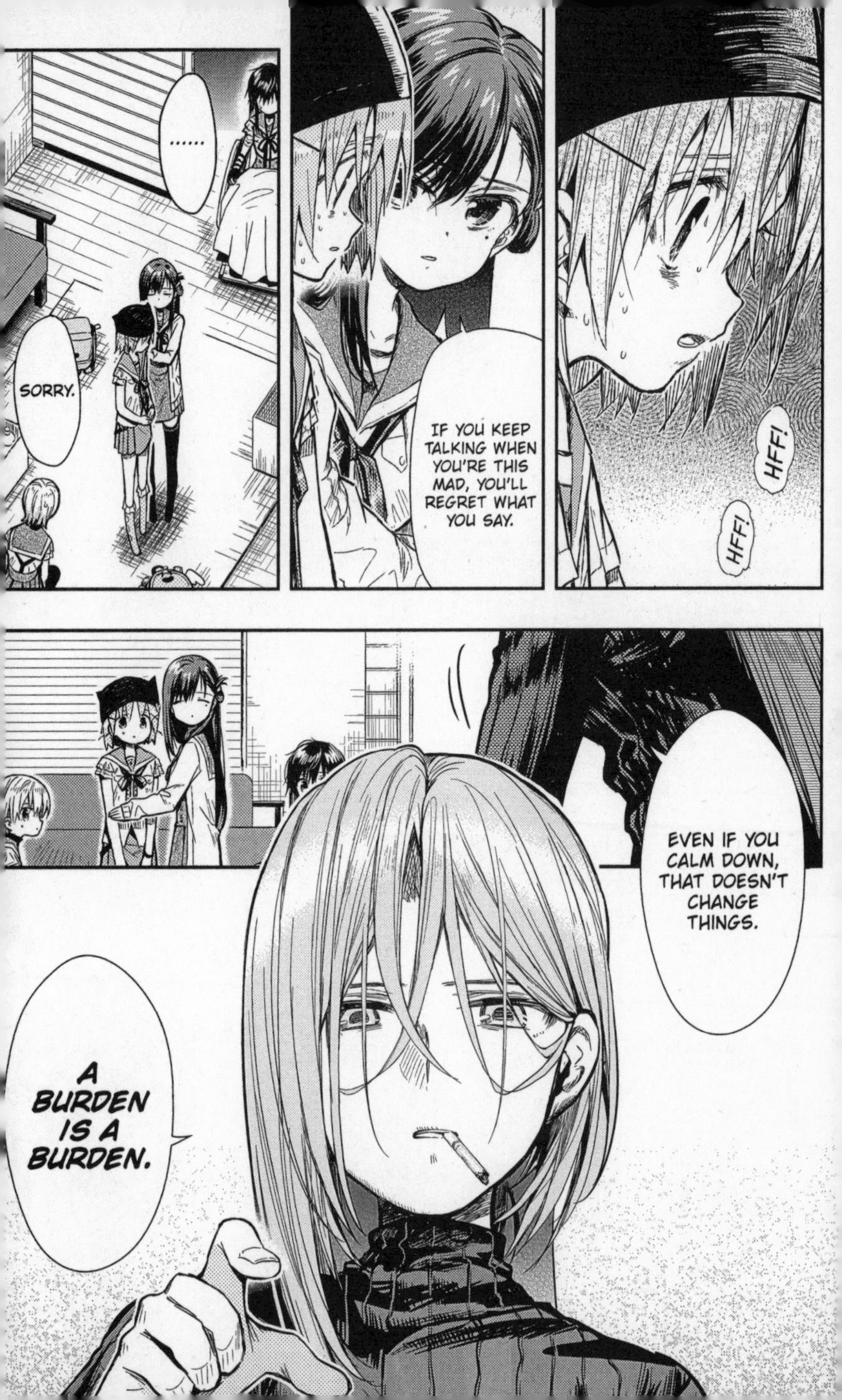
HFF!
HFF!
IF YOU KEEP TALKING WHEN YOU'RE THIS MAD, YOU'LL REGRET WHAT YOU SAY.
......
SORRY.
EVEN IF YOU CALM DOWN, THAT DOESN'T CHANGE THINGS.
A BURDEN IS A BURDEN.

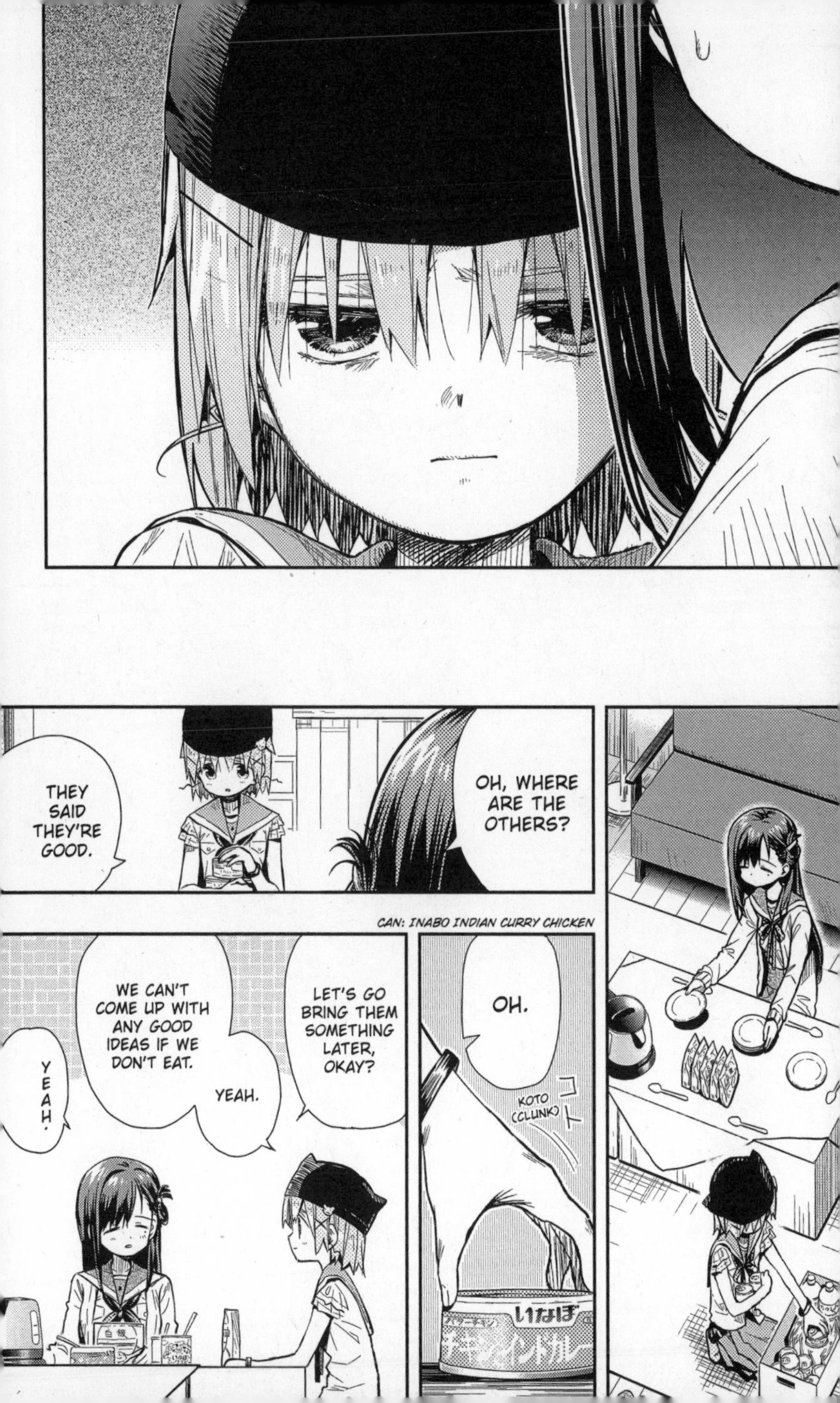
OH, WHERE ARE THE OTHERS?
THEY SAID THEY'RE GOOD.
CAN: INABO INDIAN CURRY CHICKEN
OH.
KOTO (CLUNK)
いなぼ
LET'S GO BRING THEM SOMETHING LATER, OKAY?
YEAH.
WE CAN'T COME UP WITH ANY GOOD IDEAS IF WE DON'T EAT.
YEAH.

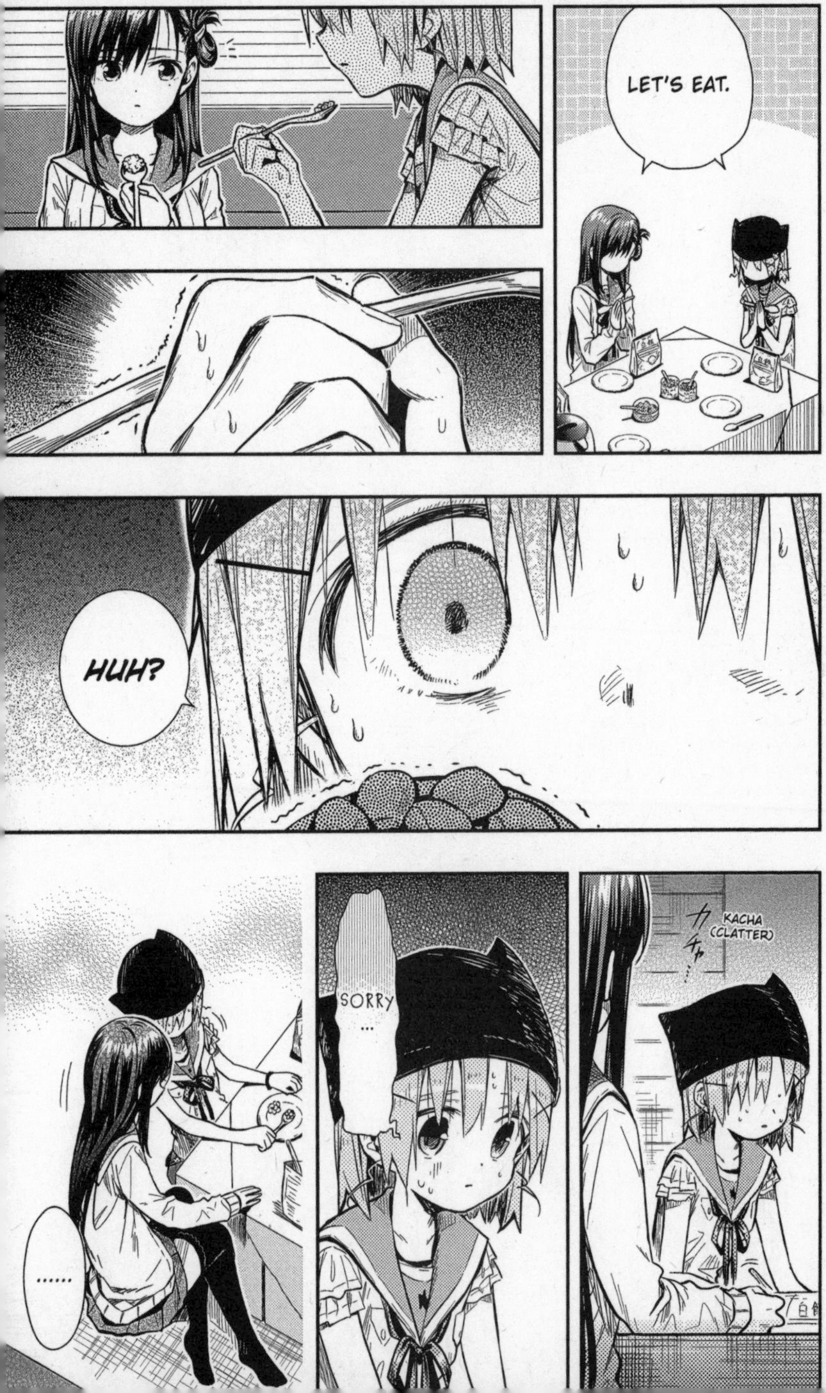
LET'S EAT.
HUH?
カチャ…
KACHA (CLATTER)
SORRY...
......

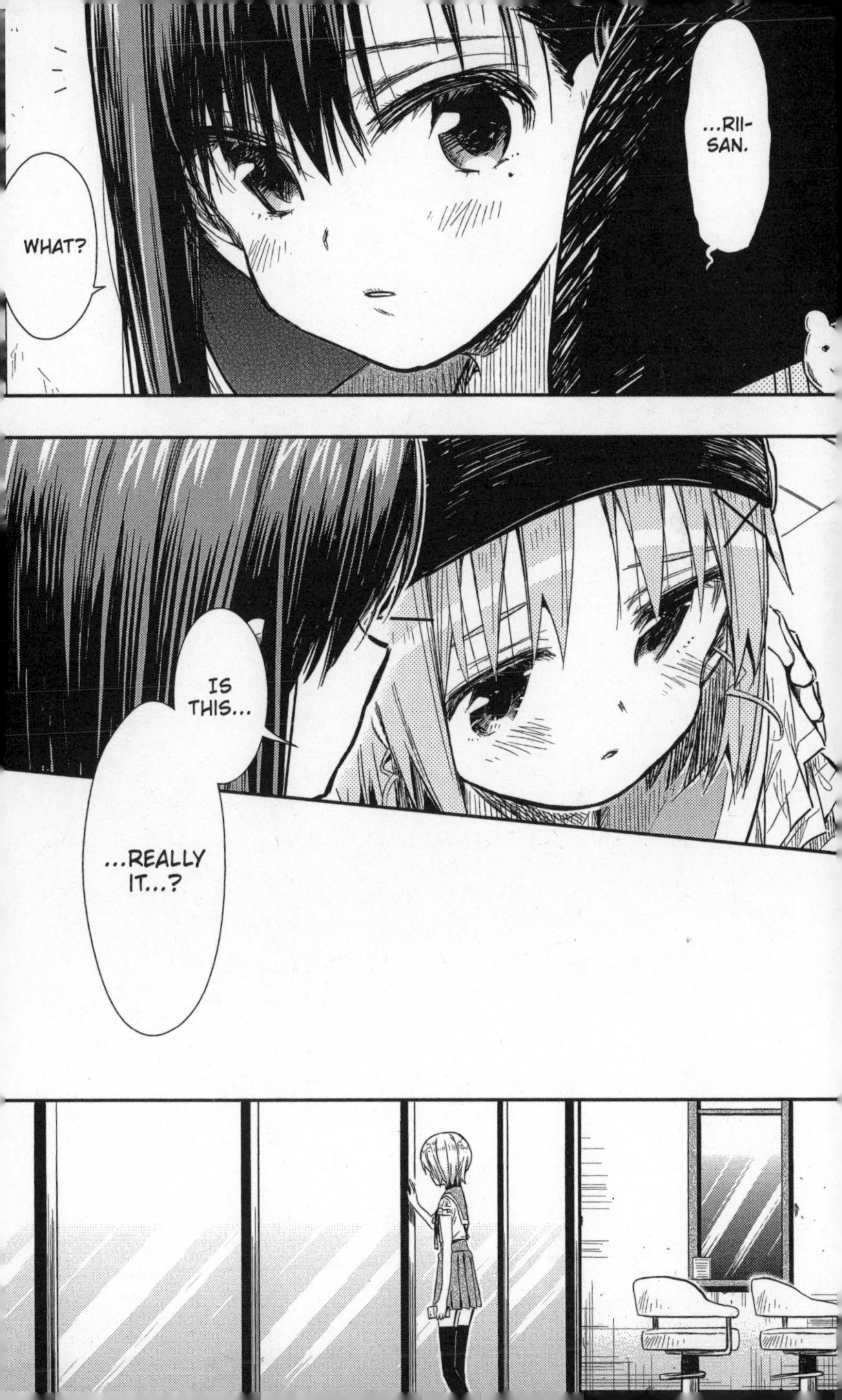
...RII-SAN.
WHAT?
IS THIS...
...REALLY IT...?

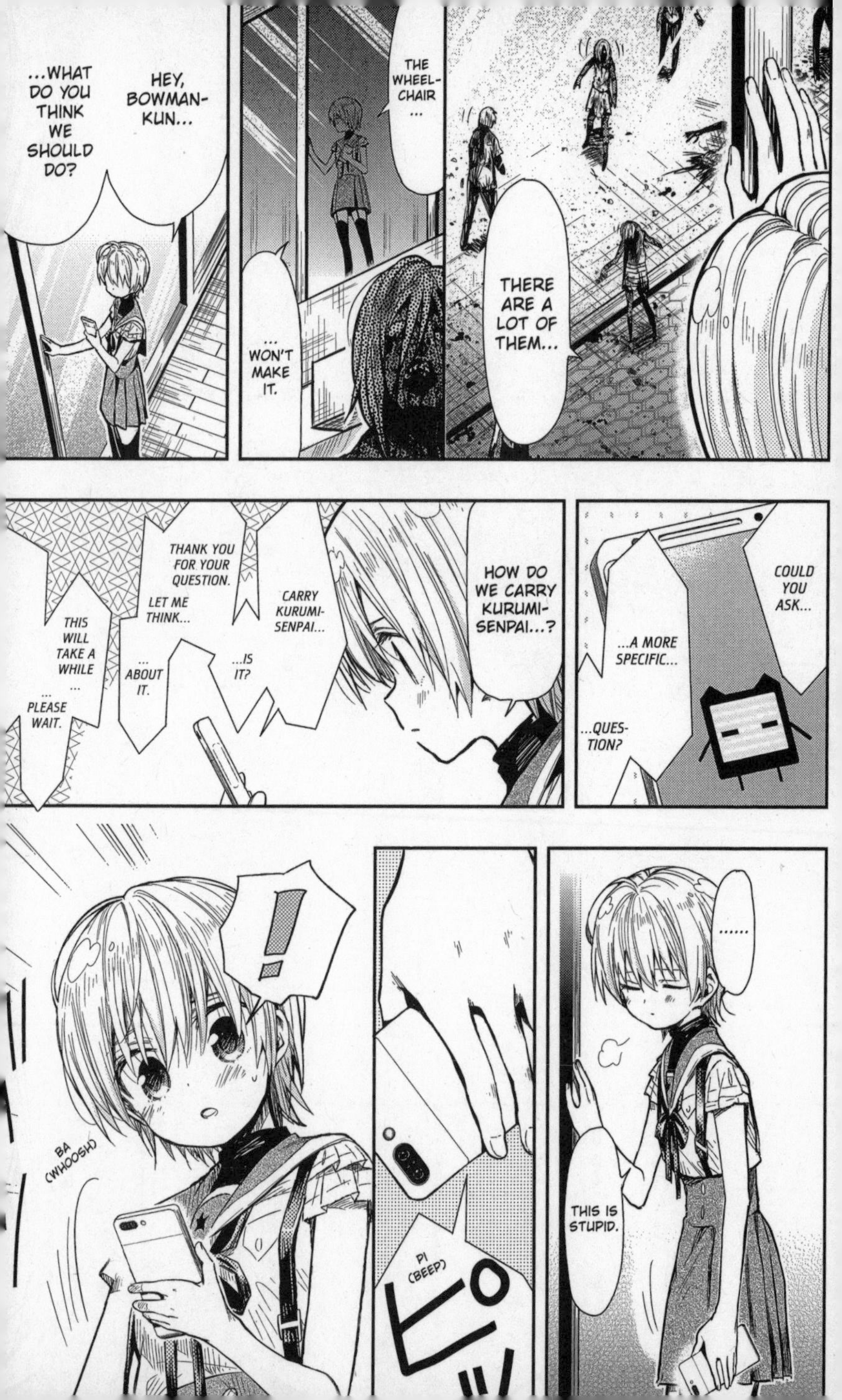
THERE ARE A LOT OF THEM...
THE WHEEL-CHAIR ...
... WON'T MAKE IT.
HEY, BOWMAN-KUN...
...WHAT DO YOU THINK WE SHOULD DO?
COULD YOU ASK...
...A MORE SPECIFIC...
...QUES-TION?
HOW DO WE CARRY KURUMI-SENPAI...?
CARRY KURUMI-SENPAI...
...IS IT?
THANK YOU FOR YOUR QUESTION.
LET ME THINK...
... ABOUT IT.
THIS WILL TAKE A WHILE ...
... PLEASE WAIT.
......
THIS IS STUPID.
PI (BEEP)
ピッ
!
BA (WHOOSH)

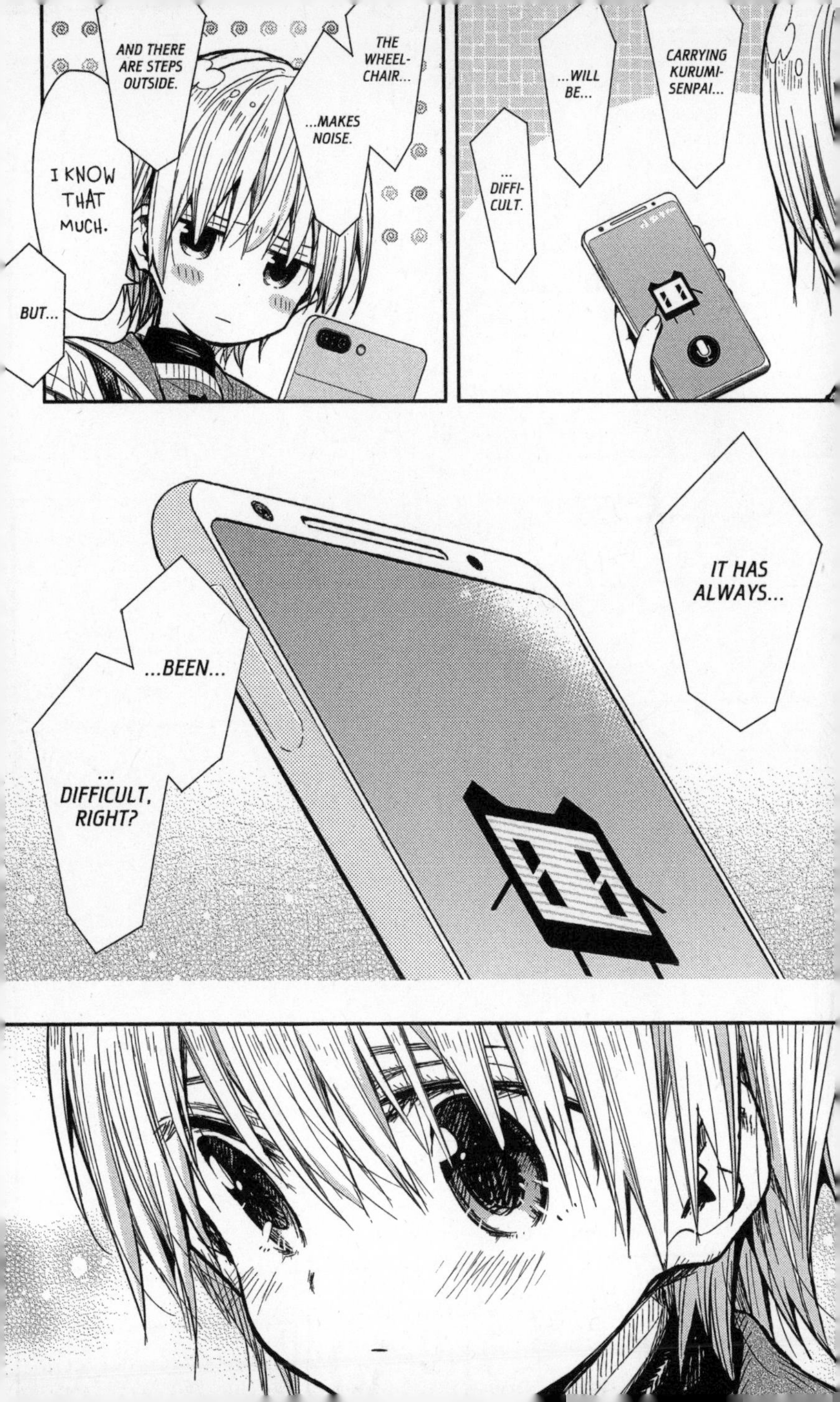
CARRYING KURUMI-SENPAI...
...WILL BE...
...DIFFICULT.
THE WHEEL-CHAIR...
...MAKES NOISE.
AND THERE ARE STEPS OUTSIDE.
I KNOW THAT MUCH.
BUT...
IT HAS ALWAYS...
...BEEN...
...DIFFICULT, RIGHT?

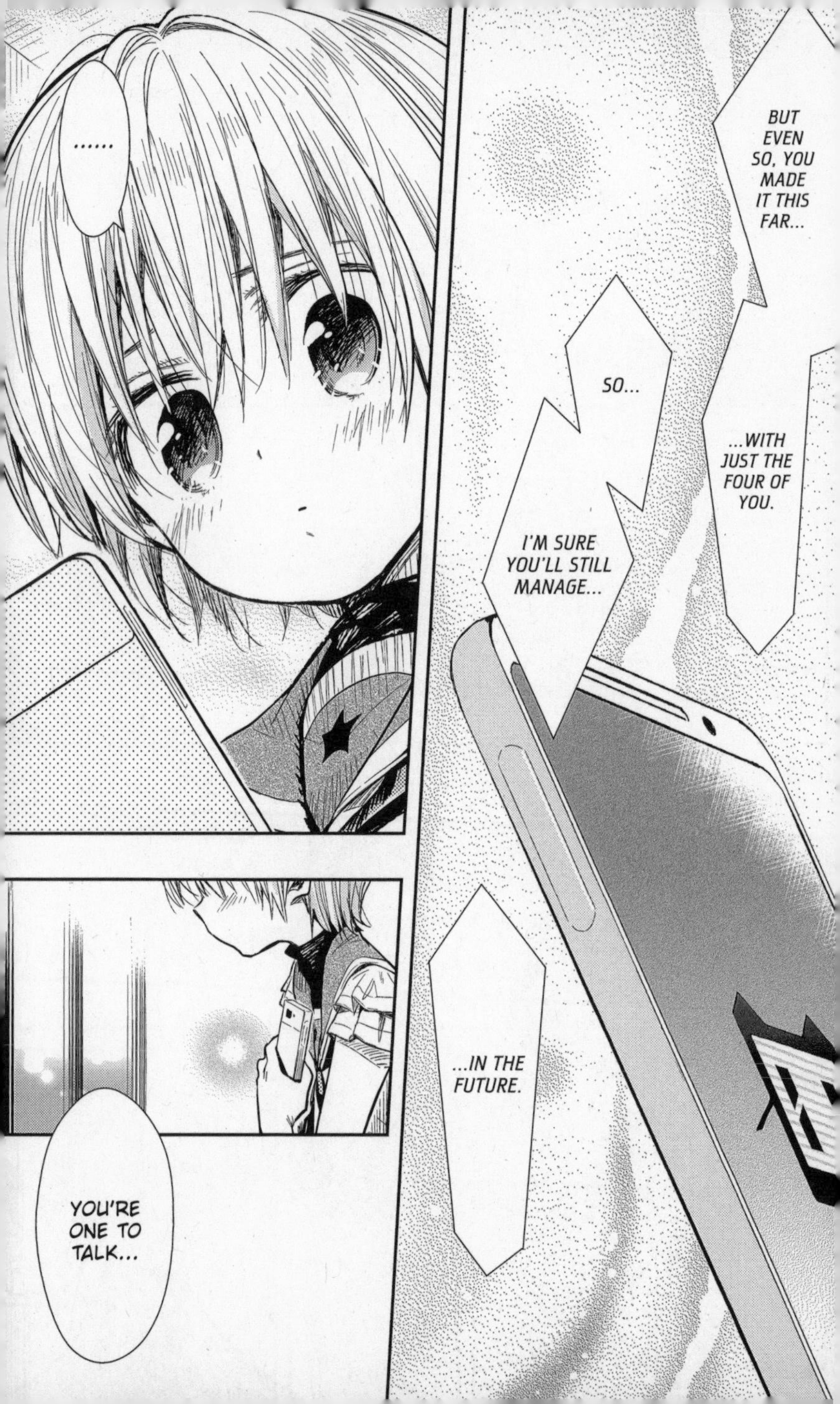
BUT EVEN SO, YOU MADE IT THIS FAR...
...WITH JUST THE FOUR OF YOU.
SO...
I'M SURE YOU'LL STILL MANAGE...
...IN THE FUTURE.
......
YOU'RE ONE TO TALK...

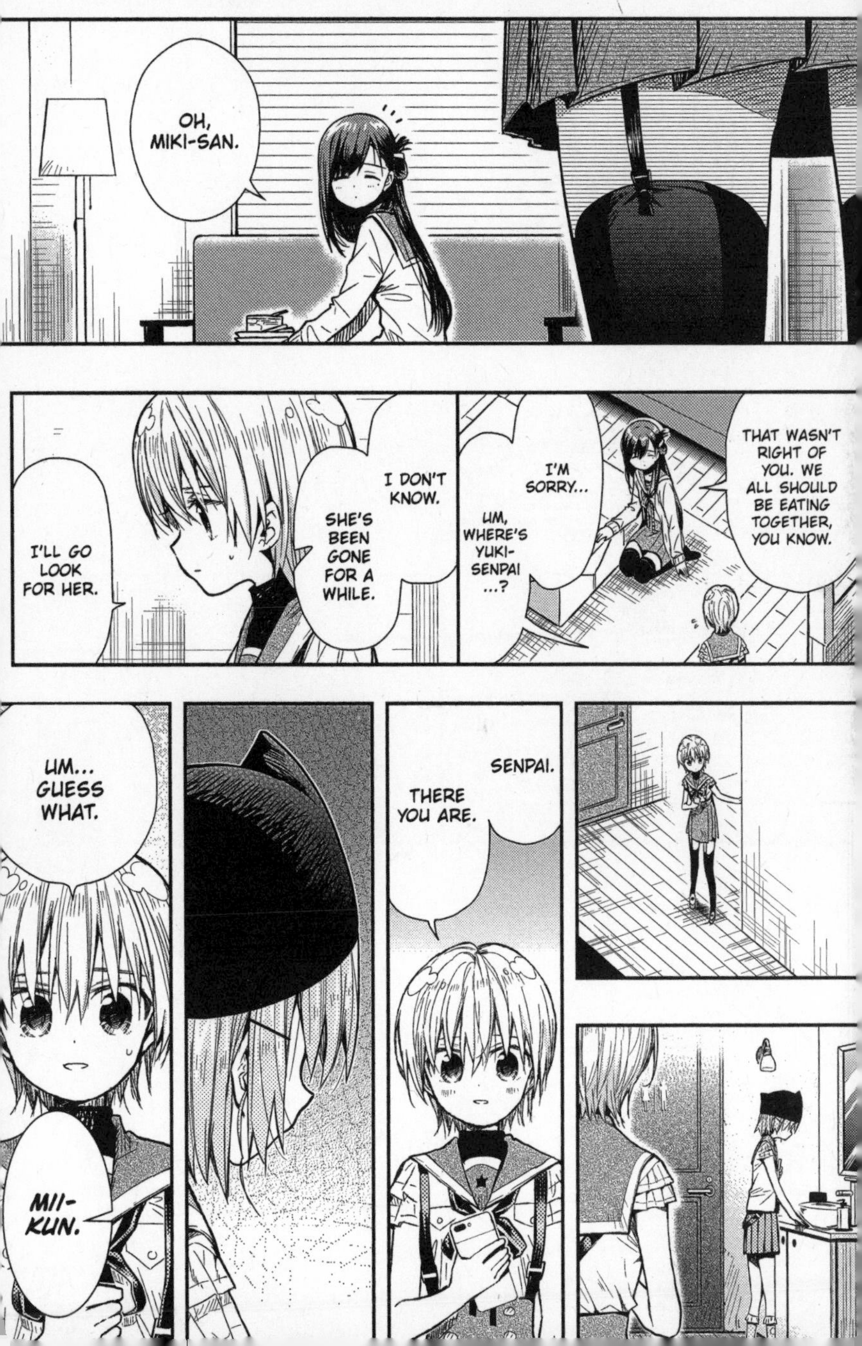
OH, MIKI-SAN.
THAT WASN'T RIGHT OF YOU. WE ALL SHOULD BE EATING TOGETHER, YOU KNOW.
I'M SORRY...
UM, WHERE'S YUKI-SENPAI ...?
I DON'T KNOW.
SHE'S BEEN GONE FOR A WHILE.
I'LL GO LOOK FOR HER.
SENPAI.
THERE YOU ARE.
UM... GUESS WHAT.
MII-KUN.

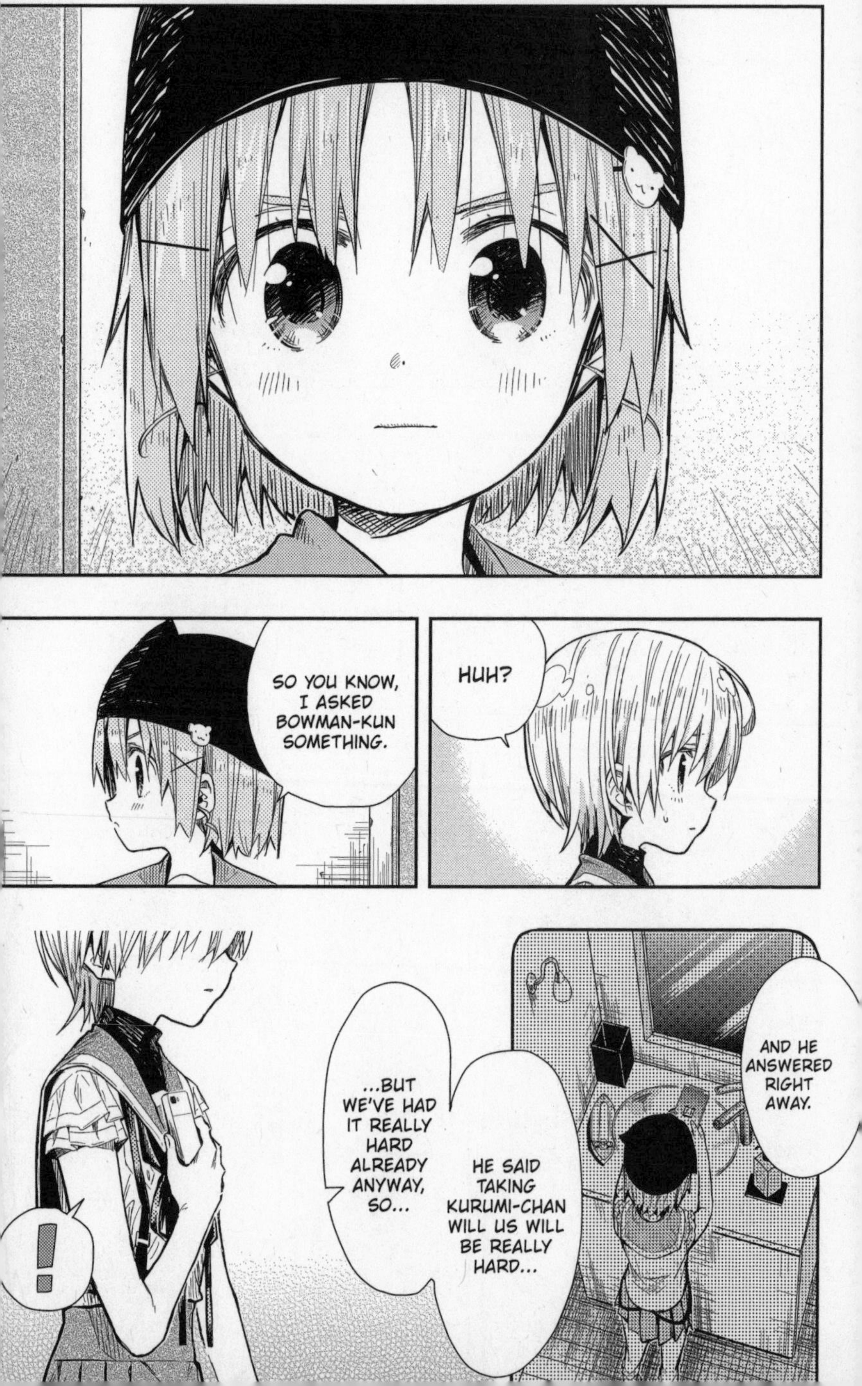
HUH?
SO YOU KNOW, I ASKED BOWMAN-KUN SOMETHING.
AND HE ANSWERED RIGHT AWAY.
HE SAID TAKING KURUMI-CHAN WILL US WILL BE REALLY HARD...
...BUT WE'VE HAD IT REALLY HARD ALREADY ANYWAY, SO...
!

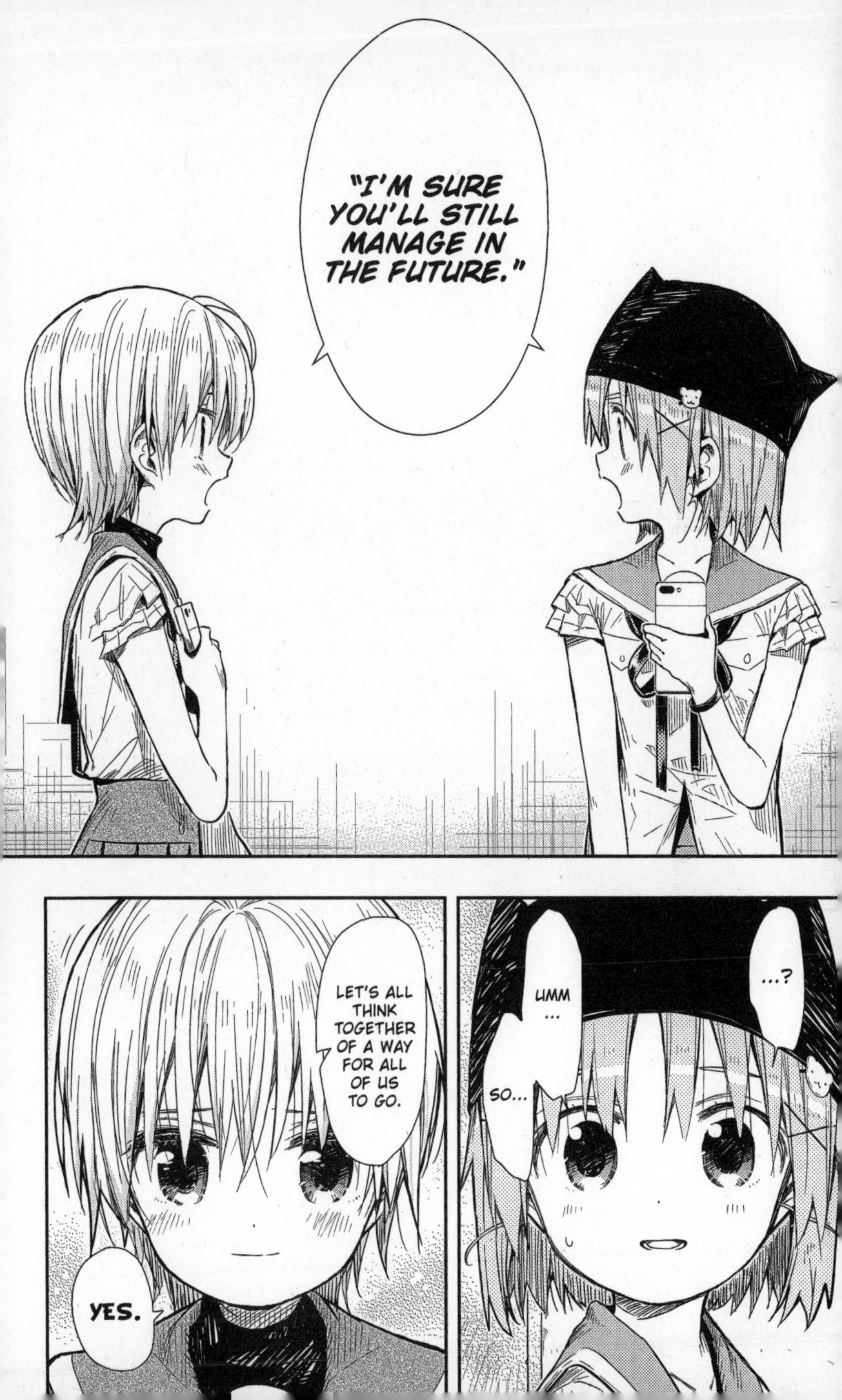
"I'M SURE YOU'LL STILL MANAGE IN THE FUTURE."
...?
UMM ...
SO...
LET'S ALL THINK TOGETHER OF A WAY FOR ALL OF US TO GO.
YES.

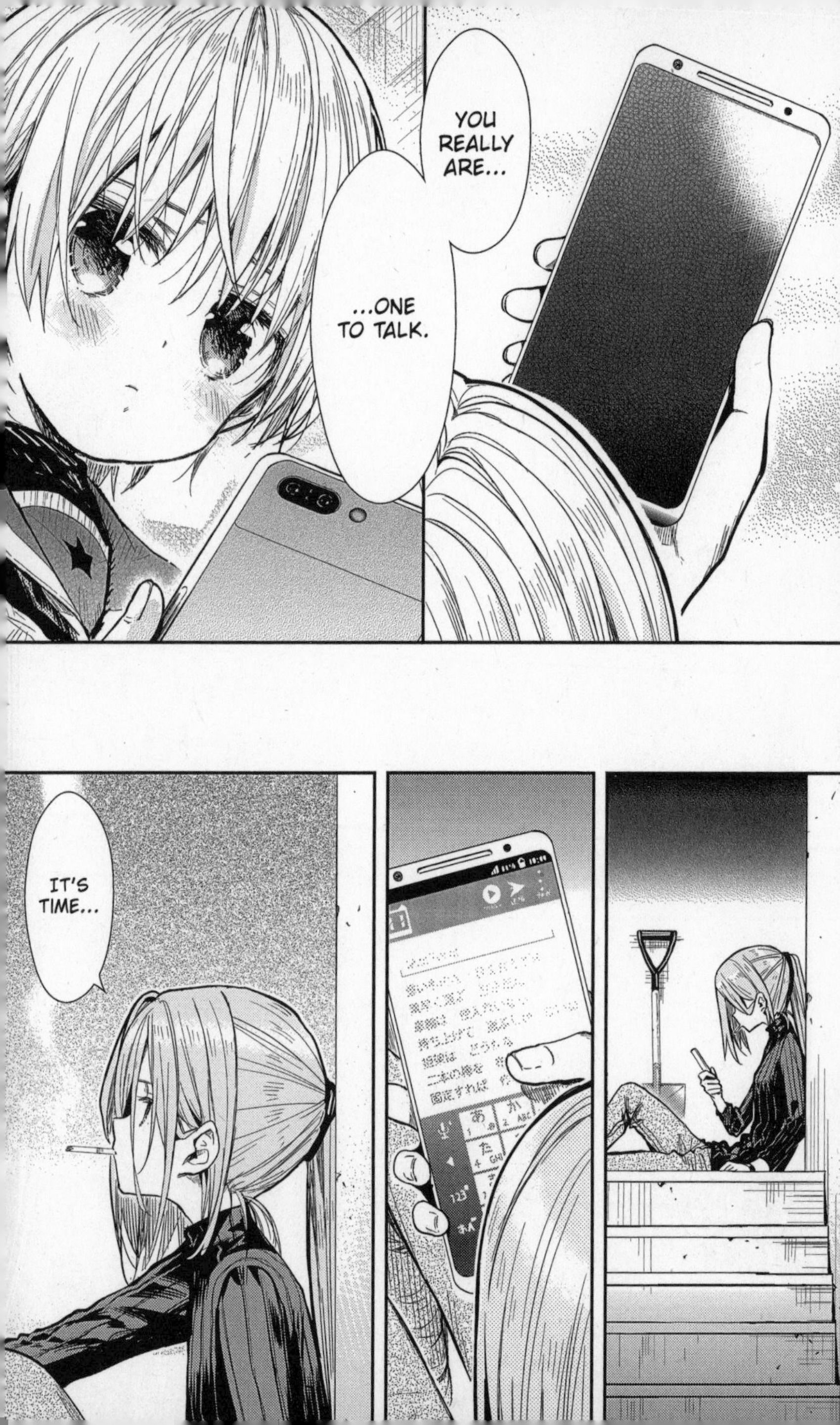
YOU REALLY ARE...
...ONE TO TALK.
IT'S TIME...

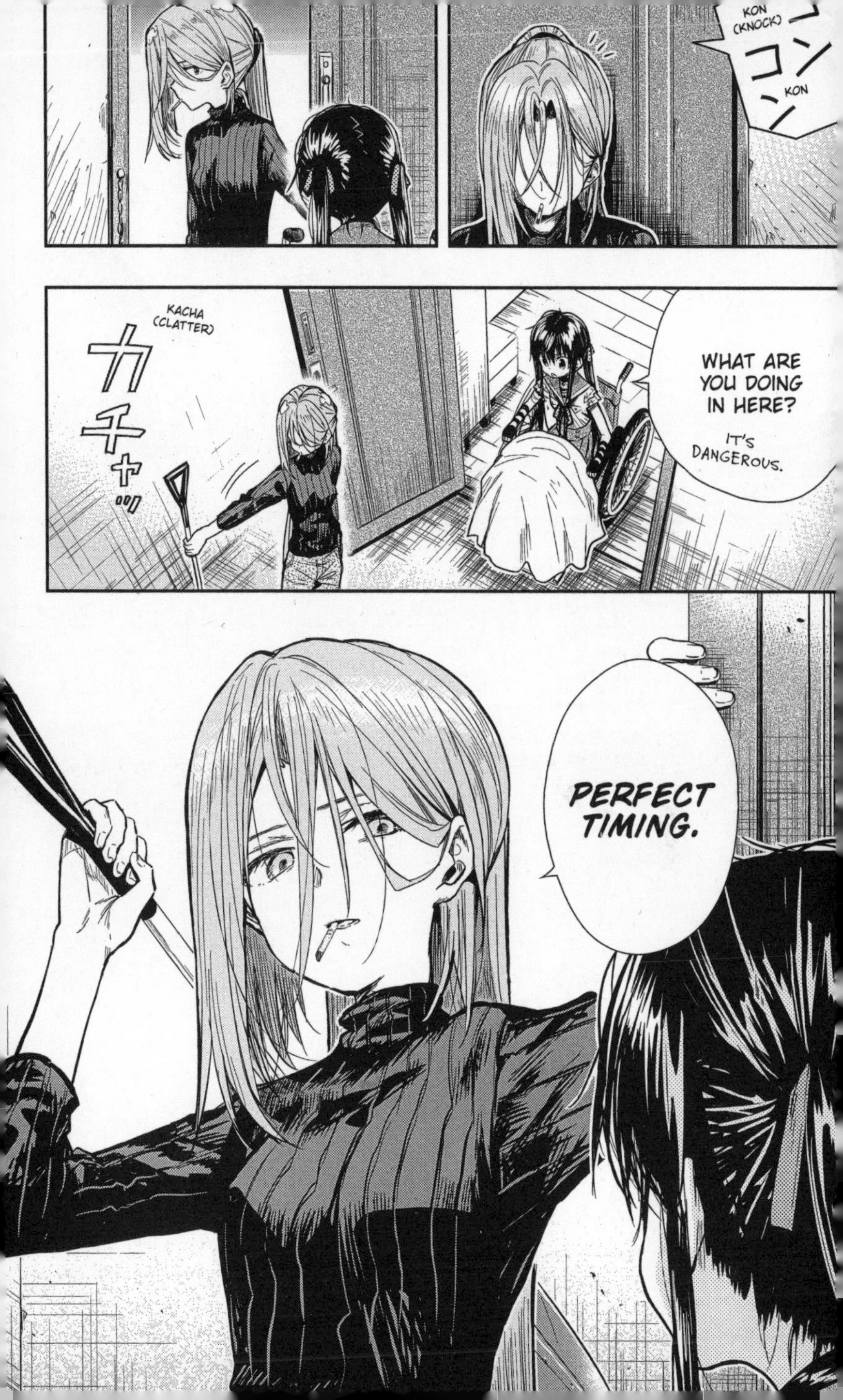
KON (KNOCK)
コン
KON
コン
WHAT ARE YOU DOING IN HERE?
IT'S DANGEROUS.
KACHA (CLATTER)
カチャッ
PERFECT TIMING.

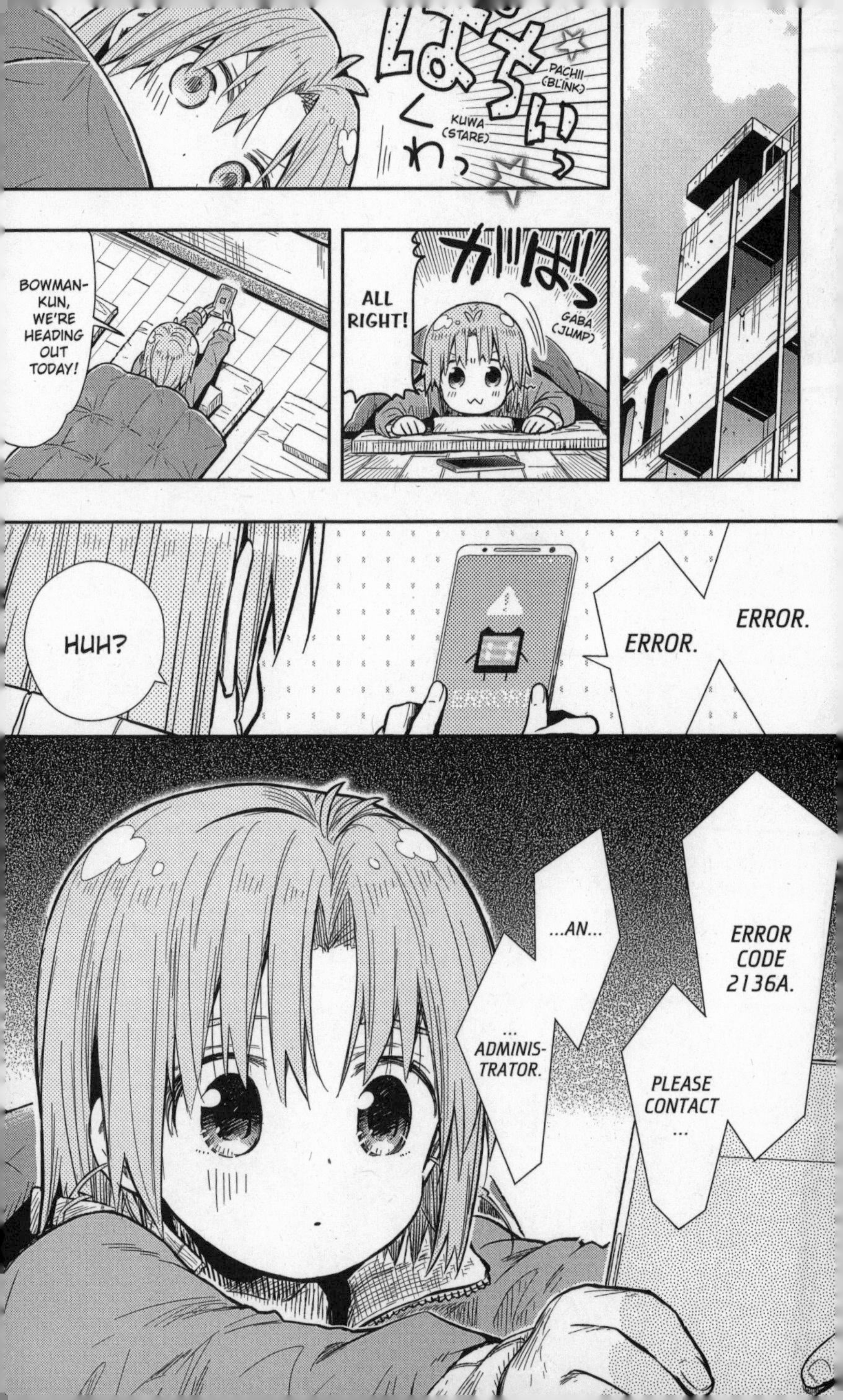
はちぃ
PACHII (BLINK)
くわっ
KUWA (STARE)
がばっ
GABA (JUMP)
ALL RIGHT!
BOWMAN-KUN, WE'RE HEADING OUT TODAY!
ERROR.
ERROR.
HUH?
ERROR CODE 2136A.
PLEASE CONTACT ...
...AN...
... ADMINISTRATOR.

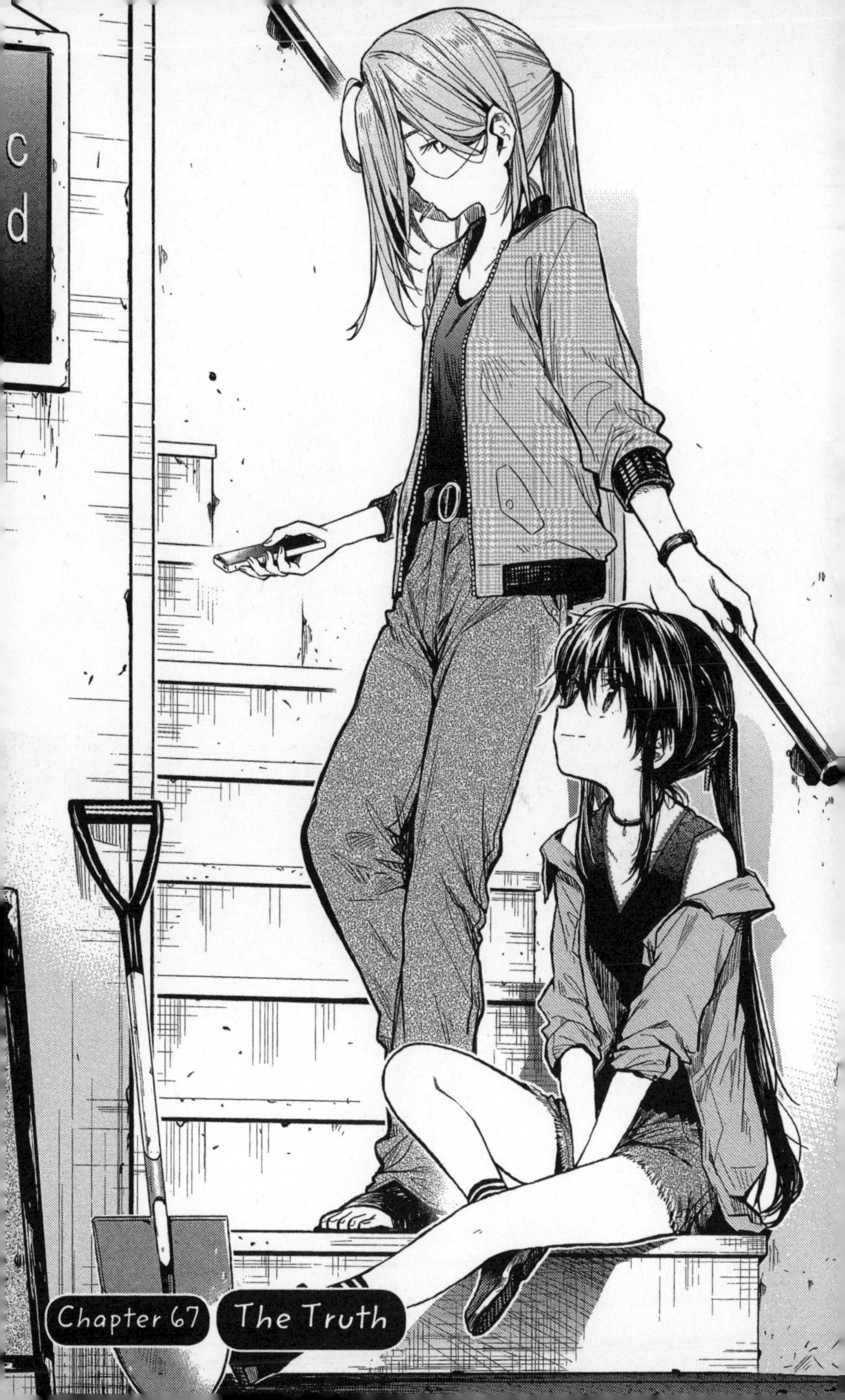
c
d
Chapter 67
The Truth

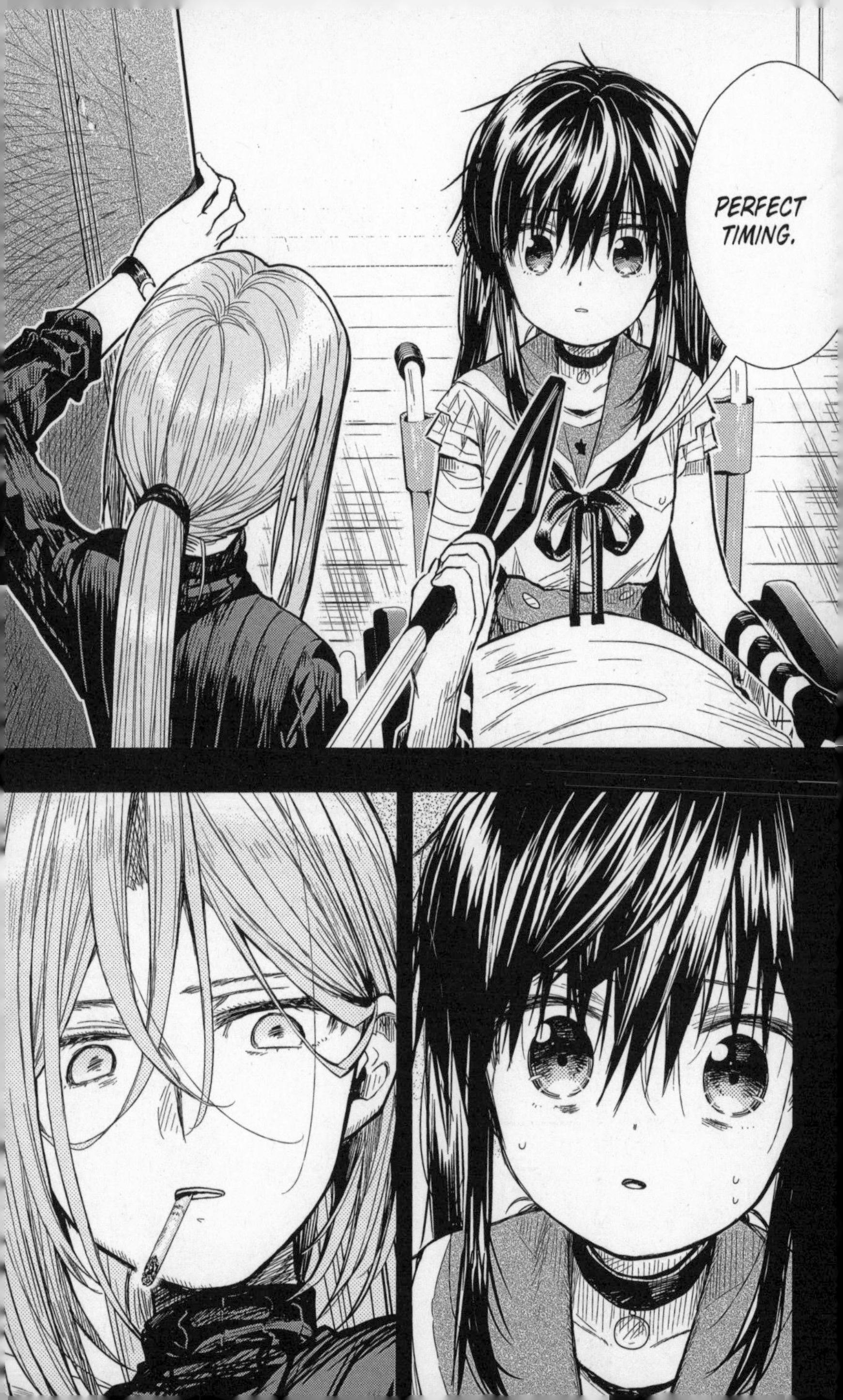
PERFECT TIMING.

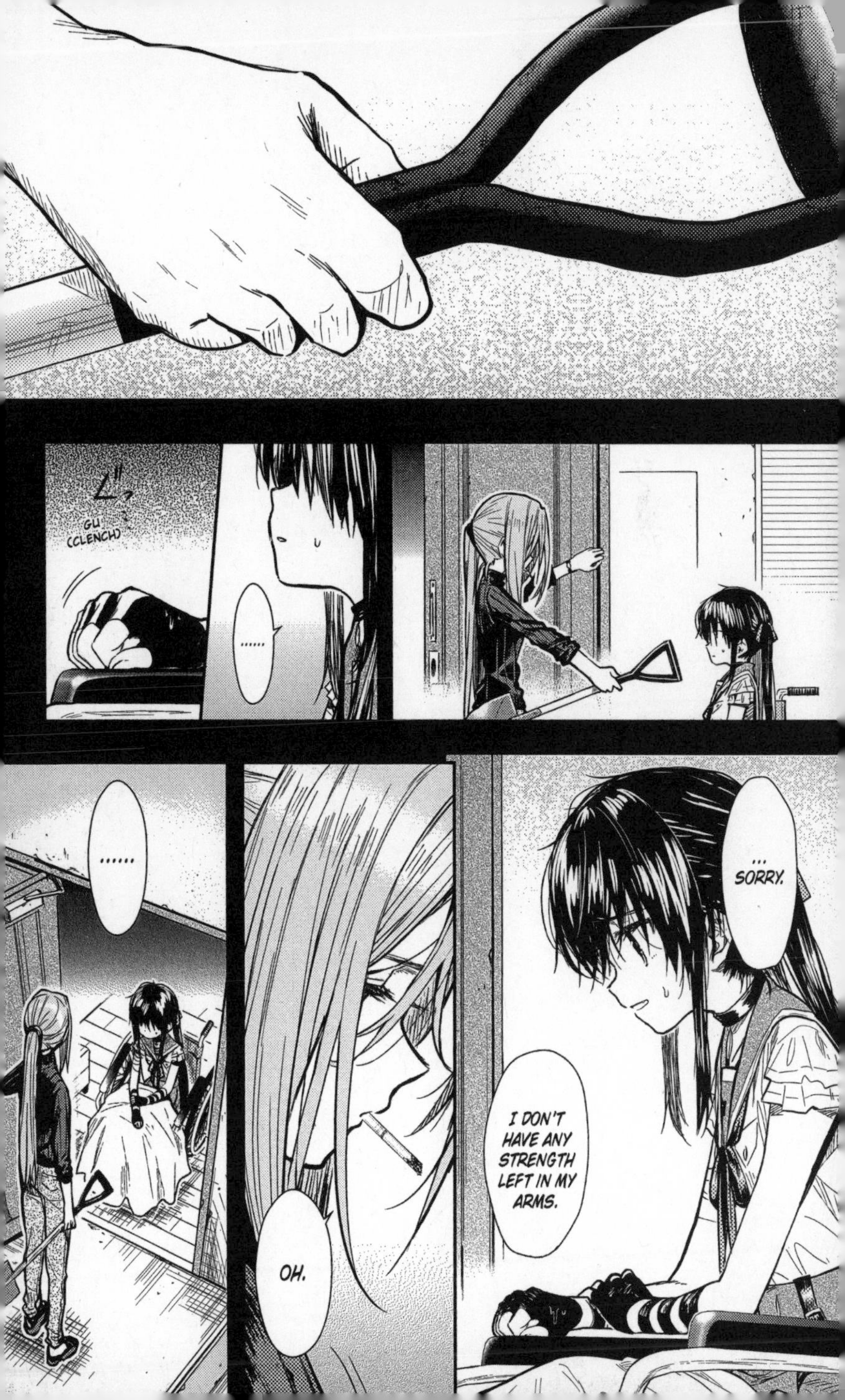
GU (CLENCH)
......
... SORRY.
I DON'T HAVE ANY STRENGTH LEFT IN MY ARMS.
OH.
......

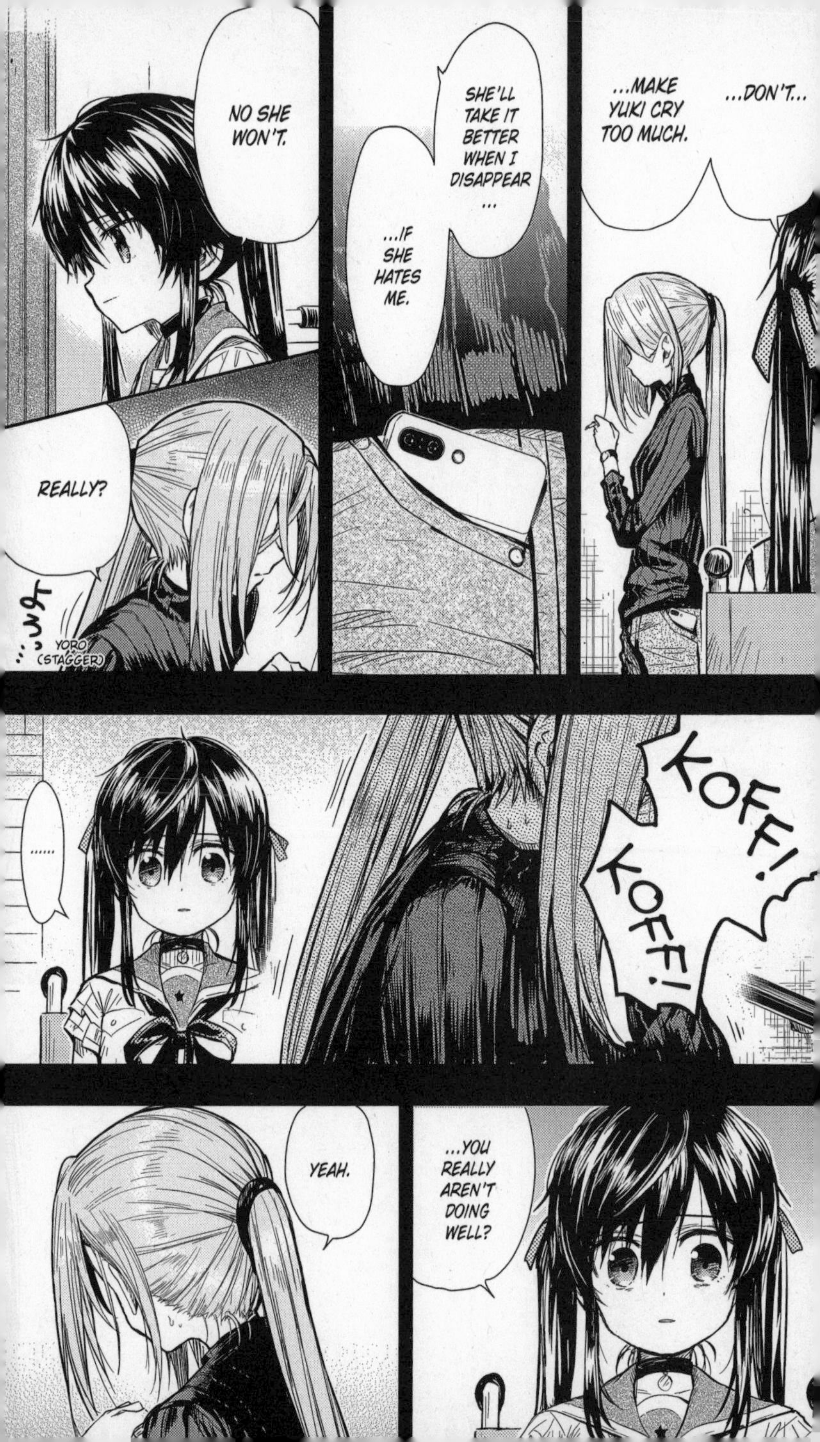
...DON'T...
...MAKE YUKI CRY TOO MUCH.
SHE'LL TAKE IT BETTER WHEN I DISAPPEAR ...
...IF SHE HATES ME.
NO SHE WON'T.
REALLY?
YORO (STAGGER)
KOFF! KOFF!
......
...YOU REALLY AREN'T DOING WELL?
YEAH.

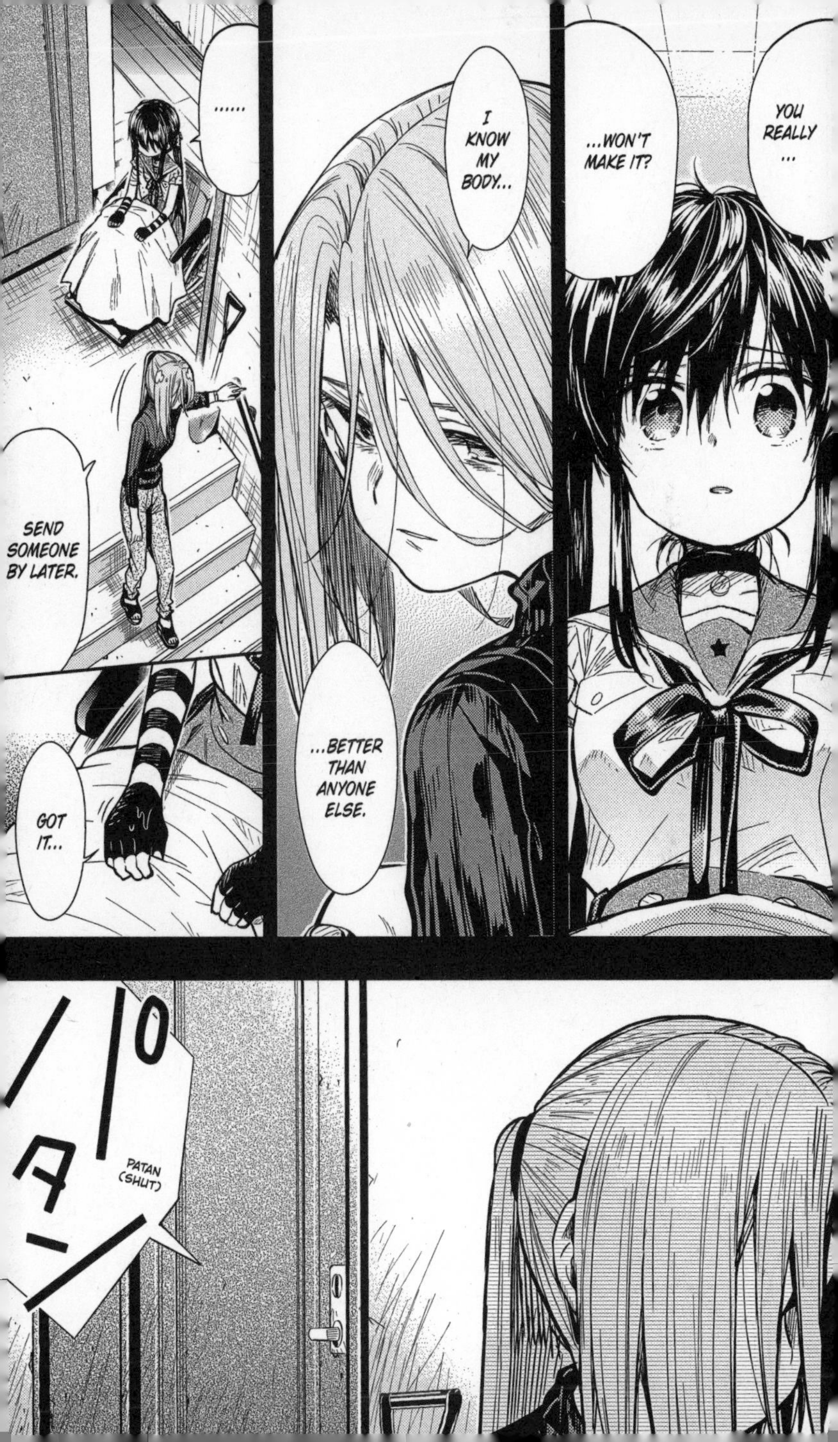
YOU REALLY...
...WON'T MAKE IT?
I KNOW MY BODY...
...BETTER THAN ANYONE ELSE.
......
SEND SOMEONE BY LATER.
GOT IT...
PATAN (SHUT)

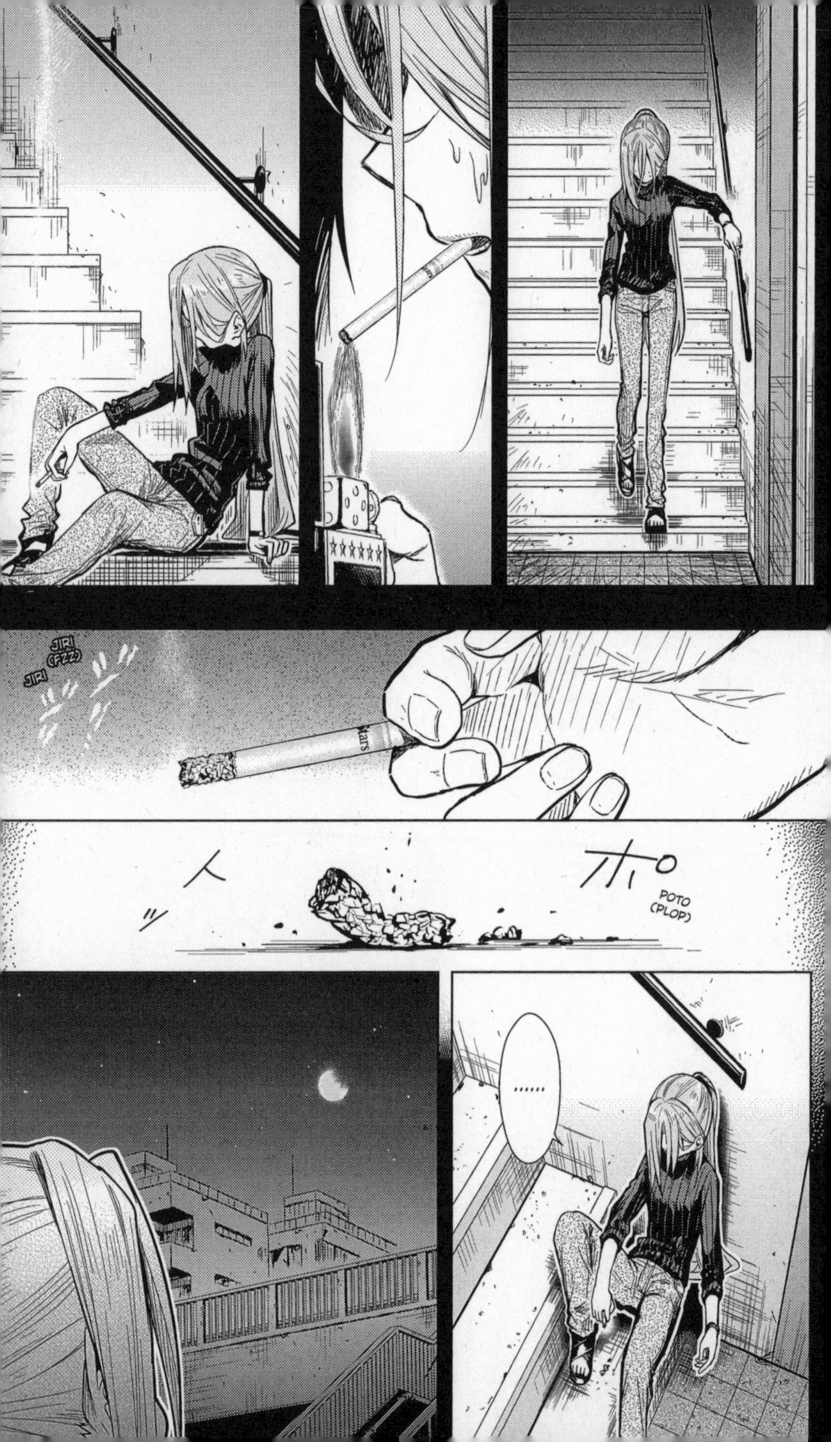
JIRI (FZZ)
JIRI
POTO (PLOP)
......

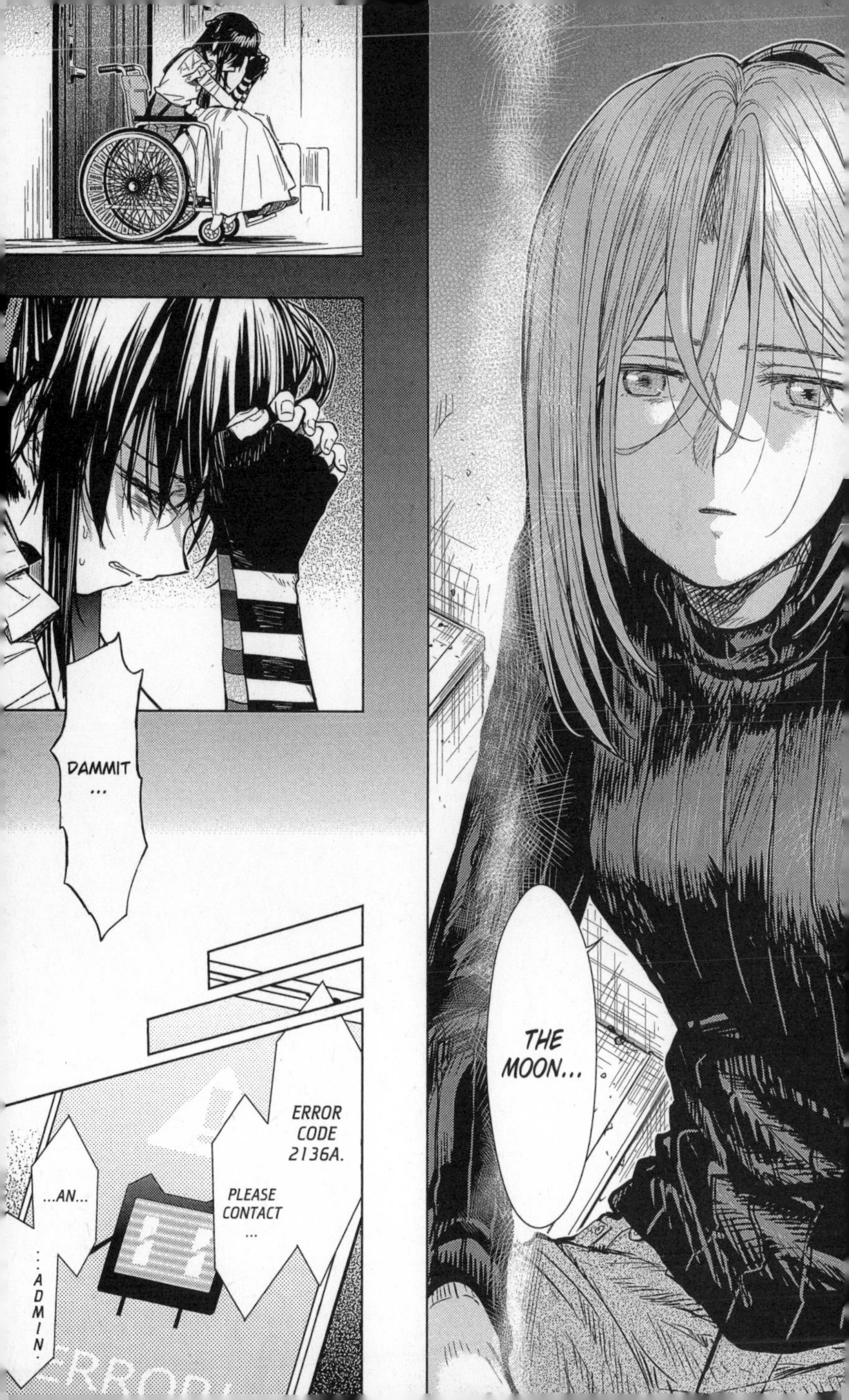
THE MOON...
DAMMIT...
ERROR CODE 2136A.
PLEASE CONTACT...
...AN...
...ADMIN.

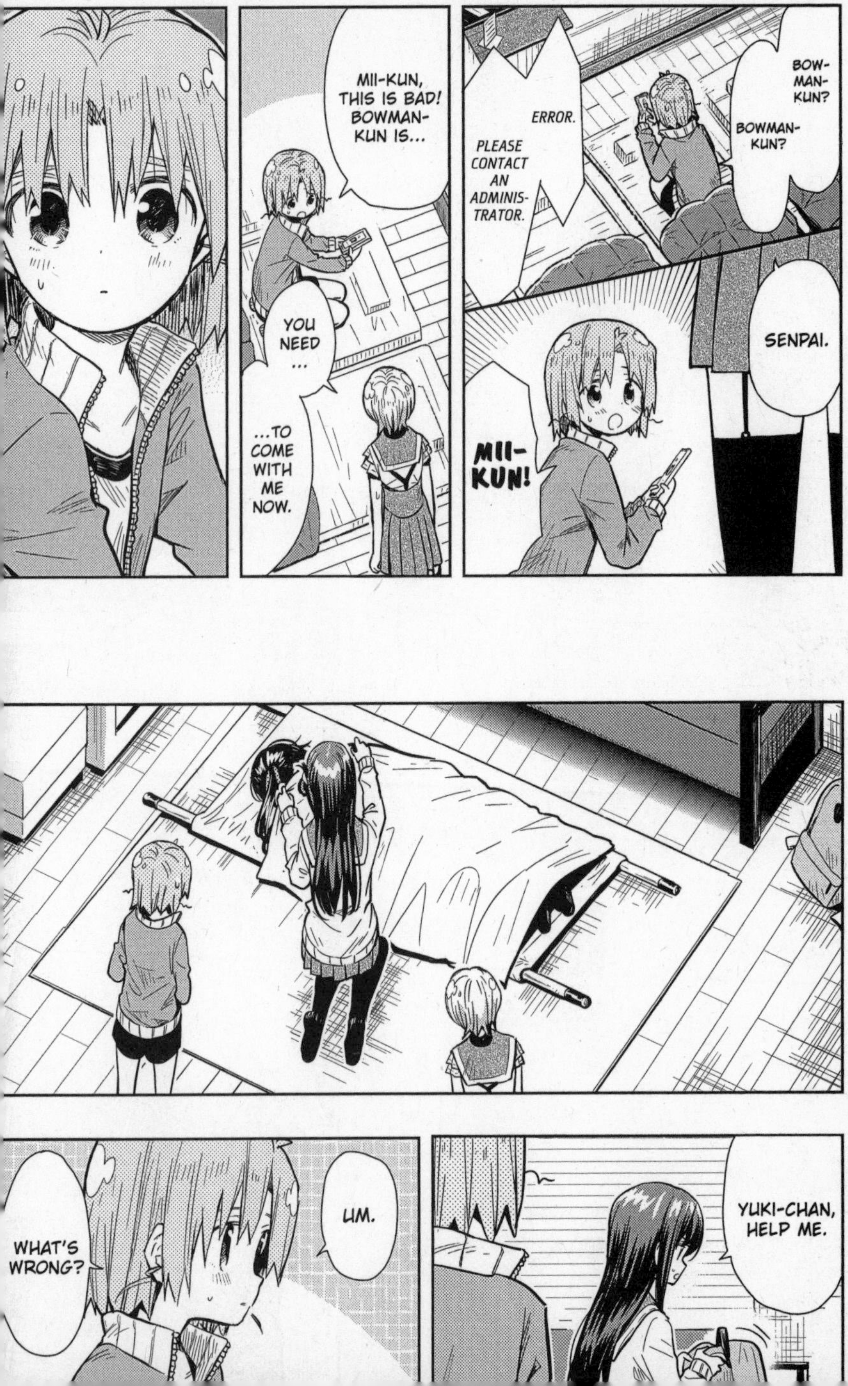
BOW-MAN-KUN?
BOWMAN-KUN?
ERROR.
PLEASE CONTACT AN ADMINIS-TRATOR.
SENPAI.
MII-KUN!
MII-KUN, THIS IS BAD! BOWMAN-KUN IS...
YOU NEED ...
...TO COME WITH ME NOW.
YUKI-CHAN, HELP ME.
UM.
WHAT'S WRONG?

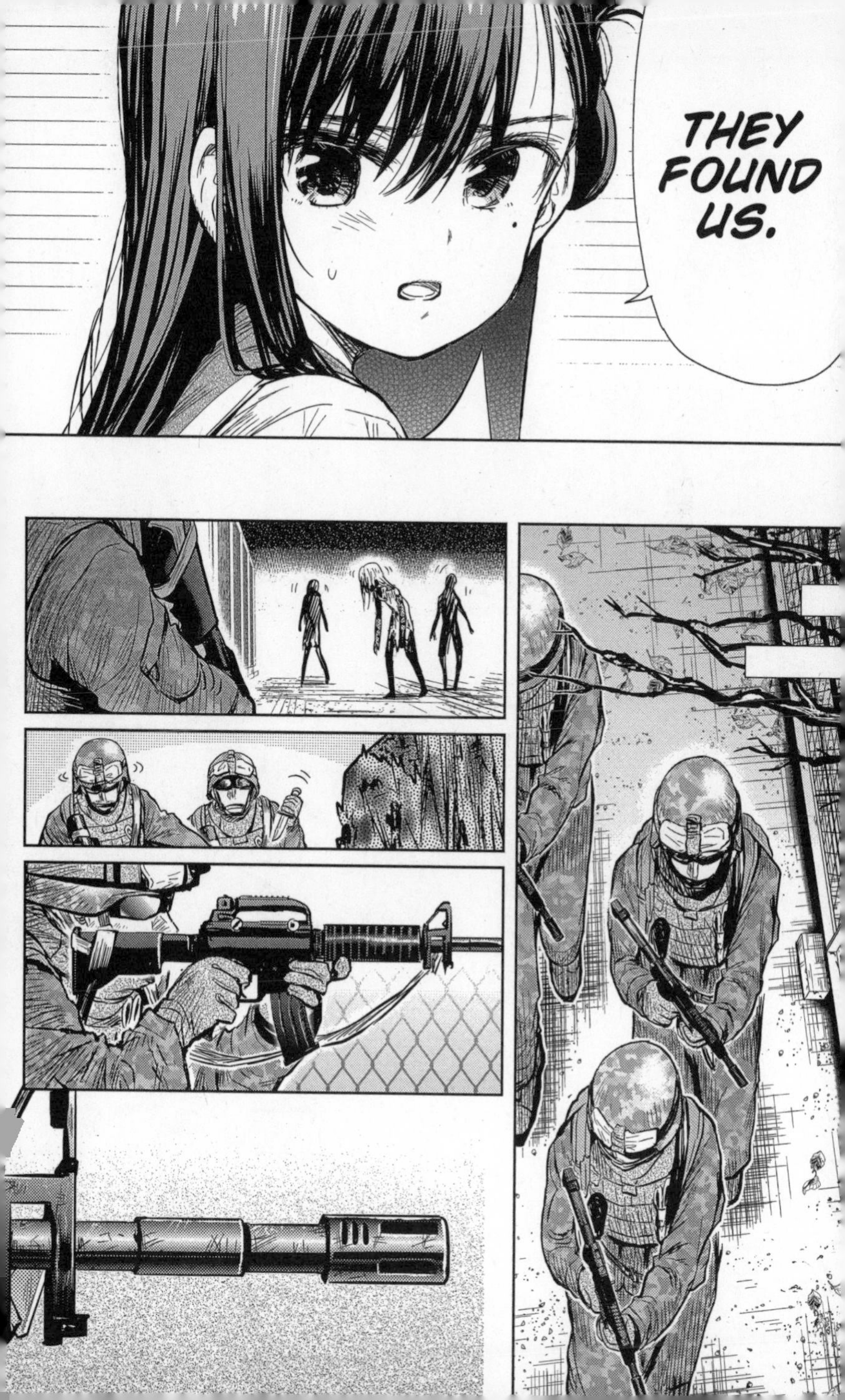
THEY FOUND US.

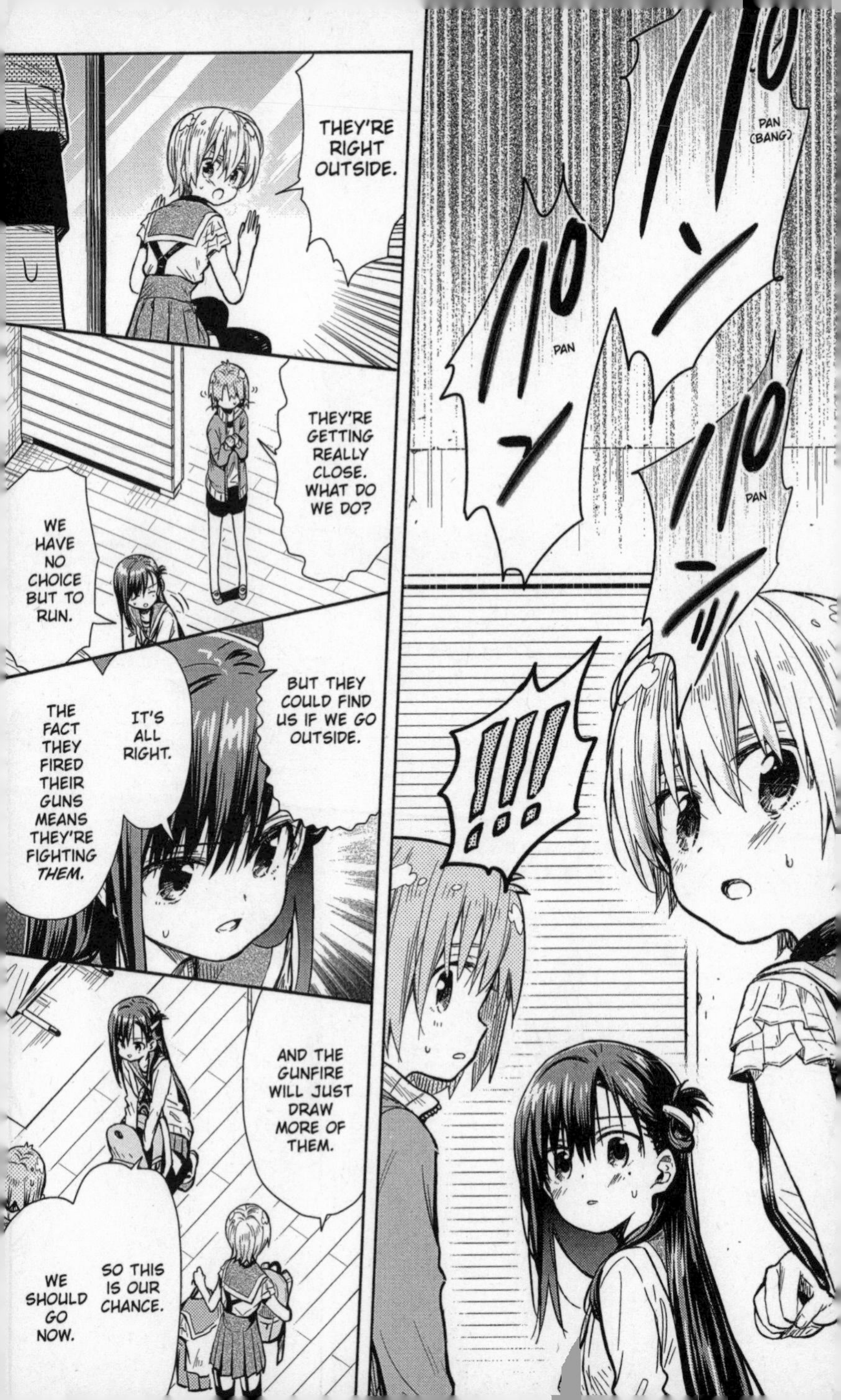
PAN (BANG)
PAN
PAN
!!!
THEY'RE RIGHT OUTSIDE.
THEY'RE GETTING REALLY CLOSE. WHAT DO WE DO?
WE HAVE NO CHOICE BUT TO RUN.
BUT THEY COULD FIND US IF WE GO OUTSIDE.
IT'S ALL RIGHT.
THE FACT THEY FIRED THEIR GUNS MEANS THEY'RE FIGHTING *THEM*.
AND THE GUNFIRE WILL JUST DRAW MORE OF THEM.
SO THIS IS OUR CHANCE.
WE SHOULD GO NOW.

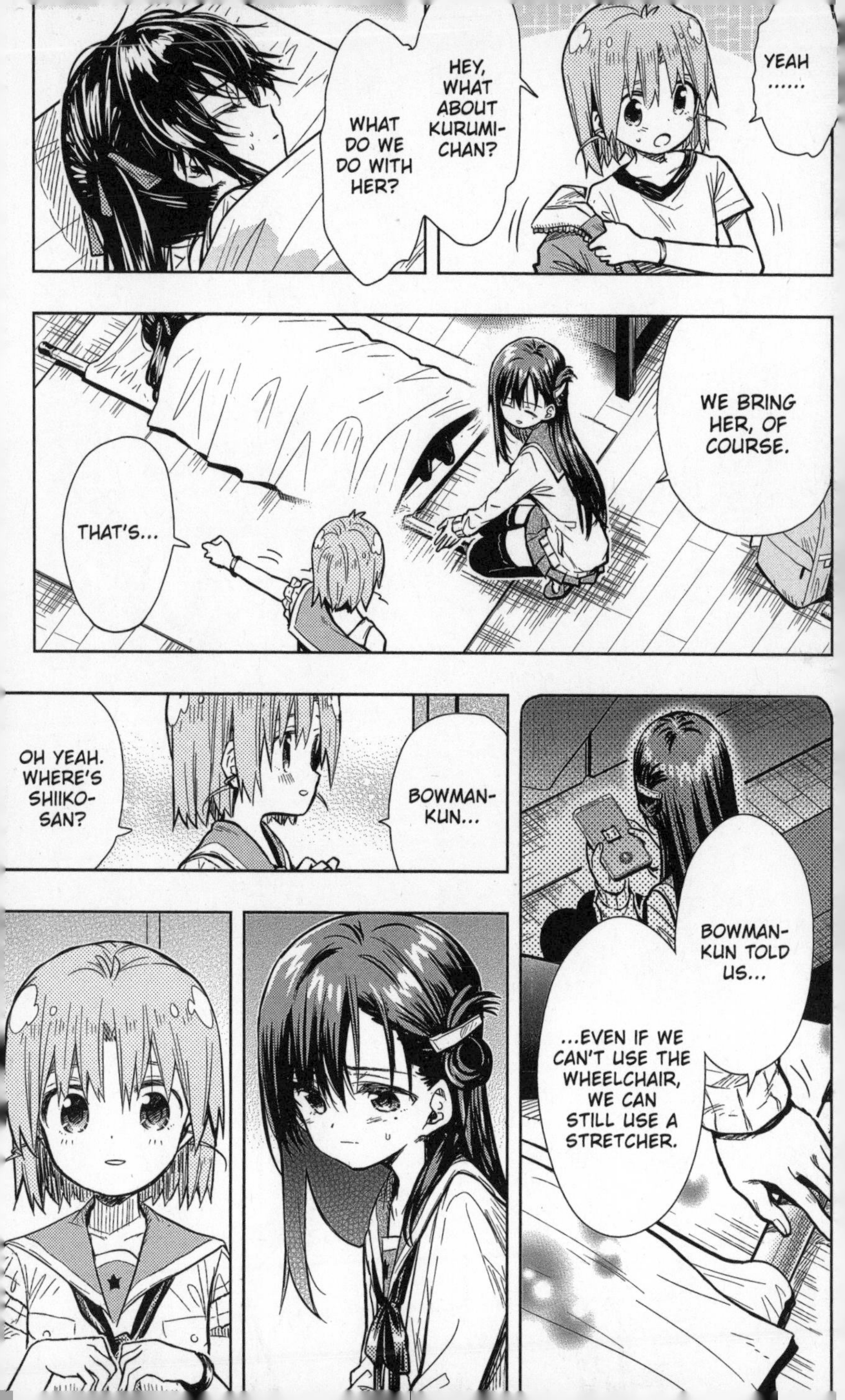
YEAH ......
HEY, WHAT ABOUT KURUMI-CHAN?
WHAT DO WE DO WITH HER?
WE BRING HER, OF COURSE.
THAT'S...
BOWMAN-KUN TOLD US...
...EVEN IF WE CAN'T USE THE WHEELCHAIR, WE CAN STILL USE A STRETCHER.
BOWMAN-KUN...
OH YEAH. WHERE'S SHIIKO-SAN?

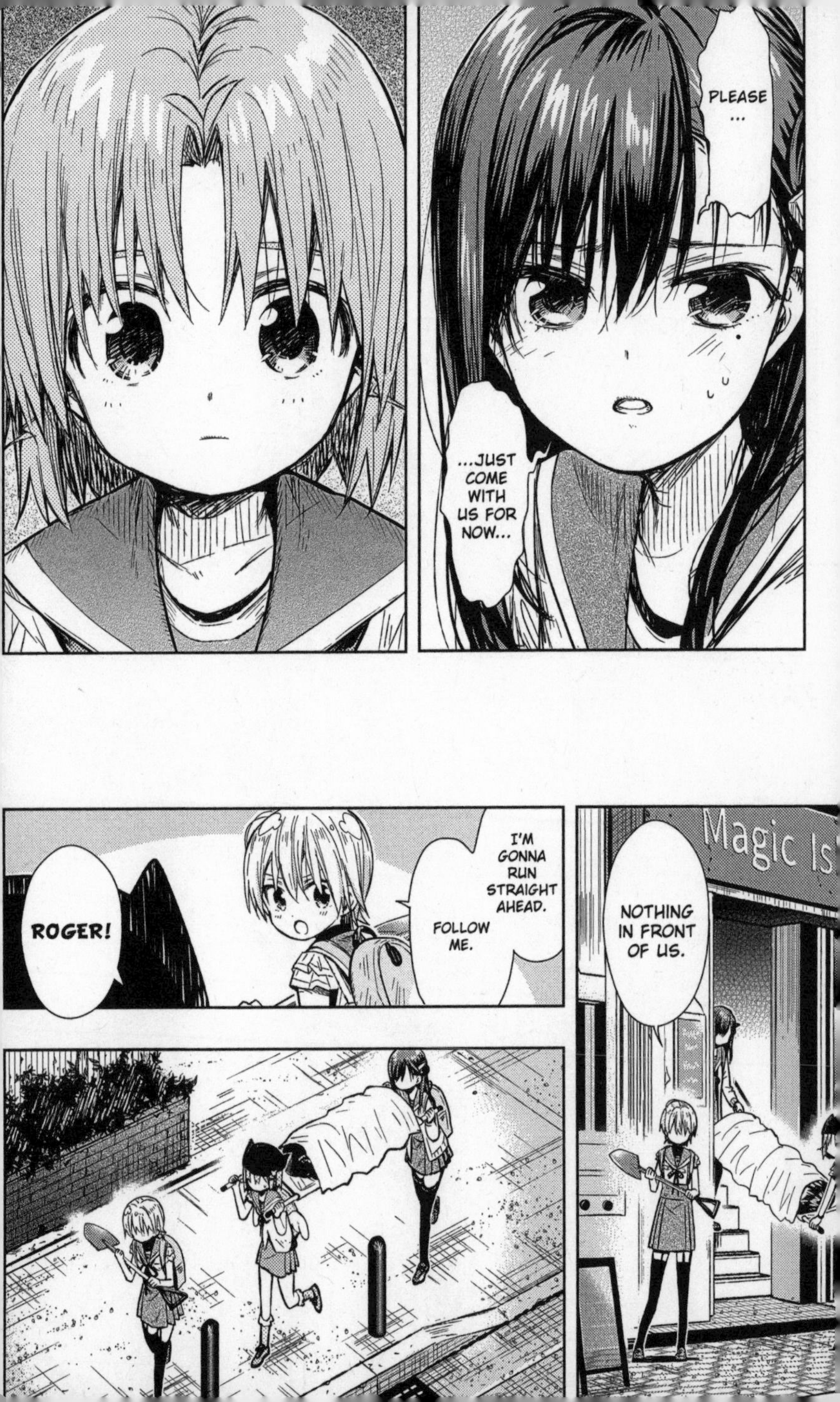
PLEASE ...
...JUST COME WITH US FOR NOW...
Magic Is
NOTHING IN FRONT OF US.
I'M GONNA RUN STRAIGHT AHEAD.
FOLLOW ME.
ROGER!

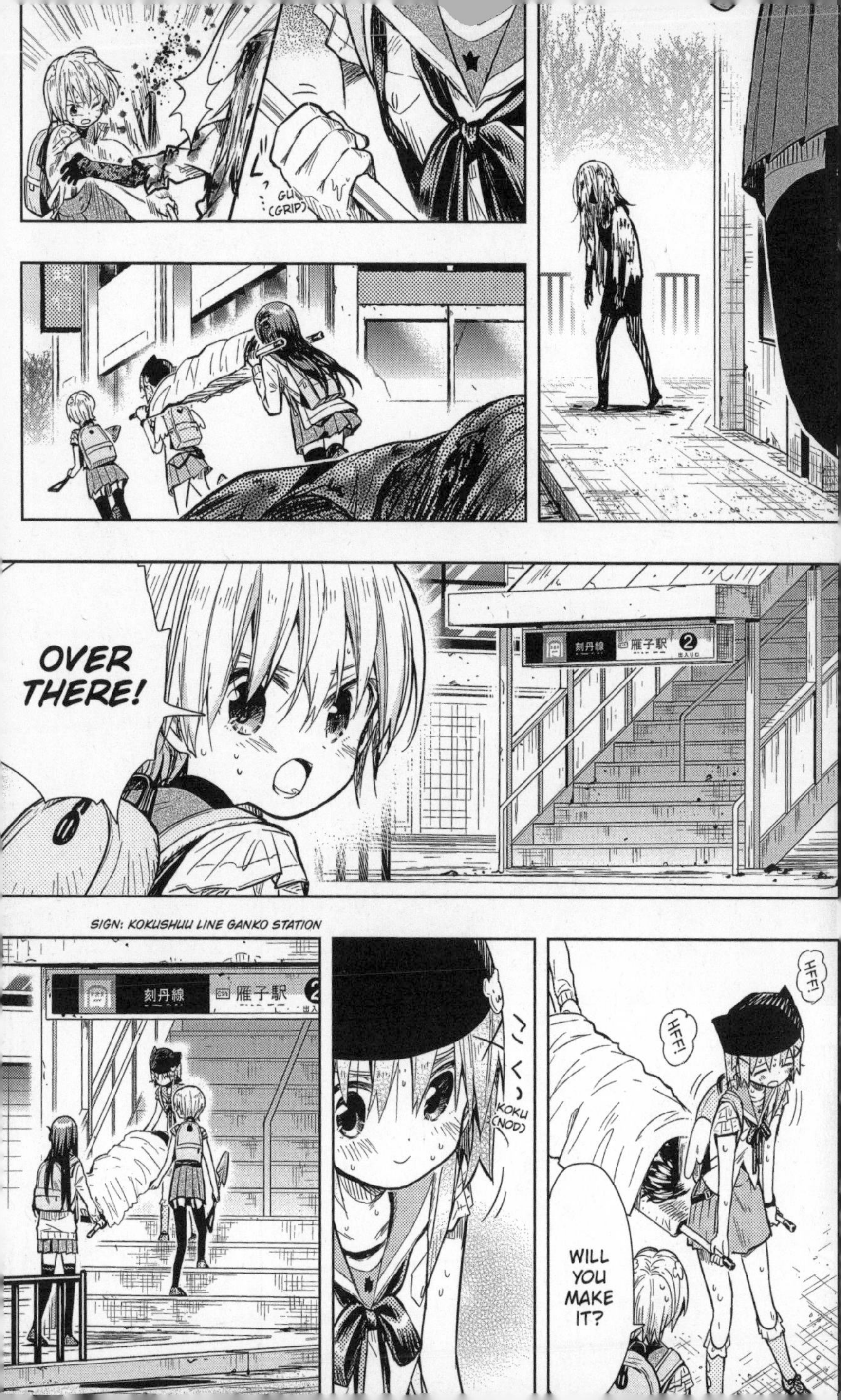
GU
(GRIP)
OVER THERE!
刻丹線
雁子駅
2
出入り口
SIGN: KOKUSHUU LINE GANKO STATION
HFF!
HFF!
WILL YOU MAKE IT?
こくっ
KOKU
(NOD)
刻丹線
雁子駅

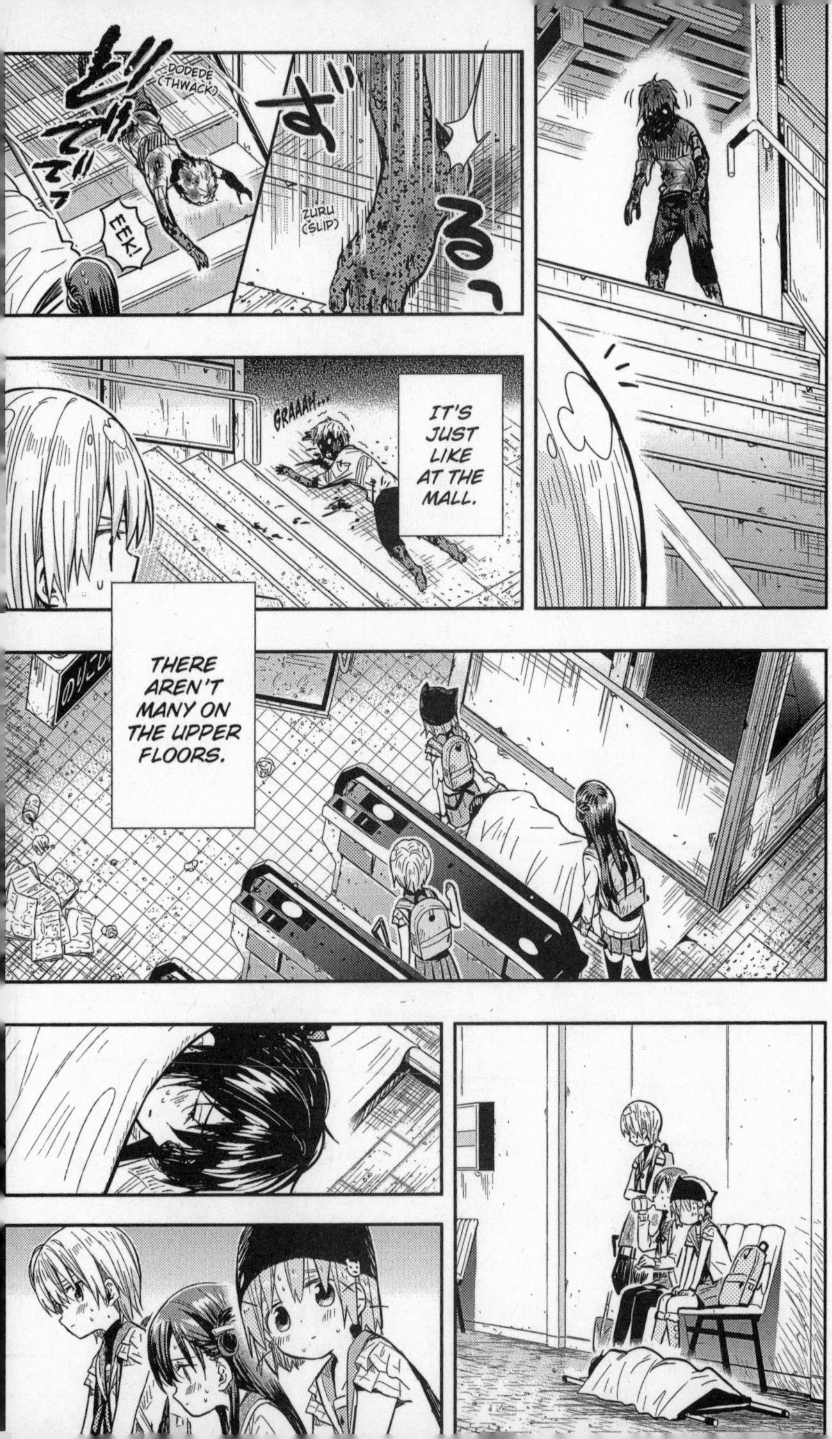
ZURU
(SLIP)
DODEDE
(THWACK)
EEK!
GRAAAH...
IT'S JUST LIKE AT THE MALL.
THERE AREN'T MANY ON THE UPPER FLOORS.

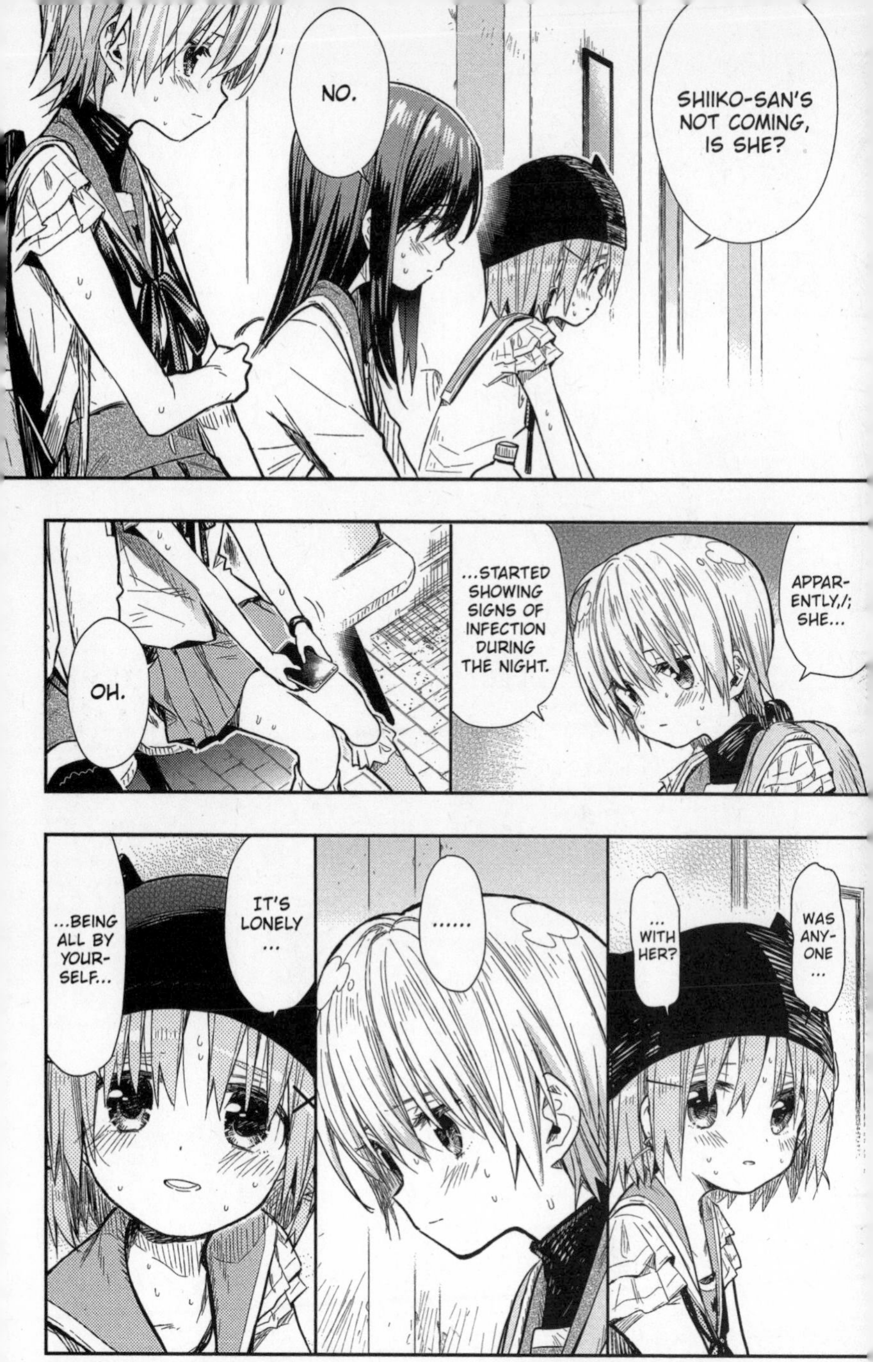
SHIIKO-SAN'S NOT COMING, IS SHE?
NO.
APPAR-ENTLY,/; SHE...
...STARTED SHOWING SIGNS OF INFECTION DURING THE NIGHT.
OH.
WAS ANY-ONE ...
... WITH HER?
......
IT'S LONELY ...
...BEING ALL BY YOUR-SELF...

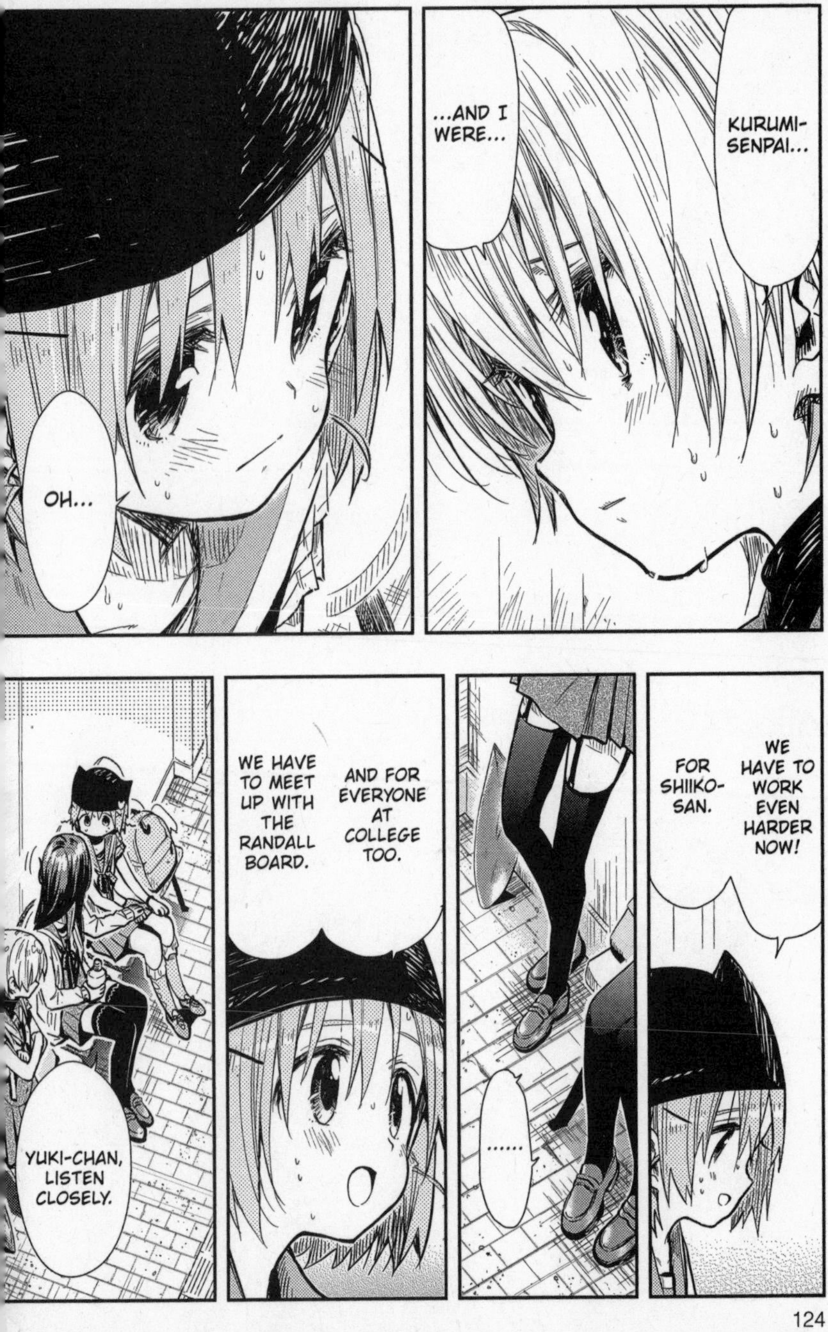
KURUMI-SENPAI...
...AND I WERE...
OH...
WE HAVE TO WORK EVEN HARDER NOW!
FOR SHIIKO-SAN.
......
AND FOR EVERYONE AT COLLEGE TOO.
WE HAVE TO MEET UP WITH THE RANDALL BOARD.
YUKI-CHAN, LISTEN CLOSELY.

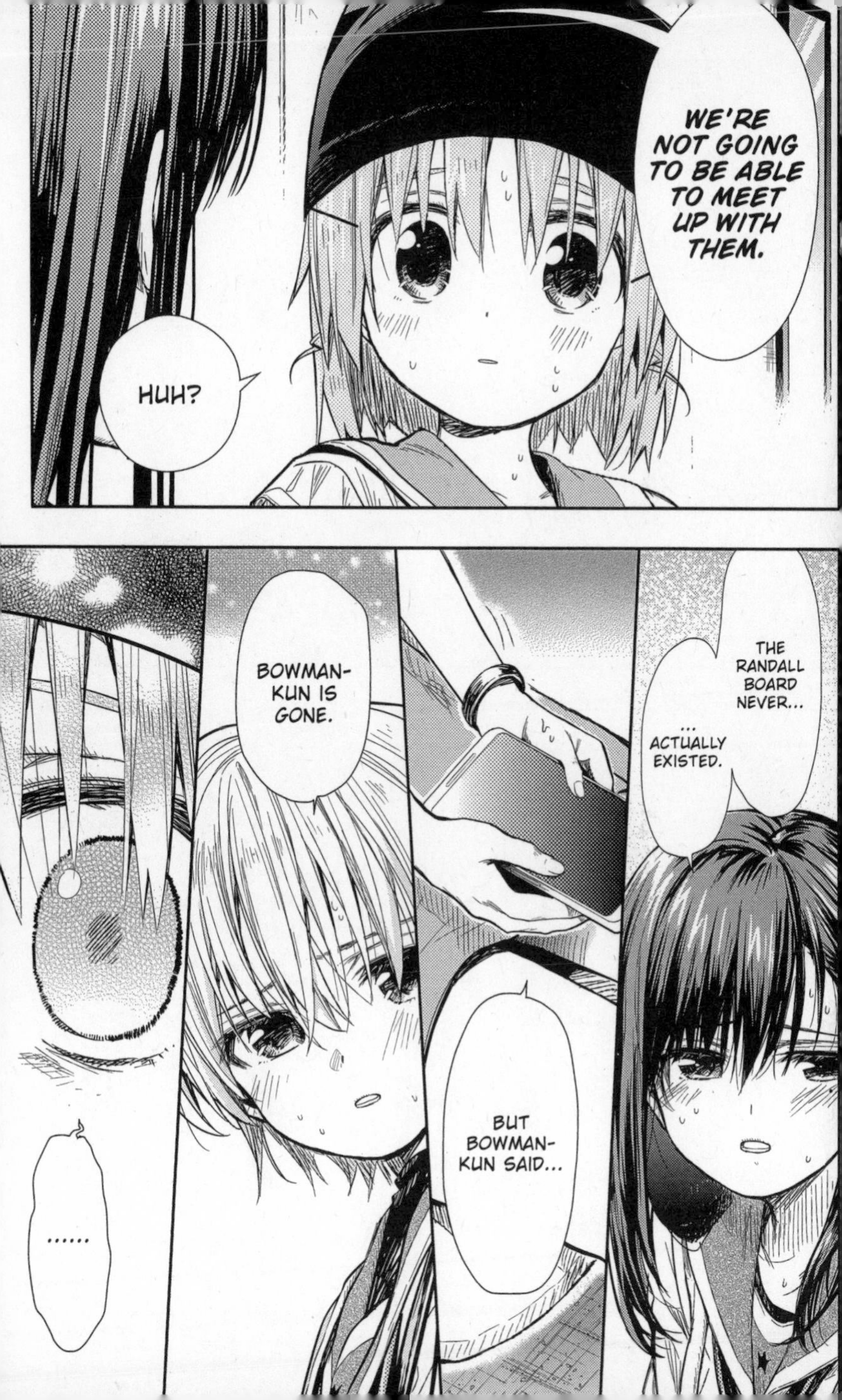
WE'RE NOT GOING TO BE ABLE TO MEET UP WITH THEM.
HUH?
THE RANDALL BOARD NEVER...
...ACTUALLY EXISTED.
BUT BOWMAN-KUN SAID...
BOWMAN-KUN IS GONE.
......

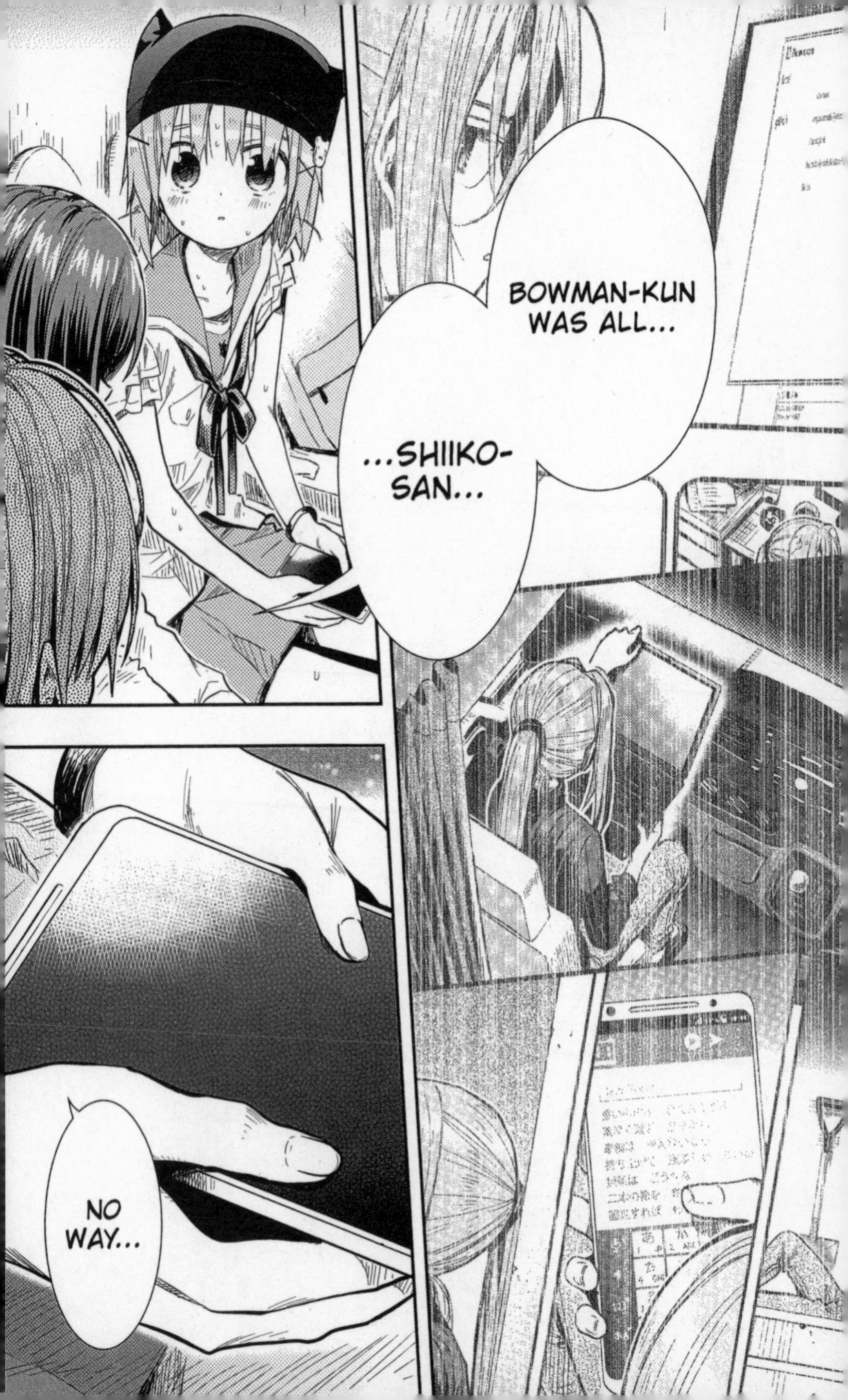
BOWMAN-KUN WAS ALL...
...SHIIKO-SAN...
NO WAY...

SCHOOL-LIVE!

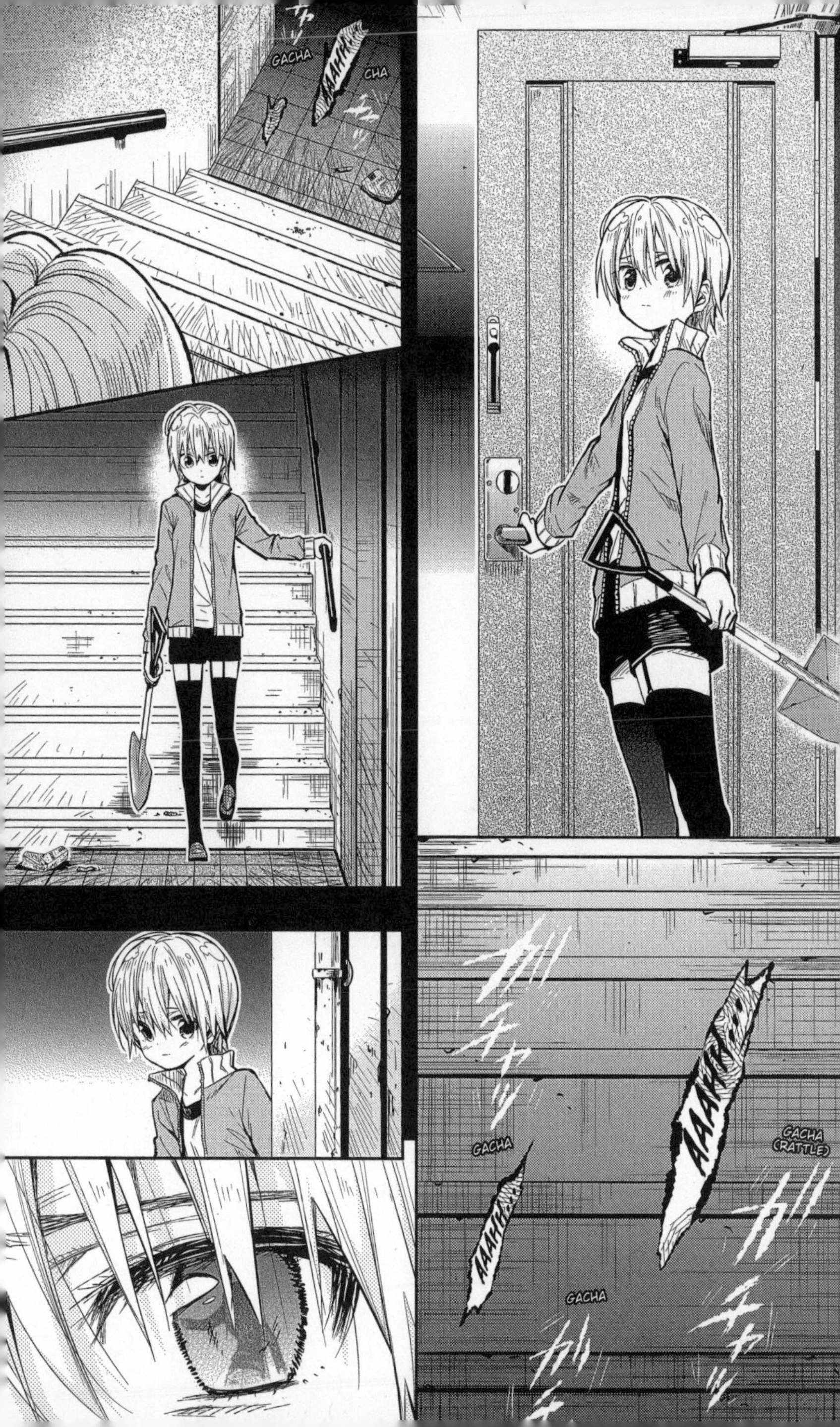
GACHA
(RATTLE)
AAAH...
GACHA
AAAHH...
GACHA
CHA
GACHA

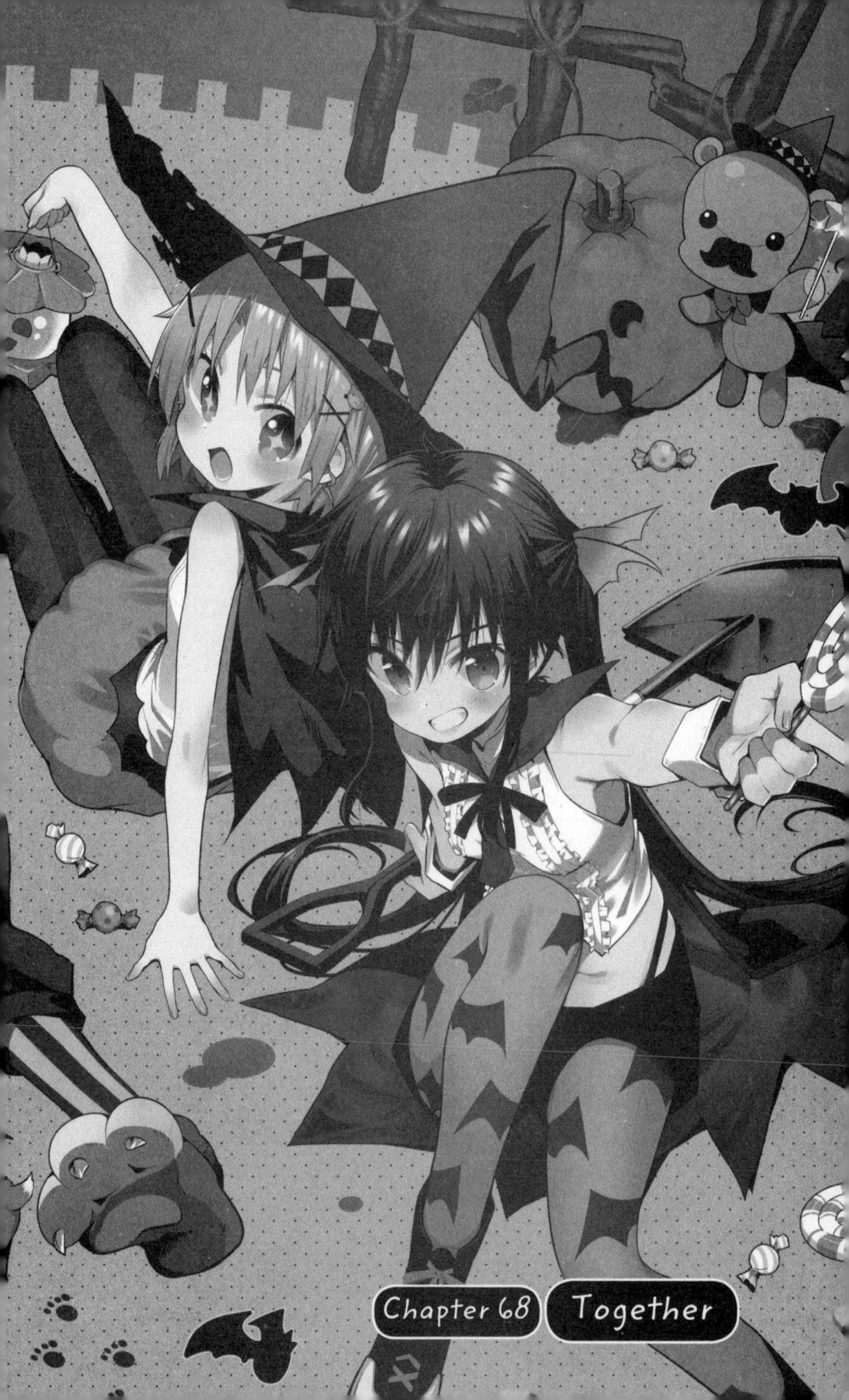
Chapter 68
Together

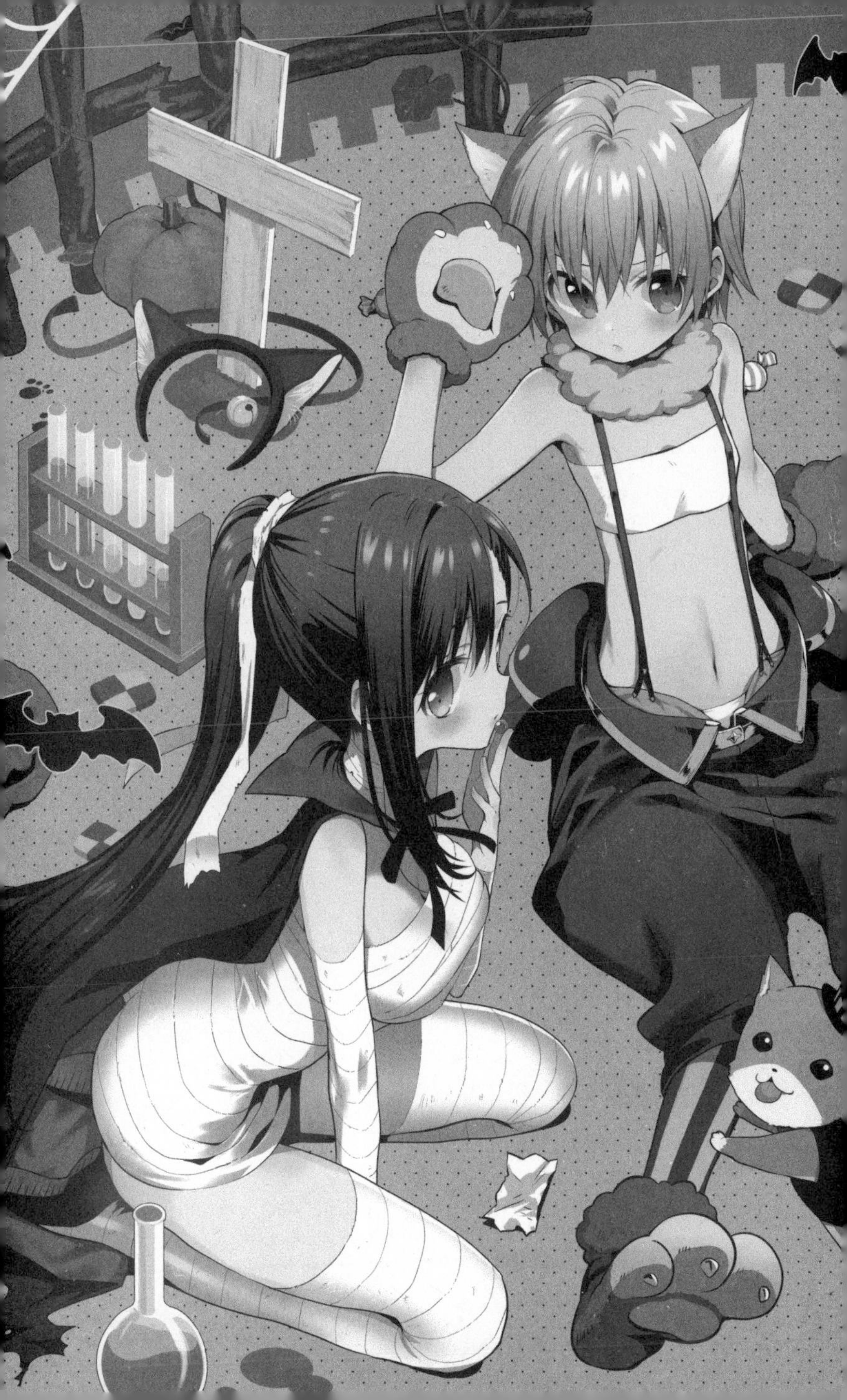

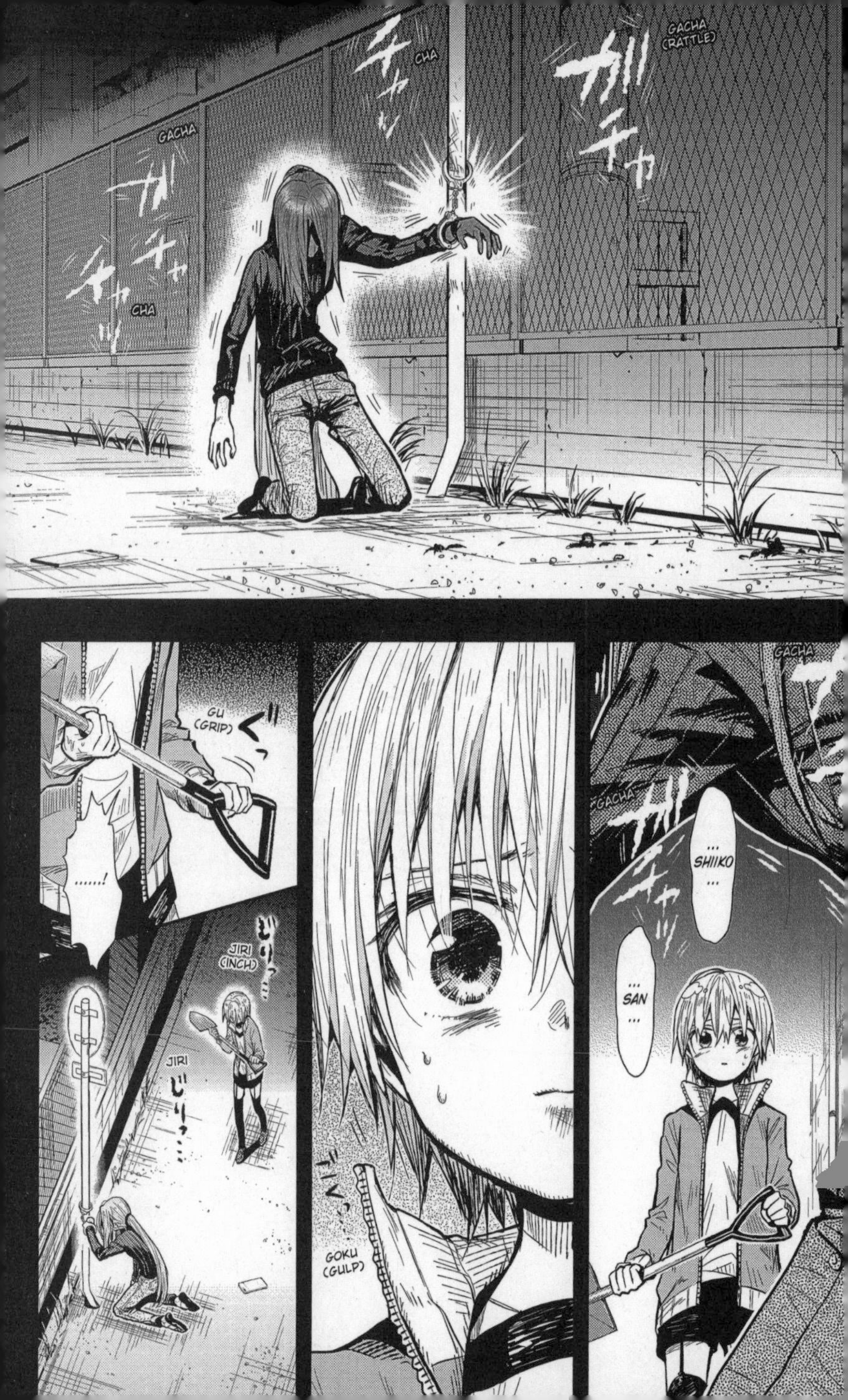
GACHA (RATTLE)
CHA
GACHA
CHA
GACHA
GACHA
... SHIIKO ...
... SAN ...
GOKU (GULP)
GU (GRIP)
......!
JIRI (INCH)
JIRI

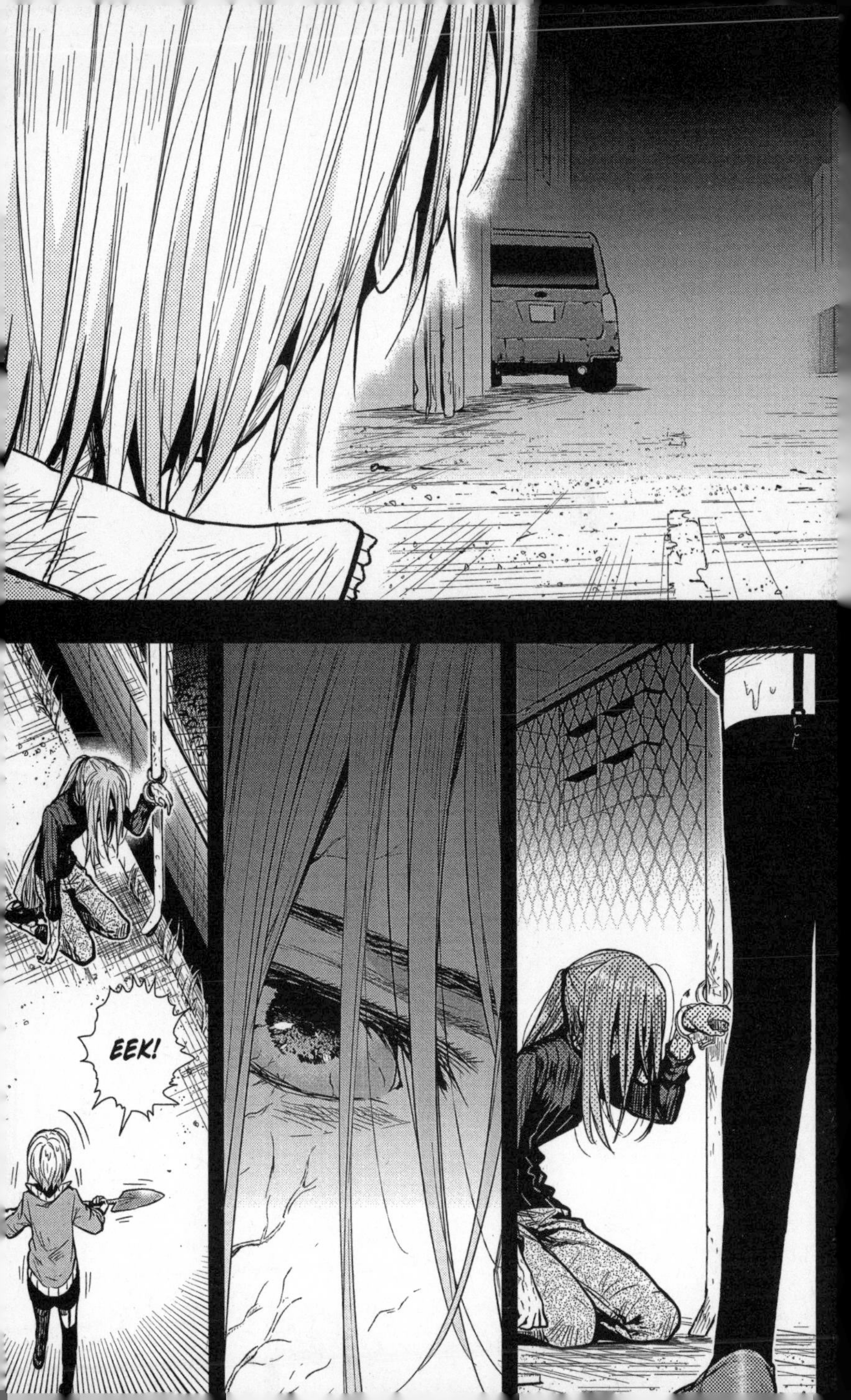
EEK!

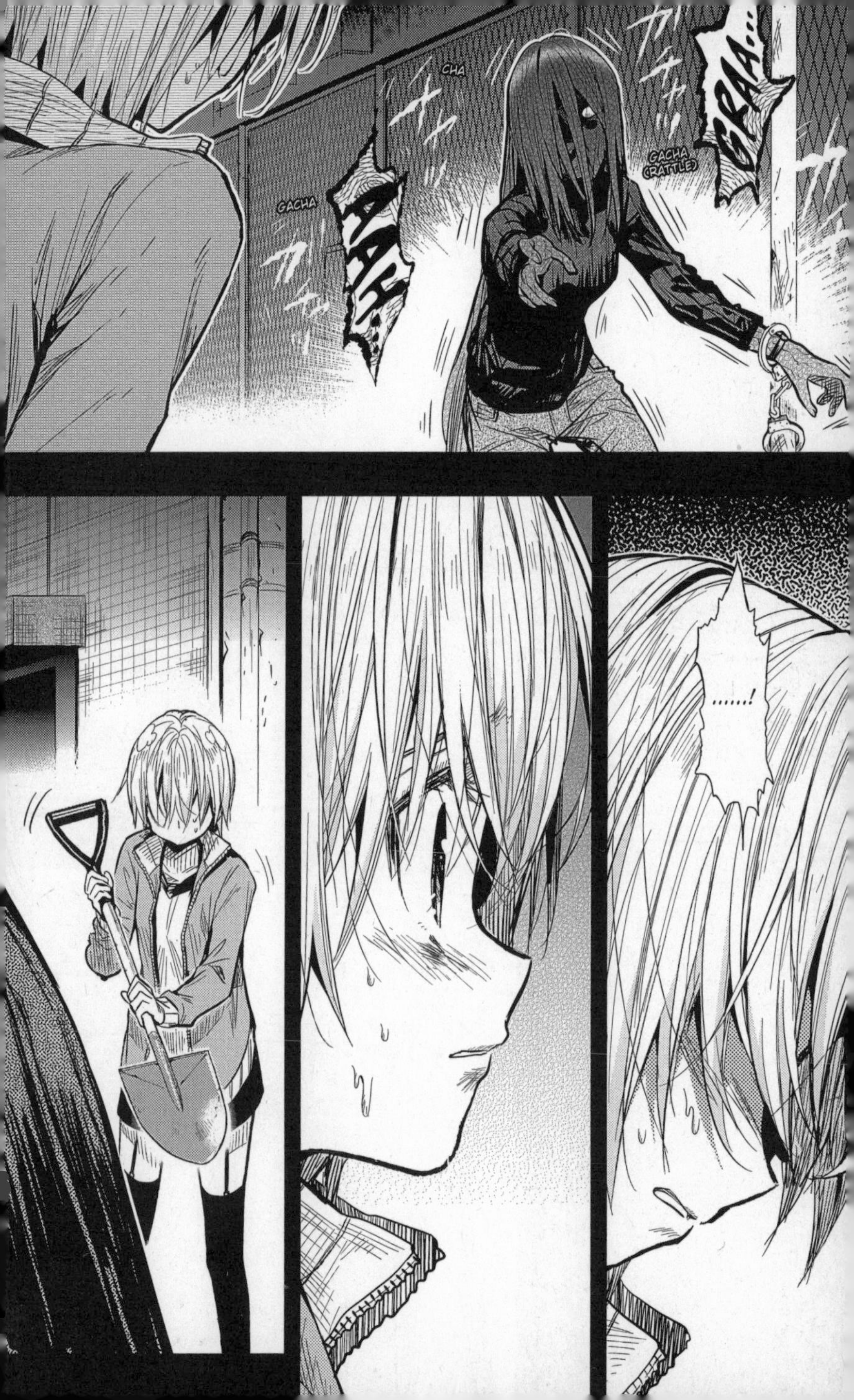
GRAA...
GACHA (RATTLE)
CHA
AAAH...
GACHA
......!

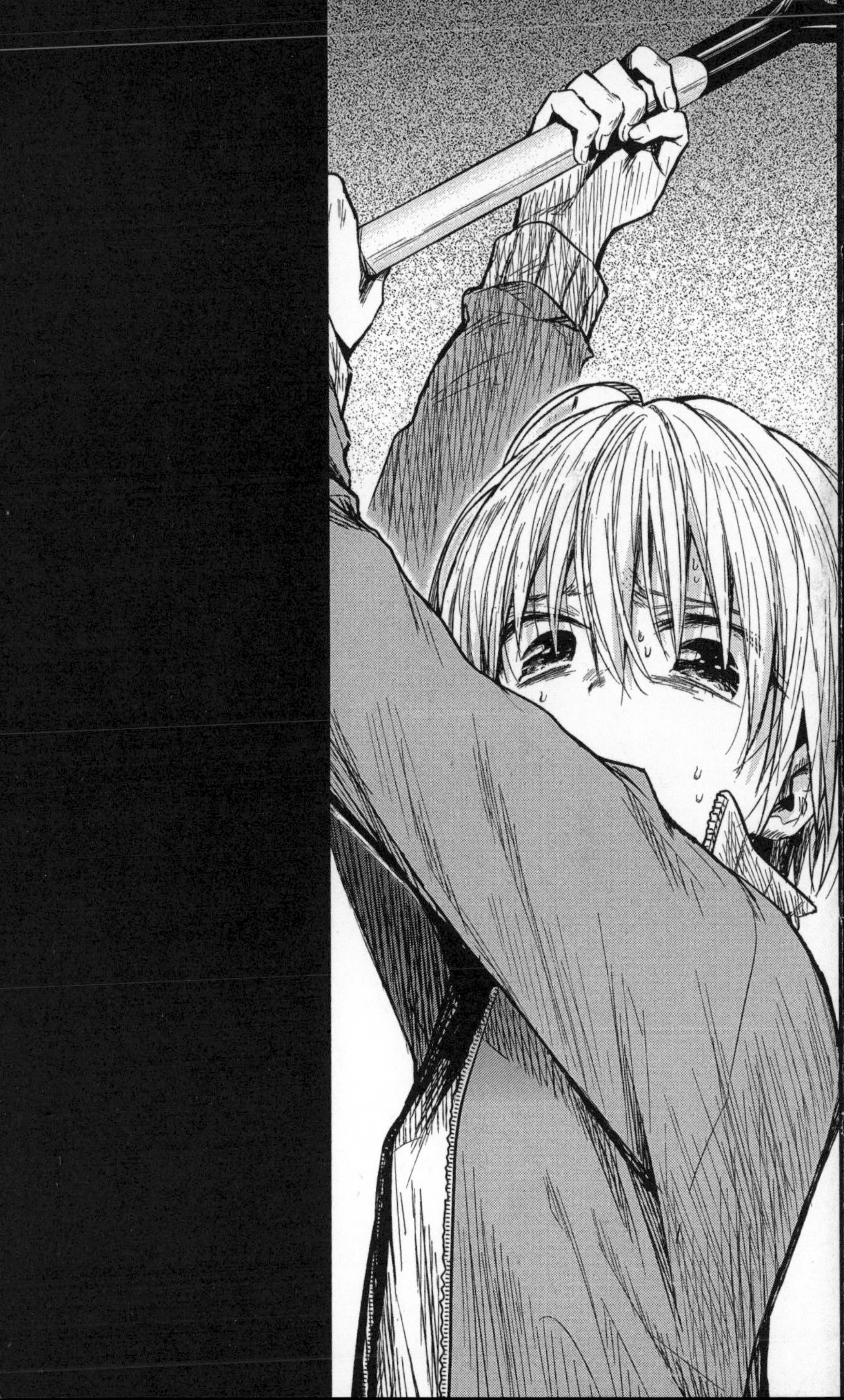

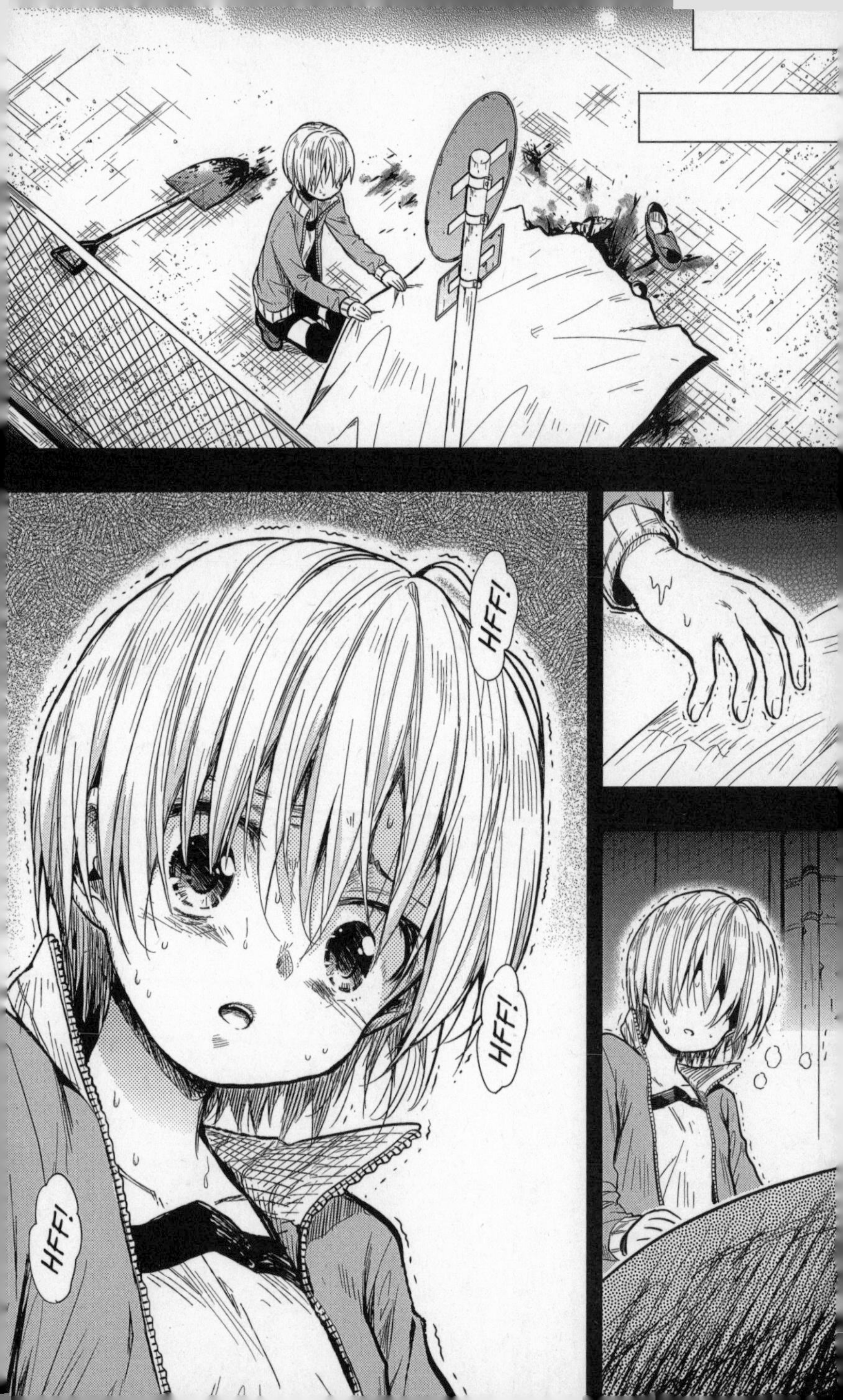
HFF!
HFF!
HFF!

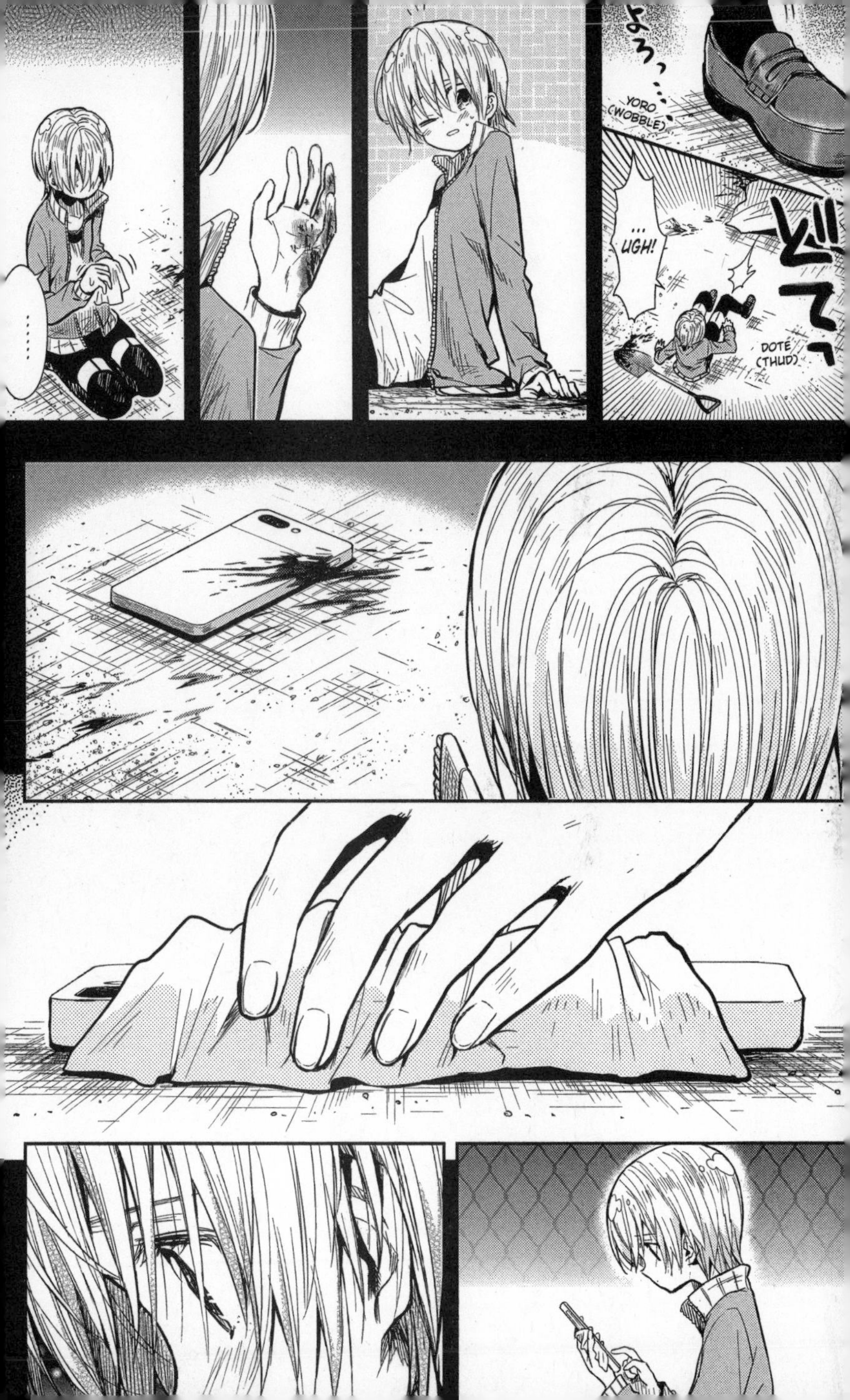
よろっ
YORO (WOBBLE)
どてっ
...UGH!
DOTE (THUD)
......

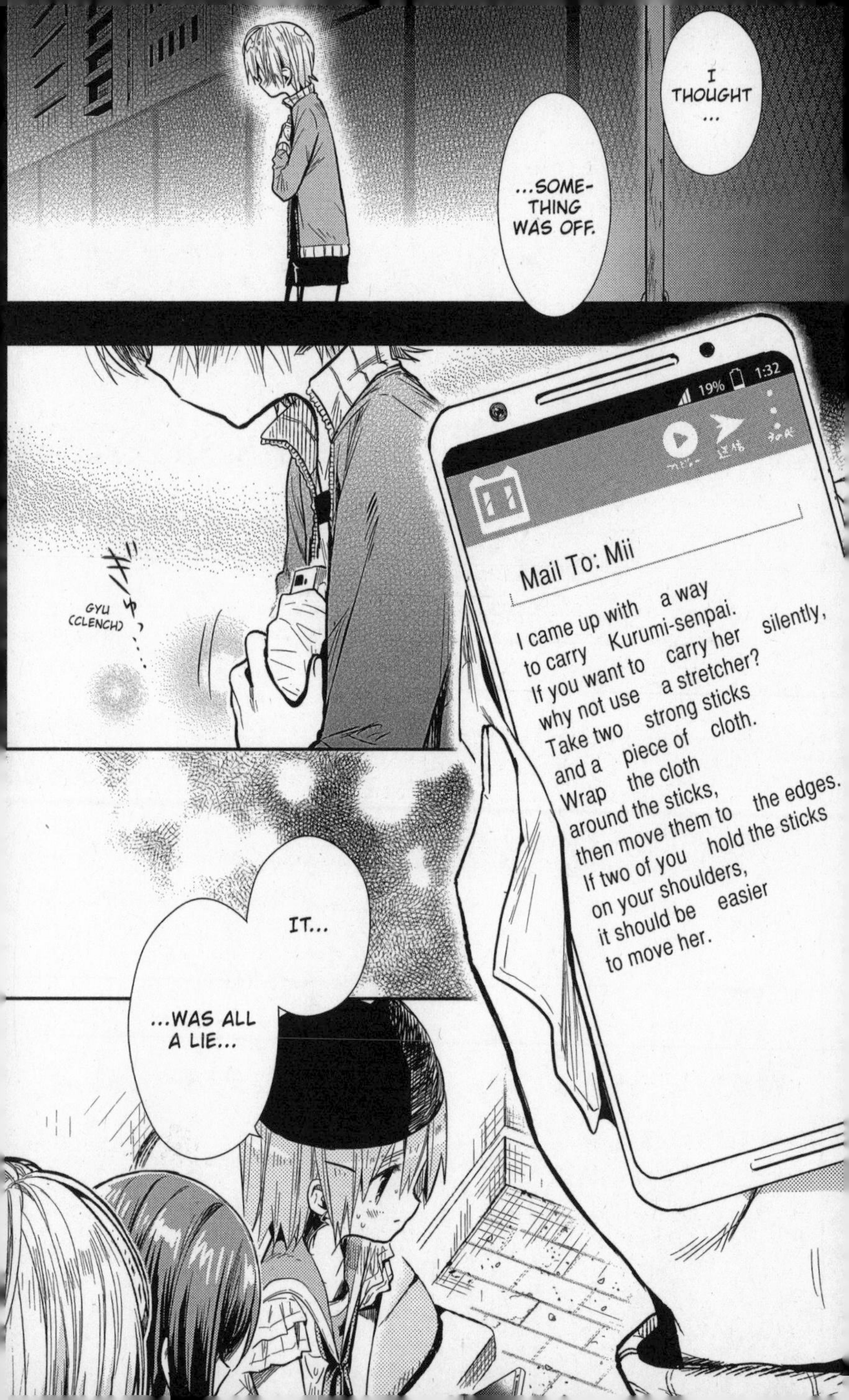
I THOUGHT...
...SOME-THING WAS OFF.
19% 1:32
Mail To: Mii
I came up with a way to carry Kurumi-senpai. If you want to carry her silently, why not use a stretcher? Take two strong sticks and a piece of cloth. Wrap the cloth around the sticks, then move them to the edges. If two of you hold the sticks on your shoulders, it should be easier to move her.
GYU (CLENCH)
IT...
...WAS ALL A LIE...

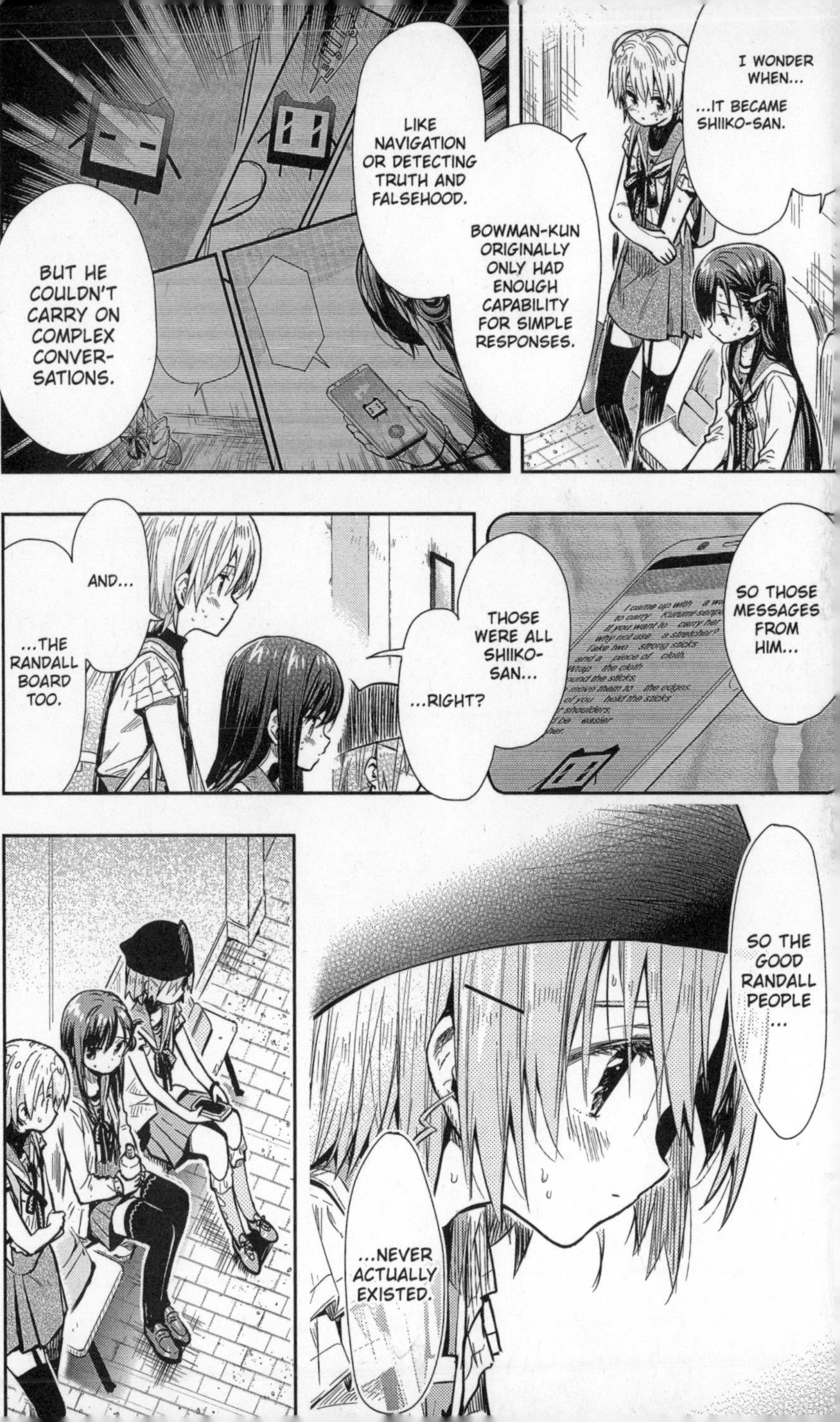
I WONDER WHEN...
...IT BECAME SHIIKO-SAN.
BOWMAN-KUN ORIGINALLY ONLY HAD ENOUGH CAPABILITY FOR SIMPLE RESPONSES.
LIKE NAVIGATION OR DETECTING TRUTH AND FALSEHOOD.
BUT HE COULDN'T CARRY ON COMPLEX CONVER-SATIONS.
SO THOSE MESSAGES FROM HIM...
THOSE WERE ALL SHIIKO-SAN...
...RIGHT?
AND...
...THE RANDALL BOARD TOO.
SO THE GOOD RANDALL PEOPLE...
...NEVER ACTUALLY EXISTED.

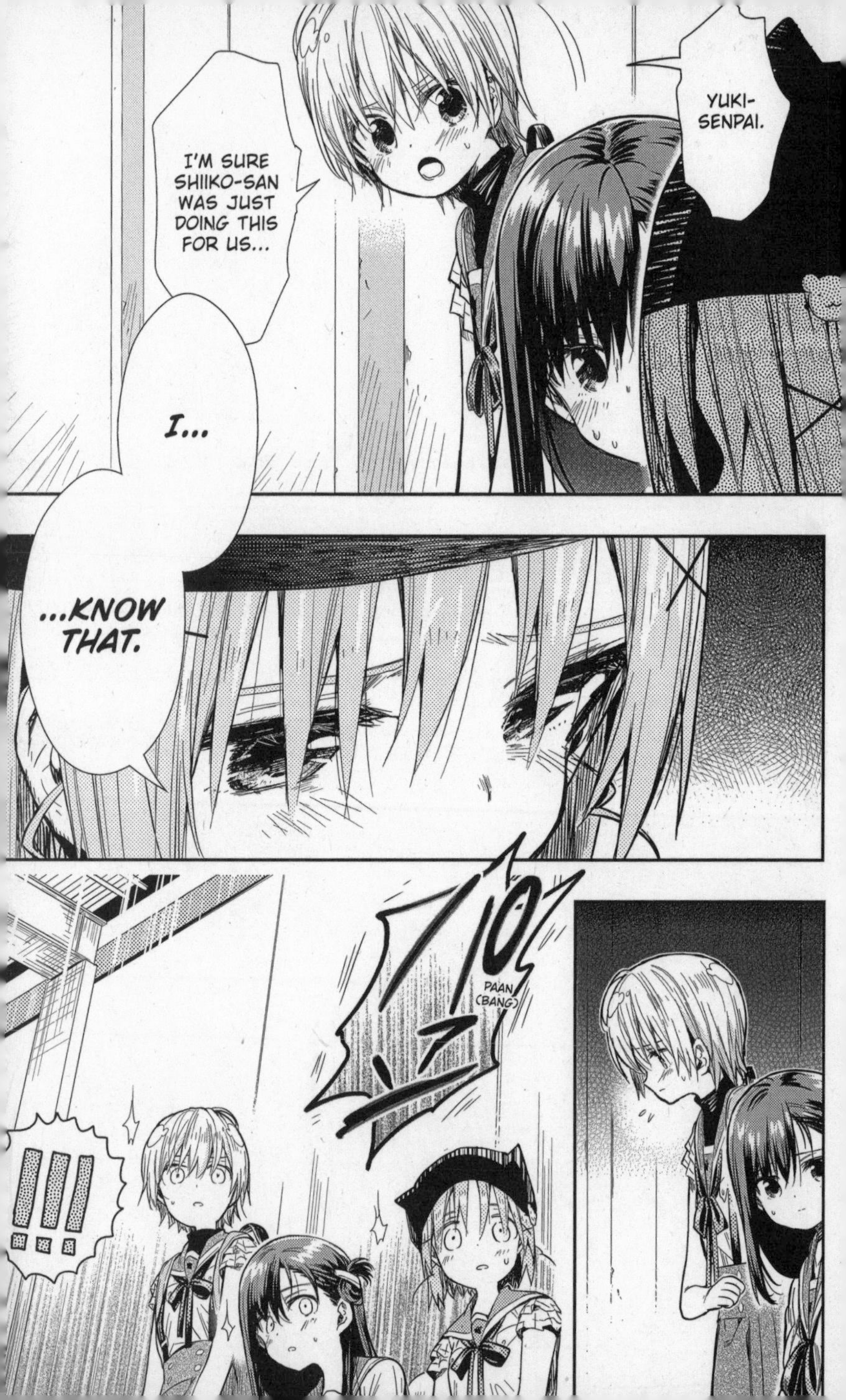
YUKI-SENPAI.
I'M SURE SHIIKO-SAN WAS JUST DOING THIS FOR US...
I...
...KNOW THAT.
PAAN (BANG)
!!!

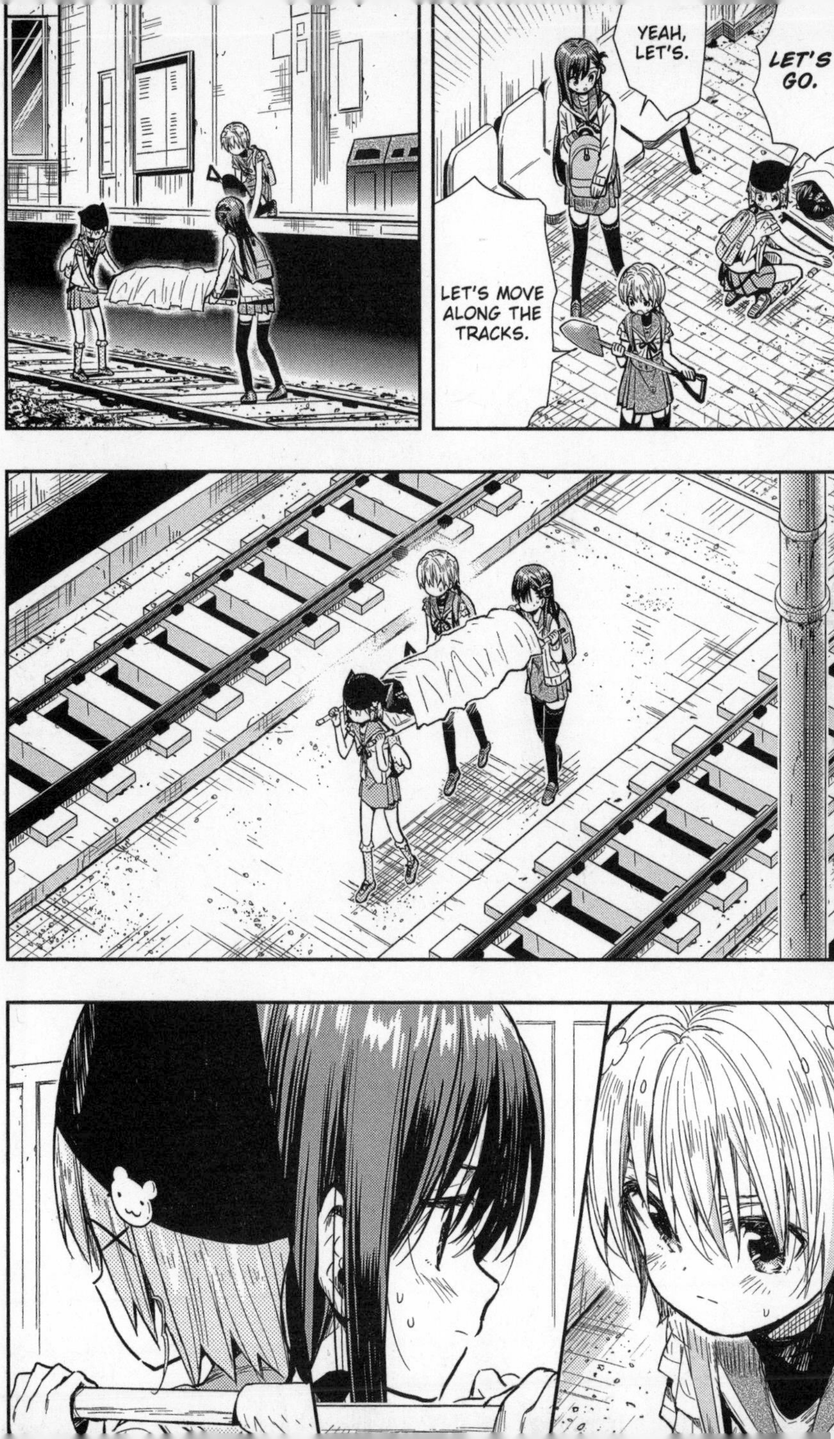
LET'S GO.
YEAH, LET'S.
LET'S MOVE ALONG THE TRACKS.

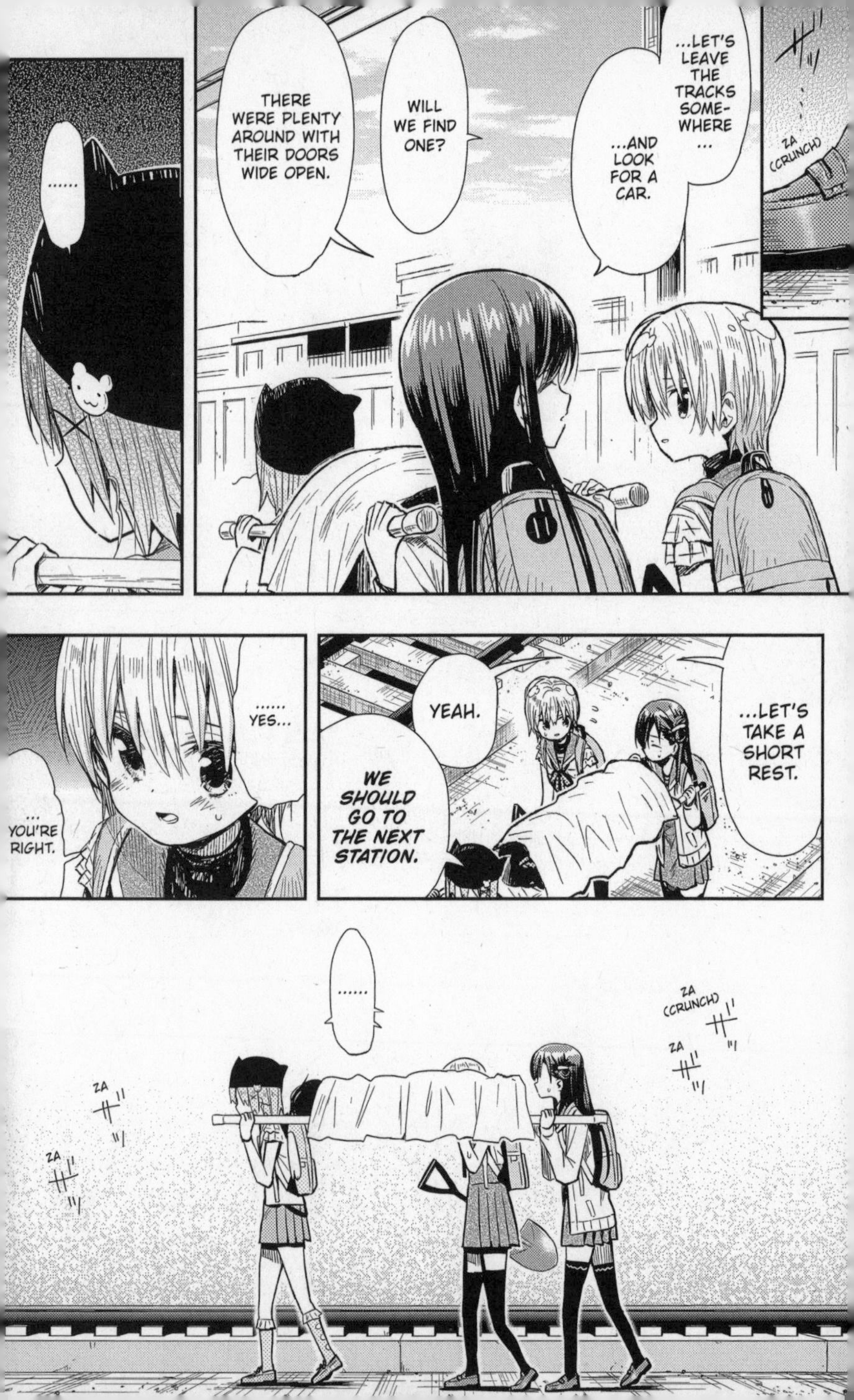
ZA (CRUNCH)
...LET'S LEAVE THE TRACKS SOMEWHERE...
...AND LOOK FOR A CAR.
WILL WE FIND ONE?
THERE WERE PLENTY AROUND WITH THEIR DOORS WIDE OPEN.
......
...LET'S TAKE A SHORT REST.
YEAH.
WE SHOULD GO TO THE NEXT STATION.
...... YES...
... YOU'RE RIGHT.
......
ZA (CRUNCH)
ZA
ZA
ZA

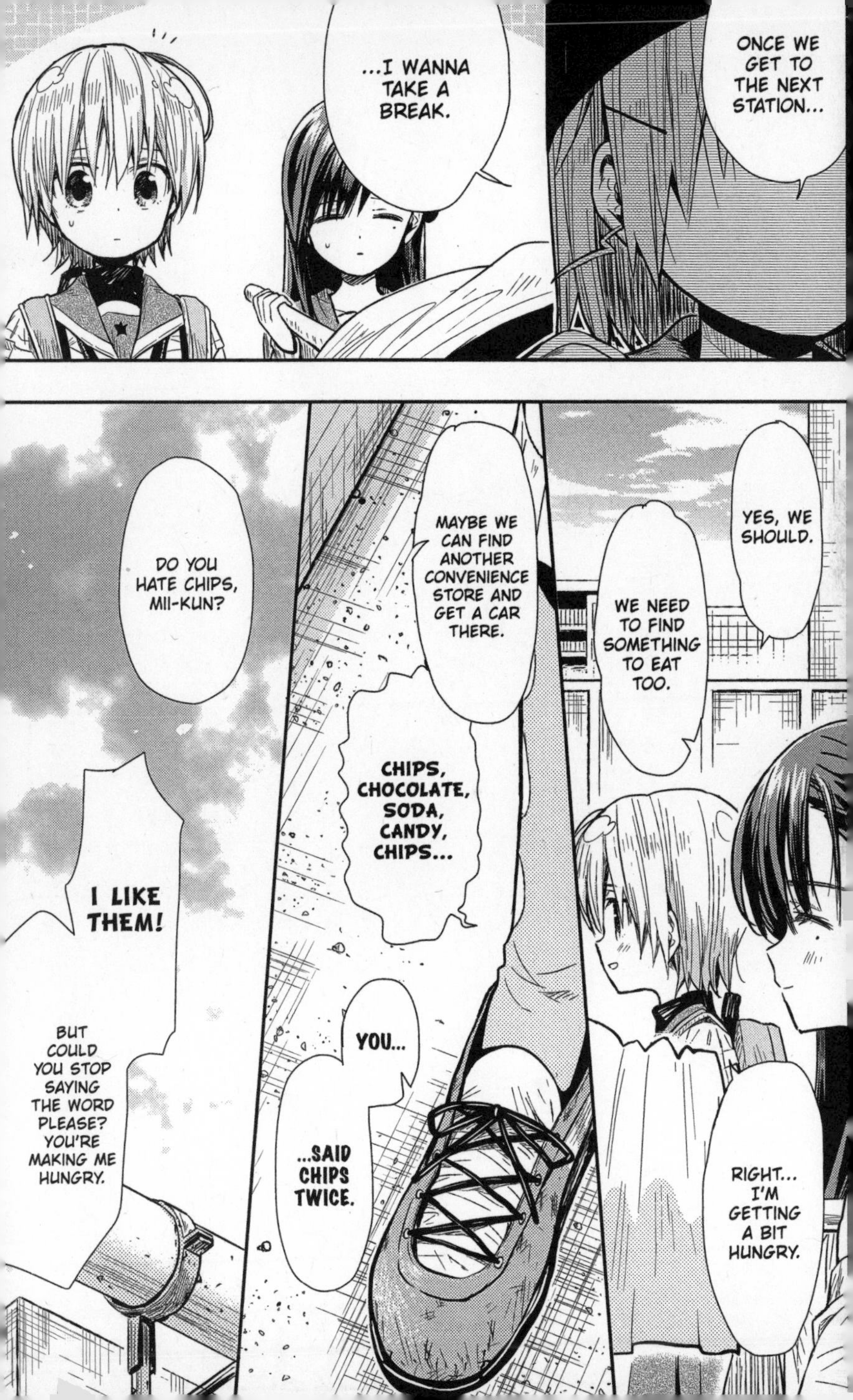
ONCE WE GET TO THE NEXT STATION...
...I WANNA TAKE A BREAK.
YES, WE SHOULD.
WE NEED TO FIND SOMETHING TO EAT TOO.
RIGHT... I'M GETTING A BIT HUNGRY.
MAYBE WE CAN FIND ANOTHER CONVENIENCE STORE AND GET A CAR THERE.
CHIPS, CHOCOLATE, SODA, CANDY, CHIPS...
YOU...
...SAID CHIPS TWICE.
DO YOU HATE CHIPS, MII-KUN?
I LIKE THEM!
BUT COULD YOU STOP SAYING THE WORD PLEASE? YOU'RE MAKING ME HUNGRY.

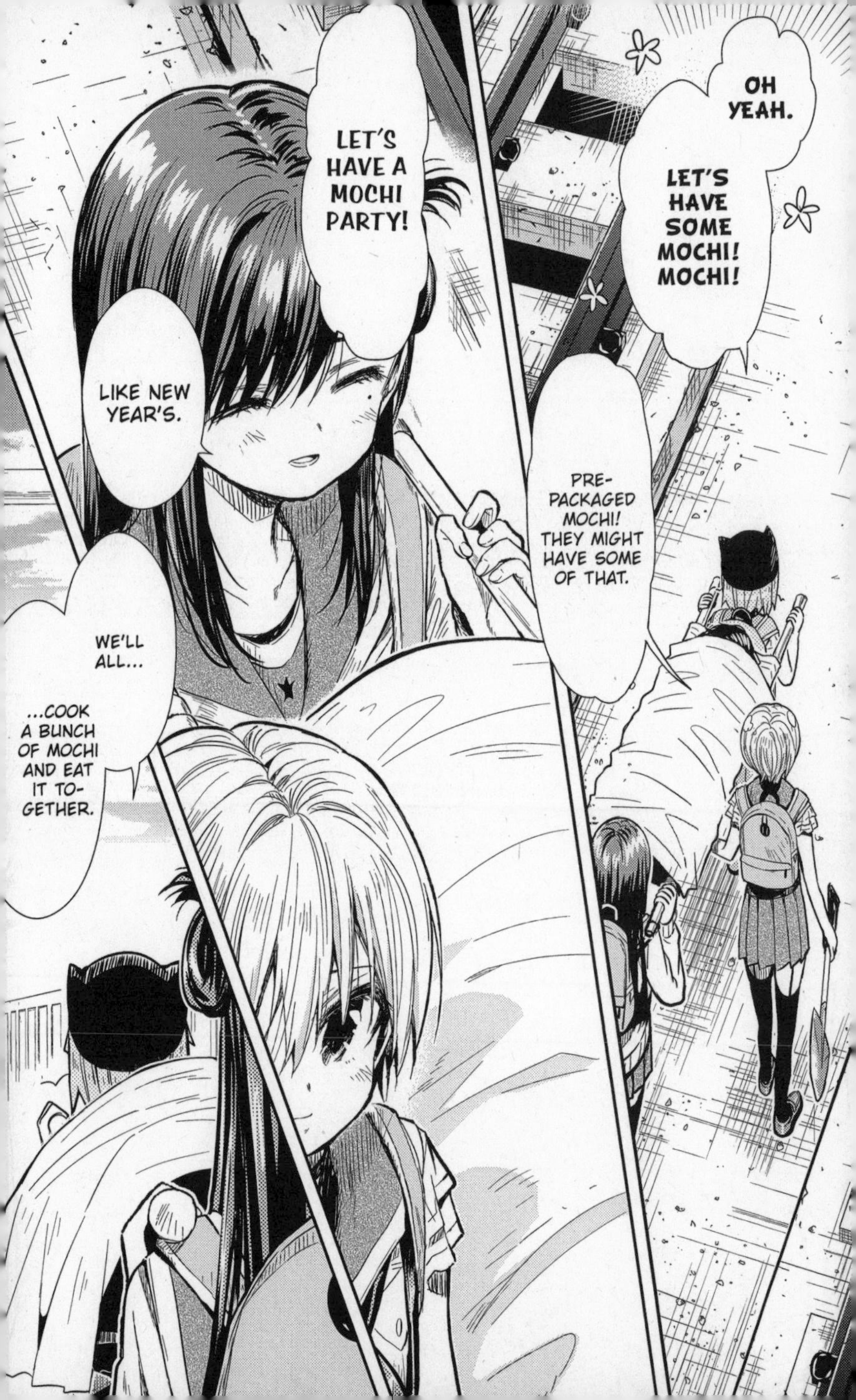
OH YEAH.
LET'S HAVE SOME MOCHI! MOCHI!
PRE-PACKAGED MOCHI! THEY MIGHT HAVE SOME OF THAT.
LET'S HAVE A MOCHI PARTY!
LIKE NEW YEAR'S.
WE'LL ALL...
...COOK A BUNCH OF MOCHI AND EAT IT TO-GETHER.

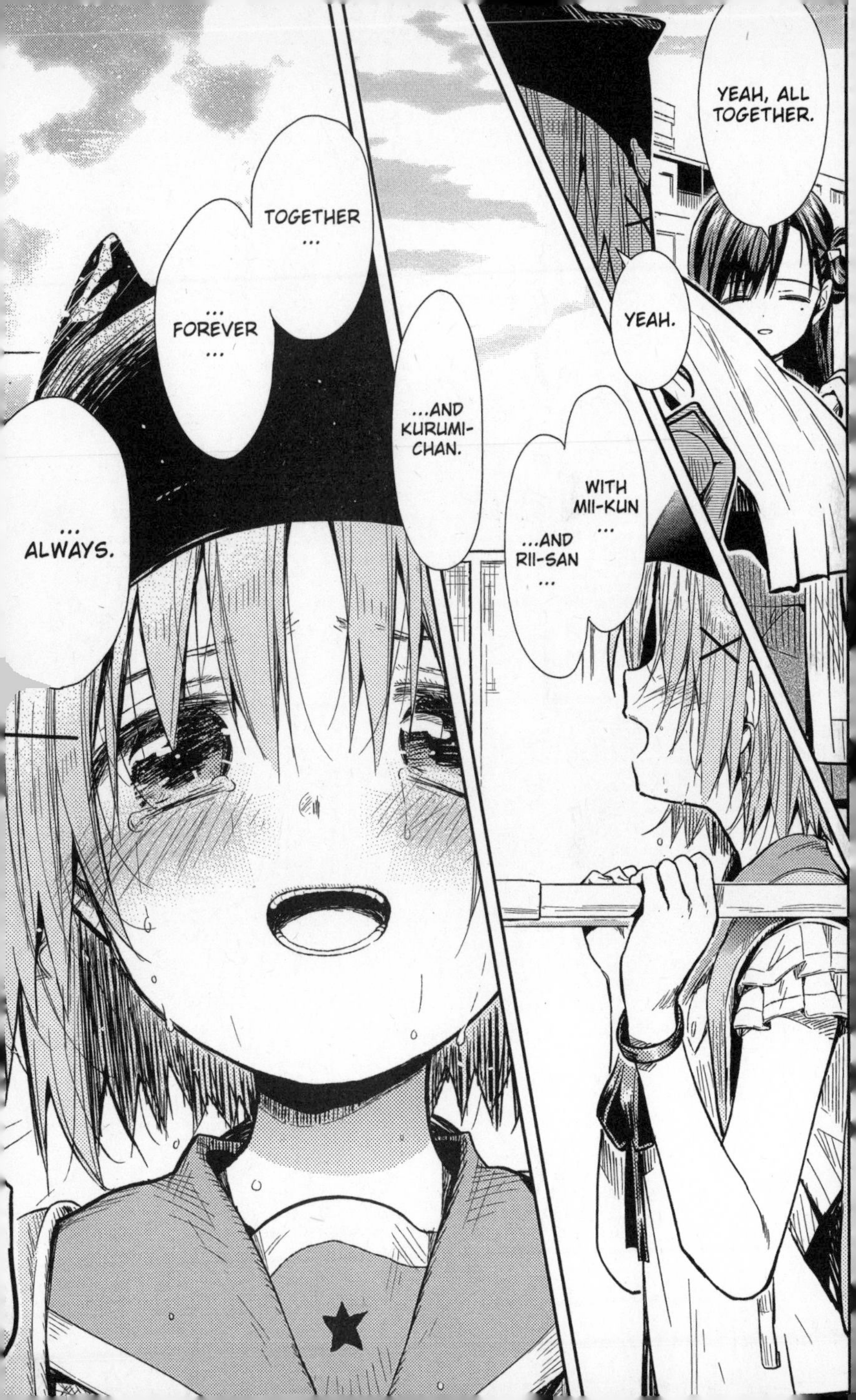
YEAH, ALL TOGETHER.
YEAH.
WITH MII-KUN ... ...AND RII-SAN ...
...AND KURUMI-CHAN.
TOGETHER ...
... FOREVER ...
... ALWAYS.

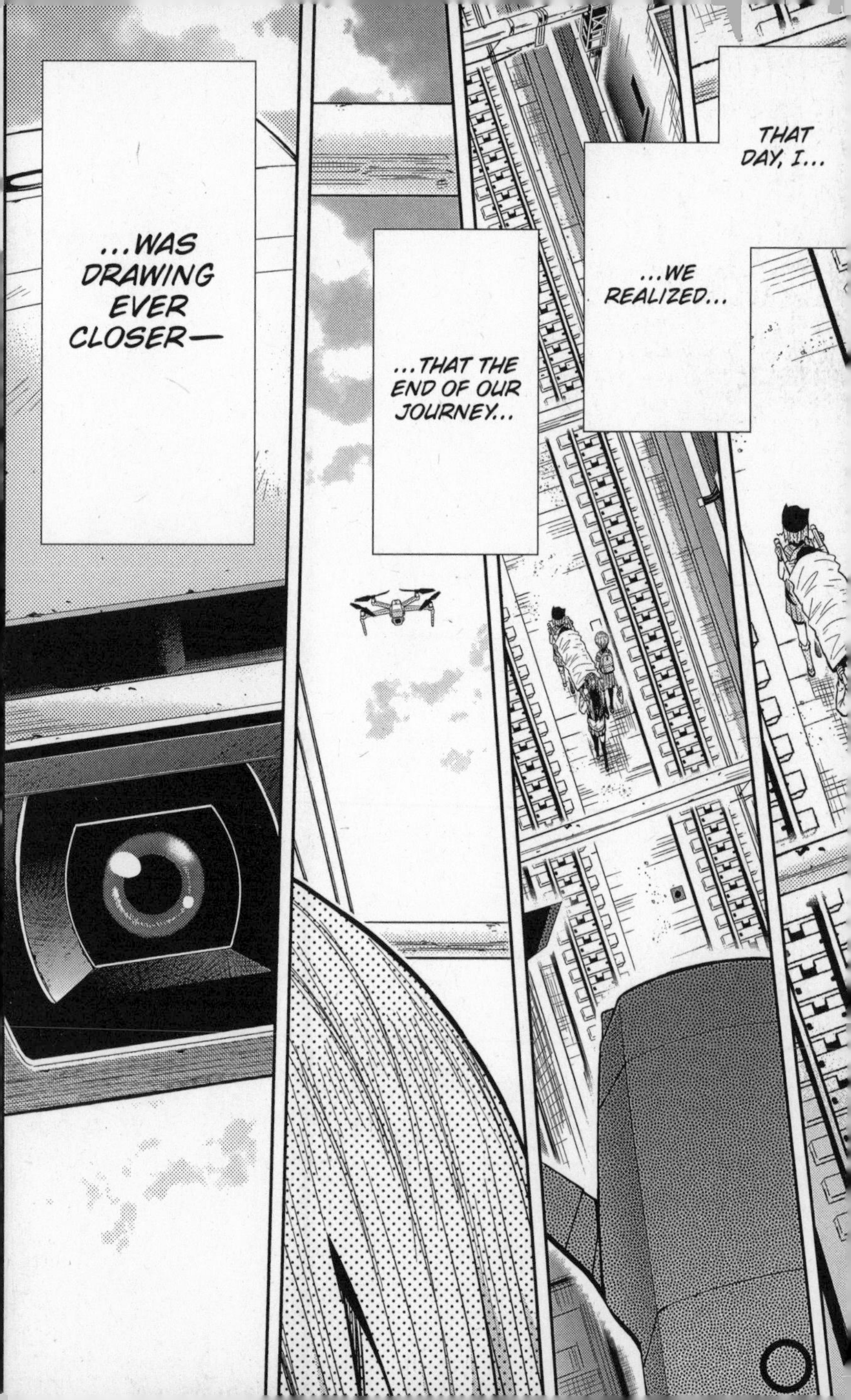
THAT DAY, I...
...WE REALIZED...
...THAT THE END OF OUR JOURNEY...
...WAS DRAWING EVER CLOSER—

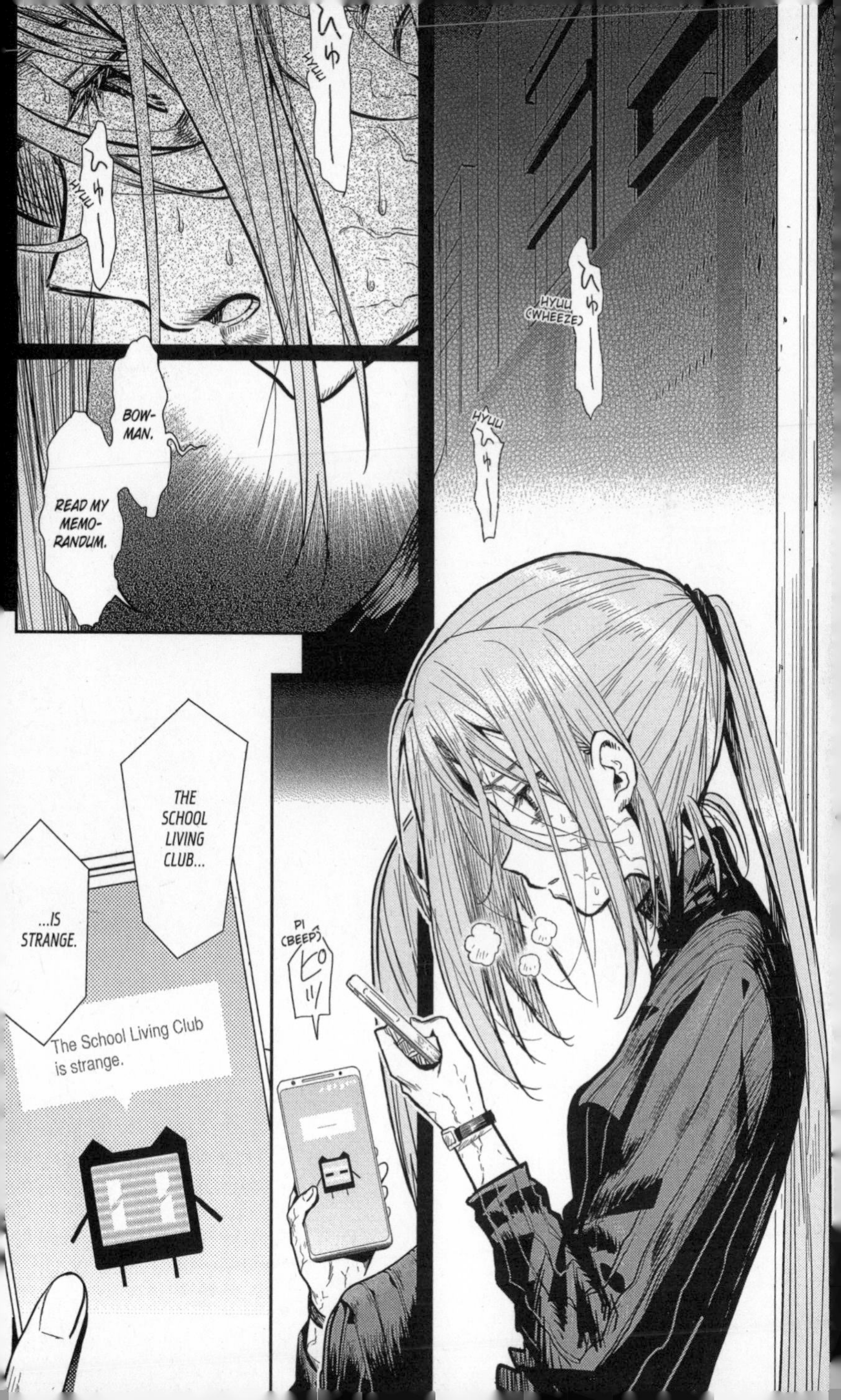

ひゅー
HYUU (WHEEZE)
ひゅー
HYUU
ピッ
PI (BEEP)
ひゅー
HYUU
ひゅー
HYUU
BOW-MAN.
READ MY MEMO-RANDUM.
THE SCHOOL LIVING CLUB...
...IS STRANGE.
The School Living Club is strange.

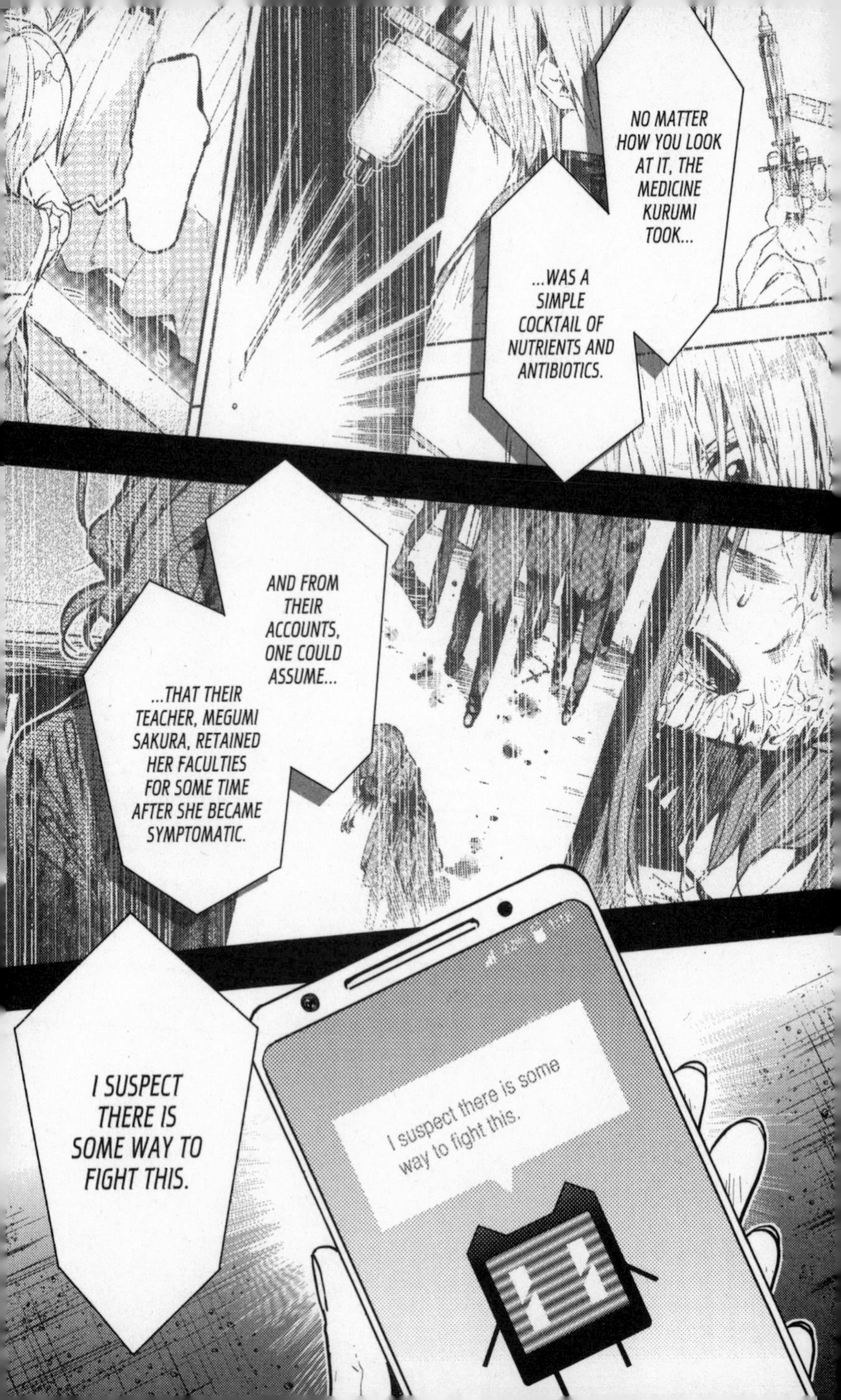
NO MATTER HOW YOU LOOK AT IT, THE MEDICINE KURUMI TOOK...
...WAS A SIMPLE COCKTAIL OF NUTRIENTS AND ANTIBIOTICS.
AND FROM THEIR ACCOUNTS, ONE COULD ASSUME...
...THAT THEIR TEACHER, MEGUMI SAKURA, RETAINED HER FACULTIES FOR SOME TIME AFTER SHE BECAME SYMPTOMATIC.
I suspect there is some way to fight this.
I SUSPECT THERE IS SOME WAY TO FIGHT THIS.

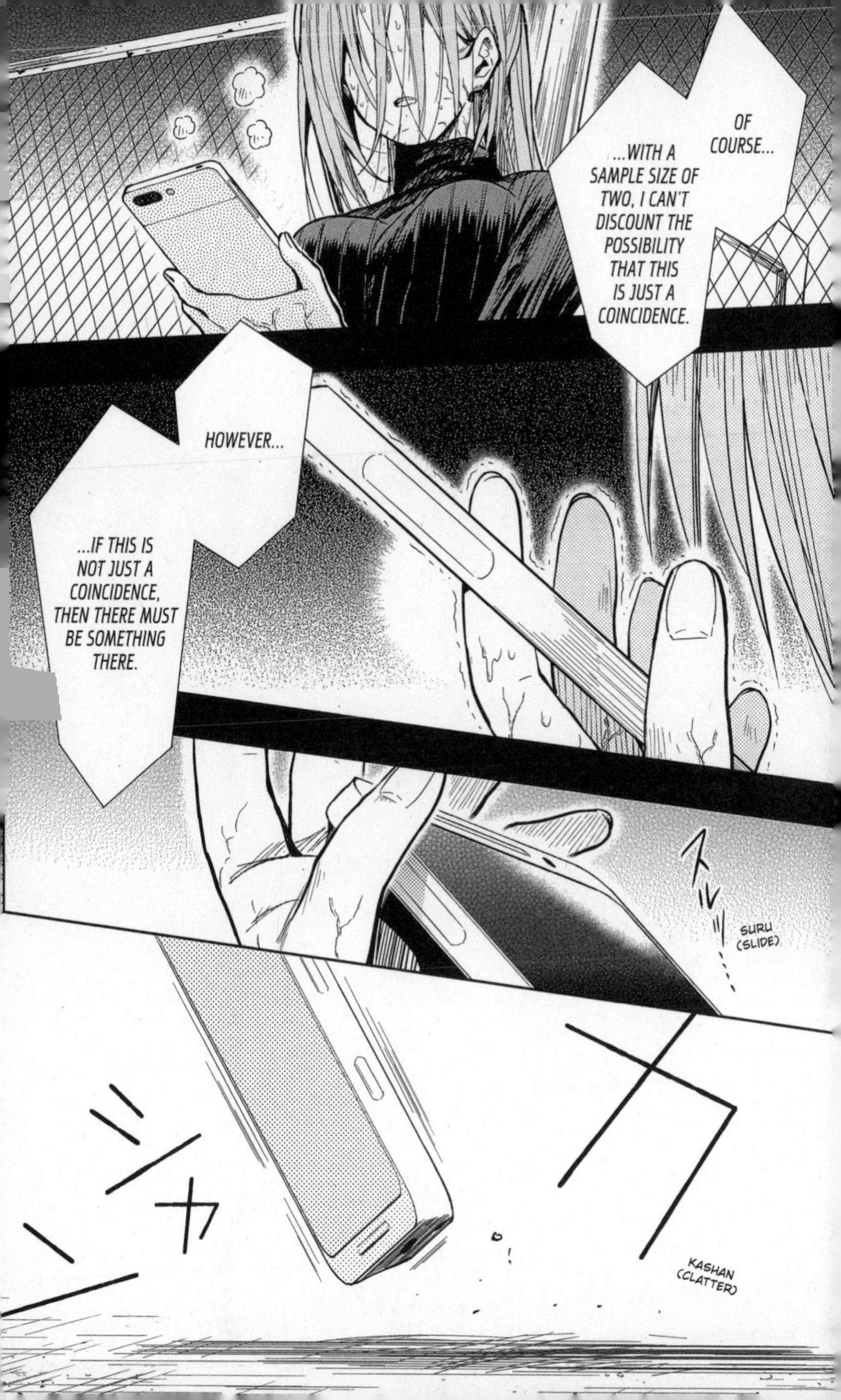
OF COURSE...
...WITH A SAMPLE SIZE OF TWO, I CAN'T DISCOUNT THE POSSIBILITY THAT THIS IS JUST A COINCIDENCE.
HOWEVER...
...IF THIS IS NOT JUST A COINCIDENCE, THEN THERE MUST BE SOMETHING THERE.
SURU (SLIDE)
KASHAN (CLATTER)

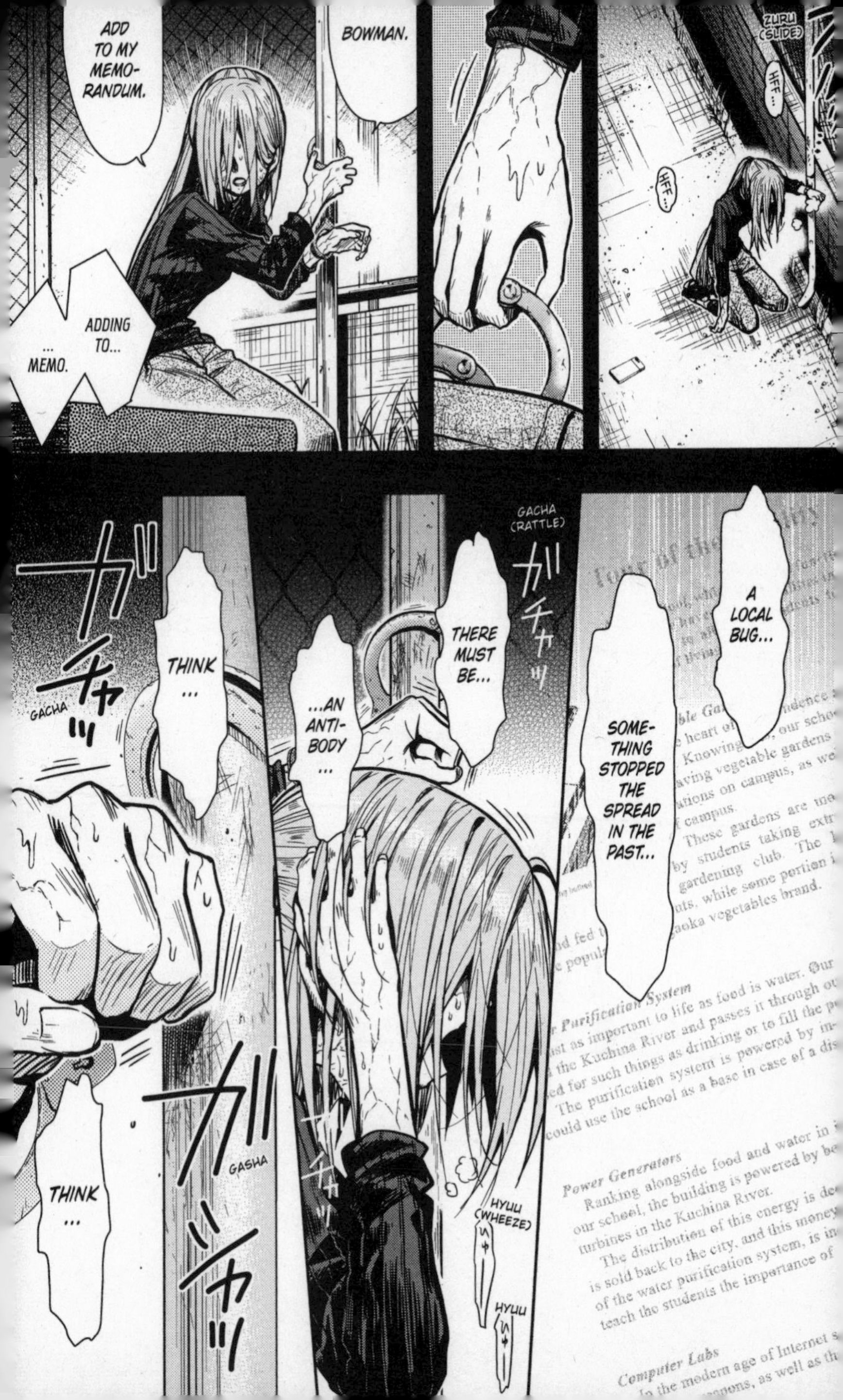
ZURU (SLIDE)
HFF...
HFF...
BOWMAN.
ADD TO MY MEMO-RANDUM.
ADDING TO...
... MEMO.
A LOCAL BUG...
SOME-THING STOPPED THE SPREAD IN THE PAST...
Power Generators
Computer Labs
GACHA (RATTLE)
THERE MUST BE...
...AN ANTI-BODY ...
HYUU (WHEEZE)
HYUU
THINK ...
GACHA
GASHA
THINK ...

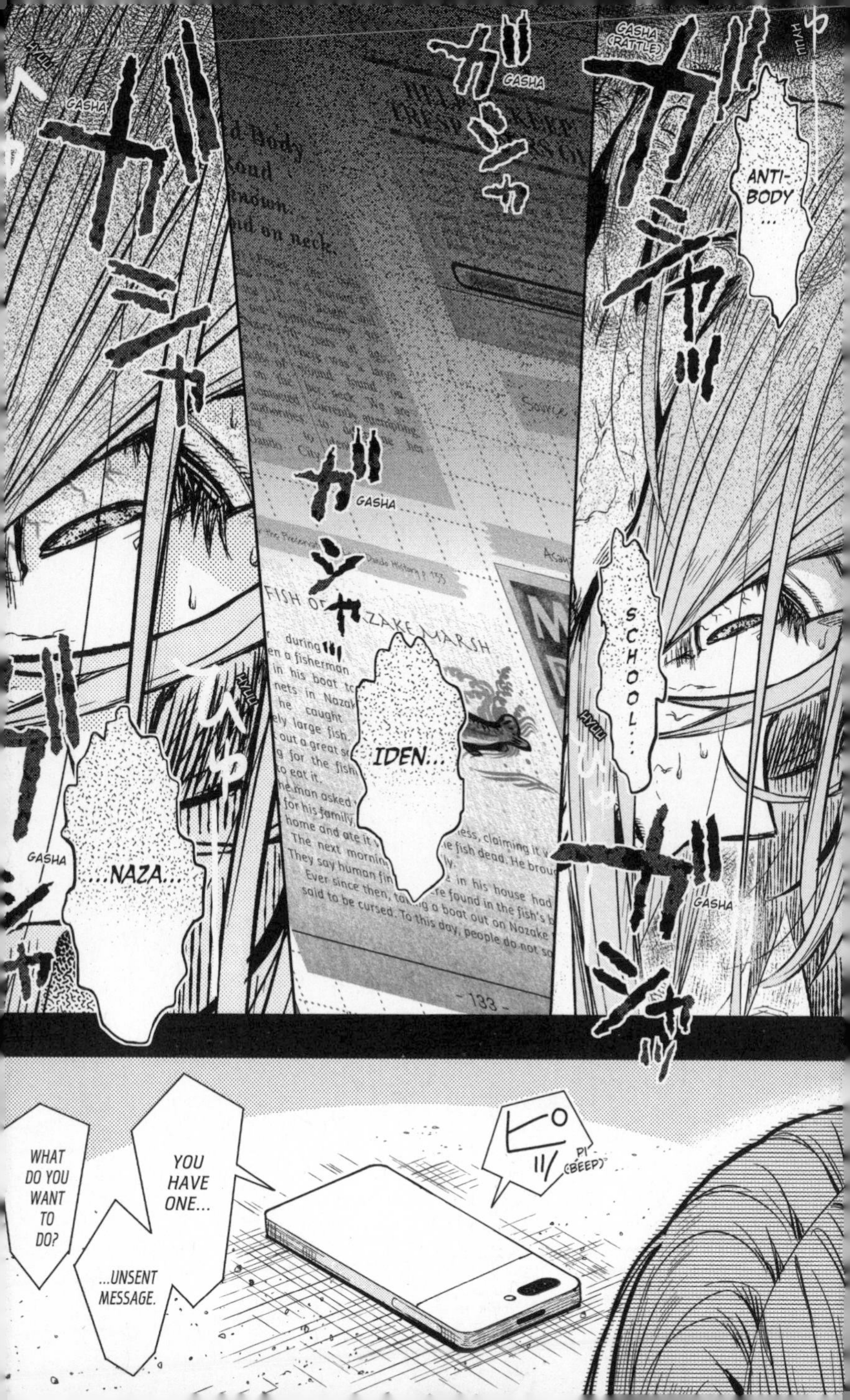
HYUU
GASHA (RATTLE)
ANTI-BODY...
SCHOOL...
HYUU
GASHA
GASHA
GASHA
IDEN...
HYUU
GASHA
HYUU
...NAZA...
GASHA
PI (BEEP)
YOU HAVE ONE...
...UNSENT MESSAGE.
WHAT DO YOU WANT TO DO?

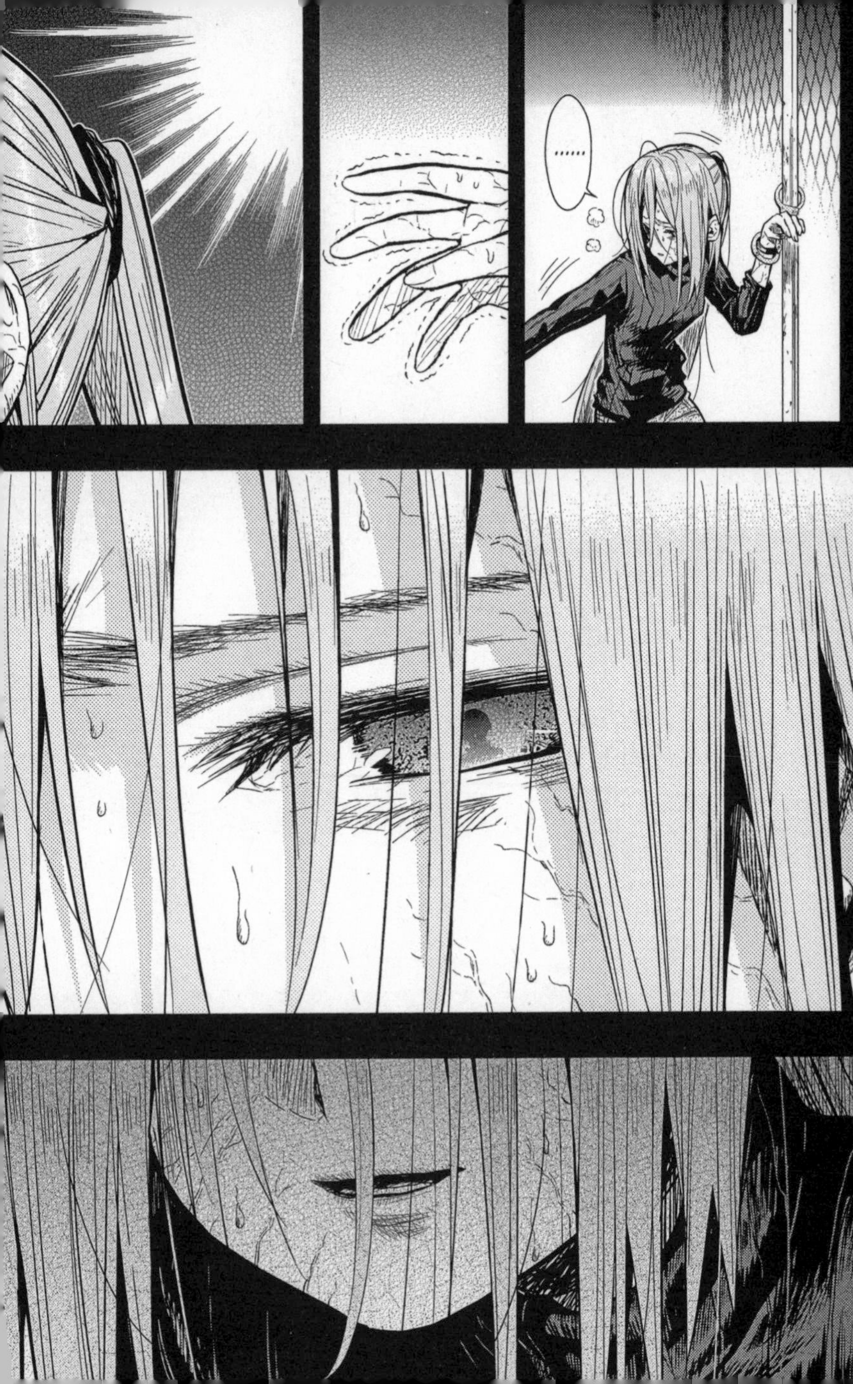
……

Chapter 69　Good Night

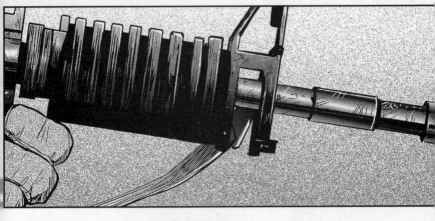

BOTTLE: IRUHASU SPRING WATER

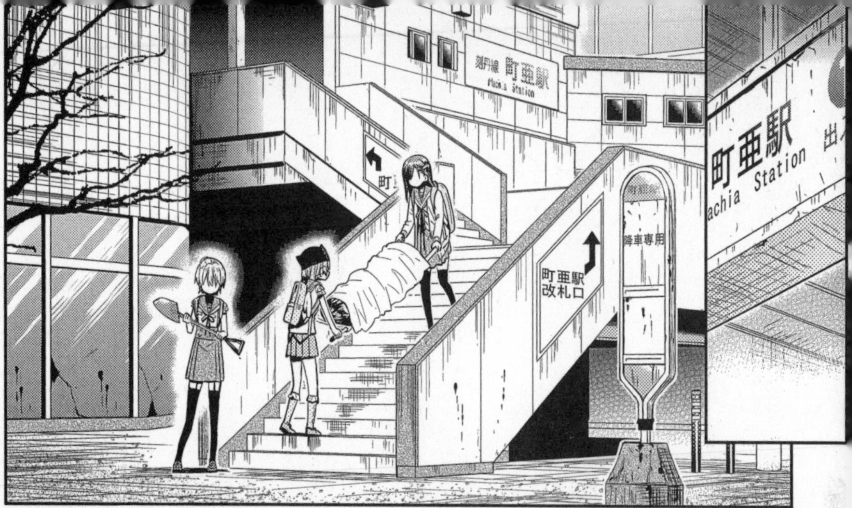
町亜駅
Machia Station
町亜駅
改札口
降車専用

SIGN: MACHIA STATION TICKET GATE

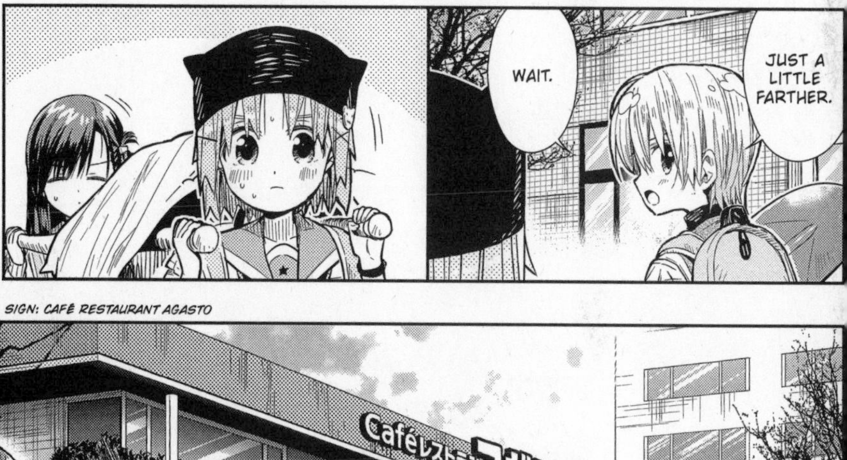
JUST A LITTLE FARTHER.
WAIT.

SIGN: CAFÉ RESTAURANT AGASTO

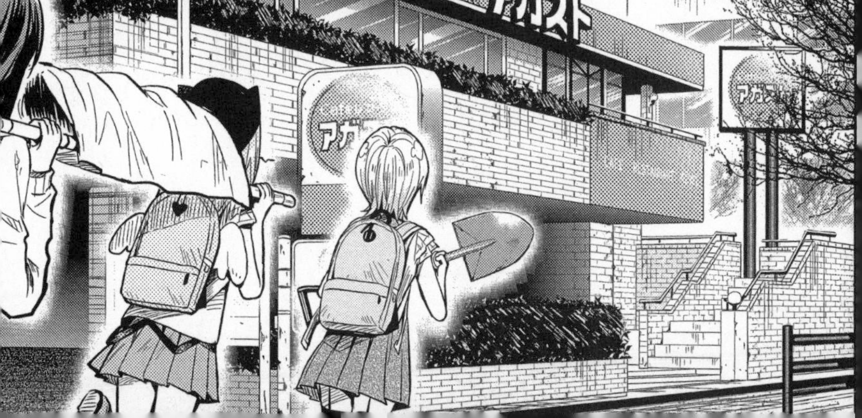
Caféレストラン アガスト

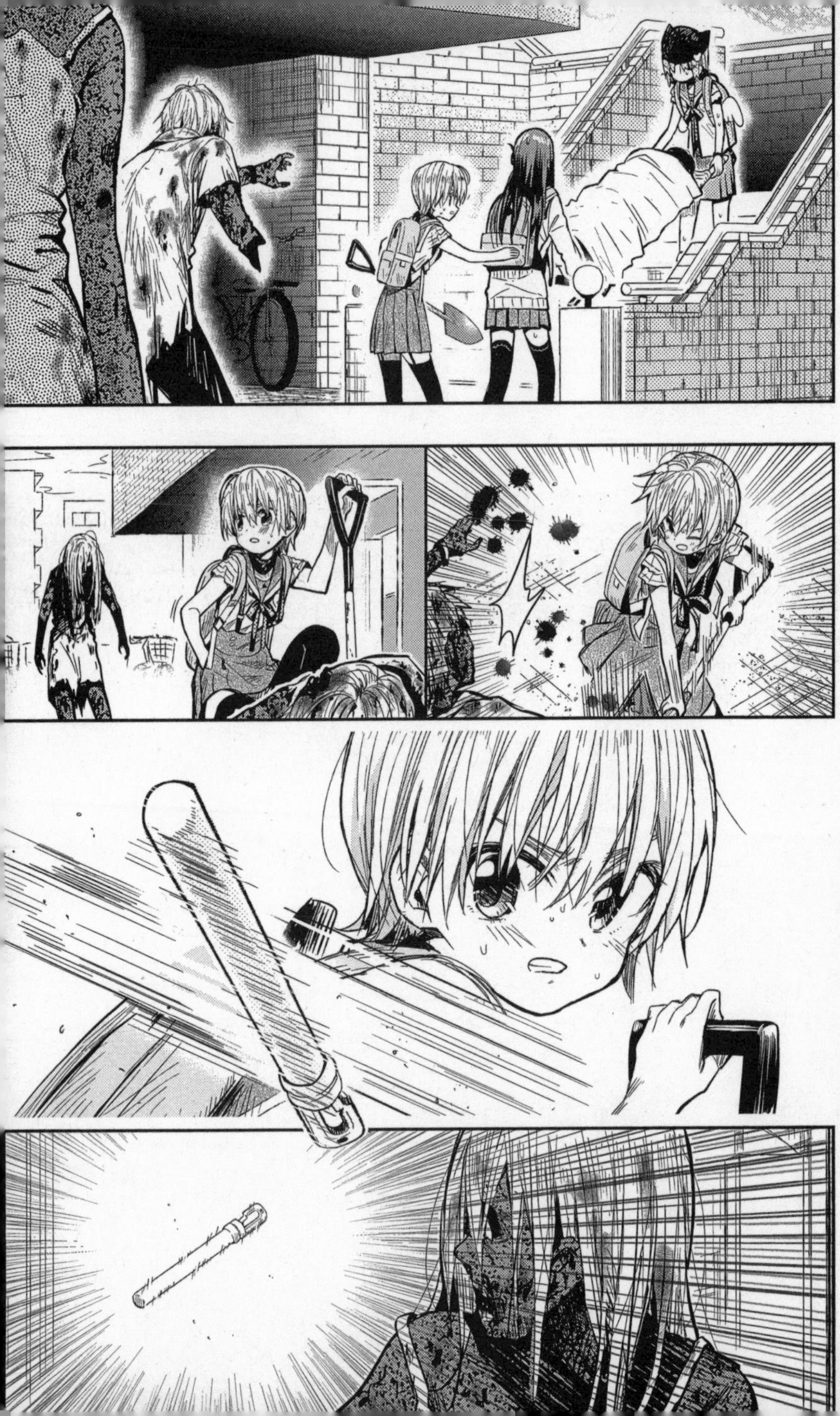

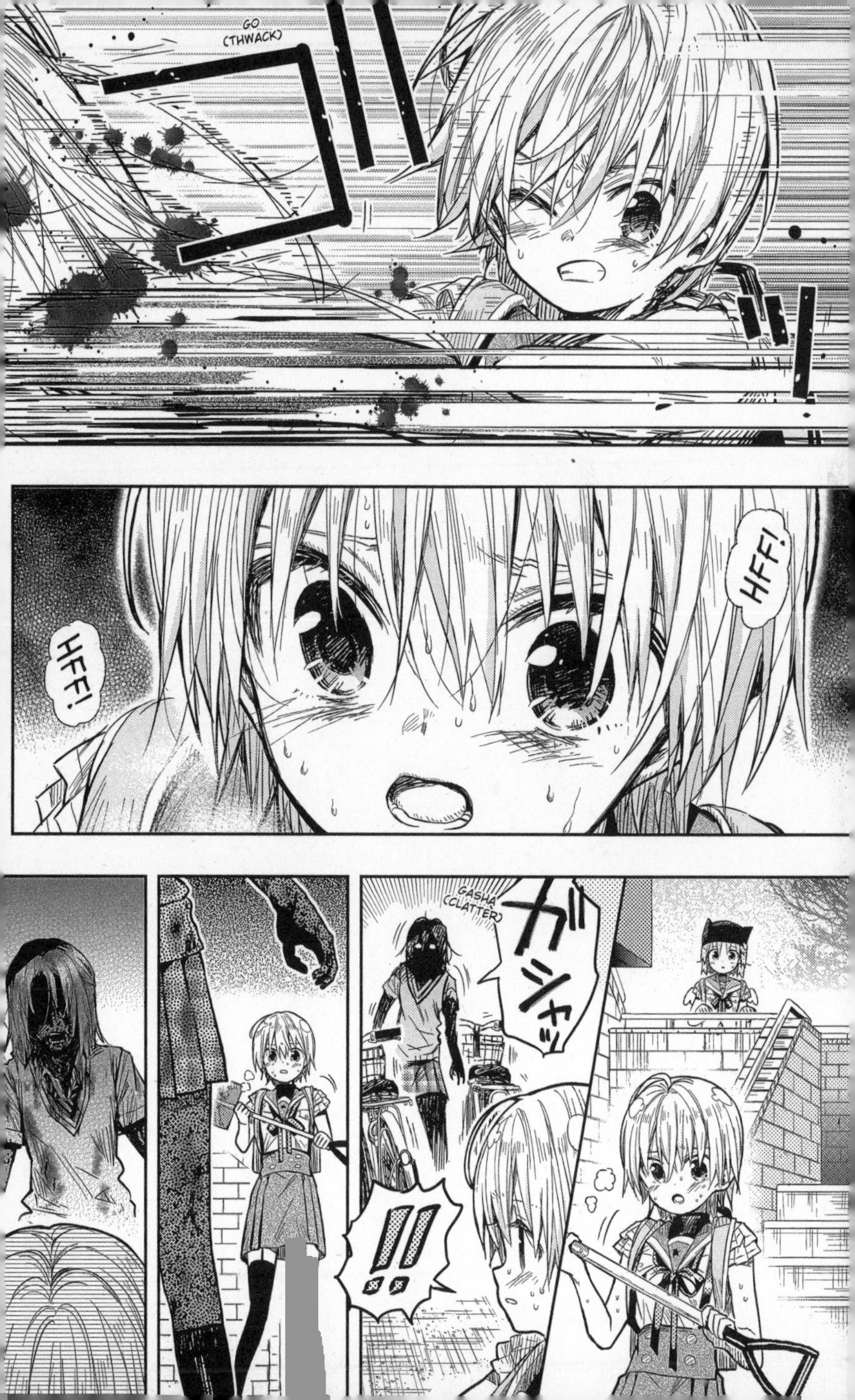
GO (THWACK)
HFF!
HFF!
GASHA (CLATTER)
ガシャッ
!!

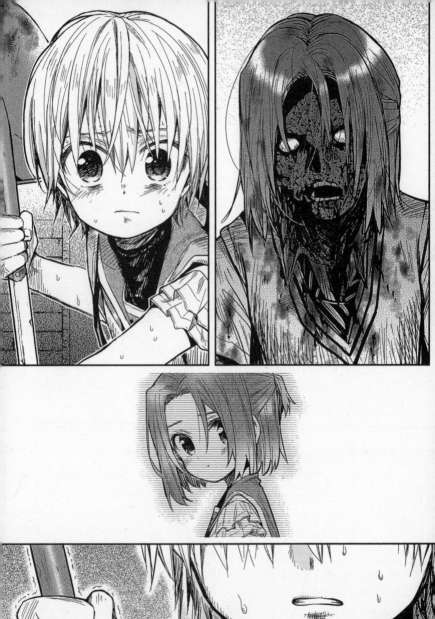

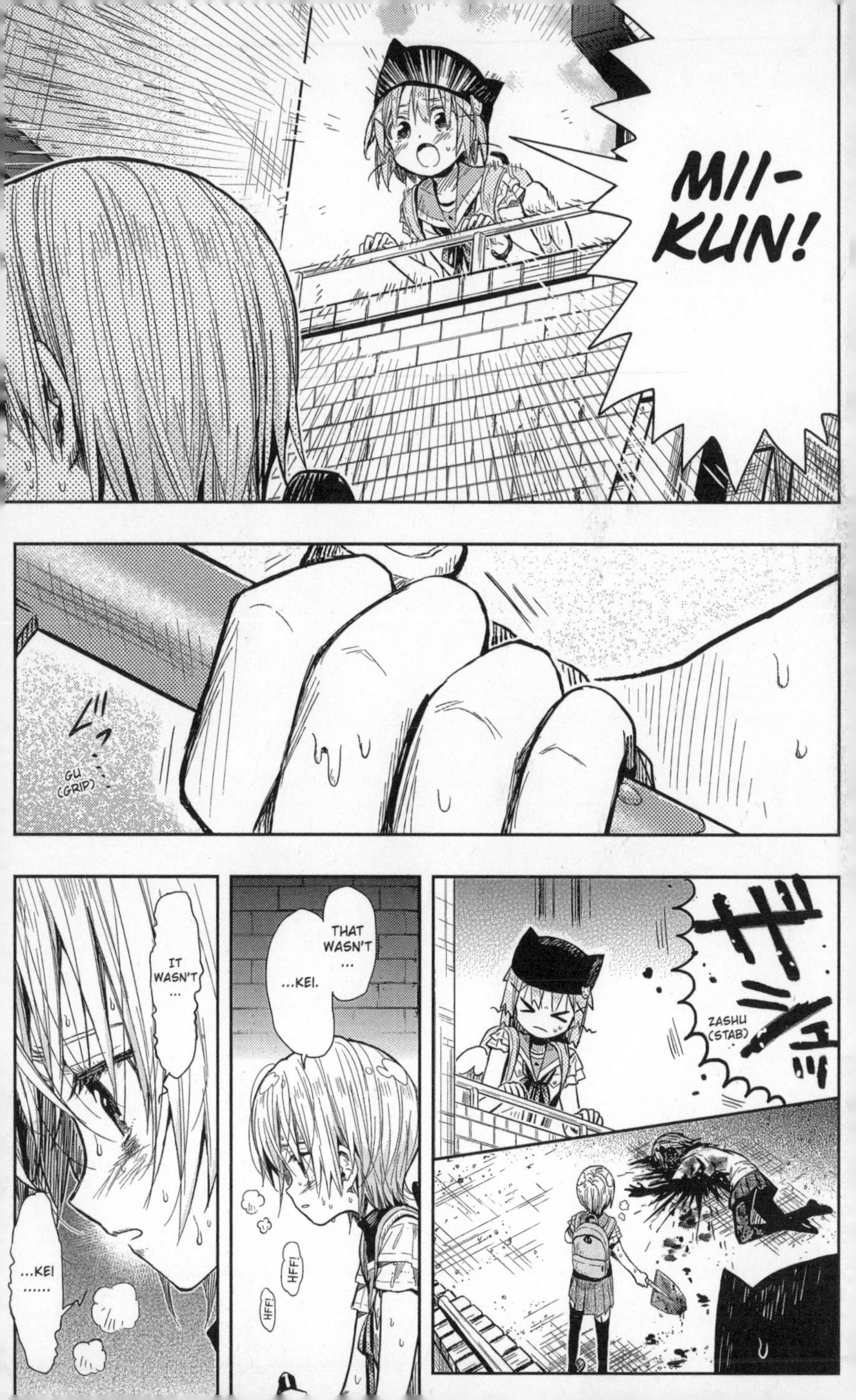
MII-
KUN!
ぐっ
GU
(GRIP)
ザシュッ
ZASHU
(STAB)
THAT
WASN'T
...
...KEI.
HFF!
HFF!
IT
WASN'T
...
...KEI
......

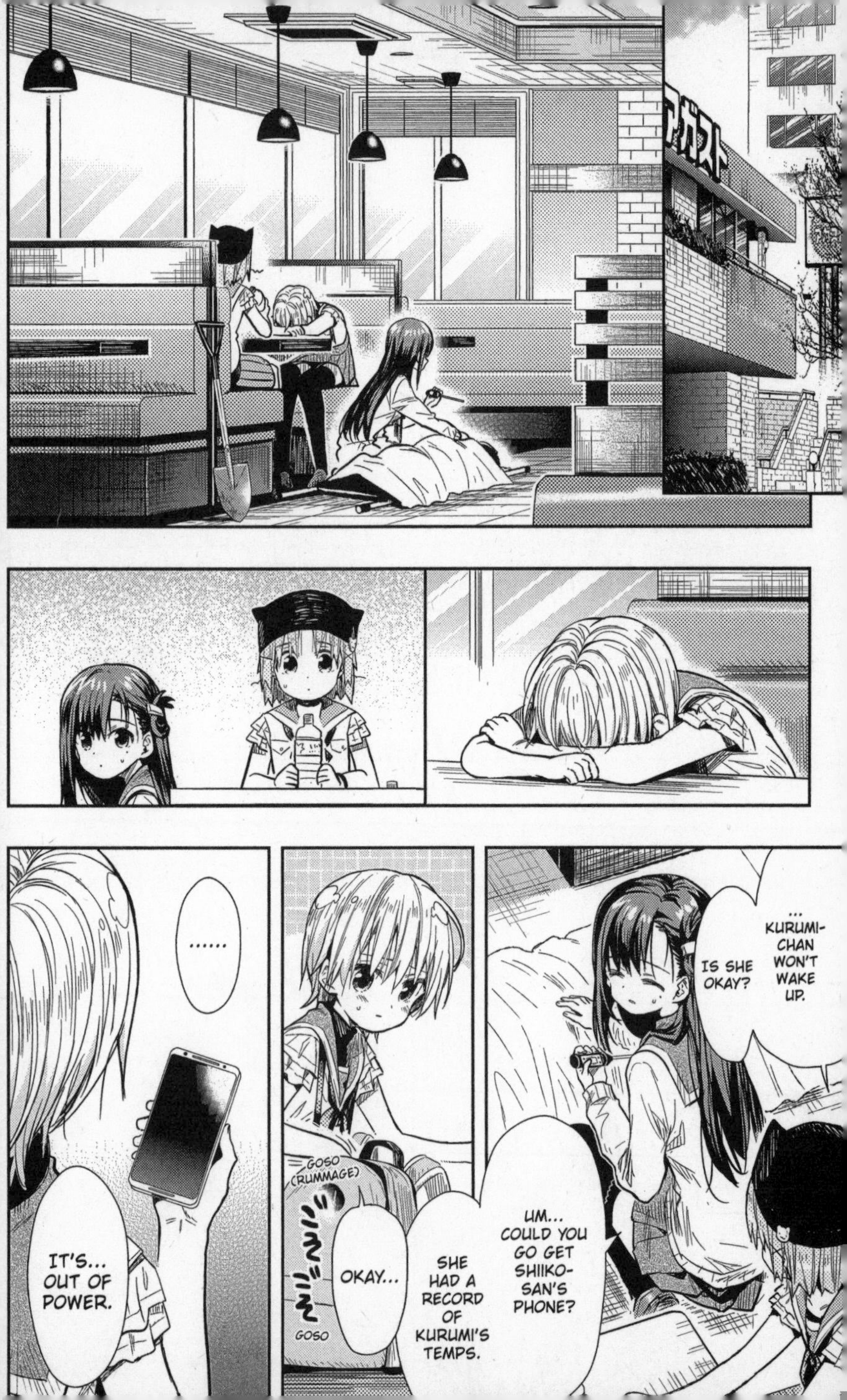
... KURUMI-CHAN WON'T WAKE UP.
IS SHE OKAY?
UM... COULD YOU GO GET SHIIKO-SAN'S PHONE?
SHE HAD A RECORD OF KURUMI'S TEMPS.
OKAY...
GOSO (RUMMAGE)
GOSO
......
IT'S... OUT OF POWER.

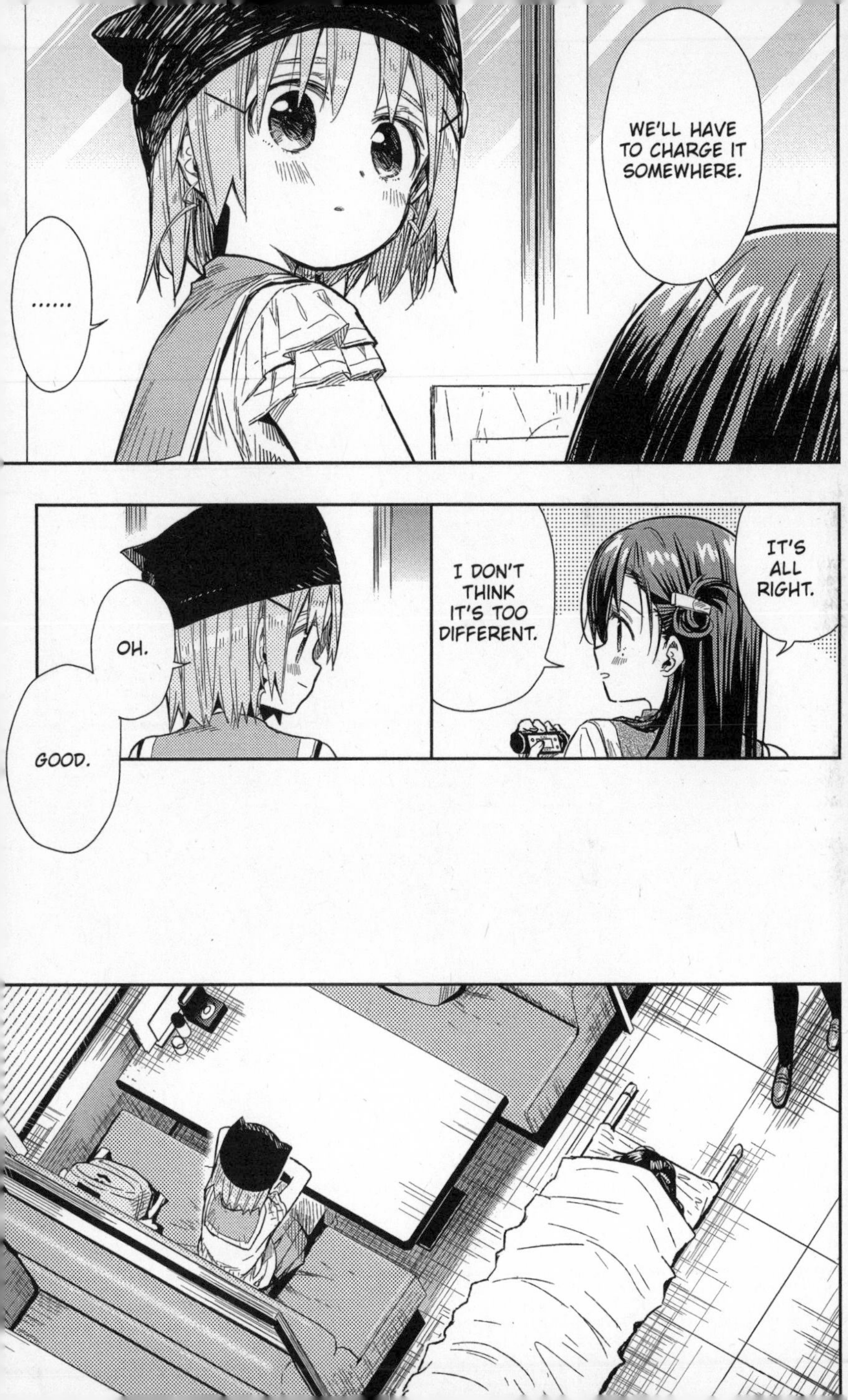
WE'LL HAVE TO CHARGE IT SOMEWHERE.
......
IT'S ALL RIGHT.
I DON'T THINK IT'S TOO DIFFERENT.
OH.
GOOD.

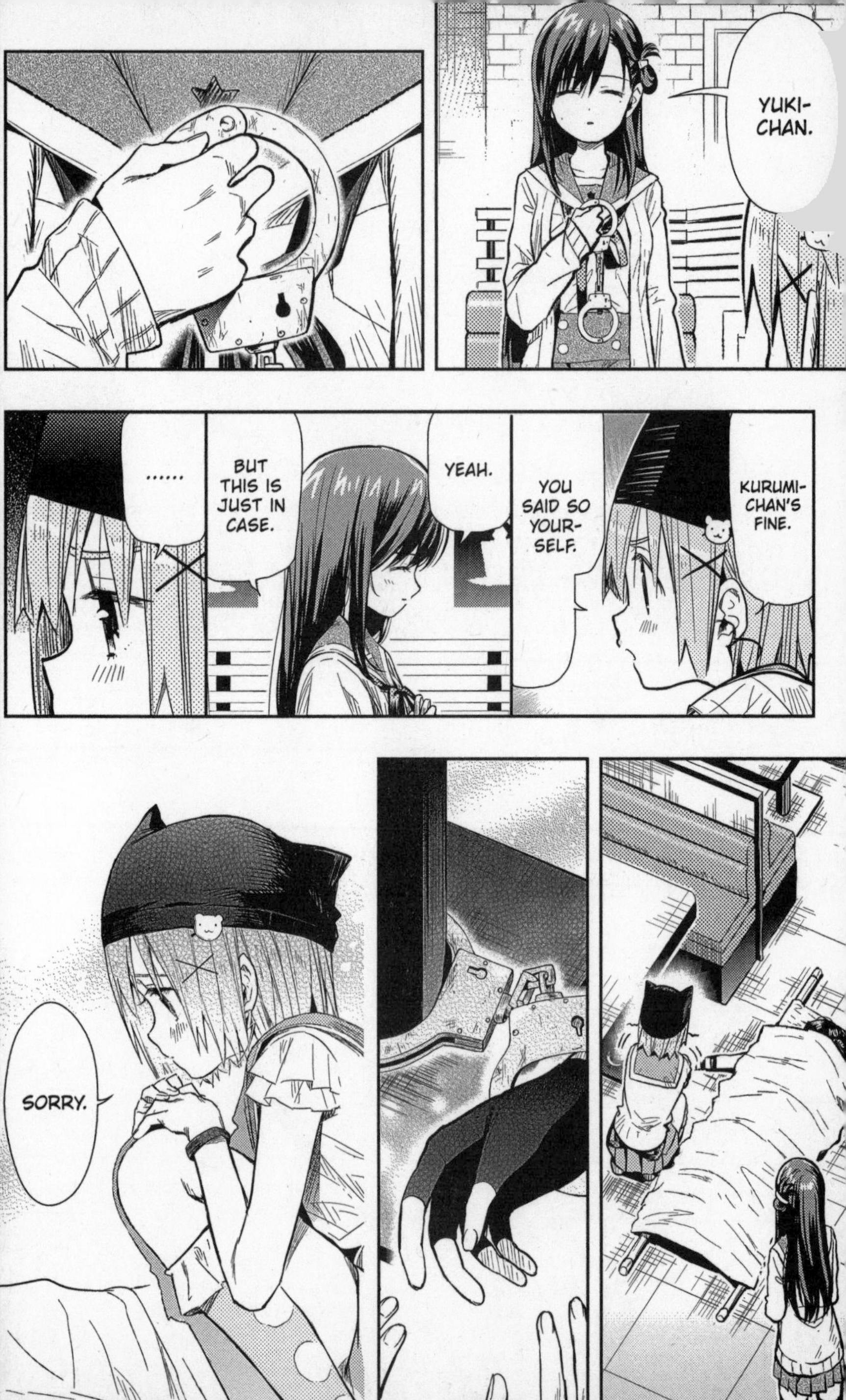
YUKI-CHAN.
KURUMI-CHAN'S FINE.
YOU SAID SO YOUR-SELF.
YEAH.
BUT THIS IS JUST IN CASE.
......
SORRY.

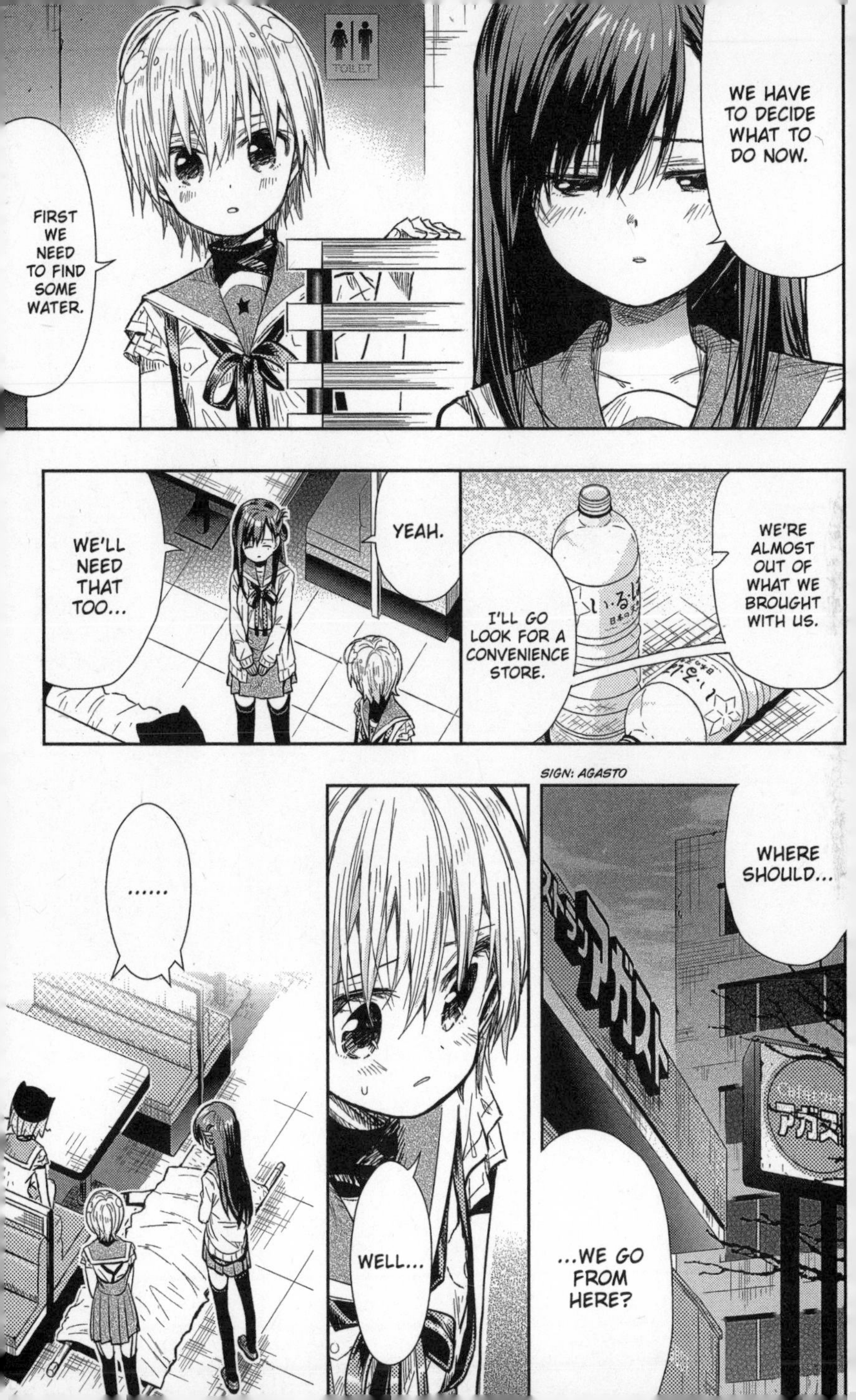
WE HAVE TO DECIDE WHAT TO DO NOW.
FIRST WE NEED TO FIND SOME WATER.
WE'RE ALMOST OUT OF WHAT WE BROUGHT WITH US.
I'LL GO LOOK FOR A CONVENIENCE STORE.
YEAH.
WE'LL NEED THAT TOO...
SIGN: AGASTO
WHERE SHOULD...
...WE GO FROM HERE?
WELL...
......

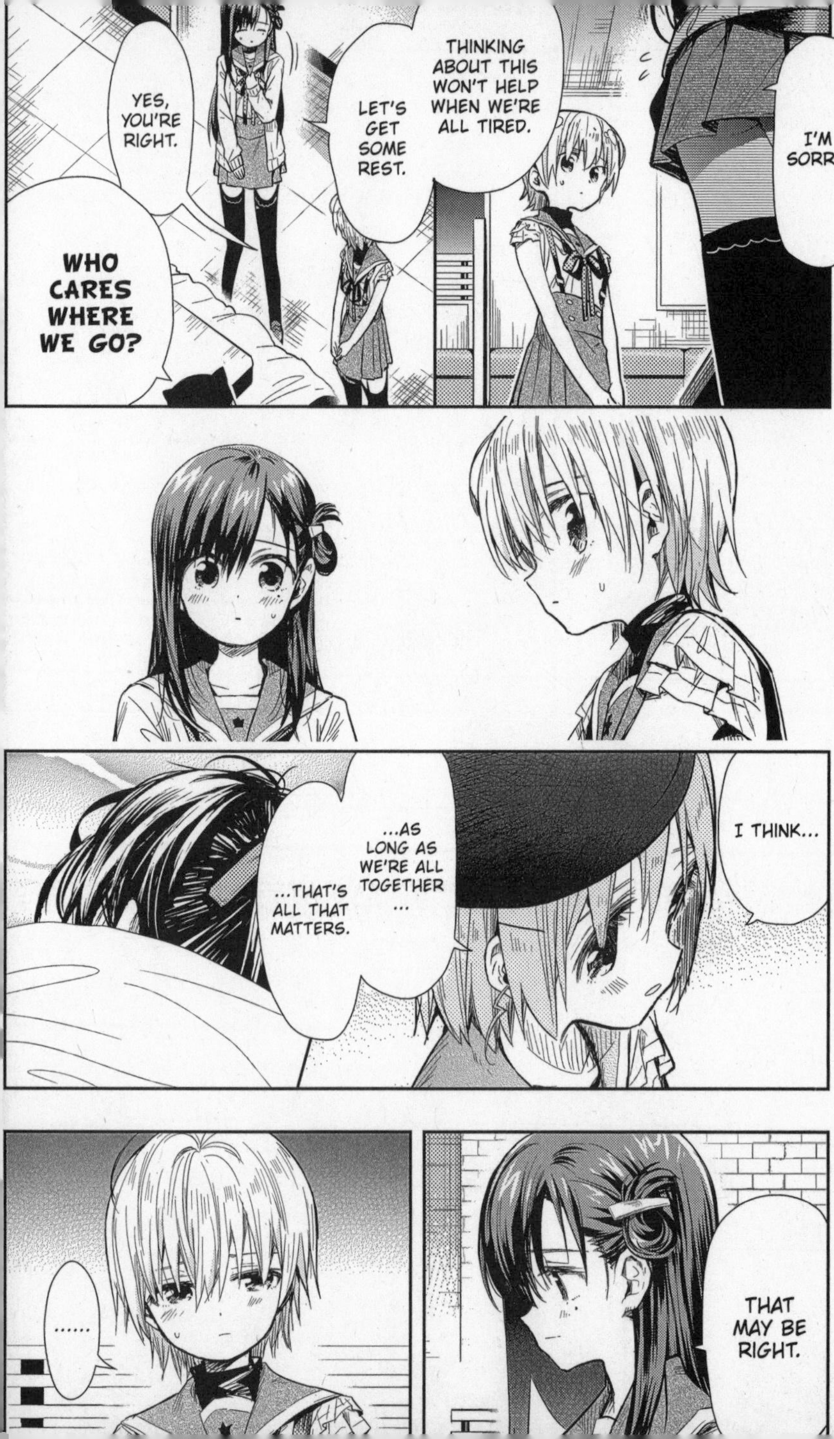
I'M SORRY.
THINKING ABOUT THIS WON'T HELP WHEN WE'RE ALL TIRED.
LET'S GET SOME REST.
YES, YOU'RE RIGHT.
WHO CARES WHERE WE GO?
I THINK...
...AS LONG AS WE'RE ALL TOGETHER...
...THAT'S ALL THAT MATTERS.
THAT MAY BE RIGHT.
......

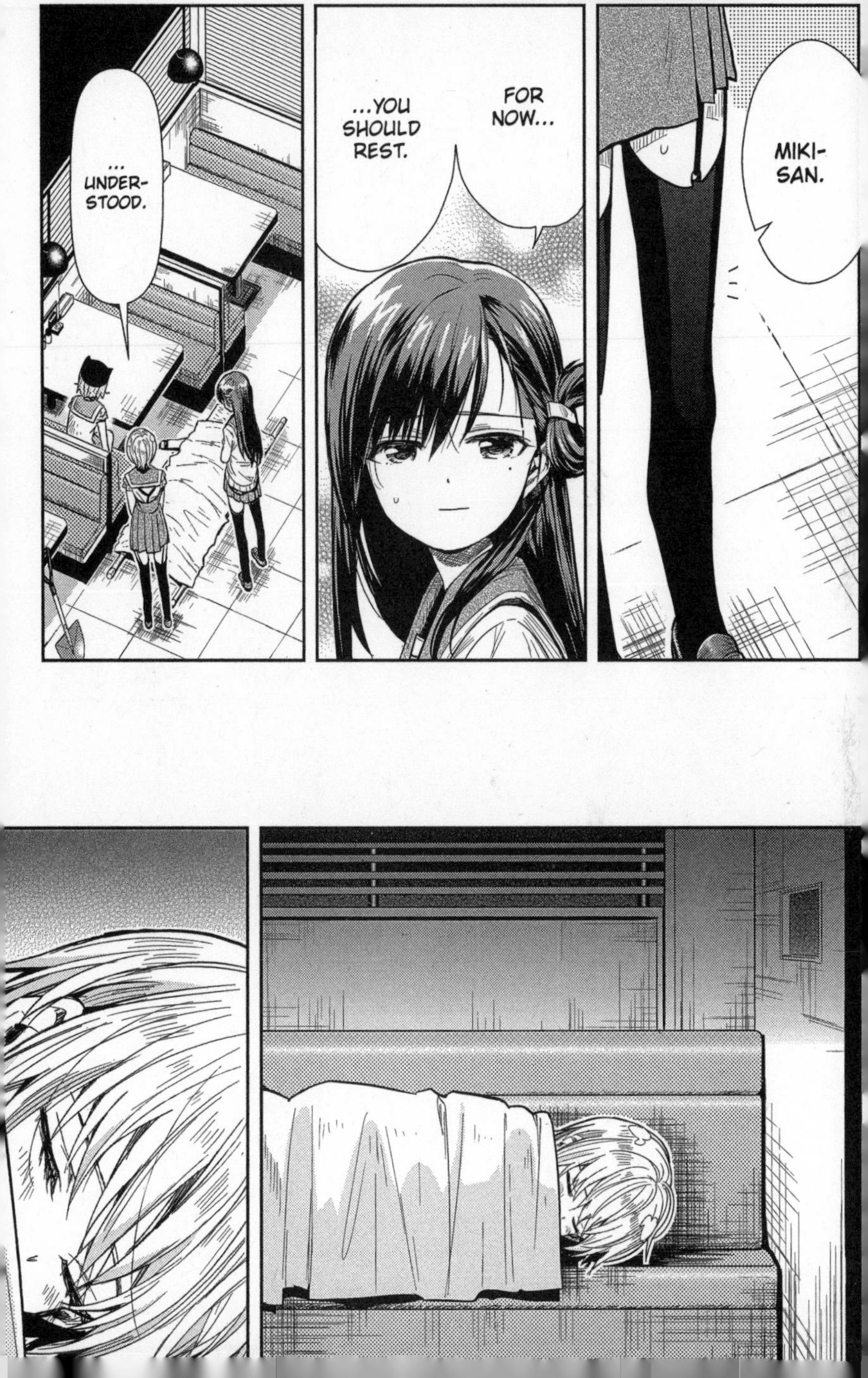
MIKI-SAN.
FOR NOW...
...YOU SHOULD REST.
... UNDER-STOOD.

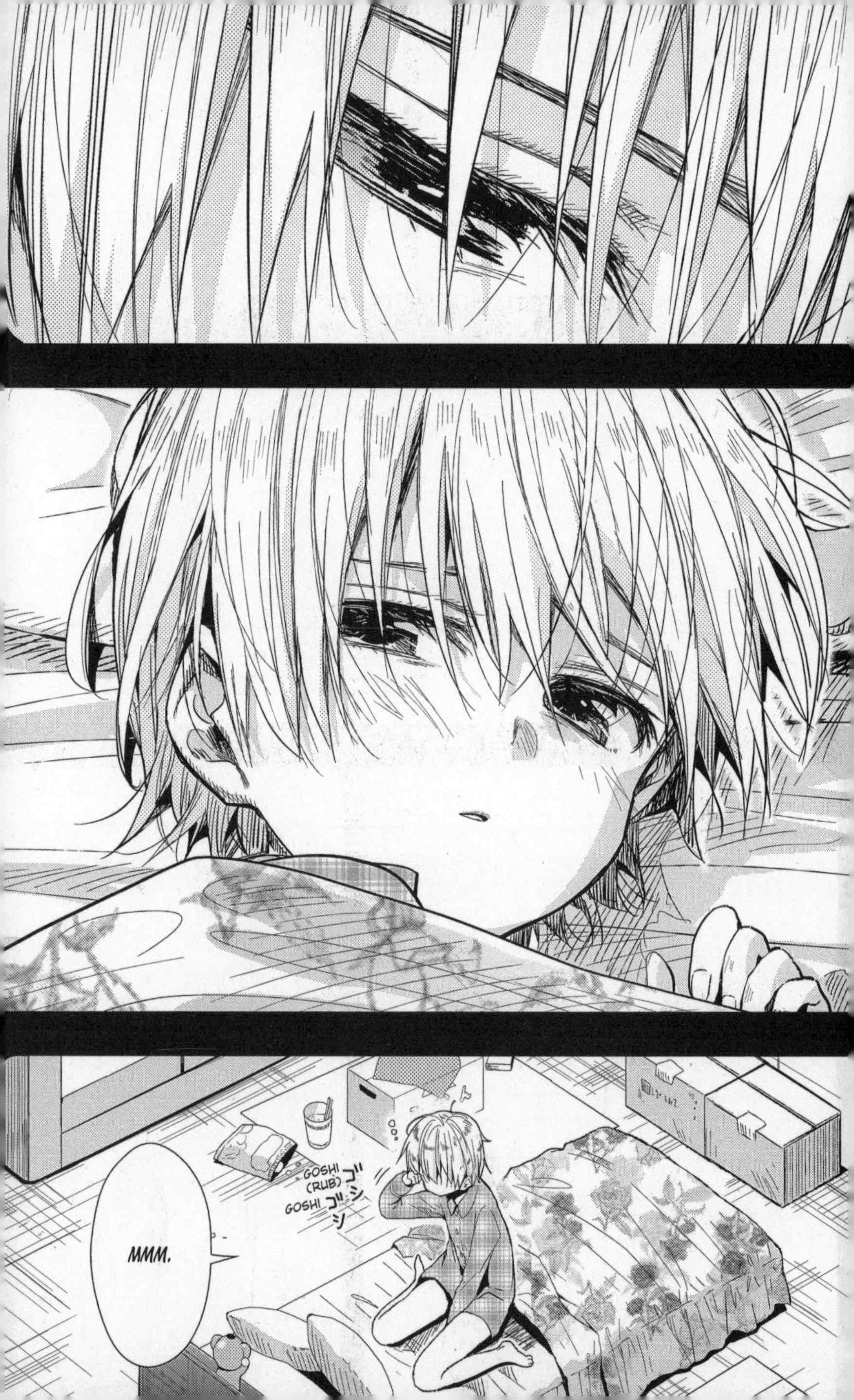
GOSHI (RUB) GOSHI
ゴシゴシ
MMM.

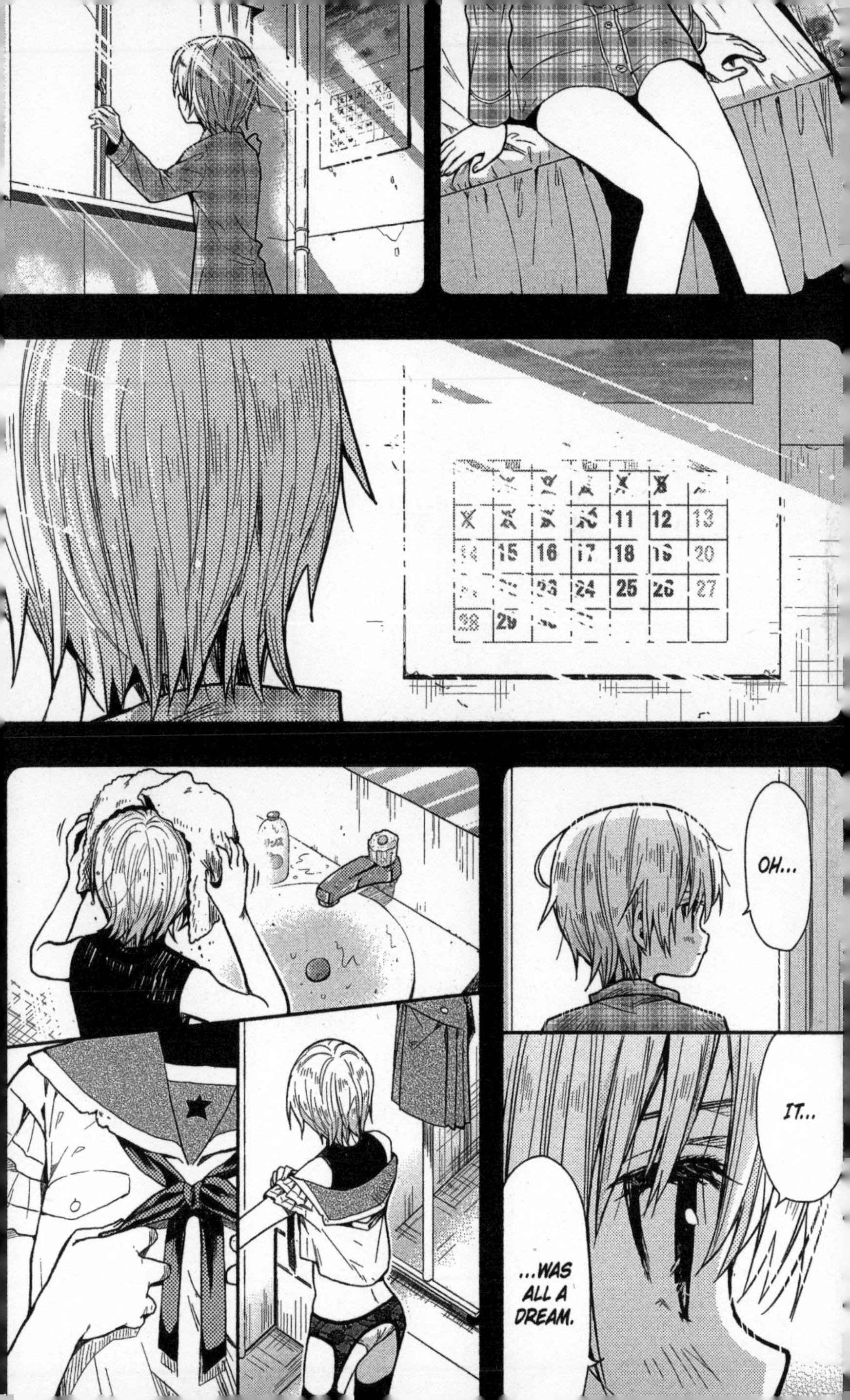
OH...
IT...
...WAS ALL A DREAM.

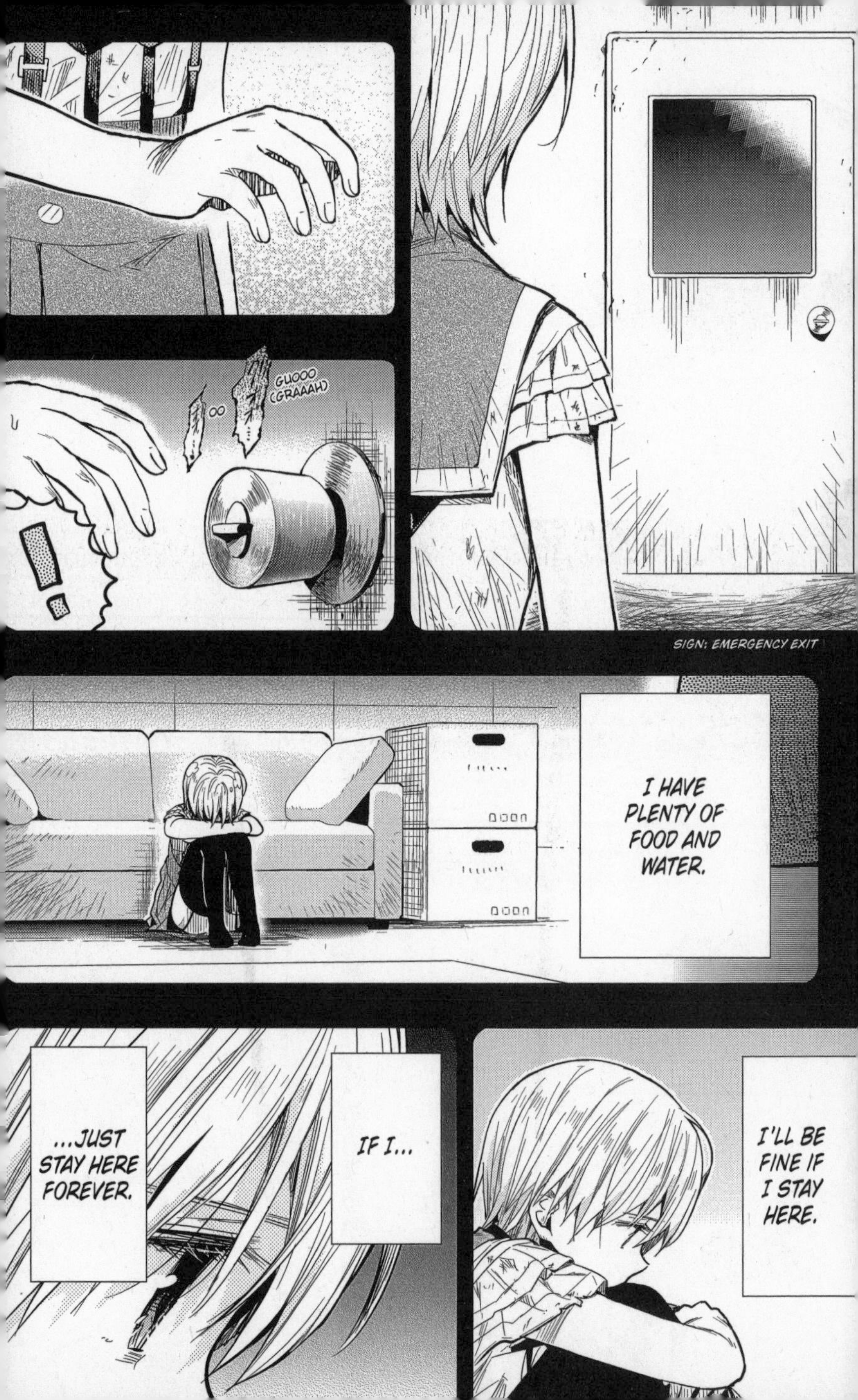
GUOOO (GRAAAH)
!
SIGN: EMERGENCY EXIT
I HAVE PLENTY OF FOOD AND WATER.
I'LL BE FINE IF I STAY HERE.
IF I...
...JUST STAY HERE FOREVER.

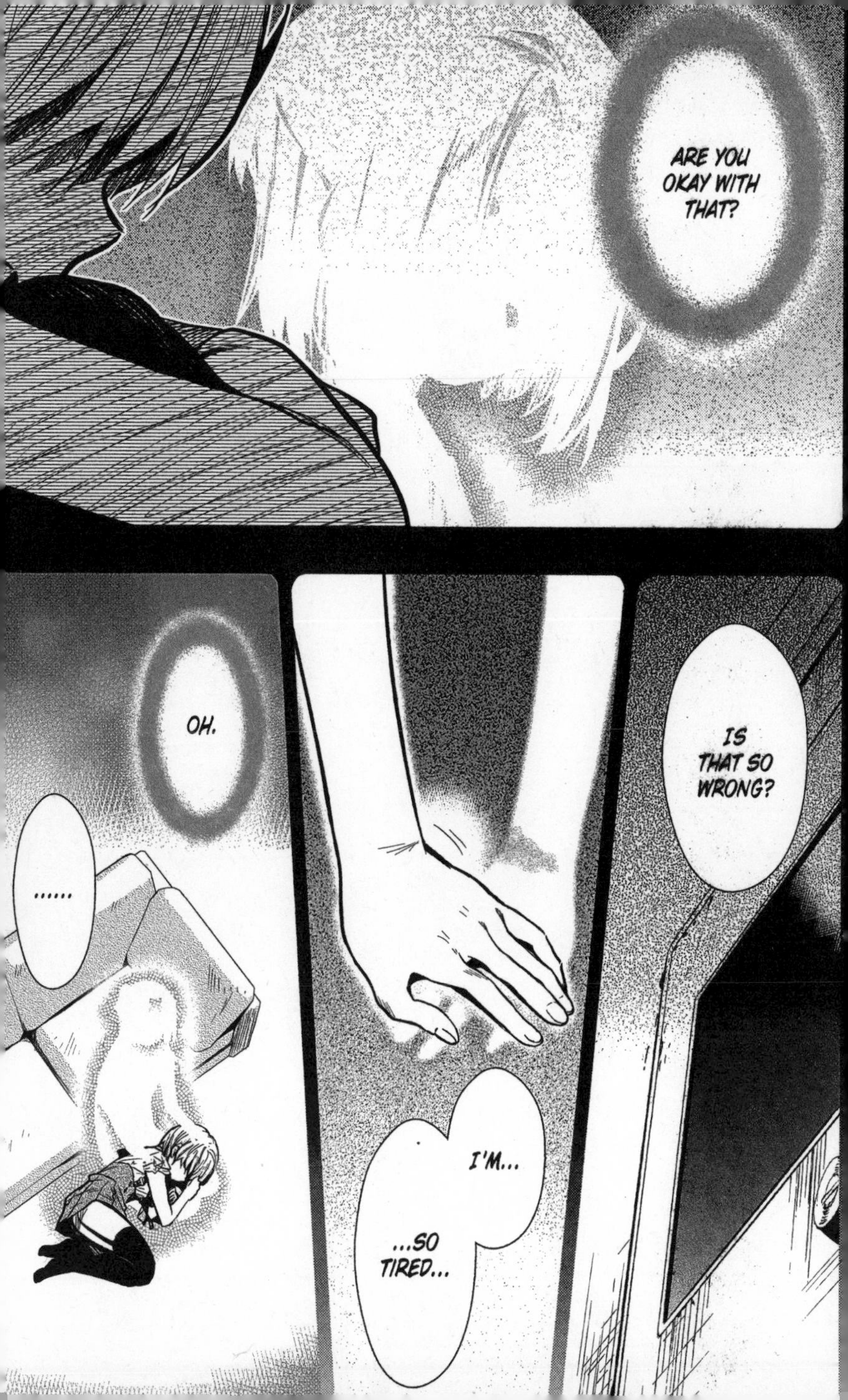
ARE YOU OKAY WITH THAT?
IS THAT SO WRONG?
I'M...
...SO TIRED...
OH.
......

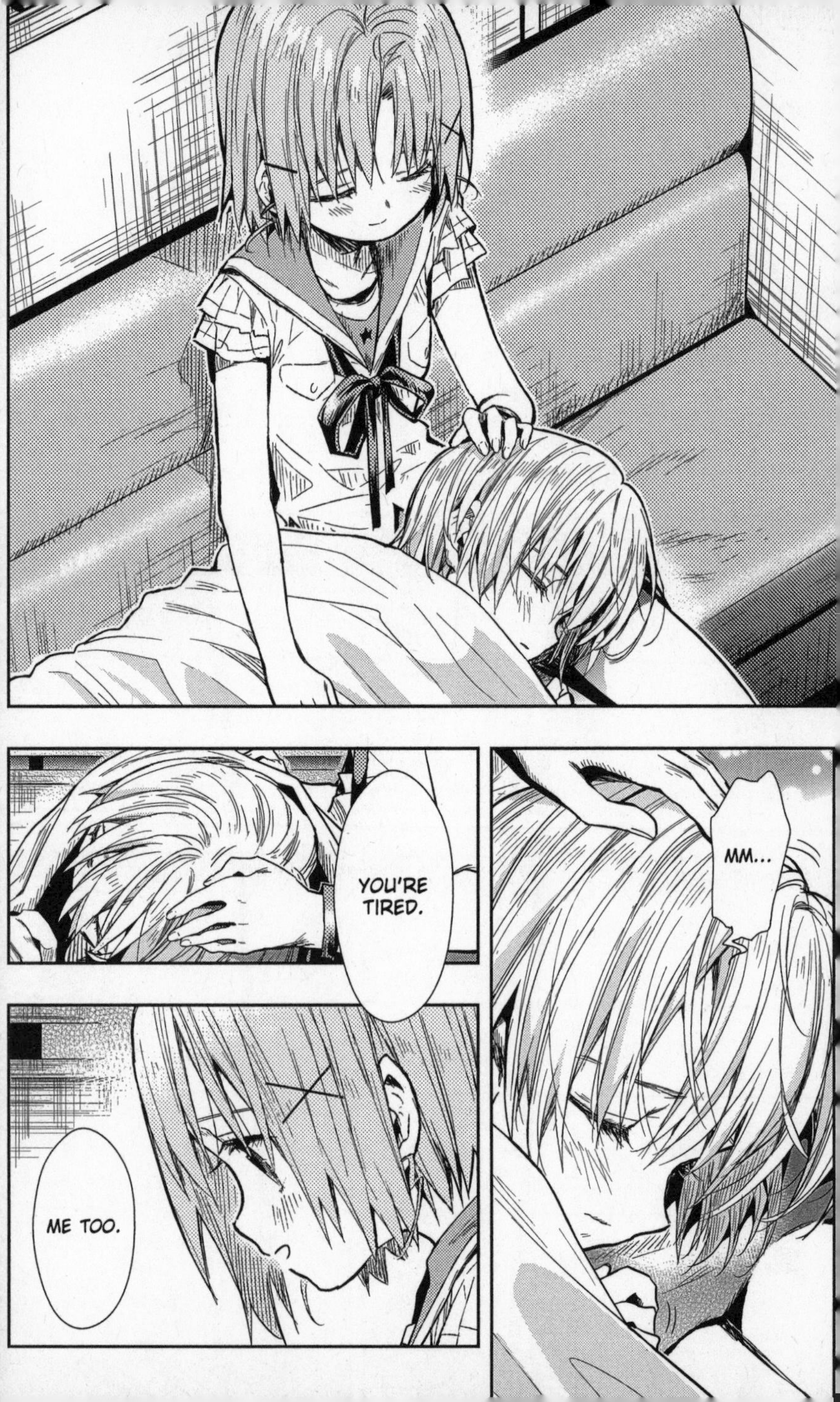
MM...
YOU'RE TIRED.
ME TOO.

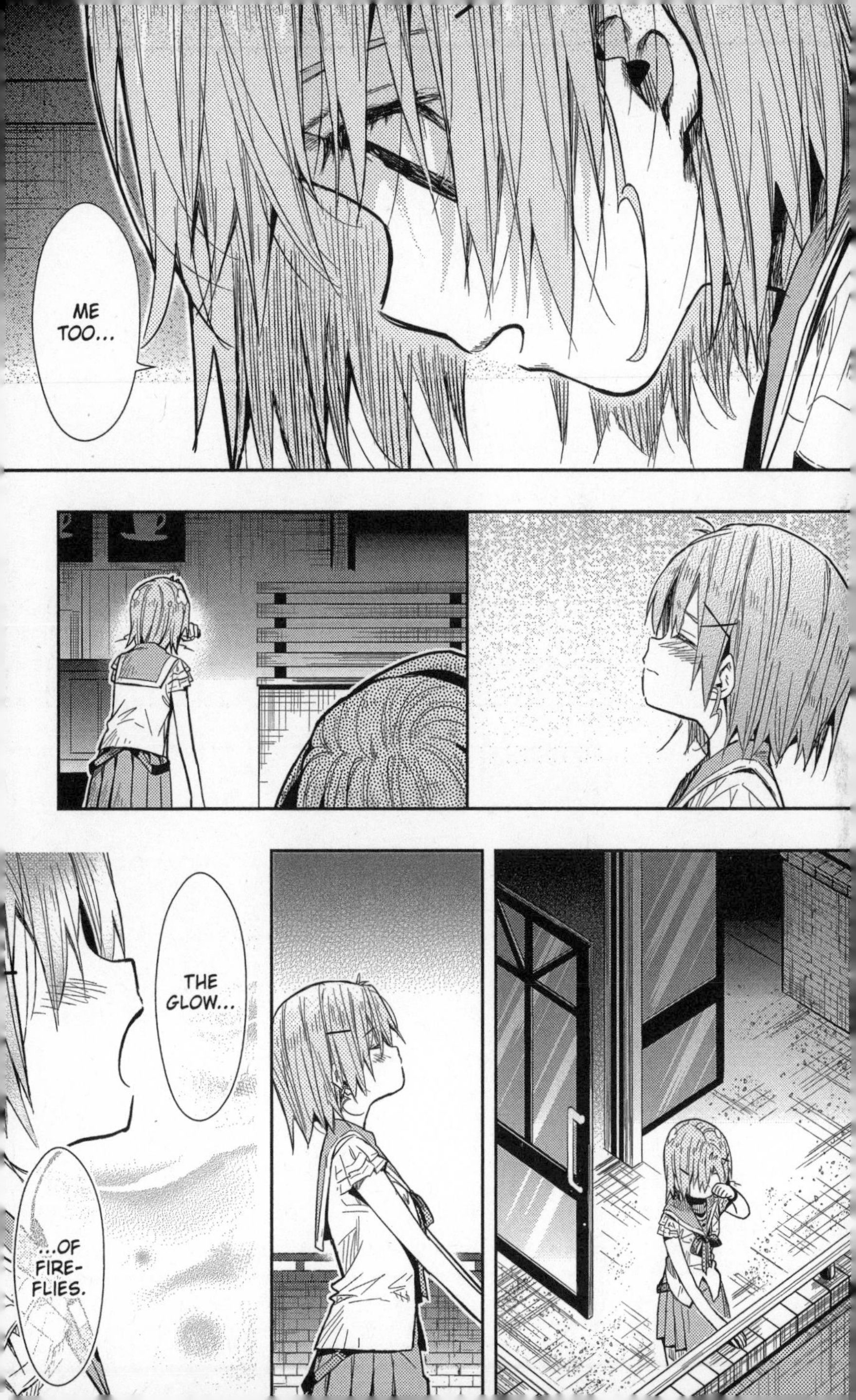
ME TOO...
THE GLOW...
...OF FIRE-FLIES.

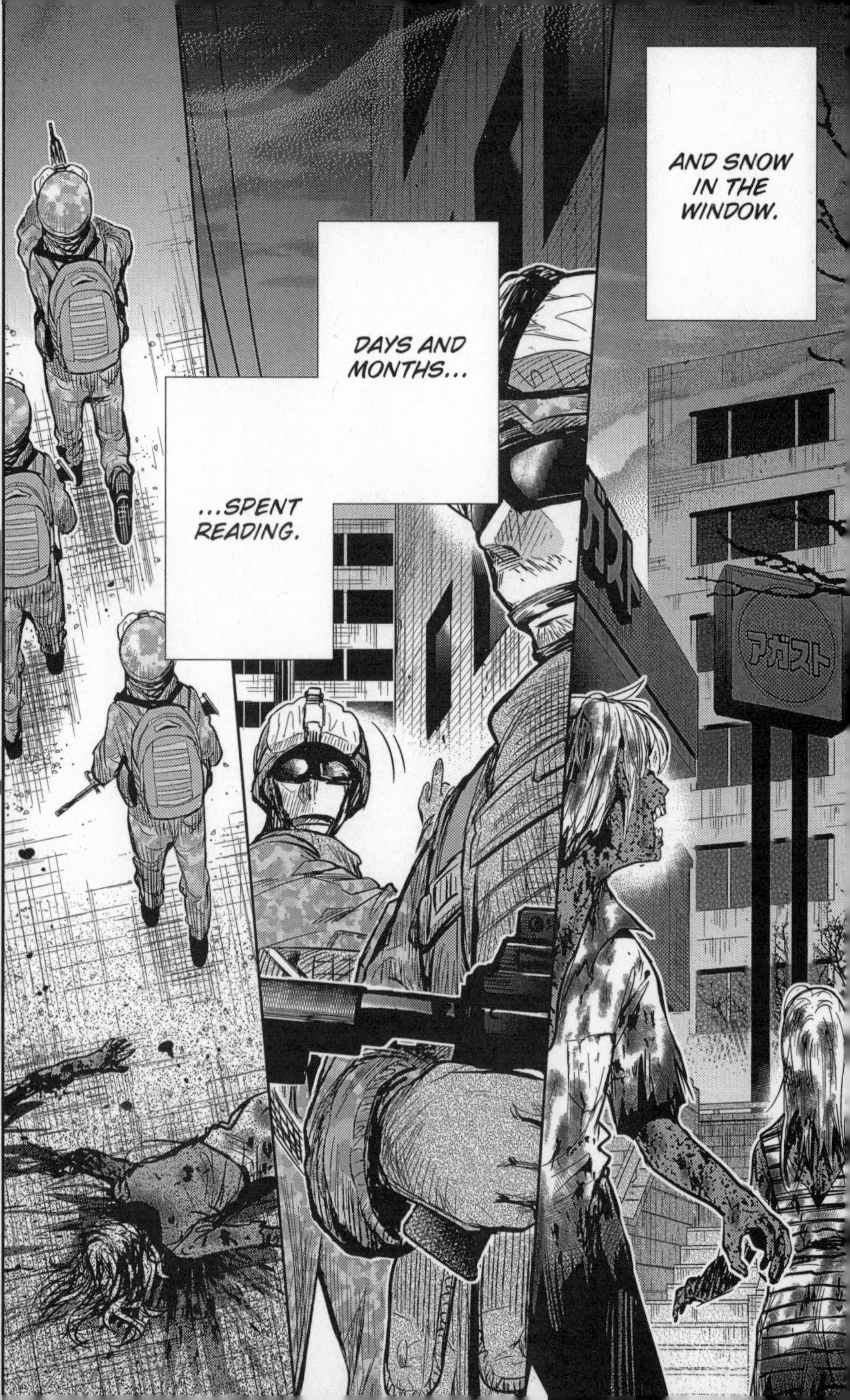
AND SNOW IN THE WINDOW.
アガスト
DAYS AND MONTHS...
...SPENT READING.

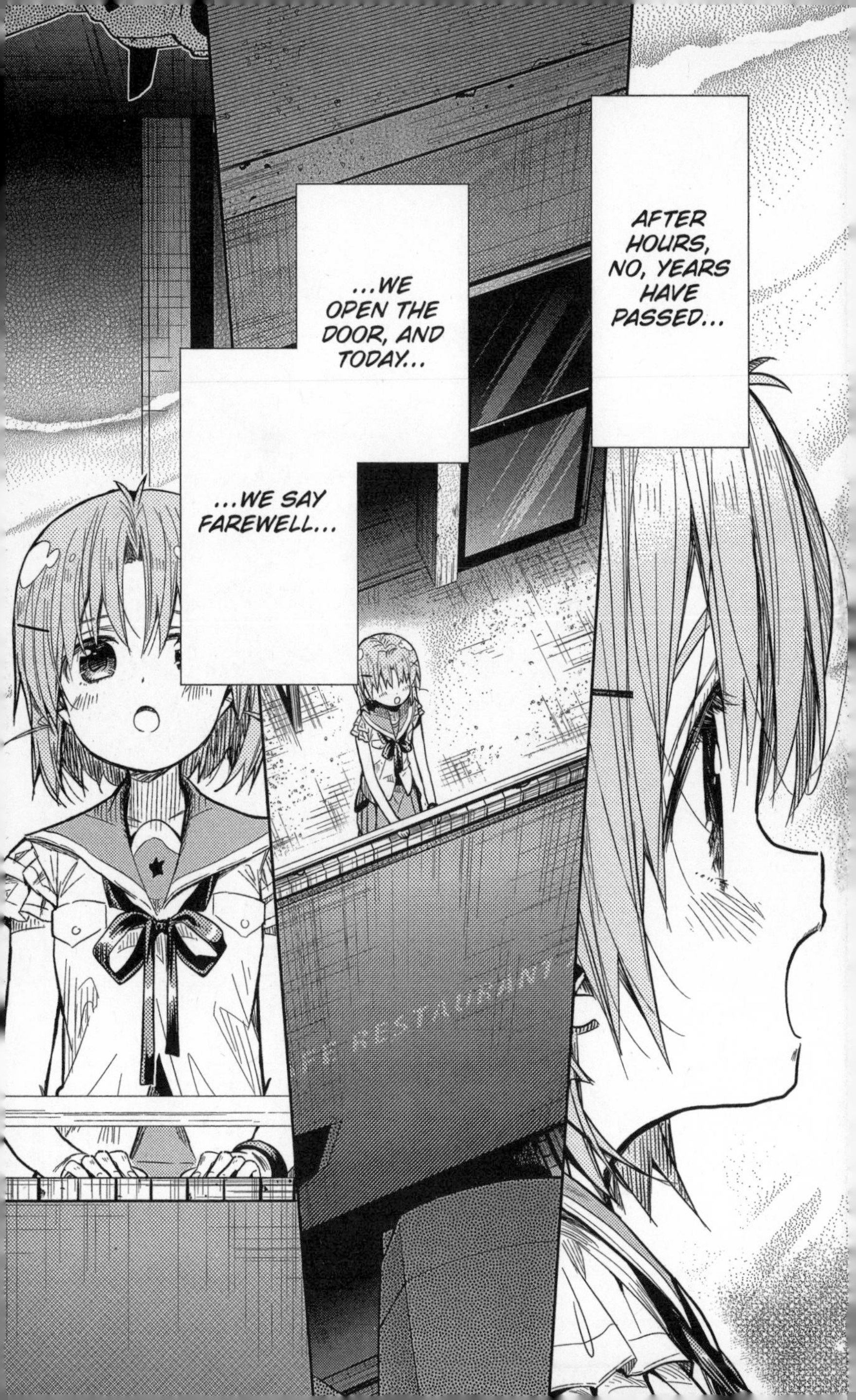
AFTER HOURS, NO, YEARS HAVE PASSED...
...WE OPEN THE DOOR, AND TODAY...
...WE SAY FAREWELL...

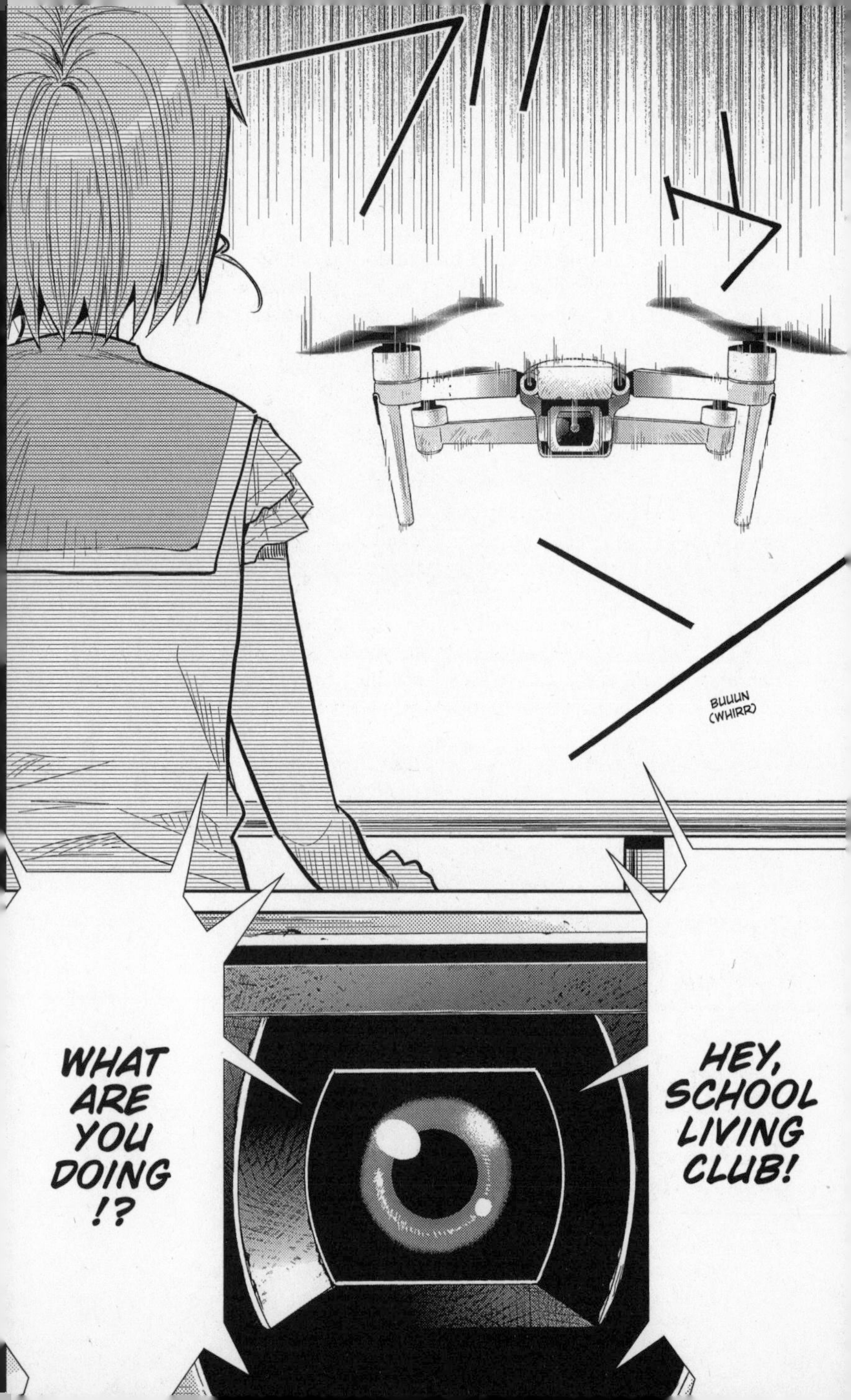
BUUUN (WHIRR)
HEY, SCHOOL LIVING CLUB!
WHAT ARE YOU DOING!?

I'm a fairly happy-go-lucky person in general, but in the course of my life, I've run into some big trouble a couple of times. Thinking back on those times, I was usually all alone when I ran into that trouble. For some reason, I would take everything on myself and just make things worse.

This trouble was only trouble because my way of doing things couldn't handle the situation, so what I needed to do was change how I dealt with it. If it's not taking it on head-first, it's running away, avoiding it, burying it, or all sorts of other ways. But when you're desperately trying to fix something, you just can't get your head wrapped around that thought. Taking to someone else can help spark some ideas.

And even if you can't come up with a good idea, just having someone to worry about things with you can make you feel better.

Some people are always ready for trouble to turn into a disaster. Those people are usually pretty much trash, but they're also the people who will get excited and act without hesitation when thrust into an obviously impossible situation.

When someone like that helps you, you're painfully reminded that human potential and aptitude aren't confined to just one type. Ah, I'm usually such a boring person it makes you want to look away.

Yuki and the others have fought many troubles and sustained some wounds, but now they're headed for their final battle.

The next volume of *School-Live!* will be the final one.

Norimitsu
Kaito

It's always darkest
before the dawn.

Special Thanks:
Itsuka Yamada (Project Bowman code-editing screen design)
Tsukasa Tsuchiya (help writing the Project Bowman code)
The Project Bowman code references Accord.net.

School-Live!

Thank you so much for happily reading! Next volume is the last.
Please stick with us right to the end.

2019.01 Sadoru Chiba 千葉サドル㊞

Special Thanks!

KAIHOU-SENSEI, NITROPLUS-SAN, MY EDITORS K-SAN & M-SAN,
BALCOLONY-SAMA, MY ASSISTANT KESHI SUGITA-SAN,
THE PRINTERS, AND ALL OF THE READERS!

SCHOOL-LIVE!

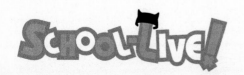

SCHOOL-LIVE! 11

SADORU CHIBA

NORIMITSU KAIHOU

(Nitroplus)

Translation: Leighann Harvey

Lettering: Alexis Eckerman

GAKKOU GURASHI! Vol. 11
©Nitroplus / Norimitsu Kaihou, Sadoru Chiba, Houbunsha. All rights reserved. First published in Japan in 2019 by HOUBUNSHA CO., LTD., Tokyo. English translation rights in United States, Canada, and United Kingdom arranged with HOUBUNSHA CO., LTD through Tuttle-Mori Agency, Inc., Tokyo.

English translation © 2019 by Yen Press, LLC

Yen Press
150 West 30th Street, 19th Floor
New York, NY 10001

Visit us at yenpress.com
facebook.com/yenpress
twitter.com/yenpress
yenpress.tumblr.com
instagram.com/yenpress

First Yen Press Edition: October 2019

Yen Press is an imprint of Yen Press, LLC.
The Yen Press name and logo are trademarks of Yen Press, LLC.

Library of Congress Control Number: 2015952613

ISBNs: 978-1-9753-5865-5 (paperback)
       978-1-9753-0642-7 (ebook)

10 9 8 7 6 5 4 3 2 1

BVG

Printed in the United States of America